A WORD OF APPRECIATION
We would like to thank all those
who have donated their bodies,
without whom this exhibition
would not have been possible.

Gunther von Hagens'
BODY WORLDS
The Original Exhibition of Real Human Bodies

Catalogue on the Exhibition

BODY WORLDS is also known as
KÖRPERWELTEN and LE MONDE DU CORPS in some countries.

TABLE OF CONTENTS

Wilhelm Kriz

Foreword

BODY WORLDS and thus this catalogue display something unusual: anatomical specimens, produced and preserved according to a new process developed by Gunther von Hagens. This process – called plastination – makes it possible to lend rigidity even to soft body parts (e.g., individual muscles, organs such as the lungs, or a single nerve). As a consequence, even specimens of the entire body can be inherently stabilised and posed in such a way that they are actually capable of standing, which was formerly restricted to skeletons.

A collection of plastinates was first shown in Germany at the Museum for Technology and Labour in Mannheim during the winter of 1997/98. The exhibition's success surpassed the most optimistic expectations.

This applies first of all to the number of visitors. Nearly 780,000 people saw the exhibition within the relatively short period of only four months; toward the end, the exhibition had to remain open around the clock to make this at all possible. Secondly, this applies to the response. A representative sampling of public opinion showed that 95% of those attending this demonstration of the inner realms of the human body gave it high marks. Critics were few but harsh. The harshest critics were those who had not even seen the exhibition.

From this mixture of a break that flouted social conventions, enthusiastic acceptance and vehement rejection – and more highly publicised than hardly any other – a public discussion was conducted that was sometimes highly emotional, sometimes seriously pensive and that was ultimately embraced by the entire country. Here I would like to respond to both the acceptance and the criticism as the long-time mentor of Gunther von Hagens, and from the vantage point of an anatomist.

There certainly were several reasons for the generally positive resonance among the public. I would like to single out three of them: 1) The creator of these specimens is an unusual personality; 2) his works show things that are new and have never before seen; and 3) exhibiting them also permits visitors without a medical background to free themselves from a taboo.

The Plastinator

Gunther von Hagens, who produced this exhibition, took over a position as a research assistant at the Institute for Anatomy and Cellular Biology at the University of Heidelberg in 1978. Right at the beginning, he stumbled by chance onto a neglected and fallow field of research, namely using plastics to preserve anatomical specimens. He was fascinated by the possibilities that had remained unused until then to such an extent that he literally sank his teeth into this subject matter right from the start – and thus we come directly to the essence of his personality.

This I had to accept, which was not necessarily difficult for me, because producing durable anatomical specimens is definitely recognised as an essential aspect of our field. It soon became clear that any attempt to dissuade von Hagens and to interest him in another research project would have been in vain. No other quality characterises him as does unswerving dedication to achieving a goal once he has set it for himself. Identification with that goal, which he had then made his own, has attained a level over the course of years that hardly allows of a distinction between the person and the profession. Gunther von Hagens embodies his work.

I have accompanied him in his work at the Institute for almost 20 years. As he enthusiastically reported every bit of progress, no matter how small, immediately and expected that we discuss it extensively, a continual professional conference was virtually the order of the day. This made me his critic as well as his partner and rival in a relationship that has remained free of dissonance over the entire period of our association. His commitment and his dedication grew from year to year; despite many setbacks, despite much that did not work out – his persistence and tenacity could not be shaken. He was thus able to discover and to invent new and more innovative improvements, new modifications of his dissection and preservation techniques that ultimately enabled the production of such spectacular whole-body plastinates as those that were mainly responsible for the success of the Mannheim exhibition.

New Vistas

The second reason for the interest of both the public and the media in BODY WORLDS is, as mentioned above, the fact that the exhibits showed things never before seen. A short historical excursion should make this easier to understand.

Even before Andreas Vesalius (1514-1564) published the first book on anatomy, Leonardo da Vinci (1452-1519) had been dissecting cadavers in order to understand the vital relief of the human body from its structures beneath the surface. Leonardo also drew whatever he discovered this way. This was at a time when nothing could be done to prevent decomposition – not a very pleasant activity, as he noted: "… if you feel like doing such things, your stomach prevents you from it; and if this does not prevent you, then your fears will keep you from associating with quartered and excoriated, dreadful to look at dead people at night." However, anatomical science and modern medicine developed from just such beginnings.

Since the last century, anatomy has made the fine structures of organs and tissue the focus of its research with the aid of the microscope, devoted itself to submicroscopic cell and cellular systems in this century and in the meantime is occupied with molecular structures and their functions – as in all other basic subject areas in medicine. Nevertheless, classic, macroscopic anatomy still provides an indispensable foundation of medical training. The necessary knowledge is imparted in dissection courses and with the aid of anatomical models and specimens of various types.

Collections of such specimens in anatomical and pathological institutes have long since been accessible to laypersons; and there are some that are outstanding, for example at the Charité in Berlin, in Basel, and in Vienna. They frequently arouse the spectre of a horror show as exhibits of abnormalities dominate in many places: a still-born child with anencephaly, in which the brain has not developed properly, and on top of that they are preserved in jars filled with formaldehyde. This is usually the lasting impression imparted to unsuspecting visitors.

This changed radically with the advent of plastinates. In them, skillful dissection of details is combined with innovative preservation and aesthetic presentation. Their production is naturally based on a differentiated process with very many individual steps: originating, testing and developing this innovative process. This in substance is what we have gained from the work of Gunther von Hagens.

However, visitors at an exhibition rarely admire the technology with which an exhibit has been made, but rather the finished product itself. Consequently, I would like to discuss the reasons for the attractiveness of whole-body plastinates using a concrete example, the specimen known as *The Chess Player* or *The Thinker*.

This is a body in a sitting position, in which the spinal column and the peripheral nerves are shown in detail. I have heard several professional colleagues offer the opinion that this is the best specimen of the nerves of the spinal column that they have ever seen. Such a specimen thus epitomises the art of dissection and craftsmanship to perfection. Up to this point, this has had little to do with plastination. It only comes into play after dissection, namely with the possibility of lending the specimens rigidity and a pose. A specimen can thus gain a natural aspect: this whole-body plastinate awakens the impression that it is sitting to think or to play chess.

This type of anatomical specimens is not only something new, but also opens to everyone an accessibility never before experienced by anyone. Even for medical laypersons, the impression wears off that this is a corpse. It becomes easier for them to overcome their timidity at the sight of the specimens, to approach them and to look at the uncovered and projecting structures of the inner realms of the body. They see things that they have never seen before and that they could not have imagined. They are amazed.

It is surprising that many visitors to BODY WORLDS consider some exhibits to be works of art. As an anatomist, I can attest to the fact that the specimen called *The Chess Player* or *The Thinker* was dissected with a high degree of skill and artistic craftsmanship and that the objective, namely of presenting the peripheral nervous system, has been achieved in an exceptionally brilliant and professional fashion as well as in a highly appealing manner.

Breaking with Taboos

There is also a third reason for the success of public exhibitions of such specimens: they touch on the taboo of death. In our society, death is repressed, blocked out, so to speak and the corpses of other people, at least, are viewed with a revulsive shudder – drilled into us through daily assaults by the same media pictures.

Many people went to see the Mannheim exhibition with such expectations and experienced that this revulsion actually decreased as they viewed the specimens, that it was lost completely and instead both amazement and a thirst for knowledge began to manifest themselves.

For each visitor, this was ultimately a personal victory. They had overcome the taboos that surround human corpses. They were able to look at these specimens quietly and with interest in anatomical details. In doing so, they were able to pick out those organs or other tissue structures that particularly touched their lives due to a personal experience with a disease or for any other reason whatsoever. And they succeeded in doing this with frankness and without having to be on the defensive. This transition from expecting revulsion to looking at the specimens freely and uninhibitedly amounts to a personal break with these taboos. Many visitors to BODY WORLDS have spoken about this and thus encouraged family, friends and acquaintances to have the same experience.

Concerns and Answers

And it was just this point, the break with the taboos of death and corpses, that also ignited the opposition to the Mannheim exhibition. Although the number of opponents was relatively small, the criticism of individuals was nonetheless all the harsher. Criticism came primarily from academics – from theologians as well as pathologists and anatomists.

It was just this vehement and emotional rejection expressed by several anatomists that appears less and less understandable to me the more time passes since the exhibition. I am not convinced by the explanation frequently offered for it, namely to avert the loss of a kind of 'sacrosanct' knowledge. Dissection and autopsies are indeed privileges of physicians; however, knowledge of anatomy has long since ceased to be some kind of elite intellectual property, on which anatomists were able to base their identity.

Whatever the motives – both the harshness and types of criticism remain regrettable when it came from the anatomical to the community. The reason is that unbiased eye skill in anatomical dissection and an innovative process of preservation were presented in a very respectable fashion; the general public in turn responded to the Mannheim exhibition with immense interest and by far with a predominantly positive resonance.

The main argument of the opponents of BODY WORLDS was that a public exhibition of authentic human anatomical specimens would violate the dignity of the individual, and more precisely that of the deceased. For an anatomist, this argument has a particular aspect. As mentioned above, dissecting cadavers has been an integral part of studying medicine from time immemorial. In my 30 years of experience, I can guarantee that students in anatomical courses have never shown anything but the highest respect for those who had donated their bodies for that purpose.

Visitors to the Mannheim exhibition were also not lacking in showing the same respect. On the contrary, it was constantly apparent and could sometimes even be distinctly felt. Dissecting cadavers within the framework of medical studies has been explained and justified by its expediency in educating future physicians. Nevertheless, in an advanced society today, educating the public in general is not a matter of any less importance or any less ethical priority than academic education. Medical laypersons too have the right to ask questions about how the human body looks on the inside, and they too have a right to want to see it. They have a right to learn where and how a disease occurs and how it might be prevented if possible or where what happens during surgery. To make a privilege out of this for physicians is no longer justifiable. On the contrary, there is considerable demand for educating laypersons on anatomical facts as well as for an objective, free and open discussion about taboos on death and dealing with dead bodies that have existed until now.

To do justice to the objective of clarification, this BODY WORLDS book includes – in addition to the current catalogue of specimens together with explanations on the anatomy and functions of the human body by Angelina Whalley – contributions on essential questions raised by the exhibition: Psychologist Ernst D. Lantermann presents an in-depth look at the methods and results of a visitor poll. State Lutheran bishop Ulrich Fischer represents the criticism based on moral-theological grounds; medical ethicist Axel W. Bauer presents the scientific position in this regard and philosopher Franz Josef Wetz deals extensively with the term 'human dignity'. Finally, art historian Bazon Brock looks at plastination as practiced by Gunther von Hagens under the aspect of applied science as a cultural achievement. Gunther von Hagens himself explains, inter alia, the technology of his process.

Controversial reactions such as experienced at the time of the Mannheim exhibition only serve to show that information on the natural facts of our bodies will always have to be reasserted. The reason is that expectations of revulsion followed by fascination after all can also be found, for example, in a 260-year-old instructional poem about a comparable event, namely a public anatomical dissection:

Hardly had I cast a glance at that dissected wench,
Hardly had I seen that corpse, partially denuded of skin,
I could hardly even look at the bloody muscles, when at that
very moment a vile and repulsive horror seized me.

However, the sage anatomist had hardly begun, he let us shortly see the wise wonders that forming Nature had given to it, so that my first impression had to make room for a far sweeter one.

Fear, horror, disgust were gone in a moment, admiration first struck me, then amazement, followed gradually by humility and awe, and then by praise, and our pensiveness.

A bright fire of holy lust began to burn in my breast that was filled with thankfulness to the glory of God to the honor of Him Who so wonderfully wrought this wonder of anatomy.

I did not even know myself how I really felt. The Creator shows Himself most clearly to mankind in man himself. It seems that one could notice in these works of wonder, in this masterpiece of forming Nature, a bright trace of our Creator even here, quite convincingly clear and at the same time visible.

Aha! I cried. Let this be written at this scene:
here atheists can no longer remain atheists!
Author Barthold Hinrich Brockes (1680-1747) was a Hamburg patrician and scholar devoted to the Enlightenment.

The quote comes from his main work, *Irdisches Vergnügen in Gott* (Earthly Joy in God), Volume 6, Hamburg, 1739: p. 298

Wilhelm Kriz has been a professor of anatomy at the University of Heidelberg since 1974 and is the chairman of the Institute for Anatomy and Cellular Biology I; he is also the director of this institute. He studied medicine at the University of Giessen and at the Free University of Berlin; he obtained his doctorate in 1963. In 1971, he completed his credentials (Habilitation) for a professorship at the University of Münster where he served as an instructor, scientific lecturer and professor before receiving an appointment in Heidelberg. He has published about 150 scientific articles and three medical books. His research has focused on the functional structure of the kidneys, development of these organs and their loss of function from chronic kidney failure. In 1990, the University of Göttingen awarded Kriz the Jakob Henle Medal and the German Dialysis Society honoured him with the Bernd Tersteegen Prize in 1998.

Gunther von Hagens

Anatomy and Plastination

1. The History of Anatomy

Anatomy and Hunting; Ritual Anatomy

Anatomy refers to the science of investigating the body's internal structures. There have always been specialists on the body's interior; hunters were among these specialists in man's early history. Animals killed during the hunt had to be gutted, and the meat had to be removed from the bones; a certain understanding of anatomy was an advantage in this regard. 'Kitchen anatomy' therefore concerned the anatomy of animals. Initial interest in human anatomy presumably arose among cannibals, whose motives were primarily ritual in nature. They believed that by consuming their enemies they could absorb their strength. In the earliest advanced civilizations, procedures were developed for immortalising the bodies of the dead – at least when the deceased had been persons of importance. Preserving entire corpses in this way was known in many cultures. The most famous instance is that of the mummies of ancient Egyptian pharaohs and other dignitaries, whose gutted bodies had been treated with fragrant resins and sodium bicarbonate, and then dried; this was to allow the deceased to live on after death. At its high point in South America, mummification even led to the establishment of entire cities of the dead. Ritual anatomy did not achieve any great anatomical insights, however, because the focus of preservation efforts was the mortal shell of the person, the skin in particular. The organs themselves, the failure of which was responsible for the individual's death, fell prey to decay.

The major impetus for acquiring detailed anatomical knowledge has always come from medicine. At first, this knowledge lay in the hands of shamans and priests; shortly before the beginning of the Common Era (A.D.), the profession of physician came into being, a vocation for which training was largely of a philosophical nature.

First Anatomical Studies in Greece and Egypt

At around 500 BC, the Greeks founded medical schools such as those in Crotona (lower Italy) and Cyrene (Africa), where they explored the anatomy of animals, examining even such tiny structures as the organ of equilibrium located in the temples. Aristotle (384–327 BC) was the first known anatomist, even though he is better known today for his philosophical writings. A student of Plato and a teacher to Alex-

ander the Great, Aristotle drew a distinction between nerves and tendons, and described how major arteries branched out into smaller blood vessels.

Shortly after 400 BC, the Greek philosopher Plato came to the conclusion that there must be a fundamental difference between body and soul. He saw the body as only a temporary housing for the soul. This school of thought, known as the dualism of body and soul, provided the necessary foundation for preserving human specimens. The conviction that the soul exists independently of the body made it permissible to open up the body once the soul had departed after death. It was in this spirit that Herophilos and Erasistratos undertook the first dissections of human bodies in Alexandria, where, following the death of Alexander the Great, King Ptolemy I had established a medical school in 320 BC. Dissections were performed on the bodies of executed prisoners – probably in public.

Although first expressed by Plato, the philosophical premise of the dualism of body and soul later finds its way into the Bible, where Paul says the following about the new body to come after the resurrection: "But someone will ask, 'How are the dead raised? With what kind of body will they come?' … But God will give them a body as he sees fit…" (Cor. I, 15:35-38)

Anatomy in Europe in the Common Era

When the Romans conquered Egypt in 30 BC, the medical school of Alexandria declined in importance. The teachings of Galen of Pergamum (131-201 AD), a doctor whose conclusions were based on the study of animals, would now dominate the field. Having studied in Alexandria, Galen settled in Rome and produced some 150 medical writings. It is assumed that he never dissected human bodies, but instead studied monkeys and other animals – his anatomical works were flawed accordingly. Galen was a difficult, high-handed individual, whose arrogance was expressed in his books as follows: "Anyone looking for fame simply has to familiarise himself with all that I have achieved." Galen did, in fact, enjoy an excellent reputation as a doctor – even Emperor Marcus Aurelius refused to go without his services.

Over the course of time, Galen published 200 books and influenced anatomical thought and medicine for the next 1,300 years. During this time, dissections of the human body remained an exception to the rule. Only a very few historical sources confirm that doctors dissected human bodies, but these dissections served mainly to preserve the identity of the medical profession at that time. A professor would read from Galen's books while his assistants dissected a cadaver, lending the words of the ancient master more significance than was attributed to any anatomical findings revealed by opening the body. Anatomical drawings were correspondingly faulty.

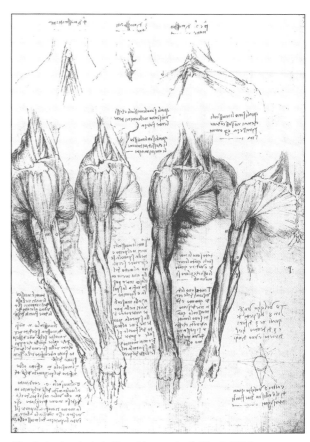

Fig. 2: Anatomical studies of Leonardo da Vinci, 1510

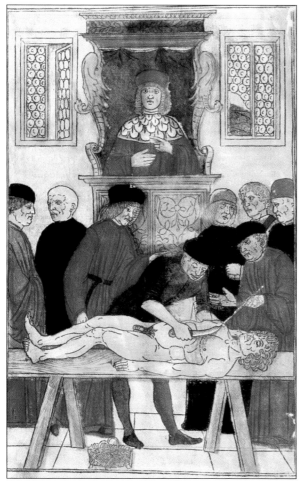

Fig. 1: Fasciolo de Medicina, drawing of an anatomy lecture, 1493. The professor read from the books of Galen, while his assistants performed the dissection.

Fig. 3: Towards the end of the Middle Ages, artists began studying the structure of the human body. This illustration presumably shows Michelangelo dissecting a corpse.

A change in attitude towards the teaching of anatomy first appeared at the end of the Middle Ages, when artists in particular began to investigate the structure of the human body. Today the most well-known artist and scientist of that time is Leonardo da Vinci (1452-1519), who privately performed anatomical dissections of human corpses. These formed the basis for his famous, highly detailed anatomical sketches. For the first time, he provided realistic, correctly proportioned illustrations of the body's interior, even though the details of his drawings were often incorrect. Leonardo da Vinci's work made a significant contribution to society's acceptance of studying human bodies.

Leonardo da Vinci passionately studied the human body. Under cover of night, he climbed cemetery walls, stole bodies, and dragged them into his studio. In his notebook he wrote presumably around 1510:

"I have dissected more than ten human corpses, digging deep into each limb, pulling back the minutest bits of flesh. If this subject excites you, you may feel a natural repulsion, or even if you're not put off, you may still dread spending the night among cut-up, flayed, ghastly-looking cadavers. If all that still doesn't deter you, you may lack the artistic talent indispensable for this science."

Fig. 4: Andreas Vesal (1514–1564), founder of the science of anatomy

A short time later, the famous anatomist Andreas Vesalius (1514-1564) had the courage to criticise publicly the practice of limiting anatomical dissections to animals. In his monumental work De fabrica humani corporis, Vesalius describes the anatomy of the human body according to what he had observed at recently introduced public dissections at the "Theatre of Anatomy." He is considered the founder of the science of anatomy. The drawings by his illustrator Kalkar were more exact than anything that had been previously produced. The sketches also introduced a new aesthetic quality, showing dissected bodies in nearly life-like poses, standing in nature and surrounded by everyday items. According to available evidence, Andreas Vesalius was also the first person to assemble real bones into an upright structure. He called this a skeleton after ho skeletos, which means 'dried up' in Greek. This was revolutionary, as no one had ever before dared to do anything similar with cadavers; he more or less pulled the dead out of their graves and put them back into society. A skeleton assembled by Vesalius can still be found at the Institute of Anatomy of the University of Basel.

Anatomy as it was shown in the drawings of that time was initially a very individual type of anatomy. The specimen and all of its unique anatomical features were copied in as great detail as possible. Certain artistic means were employed to demonstrate the authenticity and individuality of the illustration; shadows caused by the light coming in through a window, for example, made it clear what time of day that particular specimen was dissected. A fly on the drawing symbolised the momentary nature of the illustrator's art, as in a photograph.

That all changed with Bernhard Albinus (1697-1747), whose illustrator Wandelaer not only enriched contemporary understanding of anatomy with his drawings of animals; he also compiled the many variations that he found into a standard, thereby clearing the way for the statistically average anatomy. Organs were no longer sketched individually or as they were found in the body; instead, they were drawn together with their associated functional structures, thus emphasising systems of organs. A kidney, for example, was not just drawn along with the adrenal gland in the surrounding fatty tissues; the ureters and bladder were included as well. The brain was no longer shown solely from the perspective of the open skull; it was now sketched along with the spine and the peripheral nerves. This provided the foundation for developing schematic diagrams of the anatomy – an abstraction that arose from a more functional understanding of the body.

Anatomical Theaters

Artistic passion inspired the anatomists of the Renaissance, and interest in anatomy grew among the masses. More and more, physicians, as well as the general public, wanted to see the human body with their own eyes. "Autopsy" hails from the Greek phrase, "To see with one's own eyes." Anatomical theaters were built in many cities. Rich and poor alike would flock to the public dissection presentations.

The picture on the left is the frontispiece illustration for Andreas Vesal's seven-volume opus *On the Fabric of the Human Body*. It shows Vesalius performing a dissection in a crowded theatre. Like many Renaissance paintings, this illustration is filled with symbolisms and allegories. Here are a few that have been deciphered:

(1) Cherubs hold up Vesalius's coat of arms, showing three weasels.
The name Vesalius is a Latin version of the Flemish surname von Wesel.

(2) The writing on the plaque states, "Andreas Vesalius of Brussels,
Professor in the School of Physicians of Padua; his seven books
On the Fabric of the Human Body".

(3) The hooded figure, perhaps a monk, represents the Church
watching over Vesalius's work.

(4) The large skeleton symbolises that humans are mortal and that death is in the room.
The skeleton looks toward heaven, striking a pose used by Renaissance artists when
depicting saints or Christ.

(5) Many in the crowd are thought to have been members of the wealthy nobility.
Some of these noblemen may have financially or politically supported Vesalius's work.

(6) Andreas Vesalius carries out the dissection himself. In previous times, a barber-surgeon
would have performed the dissection, while a professor lectured from a nearby lectern.

(7) The cadaver is female. During the Renaissance, nature was often seen as having a female
persona. Vesalius exploring the female cadaver implies that he is exploring nature and
is part of the great line of natural scientists.

(8) The robed man may represent the classical anatomist Galen (129-200 AD).
Galen's books on human anatomy dominated medicine up until the Renaissance.
Galen's information was based on the dissection of pigs, large monkeys and
other animals, since the dissection of humans was forbidden by Roman law.
Vesalius was one of the first to publish tracts on human anatomy based on
his dissections of human bodies.

(9) The two men represent barber-surgeons. With Vesalius doing the dissection himself,
the gentlemen are left to just sharpen the scalpel-knives. Normally barber-surgeons did
the dissections.

(10) The dog (and the monkey on the left side) symbolise Galen's study of human anatomy
through the dissection of animals. Vesalius admired Galen, but through the examination
of human cadavers, he soon realised that Galen had made a number of mistakes. These
mistakes are symbolised by the dog's rear foot, which is clearly human.

The father of cross-sectional anatomy was Russian anatomist Nikolas Pirogov (1810-1881). In his Anatomia topographica, sectionibus per corpus humanum, he published two hundred and thirteen cross-sectional illustrations of the human body, including one of a pregnant woman. The cadavers were frozen during the Russian winter in St. Petersburg. The stone printing plates used for his work exist to this day.

The introduction of the microscope allowed 17th century anatomists to study the microstructure of the body; as a result, many anatomists lost interest in macroscopic anatomy, which was increasingly considered to have no more research potential. This trend was magnified in the West during the 1950's, when the electron microscope came into use in the field of anatomy; the same has also been true over the past 20 years due to anatomical research in the fields of cell and molecular biology. As a result of their research in cell biology, western anatomists have lost nearly all interest in anatomical studies on cadavers.

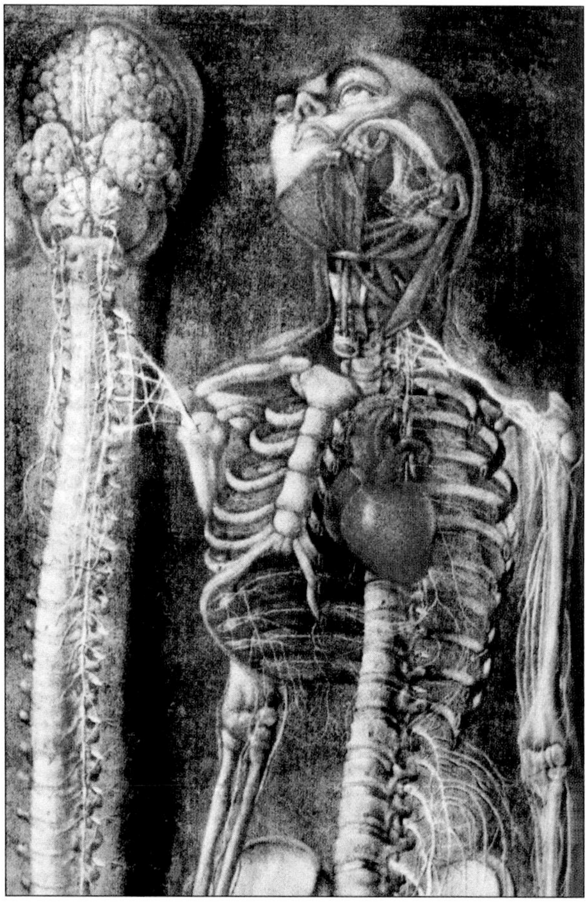

Anatomy and Art

In the 16th century, the human body was the focus of an entire era in the history of art. At precisely that moment in history when the sculptures and paintings of the Renaissance had elevated the beauty of the human body to an aesthetic ideal, and natural beauty stood at the heart of our understanding of art, artists also discovered the beauty of the body's interior. In their longing for perfection, painters and sculptors wanted to see the actual muscles upon which they modelled their works of art. First, they observed anatomists, but it was not long before they took the scalpel into their own hands. In Italy and the Netherlands, guilds of doctors, apothecaries and artists even banded together.

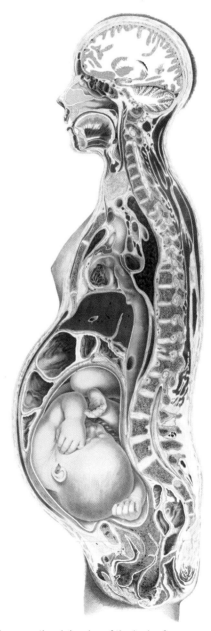

Fig. 6: Bernhard Siegfried Albinus. As anatomy became better understood, organs were sketched more and more frequently in systems representing specific functions.

Fig. 7: Cross-sectional drawing of the body of a pregnant woman by Russian anatomist Nikolas Pirogov, 1855.

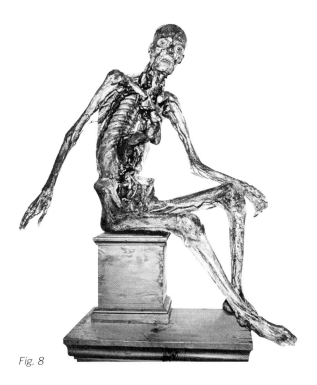

Fig. 8

Only when the skeletal systems and musculatures of entire bodies had been studied in detail could the famous paintings and sculptures of the day come into being. During this era, when artistic talent and anatomical knowledge were combined, the most artistic works in the history of anatomy were created. Surviving anatomical illustrations, which are now considered part of man's cultural heritage, were clearly not drawn from memory – real specimens served as models. Due to the lack of appropriate preservation techniques, however, cadavers decom-posed shortly after they had been dissected.

Only a very few of them could be preserved, and these can still be seen today at the Italian Museum of Anatomy. Bodies were first dried and their surfaces were treated with oils; in some cases, specimens were injected with metal alloys as a means of highlighting arteries.

The dissected bodies were displayed in aesthetically pleasing, life-like poses that are expressive in a way that brings out the individual character of their anatomy. Some of the bodies are even shown in a manner that makes them seem to exude charm and humour. What is so fascinating about surviving pictures is that, in addition to providing a detailed depiction of the specimen, they also surround the specimen with ancient landscapes. The resulting surreal atmosphere created by these illustrations is astonishing; take, for instance, a drawing in which a rhinoceros makes its way into the scene, its proverbial thick skin forming a contrast to the dissected, skinless human being. BODY WORLDS is presented here as natural art. The beauty of the mediaeval specimens manifests itself in their perfection, in the harmonious contours of

the specimens, in the pleasing, perfect balance of their components and the clarity of anatomical detail. By performing precise studies of anatomical relationships and sharing the results of these studies, anatomy artists established anatomy as a science. They sought the source of truth in the original and made seeing for themselves, i.e., the 'autopsy,' the foundation of their scientific endeavours. As the science of anatomy developed further, the significance of the artist as such was increasingly relegated to the background. Anatomy was gradually reduced to medical courses on dissection and dissection in the service of pathology; as a result, it gradually became the sole privilege of doctors. Finally, the invention of photography made artists largely dispensable.

Today an artist's place in the science of anatomy is mostly limited to occasional modifications to existing anatomical illustrations and to sketching anatomical findings yielded by surgery. If artists wished to study a real cadaver, they would now have to go begging to anatomists; being granted this privilege, however, is generally an exception rather than the rule. It, therefore, comes as no surprise that the aesthetic quality of anatomical drawings made of the human body during the Renaissance has remained unrivalled to this day.

Fig. 8 and 9: These roughly 200-year-old whole-body anatomical specimens, which can still be seen in Florence and Modena, have been preserved with varnish.

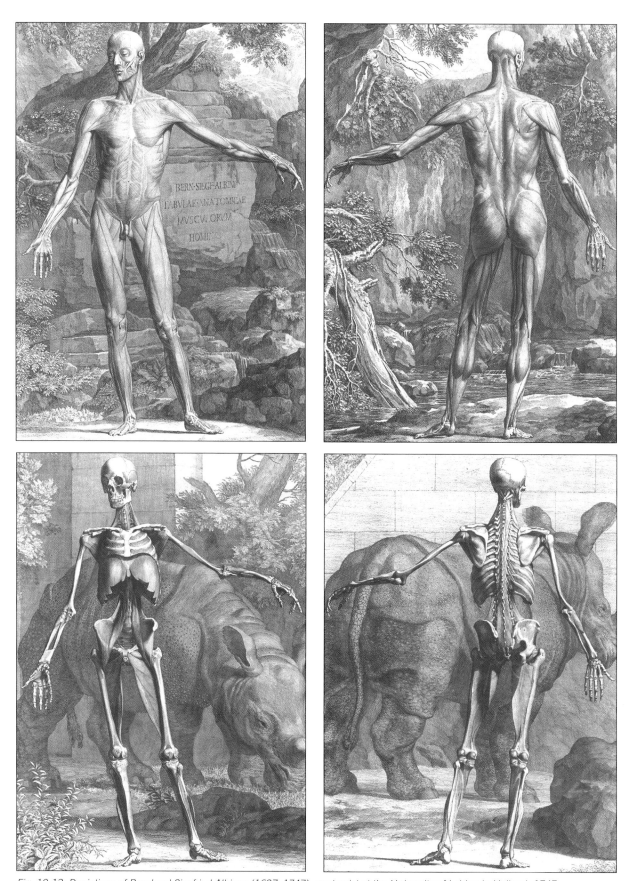

Fig. 10-13: Depictions of Bernhard Siegfried Albinus (1697–1747), anatomist at the University of Leiden in Holland, 1747.

Fig. 14: Dissected bodies were shown in life-like poses, their gestures accentuating the individuality of their anatomy.

VII expressly permitted the dissection of human cadavers in Padua and Bologna. The Museum of Anatomy in Bologna owes its existence to support from Pope Benedict XIV, who had always been very open-minded regarding modern science. Even when he was still the archbishop of Bologna, Benedict had indicated the importance of anatomy and stressed the necessity of dissecting cadavers. The Holy See expressly permitted corpses to be opened during epidemics of bubonic plague.

Without the Christian belief of the dualism of body and soul mentioned earlier, anatomical dissection would never have originated and become established in Italy, a country ruled by the papacy. Similarly, without this belief, the Catholic tradition of preserving ritual relics would never have developed. Even today, relics can be found in many Catholic churches, and many old cemeteries have what are known as ossuaries – charnel houses with stacks of bones and skulls reaching to the ceiling.

Anatomy and the Papacy

The unmitigated vanity of today's medical profession has laid sole responsibility for the over 1000-year stagnation of anatomical studies at the feet of the church. De sepulturis, the papal bull issued by Pope Bonifacius VIII in 1300, is gladly interpreted as evidence of the animosity towards anatomical science on the part of the church. The purpose of this decree was quite different, however: crusaders had begun the practice of dismembering the corpses of their fallen comrades, boiling their bones and sending them back home. The reason for this was that they could thus be buried on consecrated ground in their native lands; the time-consuming custom weakened the troops' fighting ability, however, and this was the reason that the papal bull was intended to put a stop to it. Over-zealous clerics interpreted it as a general ban on dissection.

A notable example of how well-disposed the church was towards anatomy is that the body of Pope Alexander V was dissected in the year 1410. Popes Sixtus IV and Clement

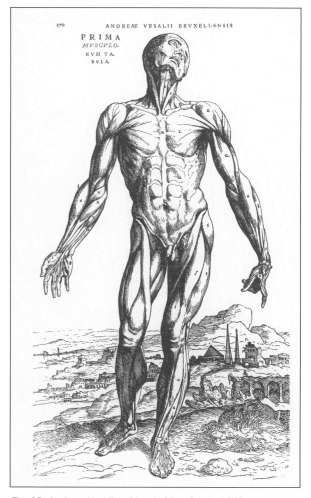

Fig. 15: Andreas Vesalius, Muscle Man, fabric, 1543

Fig. 16: In 1860, a wood carver named Frantisek Rint artistically adorned the charnel house of the All Saints Church in Kunta Hora, Czech Republic, with the bones of 40,000 people.

The History of Procuring Cadavers

Anatomists of the Renaissance dissected the corpses of executed prisoners, disputing the right of criminals to their own bodies. This was the case in England, where Henry VIII (1491-1547) commanded that the bodies of criminals hanging from the gallows be handed over to anatomists. Dabbling in anatomy became so popular, in fact, that dissections began to be carried out in public theatres of anatomy so that anyone having an interest could satisfy his or her curiosity. It was not long before bodies became so scarce that people began robbing cemeteries. Parish councils received frequent complaints; in one such complaint, it was reported that thieves had stolen seven adult cadavers and three children's bodies on the night from Thursday, January 12, to Friday, January 13, 1786. In this case, it was claimed that young anatomists had, in attempts to hide the remains from the neighbours, burned the bones and used the fat from the dead as heating fuel in the winter. Robbing graves became an established profession; its representatives were known as 'resurrection men.' Because of the public interest in educating medical students, a blind eye was turned to this practice, until 1828 when two Scots named Burke and Hare began strangling people in order to deliver the bodies directly to anatomists. The public was so horrified that the English parliament immediately passed the Anatomy Act in 1832, a law that would secure the supply of bodies to anatomists, thereby depriving grave robbers of their economic base. Since that time, England has had an official anatomy examiner bearing the title 'Her Majesty's Inspector of Anatomy.' In Germany, there was also an effort made by the state to offset short-ages of cadavers for anatomical purposes. In Prussia, for instance, circulars from 1889 saw to it that unclaimed cadavers were delivered to anatomical institutes. Bodies found, for which no survivors could be identified, formed the basis for the supply of corpses at anatomical institutes up until the 1960's. Bodies were transferred to institutes of anatomy by such public institutions as the Social Welfare Office.

In the 1960's, German anatomical institutes switched over to the practice of seeking bequeathments, in which individuals stated that, upon their deaths, their bodies should be donated to the nearest anatomical institute. Since then, the supply of cadavers has so greatly outpaced demand that most institutes of this type no longer need to accept unclaimed corpses.

How cadavers are procured for anatomical purposes varies greatly from one country to the next, and depends on the cultural and religious context. In the United States, for instance, where this is a state issue just as it is in Germany, institutes of anatomy either operate their own body-donation programs or they obtain bodies from independent, state-run organisations (State Anatomy Boards), which are responsible for supplying cadavers to interested institutes. Such organisations also run special donation programs for obtaining bodies. In addition to this, federal law holds that unclaimed cadavers are to be sent to State Anatomy Boards, where, for example in Maryland, they are chemically preserved and turned over to any interested institutions for a small fee (to cover costs).

History of Preserving Cadavers

Man's desire to be immortalised is as old as the human race. Cave paintings, Egyptian pyramids, art collections, endowments and monuments all testify to this. It, therefore, comes as no surprise that there has always been a desire in all civilizations to protect one's own body and those of relatives from decomposition, or at least to slow the process down and to prevent the body from becoming a transitory object immediately following death. In the past, however, permanent preservation was reserved for only a few wealthy individuals. Yet it was not simple death rituals that led to the development of methods for preserving cadavers; fear of apparent death also played a role. Up until the 18th century, the processes of death and dying were not well known, and people were very unclear and unsure as to when the actual moment of death occurred. It was believed that the body lived on in some diminished state, especially for however long the flesh was still on it. Comments such as "Corpses are ravenous and devour their own garments!" or "Corpses can hear!" were not uncommon in documents of the time. If the ground over a grave sank or if the gases that result from decay caused it to rise (mass graves were common at the time, and a significant amount of gas was produced as a result), the tombstone would rise and sink, thereby sending out what appeared to be encoded messages from the dead. It was not until people understood the circulatory system and the functions of the brain that the moment of death could be defined as a unique event in time. Finally, the development of appropriate preservation methods was extremely important for the advance of medicine, as the study of human anatomy had previously been greatly impeded by the process of decay.

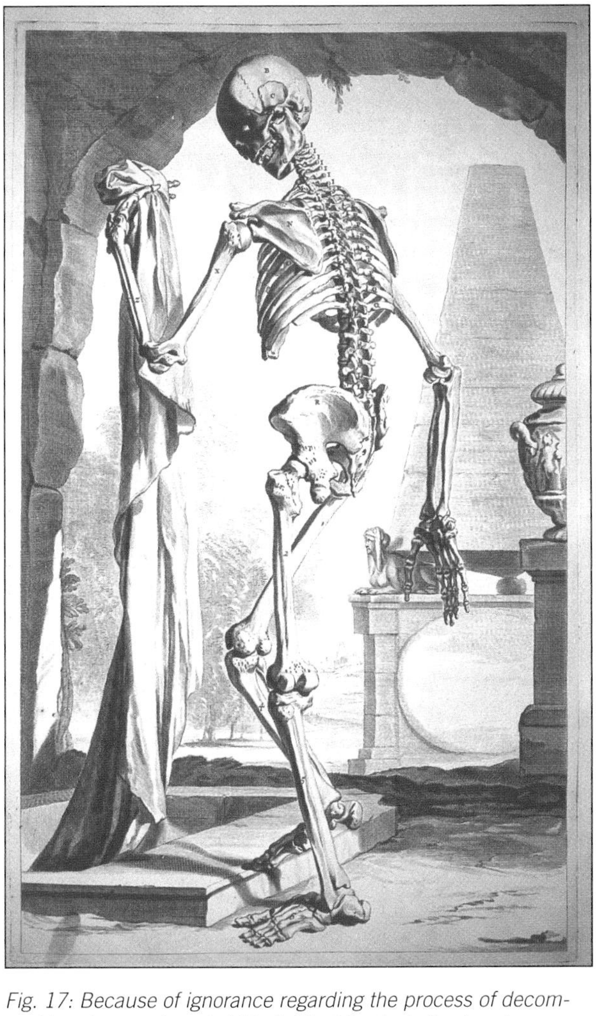

Artificial preservation methods undertaken by man are not the only means of preserving corpses. Natural preservation can also take place, and requires that the cadaver dry out in a relatively bacteria-free environment over a long period of time, as happens to a body when kept in an air-tight sarcophagus or in a crypt ventilated with dry air. The same is true for bodies buried in moors where they are preserved by the humic acid found there. Many natural mummies, including Ötzi (the oldest and most well known European mummy) prove that the degree to which they have been preserved is no worse than in the case of the mummies of the Pharaohs, for which such great pains had been taken.

Cultic Preservation of Bodies

The idea has persisted throughout nearly every epoch, culture and religion that death does not mean the end of our individual existence. When death is seen as a transition of the soul to a spiritual world, as is the case with Jews, Christians, Buddhists and other religious societies, then the body is considered to be of secondary importance; rituals accompanying death are kept relatively simple.

It was different with early cultures that were often convinced of a somatic life after death. Here the deceased were buried with a rich array of burial objects, commensurate with their social status. Moreover, the question arose on how to preserve the bodies of the dead from decomposition. Especially the Egyptians developed embalming and mummification methods over several thousand years, the results of which can even today be admired in museums throughout the world.

Why it was the Egyptians who developed such methods can presumably be explained by the following. Because of the annual flooding of the Nile Valley, the people were forced

Fig. 17: Because of ignorance regarding the process of decomposition, it was a long-held belief that the body lived on in some diminished state.

Fig. 18: "The little Inca prince", approximately 500-year-old ice mummy. National Museum in Santiago de Chile

Fig. 19: Tollund man, one of the best-preserved bog bodies from the pre-Christian era

to bury their dead beyond the reach of the floodwaters, in other words, in the dry, hot sand or rocks of the surrounding desert regions. Here the conditions were ideal for natural mummification: warm, dry sand that could dehydrate the body while at the same time stabilising it in its outward form. The steady draughts prevailing in these desert regions additionally favoured the drying-out process. Finally, finding natural mummies by the Egyptians themselves must have contributed to making the idea of a somatic afterlife a central part of their religious world view.

The art of embalming in Egypt reached its zenith in the period from 1700-1100 BC. It confined itself, however, to the 'mortal shell' of the corpses. The organs, whose failure was the cause of death, such as the lungs, liver, kidneys and brain, could not be sufficiently preserved. Their fate was as follows: First, the brain was removed through the nose with the aid of a hook. After opening the abdominal cavity through a slit along the left side of the body, the viscera were taken out except for the heart; they were then washed in palm oil and preserved in an alcohol solution in canopic jars. They nevertheless quickly fell prey to decomposition because the essences (natron, resins) only had a superficial effect. The body cavity was also washed and filled with powdered myrrh, resins and perfumes. The slit was then sewn back together. Next, the body was placed in a solution of potassium nitrate or saltpeter for 70 days.

Finally, it was again washed, rubbed with oils or resin and wrapped repeatedly in complicated layers of linen bandages. It was thus possible to preserve permanently only the skin and the bones, which could hardly rot under such dry conditions, anyway.

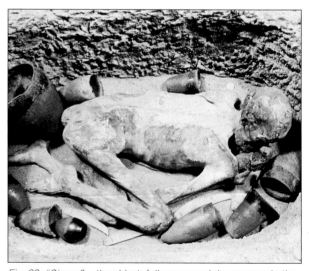

Fig. 20: "Ginger" – the oldest, fully preserved dry mummy in the world. About 3200 years ago, she was buried in the hot desert sands of Egypt. British Museum, London

Methods of preservation similar to those of the ancient Egyptians are also utilised by the natives on the Canary Islands, in Africa (Guinea, Congo, Sudan and the Ivory Coast), in Asia (inter alia, India, Sri Lanka and Tibet), in Oceania (inter alia, Melanesia and Polynesia), America (in many Indian tribes of North and South America) and in Europe. In fact, they are partially still in use even today, for example by headhunters in the Amazon region, in Assam, Burma, Malaysia and New Guinea, to produce shrunken heads as trophies.

The complex processes of mummifying corpses developed from methods used to preserve food, for example, drying (dried fruits and meats), curing with smoke, salts, acids and protective solutions (pickling fluids, honey, sugar or alcohol). Two famous examples of using methods for preserving food to protect corpses were: 1) the body of Alexander the Great, which was kept in honey for the return to Macedonia after his untimely death; and 2) the body of Horatio Nelson, which spent the return journey from the victorious battle of Trafalgar, which had ended fatally for the admiral, in brandy.

Modern Embalming

Until the 17th century, corpses were preserved with the embalming methods developed by the Egyptians. The embalming methods commonly used today differ from the old ones both in the substances employed for preservation as well as the technology. Here we can primarily mention the introduction of new chemicals for preservation, especially formaldehyde, and the development of embalming through arterial injection. The latter was first made possible when William Harvey published his revolutionary ideas on the circulatory system. During his research, Harvey had injected dyestuffs

Fig. 22: Shrunken head of a Jivaro. Trophies of human heads were supposed to convey the power and strength of an enemy to the victor

Fig. 23: Canopic jars. They were used to hold the viscera of Egyptian mummies

Fig. 21: Egyptian mummy. Vatican Museum, Rome

into the blood vessels of cadavers. This new principle of arterial injection was first used successfully by Frederick Ruysche (1665-1717), who taught anatomy in Amsterdam. Unfortunately, Ruysche neglected to record exact information about the chemicals that he used. Detailed descriptions on arterial embalming were first written by the famous Scottish anatomist, William Hunter (1718-1783). He employed a solution consisting of turpentine and resinous oils, mixed with dyes, which he chose to inject in the femoral artery. In 1868, chemist August Wilhelm von Hofmann discovered formaldehyde that was later integrated into preservation techniques. Some years before, Laskowski (1886) had already introduced his Genevan embalming fluid, glycerin (discovered by Scheele in 1779), to protect specimens from dehydration and phenol (introduced as a disinfectant by Lister in 1867) to preserve them.

The importance that these discoveries had for practical preservation is shown by a survey that was published by Grönroos in 1898. Of the 44 anatomical institutes in Europe surveyed by the study, all of them utilised arterial injection for embalming. Embalming fluids that had gained Europe-wide acceptance were those that used solutions with formaldehyde (embalming and hardening), phenol (to inhibit the formation of fungi) and glycerin (moisture-retentive as it is a humectant). By the beginning of the 20th century, all of the substances had already been introduced, which have remained relatively unchanged until today and have been most frequently used to preserve cadavers. These include formaldehyde, phenol, glycerin, ethanol and water. A typical example is the preservation fluid used in the Institute of Anatomy at the University of Heidelberg: formaldehyde 3%, lysoformin (contains formaldehyde, glutaraldehyde and a wetting solution) 1%, phenol 6%, glycerin 15%, alcohol 30% and water 45%.

2. Plastinated Specimens and Plastination

What are Plastinated Specimens?

Approximately 70% of our bodies consist of fluids. They are indispensable both for living and for decomposing. With plastination, fluids in our tissue are replaced by reactive plastics, such as silicone rubber, epoxy resin or polyester resin, in a special vacuum process. Body cells and the natural surface relief remain identical with their condition prior to preservation down to the microscopic level. The specimens are dry and odourless and are thus 'graspable' in the most literal sense of the word. Thanks to these properties, plastinated specimens are of extremely high value both in educating medical students and in enlightening interested laypersons.

With the invention of plastination, it has become possible for the first time to preserve natural anatomical specimens in a durable, realistic and aesthetic manner for instructional and research purposes as well as for general education. Natural specimens are especially valuable for medical studies and also for laypersons as the complicated structure of the locomotor system and organs as well as their relative positions and relationships to one another cannot be fully comprehended in their three-dimensional complexity when only books are used. Regardless of the quality of the pictures, they cannot replace the original. Artificial anatomical models can also make only limited contributions to understanding anatomy as they are schematised at best, are not capable of showing fine details and cannot convey the individuality of the human body. One model is the same as the next one. Anatomical variations, however, are significant from one individual to another. For this reason, a thorough, practical anatomical education for medical students using dead, human bodies has been laid down by law in most of today's advanced societies.

Beyond their didactic qualities, plastinated specimens also radiate a certain fascination, based primarily on their authenticity. Plastination stops decomposition and dehydration so completely that the insides of bodies cease to be objects of revulsion. Observers are not bothered by any kind of offensive odours.

Plastination creates beautiful specimens as a sensuous experience that are frozen at a point between death and decay. Thanks to this realistic quality, plastination represents the most attractive form of exhibiting durable human specimens. This becomes particularly evident in the transparent body slices that provide a window into structures that are indispensable to life even in areas which would normally be viewed with a magnifying glass. To achieve the unlimited durability of a specimen, an inordinately large amount of time-consuming dissection work is now justified, which was heretofore not justifiable. One thousand and more hours of dedicated work are necessary to create one whole-body specimen dissected to show minute details. Plastinated specimens far exceed the expressive power of untreated specimens, for example, when – thanks to dyed plastics – grey brain matter is more obviously distinguishable from the white matter than would be possible with an unplastinated brain.

New Types of Specimens through Plastination

Plastination permits us to produce completely new types of specimens because it makes otherwise soft body parts such as muscles or the skin rigid, for example, in 3-millimeter-thick body slices. Plastination also makes it possible to produce 'exploded-view' specimens, 'open-door' specimens and 'open-drawer' specimens. With 'exploded-view' specimens, body parts are shifted in all directions.

These specimens are particularly instructive when the body parts are 'exploded' in only one direction, for example, in the longitudinal. Instructional 'open-door' specimens also succeed in that hinges are attached in such a way that an open view into the innermost realms of the body is provided. Finally, parts of the body can be shifted forward like open drawers, thereby giving a clear insight into the body.

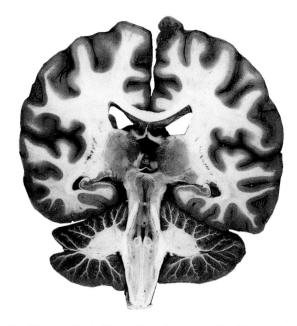

Fig. 25: In plastinated brain slices, the grey matter of the cerebral cortex and the nuclei are clearly distinguishable from the white matter.

These interstitial specimens that permit the observer to shift back the individual parts of the body to their original position in the mind's eye and reduce the body to its original shape and size contrast with traditional 'removal dissections' practiced at universities. Here, each succeeding layer is removed from the bodies. The major disadvantage of this procedure is that by the end of the course, students have often forgotten which parts were removed at the beginning.

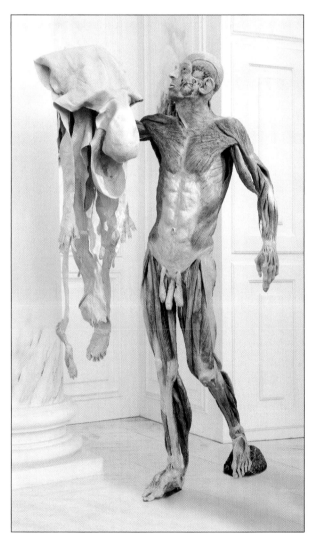

Fig. 24: A whole-body specimen in a life-like pose

The Technology of Plastination

In principle, plastination is relatively simple. As shown in the Figure 31, plastinated specimens are created through two essential exchange phases: In the first phase, bodily fluids are replaced by acetone through diffusion. In the second phase, the acetone still in the body is replaced by reactive plastics. It is then removed from the plastic bath to be cured into a fully plastinated specimen.

The decisive trick, with which liquid plastic can be infused into the last cells, is forced vacuum impregnation. Just as babies use a partial vacuum to suck the milk out of their mothers' breasts, acetone is sucked from the specimen in the vacuum. In this way, the vacuum created in the specimen keeps a steady supply of plastic flowing into the tissue. Gradually the specimen fills up with plastic. Seen physically, the process takes advantage of the difference in pressure between the volatile acetone and a plastic solution with a high boiling point. Thin body slices take only a few days for this; conversely, with whole-body specimens, this can take weeks. Only when the vacuum falls below one-hundredth of normal atmospheric levels (<5mmHg) and only individual acetone bubbles squeeze out of the specimen is it removed from the plastic bath and cured.

The advantages of this "forced impregnation with plastic in a vacuum," which is the main step in plastination, are primarily the following:

1. Impregnation can be done with a number of liquid, polymeriseable plastics.

2. By regulating the vacuum, the speed of impregnation can be adapted to the type of specimen, its thickness and the viscosity of the plastics used.

3. Impregnation can be used to minimise shrinkage at low temperatures, e.g., at –25°C.

Fig. 26: The Longitudinally Expanded Body (1996)

Fig. 27: Forced impregnation. Acetone is squeezed out of the specimen and is constantly sucked away

The Plastination Process

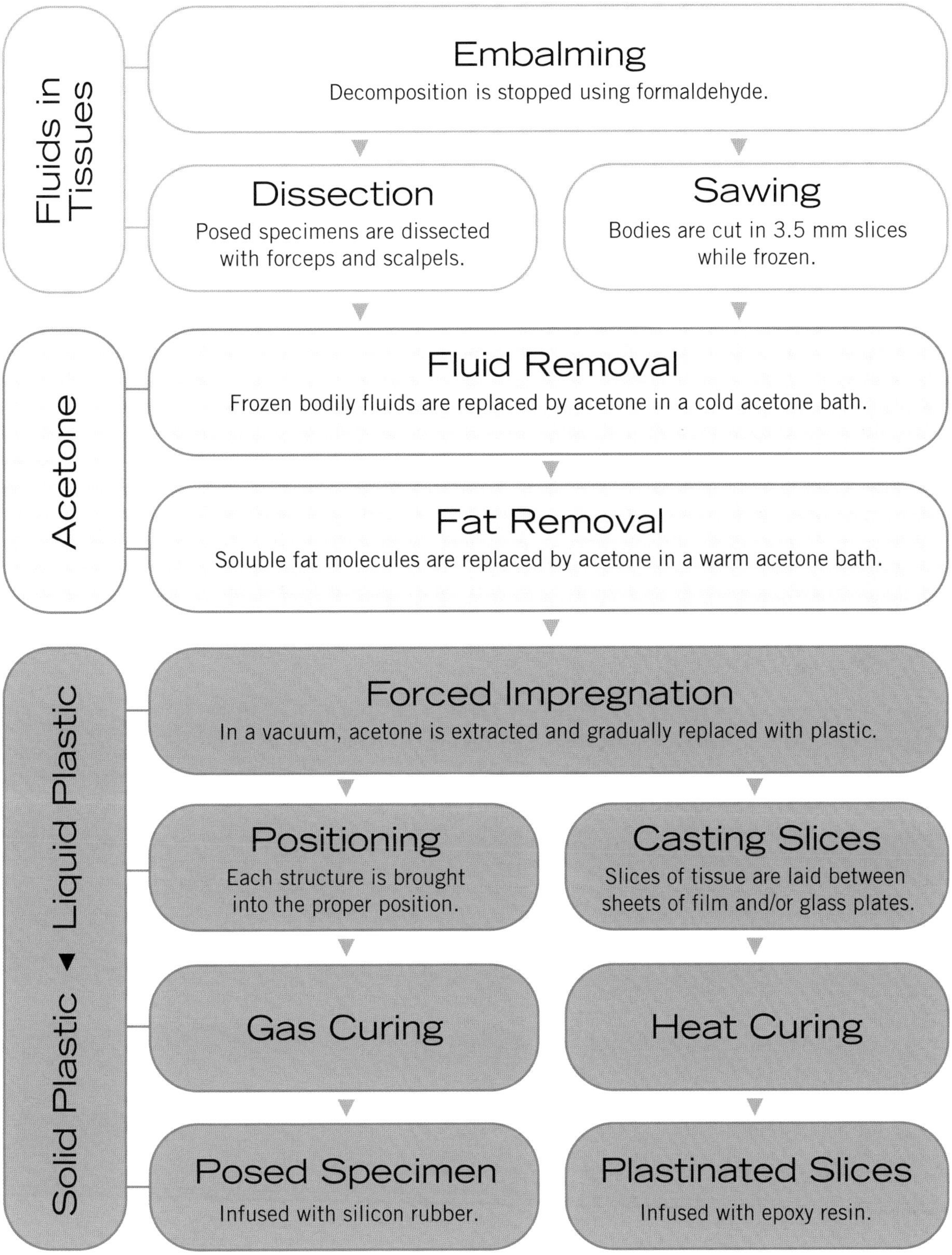

Fluids in Tissues

Embalming
Decomposition is stopped using formaldehyde.

Dissection
Posed specimens are dissected with forceps and scalpels.

Sawing
Bodies are cut in 3.5 mm slices while frozen.

Acetone

Fluid Removal
Frozen bodily fluids are replaced by acetone in a cold acetone bath.

Fat Removal
Soluble fat molecules are replaced by acetone in a warm acetone bath.

Solid Plastic ▼ Liquid Plastic

Forced Impregnation
In a vacuum, acetone is extracted and gradually replaced with plastic.

Positioning
Each structure is brought into the proper position.

Casting Slices
Slices of tissue are laid between sheets of film and/or glass plates.

Gas Curing

Heat Curing

Posed Specimen
Infused with silicon rubber.

Plastinated Slices
Infused with epoxy resin.

In this way, the plastination process permits numerous possibilities for variation. It also means that the process can be very complex in individual details on the one hand; however, its strengths come just from these complexities on the other hand. If optimum results are desired, the choice of plastics and the type of plastination technology can be adapted to the respective specimen. Here are some examples:

Most specimens, especially bones and intestines, must first be defatted in acetone at room temperature. Conversely, brains would shrink substantially in size if subjected to such a treatment. The same applies for specimens still covered with skin, such as embryos and fish, which therefore require additional infusion with plastic. Freezing specimens may also cause their volume to expand, and when this occurs too slowly, ice crystals can form. Emulsifying plastics cause swelling so that newcomers to the process often wonder why a brain plastinated with these materials no longer fits into its skull. Transparent series of slices should be approximately 6 millimetres (1/4inch) thick through the abdomen while slices of the head should be approximately 3 millimetres (1/8inch) thick. All of this depends still on a number of different factors, such as age, distribution of fat, venous congestion and others.

Fig. 28: Specimens plastinated with silicone are cured with a special gas

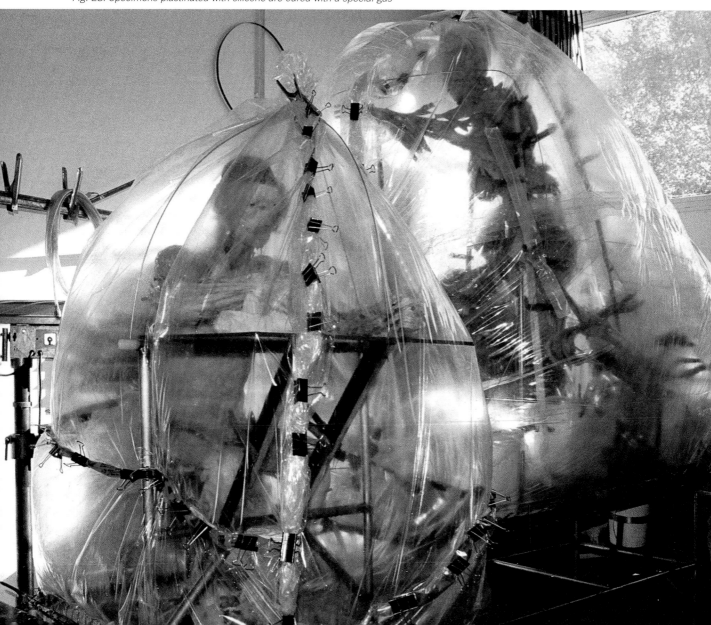

Fig. 29: A body that has been frozen at −70°C and infused with polyurethane is sawn into approximately 1/8-inch-thick slices

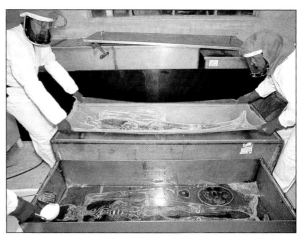

Fig. 30: Body slices dehydrated with acetone are then placed in a polymer solution

The demand for research is still enormous despite all of the progress until now. A particular focus is on retaining the colour of tissue, optimum presentation of blood vessels as well as improving the plastination of slices and treating specimens that are difficult to preserve, such as jellyfish. An International Society for Plastination, a professional journal and biennial conferences are the main forums for discussing advances in plastination.

Plastics used in Plastination

Developments in plastination have always been closely associated with development of suitable plastics, as the mechanical and optical properties of the plastics employed largely determine the character of the specimens. The plastics normally used are silicone rubber, epoxy resins and polyester resins.

After curing, silicone rubber is elastic and thus lends elasticity to the specimens. It only refracts light very weakly, which accounts for the natural look of specimens infused with silicone. For this reason, silicone rubber is used to plastinate whole organs (in contrast to slices); here plastination of whole-body specimens is a more recent development. A very thin-bodied silicone provides the best results with whole-organ packages. Gas-curing is used to harden the specimens after all of the anatomical structures have been properly positioned. Plastination with silicone rubber is the simplest of all the techniques used in this process and thus has the most users worldwide.

The highly refractive properties of epoxy resins allow the slices of saturated tissue to appear transparent when the surface is smooth. Because polymerised epoxy resin is also extremely hard, epoxy resin blends were chosen as the polymer of choice for plastinating cross-sectional specimens. The resins are heat-cured.

The use of epoxy resins for plastination is highly suitable for solving clinical problems, because plastinating bodies that have been cut into a series of slices makes it possible to perform precise, three-dimensional analyses of the specimens. In the past, this has allowed scientists to investigate such complex issues as the blood supply in the kneecaps and wrist bones, and the paths taken by the tiny muscles and nerves around the prostate gland that are critical for sexual potency.

A highly refractive polyester resin cured by ultraviolet light is only used for slices of the brain. Polymeriseable emulsions that turn white during the curing process are used for thick, natural-looking specimens.

Scientists just getting started with plastination work with one to two types of polymer systems; experienced scientists will use up to ten. Polymers utilised for plastination must have low viscosity, should withstand yellowing and should be compatible with the tissues being plastinated; also, the time available for processing these polymers should be as long as possible, or, even better, unlimited. For this reason, only special polymer blends developed specifically for plastination are used.

The Idea behind Plastination

I developed the plastination techniques at the University of Heidelberg's Institute of Anatomy in 1977, patented it between 1977 and 1982, and have been continually improving the process ever since. When, as an anatomy assistant, I saw my first specimen embedded in a polymer block, I wondered why the polymer had been poured around the outside of the specimen as having the polymer within the specimen would stabilise it from the inside out. I could not get this question out of my mind. A few weeks later, I was to prepare a series of slices of human kidneys for a research project. The usual process of embedding the kidneys in paraffin and then cutting them into thin slices seemed like too much wasted effort to me, as I only needed every fiftieth slice. Then one day, I was in the butcher shop in the university town where I was studying, and as I watched the sales woman slice ham, it dawned on me that I ought to be using a meat slicer for cutting kidneys. And so a 'rotary blade cutter,' as I called it in the project-appropriation request, became my first plastination investment. I embedded the kidney slices in liquid Plexiglas and used a vacuum to extract the air bubbles that had formed when stirring in the curing agent. As I watched these bubbles, it hit me: It should be possible to infuse a kidney slice with plastic by saturating it with acetone and placing it under a vacuum; the vacuum would then extract the acetone in the form of bubbles, just as it had extracted air before. When I actually tried this, plenty of acetone bubbles emerged, but after an hour the kidney was pitch black and had shrunk. At this point most people would have dismissed the experiment as a failure, and the only reason I went ahead and repeated it a week later using silicone rubber was because my basic knowledge of physical chemistry

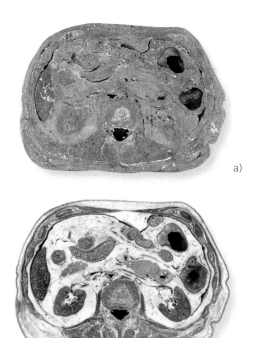

Fig. 32: Slices of bodies impregnated with a polymeriseable emulsion, a) before curing and b) after curing. Emulsification during the curing process lightens the color of the specimen.

told me that the blackening effect was due to the index of refraction of the Plexiglas, and that the shrinkage could be attributed to having permeated the specimen too quickly. The next time, I carried out this process more slowly, using three successive silicone baths as a means of preventing a single bath (along with its contents) from curing too quickly. After curing the specimen in a laboratory kiln, I had the first presentable sample of plastination. That was on January 10, 1977, the day that I decided to make plastination the focus of my life. The roots of this decision go back to January of 1968, following my arrest for unsuccessfully attempting to defect from East Germany. While I was being detained in a Bratislava jail, a Czech official gave me the opportunity to escape. I stood before an open window, but could not make up my mind to flee. I was convinced that the East German secret police would not incarcerate me – that conviction cost me two years in an East German prison for "deserting the Republic." That is the reason that in 1977 I made a clear decision in favour of uncertainty, because uncertainty always represents an opportunity.

The first round of plastinated specimens looked anything but promising. Their surfaces were smeared with polymer, transparent tissue slices were full of air bubbles, and it often happened that specimens met their end in polymer baths that had cured prematurely. Only a series of further developments over the past 20 years have made it possible for me

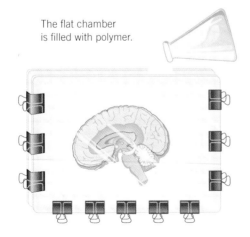

The flat chamber is filled with polymer.

Fig. 31: Cross-sectional plastination. Tissue slices that have been saturated with polymer are placed in a flat container where additional polymer is poured over them.

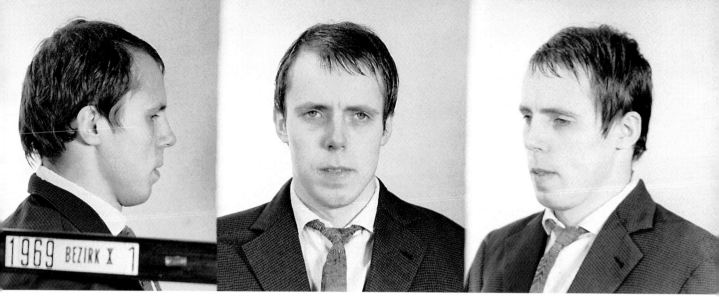

Fig. 33: Prison photo of Gunther von Hagens, taken in 1969 by the East German Ministry for State Security

to transform plastination from a largely impractical idea to an internationally recognised preservation technique. Significant innovations and developments included the following:

1. The ability to delay curing of the impregnation bath while simultaneously speeding up the curing process once a specimen has been completely infused with polymer. Specimens saturated with silicone rubber in a vacuum, for instance, are not cured until placed in a gas atmosphere. This even makes it possible for large specimens such as entire bodies to be saturated over the course of several months without running the risk that the impregnation bath will cure too early. After the specimens are taken out of the bath, they are further dissected and positioned – only then are they subjected to curing.

2. The development of plastinating slices, in which tissue sections are infused with polymer in flat glass containers or between plastic sheets.

3. The use of highly refractive polyester resin copolymers for plastinating slices of the brain. These copolymers create an excellent colour distinction between the cerebral cortex, medulla oblongata and the nuclei.

4. Development of a new class of polymers that do not emulsify until the curing process has begun, thereby yielding firm, yet natural-looking specimens.

5. The development of perfusion plastination. The first steps in this process are to drain and rinse all of the blood from an organ, position it and allow first acetone and then silicone to flow through it. The specimen is then cured by means of a gas perfusion technique that sends the curing agent through the organ's vascular system. Entire systems of organs can be plastinated in this way, yet because their vascular system is hollow (only the cells themselves are permeated with polymer), they remain light-weight and flexible.

The term 'plastination' is a word of my own invention. In my initial patents of 1977/78, I referred to the procedure as "Polymer Impregnation of Perishable, Biological Specimens," but I did not think that it was very catchy; it was also completely inappropriate for popularising the technology, particularly abroad. Because the term 'plasticise' was already used in the field of polymer chemistry to mean something else, I came up with the following little jingle during a visit to a Viennese pub in 1979: "Plastination teaches the nation, because BIODUR (a trade name for polymers used in plastination) retains the structure." In the 19th edition of the Brockhaus Encyclopedia (1992), on the other hand, the term plastination is shown to be derived from the Greek (from plassein = to mold, form).

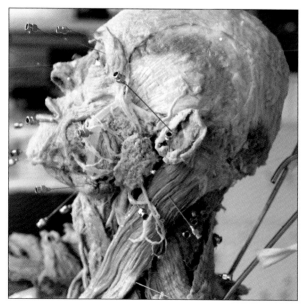

Fig. 34: Positioning anatomical structures before gas curing

The Inventive Process

Society praises its living conformists and honours its deceased rebels. As a result, people are caught up in a conflict between individuality and group consensus. If an individual conforms to the group, he will be popular. If he goes his own way, he will lose the group's approval and quickly come to be considered an oddball. The lure of this status is enhanced by ever increasing specialisation, which offers a previously unknown degree of choice and potential for personal development, thereby permitting individuality to a degree never seen before. The more individualism a society allows, the more inventors it will produce. Inventions have always been created by individuals – particularly when these have been individualists. Groups do not invent; their existence is dependent upon conformist thinking. Inventions under socialism tended, therefore, to be rare.

An invention must be new for it to be patentable; it must represent an advance in technology and must be acknowledged as surprisingly good even by experts in the field. In the language of patent law, "surprisingly good" is expressed by the words "inventive merit." As such, it is distinct from simple modifications to existing inventions. The door to invention has never been open to as many people as it is today. A computer, for example, is the only investment software developers need to begin inventing. The essential invention behind plastination, i.e., introducing polymers into every cell in a tissue sample, was not expensive.

During my twenty years of working on plastination, I have produced a whole series of individual inventions. Again and again, people have asked me how I come up with these ideas and what steps I take.

The inventive process that I utilise corresponds to the usual four stages of invention: recognising the problem, analysing it, working out solutions and applying those solutions.

(1)   Recognising the problem: I question everything as a matter of principle. Anything that is good can be improved because better is superior to good. Recognising that infusing a specimen with polymers must be superior to embedding it in a polymer block (as had been done up to that point) was the central problem that led me to develop the Plastination process. The problem was to put that idea into practice.

(2)   Analysing the problem: Not only do I try to recognise the problem at hand; I also try to imagine what sorts of additional questions might arise from the problem. This includes studying handbooks, textbooks, patent literature and company brochures, and regularly visiting trade fairs.

(3)   Solving the problem: As a matter of principle, I am never completely satisfied with a solution. Instead, I always have several irons in the fire, letting three to five potential solutions compete simultaneously with each other for a relatively long period of time. It is also important that I not settle on any one solution too soon. When following up on an approach to a solution, my gut feeling tells me that the solution in question will be the one that will work, even if I know that it is nonsense from a purely objective standpoint. I always have to go back and rethink the problem and factor in my own mistakes. When discussing suggested solutions with experts, I am often inclined to believe that the more emotionally a given potential solution is rejected, the more revolutionary and essentially feasible it must be.

(4)   Applying the solution: This is where studying company brochures and visiting trade fairs again becomes important. Constantly updating my technical expertise in the field and constantly thinking through ways of applying solutions is indispensable. As a result, I think about plastination nearly all the time: before I get up in the morning, when I am looking at my schedule for the day, when I am in the shower, driving my car, or doing my shopping. That is how a pudding mould becomes a cranium, a meat slicer becomes a cutter for making anatomical slices of the brain, a pancake turner becomes a turner for brain slices, an aquarium pump becomes a vaporizer for the gas-curing process, and clamps to hold price tags in store windows are "recycled" to hold the plates of the shallow containers used to infuse slices with polymer. Adapting and recycling established technologies in this way is the stuff that enriches the inventive spirit.

I often try out impossible, utterly ridiculous options; decisive insights frequently arise from trying out nonsense. Hence, I sometimes allow mistakes to happen or even make them consciously. Odd experiments, mistakes and coincidences are a productive part of the inventive process. A key development in plastination, for instance, was the use of a gas-curing technique for silicone rubber. This invention came about while attempting to extend as much as possible the time available for preparing a specimen. I hoped to achieve this by placing infused specimens in a curing bath; the curing agents that I was using, however, partially dissolved the polymer, causing it to leach back out again.

As the polymer leached out of a specimen, it created countless polymer bumps on its surface, nearly covering it completely. I knew this before performing an experiment, in which I left a brain in the curing bath overnight. Because the container that I was using no longer held sufficient cur-

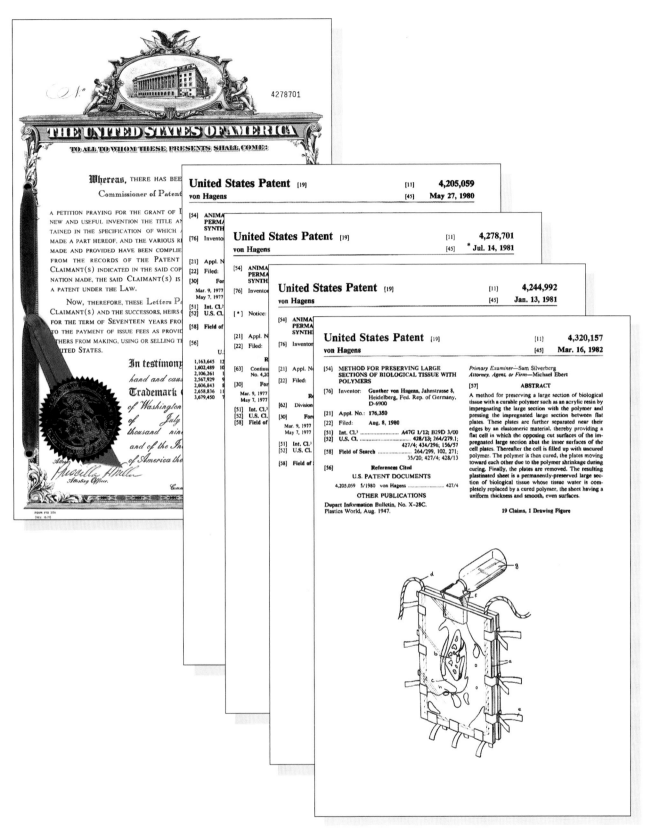

Patent Rights

The plastination process is protected by a series of patents, particularly in the United States. Plastinating specimens for non-commercial purposes such as medical instruction or museum exhibits, however, is not subject to any such limitations.

ing bath, I had propped it up at an angle so that the brain would be completely submerged. The next morning, I found that the container had fallen over, and only the base of the brain was still in the bath. This section had hardened, and, as expected, was covered with little plastic knobs that would require a great deal of effort to remove. The real excitement, however, came when, much to my surprise, I discovered that the major portion of the brain, which had been sticking out of the curing bath, had also hardened, but in fact had done so perfectly, without any annoying bumps. This could only have been the result of the evaporated curing bath, i.e., the gaseous vapors of the curing agent. I quickly repeated the experiment, having procured even more volatile hardening agents. Thus the gas-curing process was born, a technique that has significantly influenced further development of plastination with silicone polymers, and which is now used in 38 countries.

The constant effort to find new ideas, to see what has never been seen before, does, however, affect my personality. My penchant for hats, for instance, is not reflective of an artistic demeanour; it has more to do with my self-image as an inventor. My hat symbolises my internalised individualism, which is born of the conviction that an unusual outward appearance fosters non-conformist thinking. A look that flies in the face of social conventions has a nurturing effect on my creativity.

Donating Bodies for Plastination

Exhibiting real human specimens is made possible most of all by countless donors. During their lifetimes, these people willed that, upon their deaths, their bodies should be plastinated and thus made available for educating doctors and providing instruction for anyone else with an interest in medicine. They have expressly waived their right to burial. The Institute for Plastination also accepts donations of bodies that have been provided by survivors, provided that neither the deceased nor any relatives have voiced any objections. Finally, the Institute also accepts specimens from old anatomical collections when such collections are liquidated. This particular exhibition includes, for example, a plastinated hydrocephalic baby, a phenomenon that, thanks to advances in medicine, no longer occurs in today's highly developed societies. In some cases, these specimens are over 100 years old, and the Institute either purchases them outright or procures them in return for its plastinated specimens.

Because I am the director of both the Institute for Plastination of Dalian University in China as well as the Plastination Center of the State Medical Academy of Kirgizskaja, body-donation programs have been initiated at these institutions, improving cooperation and exchange of specimens between them and the Institute for Plastination in Heidelberg.

Motivations of Donors

Reasons for donation are as varied as life itself. The desire to donate one's body as a way of aiding a good cause is a common theme. Emotional rejection of decomposition and cremation, a desire to save burial expenses, or simple enthusiasm for plastination are often given as reasons. Comments such as the following indicate the wide variety of opinions (partially abridged):

"I would like to make the human body – 'the natural work of art' – more accessible to anyone who's interested."

"Through my many years of work with the Institute for Plastination I have had the opportunity to become very familiar with plastination, and it fascinates me more and more all the time."

"Since I've been helped over and over again by blood transfusions, it's important to me to help future generations by allowing research to be performed on my body."

"After my death I would prefer being like this to being consumed and metabolised by worms and tiny organisms."

"If I were displayed as a whole-body specimen, my body might make visitors stop and think."

"I've abused, neglected and ignored my body. But it still works, renews itself and tests its limits. Gratitude for that is a major reason for me to donate."

"Maintaining a grave site is just one last way of pulling the wool over other people's eyes."

"Ever since I heard about the plastination process, the prospect of my own death hasn't bothered me at all."

"Using plastination as a way of furthering the development of art and culture is what fascinates me most."

"I've always felt a need to donate my body to science, and the idea of being plastinated fills me with a sense of inner tranquillity and happiness."

"When this world comes to an end and Christ returns, He will raise me to new life with a new body, as is written in the Bible."

"I'm a Bible-believing Christian and I know that man has a soul, and when he dies, the breath of life within him will return to God, and when Christ returns I will be raised to new life in a new body, as is written in the Word of God."

"As a former Heidelberg student, I feel very attached to the city of my alma mater. I see your program as a way for me to return to Heidelberg."

"You've 'cut through' a taboo, as it were, and for that I'm particularly grateful to you. And there's one thing I'm now sure of: when I've breathed my last, my body will perform an important function for mankind. Mind and spirit will gaze upon it with envy… I even dreamed that I had been cut into fine slices and was admiring myself. It was a lovely dream."

"Plastination has added a new dimension of memory to anatomical thought. It will be my pleasure to contribute to its progress!"

"Because the medical arts have saved me from death several times, I feel a need to show at least a small token of my appreciation to medicine by donating my body."

Transforming a Cadaver into a Plastinated Specimen

Terms are usually defined according to such criteria as form, quality, function or an administrative act. Because a purely descriptive definition of a cadaver slated for burial is not clearly distinct from that of a mummy, relic, specimen, skeleton or plastinated specimen, we must draw upon additional qualities such as intent, administration and qualitative change. Intent can be seen in bodies that have been donated for plastination to promote education and research; the administrative act consists of accepting bodies for plastination, transferring documents and assuring anonymity; the qualitative change is the first plastination step, i.e., preserving the body for plastination (with formalin or by freezing). Transforming a body into a plastinated specimen (either an entire body or a part of the body) is accomplished by curing a

polymer inside the specimen. Ensuring anonymity is important for distancing the body from its plastinated counterpart, as it is the only sure way of ending the sense of reverence surrounding that body, i.e., the sense of personal and emotional attachment to the deceased. Anonymity also makes sense, because it fits in with anatomical traditions, thereby distinguishing plastinated specimens from relics and mummies of persons known by name. Conversely, the only time that plastination should be non-anonymous is in exceptional cases where there is ample justification. It goes without saying that every human specimen continues to possess human qualities. That also means that a plastinated specimen must be used for educational purposes, as dictated by the testamentary disposition of the donor.

Plastination, Art and Knowledge

Dissection and plastination are done by hand. In 1860, anatomist Joseph Hyrtl said, "Dismemberment is the heart and soul of anatomy. It is a craft, however, that requires skill if it is to be successful. The art of dismemberment must be learned. Beyond that, it also requires an innate talent for technical work. Anyone not possessing this talent will not make much progress towards solving the mysteries of the grave."

The most difficult aspect of this is plastinating entire bodies. Whole-body plastination is an intellectual achievement requiring the ability to see the finished specimen in the mind's eye just as a sculptor envisions the completed statue while he is carving it. If the specimen has soft, flexible tissues such as muscles when it leaves the silicone rubber bath, it will need to be positioned, a process guided by both aesthetic and educational considerations. The chess player's nervous system, for instance, is highlighted specifically. The plastinated pregnant woman is protecting both her genitals as well as the foetus in her uterus. Specimens that have been plastinated without such gestures often appear doll-like by comparison.

Experience at exhibitions has shown that the aesthetic aspects of posed specimens make such an impression that visitors consider a number of these to be works of art. There is no dispelling that conclusion either, because "art is in the eye of the beholder." No anatomical works of art have been created; they become works of art through the judgment of the visitors to exhibitions.

Fig. 36: A plastinated body in a realistic pose

BODY WORLDS falls within the tradition of the Renaissance when art was a product of ability; plastination has brought anatomy art a step further by making it possible to take soft tissues such as muscles or fat and fix them permanently in any given pose. This gives rise to completely new types of specimens, including slices of bodies only 3 millimetres (1/8 inch) thick, which are as transparent and colourful as stained glass. The ability to position soft tissues permanently also makes it possible to fragment the body in ways that are both aesthetic and instructive. Displacing these fragments and opening doors cut in the body provide new perspectives for viewing the body. The novel forms that arise from such techniques, such as a body that was expanded lengthwise, are necessary results of displacing fragments; they do not, however, reflect a dominant, recurring theme of the dissection process.

Even though plastinated specimens are not intended to meet any artistic demands, and even though I do not create the specimens in pursuit of any artistic goals, they may well satisfy certain artistic criteria. Like works of art, attractively posed specimens have a certain aesthetic effect and emotional content, which is attested to by, among other things, the fact that half of the visitors to the BODY WORLDS exhibition in Mannheim went precisely because of the aesthetic appeal that the specimens held for them (this according to a scientific survey taken by Dr. Lantermann of the University of Kassel's Institute of Psychology). These are qualities not generally possessed by objects that are of purely scientific interest.

Posed specimens provide an optical bridge to self-awareness. Immanuel Kant said that man's powers of awareness are two-fold. By that he was referring to emotional and rational awareness; whereas the former is conveyed more by aesthetics and feelings, the latter is imparted by intellect and instruction. Emotions and intellect are both involved when making visual sense of plastination exhibits, particularly when these are whole-body specimens. Feelings, i.e., emotional awareness, have a direct effect without our really being conscious of it. This type of insight leaves many visitors feeling fascinated and moved. The aesthetic pose, which is occasionally criticized, is what helps dispel revulsion; because it is so powerful, it also promotes emotional awareness.

From my perspective, however, plastinated specimens are not works of art, because they have been created for the sole purpose of sharing insights into human anatomy. Art, unlike the products of skilled trades and the sciences, is not created for a purpose. Unless the term 'artist' is used in the inflated sense in which Beuys uses the word, a plastinator is at most a skilled labourer in the field of art, but not an artist as such. It would be completely misguided to refer to posed specimens as works of art, because (modern) art is a term subject to interpretation; as a result, everyone projects his or her own personal understanding of art and morality onto the motivation underlying my efforts.

In order to avoid misunderstandings and to depersonalise discourse, I have introduced the term BODY WORLDS, by which I mean the "aesthetic and instructive presentation of the body's interior." 'Presentation' in this case can be understood in two ways: both in the sense of an artistic rendering and in the sense of the work performed by a skilled labourer in the field of art. The instructive component of this presentation likewise has two meanings: on the one hand, it refers to making us aware of our physical nature, of nature within us; on the other hand, it can be understood as a concrete act of sharing anatomical information. Only in this sense do I consider myself to be an artist – an anatomy artist.

In an exhibition for laypersons, who are not attending an anatomy lecture but who have instead come to the museum just to "have a look," it is especially important that objects be directly understandable without lengthy explanations. The whole-body specimens achieve this most successfully. The intellectual awareness of the visitor is aroused by com-

Fig. 37: Whole-body plastinates. Displaying these specimens in realistic, life-like poses carries on the tradition begun by the founding fathers of anatomy

ponents of whole-body specimens, such as organs, muscles and bones. Achieving awareness in this way is a greater and more satisfying accomplishment than is the case when studying individual organs or body parts. Seeing a skeleton likewise leads to a greater understanding of the body than does seeing an individual bone.

The realism of the specimens contributes greatly to the fascination and power of the exhibition. Particularly in today's media-oriented world, a world in which we increasingly obtain our information indirectly, people have retained a keen sense for the fact that a copy has always been intellectually 'regurgitated,' and as such is always an interpretation. In this respect the BODY WORLDS exhibition satisfies a tremendous human need for unadulterated authenticity.

Living Anatomy
The anatomy of a corpse is not very interesting in and of itself. It is significant only because through it we can study the anatomy of living human beings to a certain degree. Whereas the human skeleton has been standing upright ever since Vesal's work during the Renaissance, the wet, dripping corpses of anatomical institutes have had to remain on the dissecting table. Lying there, with either their front or back hidden from the researcher's view, is how an intact body has traditionally been presented.

As a student I always found it difficult to follow the advice of our anatomy professor and associate the pleasant bodies on display at the swimming pool with the utilitarian study of surface anatomy. The difference between the stiff corpse lying on the dissecting table and the interplay of muscles in swimming, running and sitting people was just too great.

Fig. 38: A woman attending the exhibition in Japan

Fig. 39: Mixed reactions at the exhibition in Japan

"Living anatomy" was always a popular subject with students, although rather neglected by classical anatomy. In this course, students would feel each other and then project and paint muscles and organs on each other's skin. Neither a hobby anatomist nor a beginning anatomy student is interested in the anatomy of the dead because a real patient is living, moving and posing. Hence, it is only natural that plastinated whole-body specimens should be positioned upright and realistically – and thus imparting the information that they are intended to convey – in the living environment from which they came.

Plastination allows us to solidify soft tissue and as a result has made it possible to stand entire bodies in upright positions. Doing so carries on the tradition begun by the founding fathers of anatomy. As the Tokyo exhibition was nearing – the first major public plastination exhibition – our colleagues at the National Science Museum in Tokyo clearly recognised the unique qualities of the posed whole-body specimens, and discussed this with us for weeks. The issue under debate was the horizontal display of whole-body specimens, but the decision that came out of the discussions favoured

living anatomy and the new dimension that it adds to the way we view the body as a whole. In the foyer of the Heidelberg Institute of Anatomy is a sign that reads, "Hic gaudet mors succurrere vitae," which means, "Here Death is happy to rush to the aid of the living." And it should do it standing upright. This realistic pose creates anatomical individuality. A whole-body specimen is attractive when its pose is compatible with dissected anatomy and its function within a living being.

The Face Within

Whole-body plastinate join the ranks of skeletons and mummies as a new means of determining our post-mortem existence for ourselves. In addition to an external face associated with our personalities, we all possess a face within. This internal face is a great deal more variable and unique than our external faces. Even slices of a head, torso or arm no more than 3 millimetres (1/8 inch) thick are individual representatives of their donors, and can be distinguished by their shape, size, colour and tissue composition. The aesthetics of the human body, celebrated during the Renaissance, visibly lives on in the body's interior – even at a microscopic level. Donors demonstrate their natural anatomical individuality, regardless of whether the body has been plastinated in its entirety or whether it is displayed as a series of slices. The manner and quality of both the dissection and the plastination work will determine which outward appearance the face within will acquire.

A posthumous change in identity is really nothing new. In Japan, the deceased have been given new names since time immemorial. Plastination, however, also represents a shift in value from a useless corpse to a plastinated specimen, which is useful, aesthetically instructive and produced by nature.

Austrian philosopher Ludwig Wittgenstein once said, "The human body is the best picture of the human soul." For a physician, that statement is only too understandable. The external face, the human countenance, has always been considered the mirror to the soul.

The soul, on the other hand, also has an effect on the body. Happiness and worry have visible effects on the face within – just look at anorexia or stomach ulcers. Does that mean that an entire plastinated body is also an embodiment, a reflection of the soul? Thinking along these lines does not, however, bring us any further in our search for the individual soul. The closest that I have come to the location of the soul is when I am plastinating a brain. The function of brain cells and the memories stored within them collapse when the person dies. That makes it likely that death also erases our ability to remember. Yet without memory there is no awareness of the self, and without awareness of the self, there is no individual soul. The decisive question is therefore whether there is not some individual capacity for memory associated with the brain. If so, does that fly away as part of the soul, leaving the brain behind as an empty container?

Plastination is the most modern, lasting and vivid means of preserving specimens of the human body for educational purposes. The process is therefore especially well suited for honouring the desire of donors to make a posthu- mous contribution to the education of future generations. Like marble statues, they outlast the lifetimes of their creators. Life is short, but Plastination will endure (and will educate) for a long time.

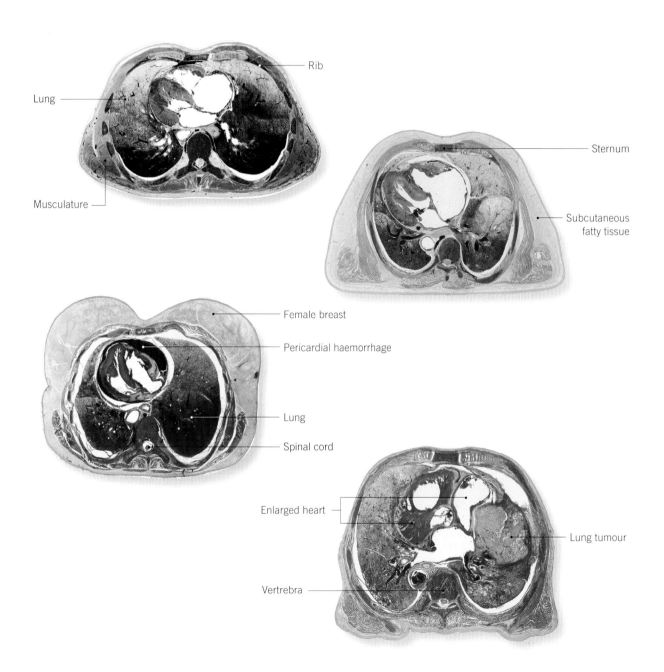

Fig. 40: The inner individuality: These chest slices were all taken from different donors. Even though they were all cut at the same height, they look completely different depending on, among other things, individual body size, distribution of fat and blood, organ size, age and disease.

A Word of Appreciation

I would like to thank those people who have donated their bodies to plastination, which in turn have made the existence of the Institute for Plastination and the development of public exhibitions of plastinates possible. I would also like to express my gratitude to my co-workers in the Plastination Institutes in Heidelberg, Germany; Bishkek, Kyrgyzstan; and Dalian, China for their dedication and commitment. I would like to thank my distinguished teacher, Prof. Wilhelm Kriz, for supporting me with unswerving foresightedness during my university years and for allowing me the room to develop that is so vital for success.

Finally, I would like to thank all of my critics for their qualified and also their unqualified criticism, which has gone a long way in helping me continually to assess and to reassess my work.

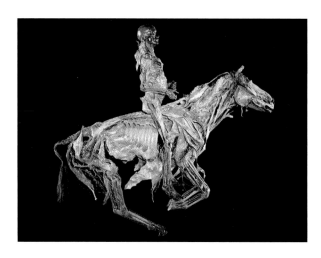

Fig. 41: Specimen by French anatomist Honoré Fragonard (1732-1799). Coloured wax was injected into the blood vessel; remaining tissue was dried and treated with varnish. The specimen may still be seen today at the "Ecole Nationale Vétérinaire d'Alfort" in Alfort near Paris.

Gunther von Hagens, the creator of Plastination, began his medical studies at the University of Jena in 1965. He was arrested after he had distributed leaflets protesting against the invasion of Czechoslovakia by Warsaw Pact troops and soon thereafter had tried to flee from East Germany. Finally, in 1970, only after the West German government had bought his freedom as well as that of other political prisoners was he able to continue his studies at the University of Lübeck, which he completed there in 1973. In 1974, he received his license to practice medicine before moving to the University of Heidelberg, where he completed his doctorate in the Department of Anesthetics and Emergency Medicine in 1975. He subsequently worked at the Institutes of Anatomy and Pathology. It was in Heidelberg starting in 1977 that he invented the basic technologies for forced infusion of anatomical specimens with reactive plastics especially developed for this purpose. It was also in Heidelberg in 1980 that he founded BIODUR® Products to market the respective polymers and equipment; finally, he founded the Institute for Plastination in 1993. 1996 he was appointed a visiting professor at the School of Medicine in Dalian in China and Director of the Plastination Center at the State Medical Academy in Bishkek, Kyrgyzstan, where he was awarded the title of an honorary professor. Since 2004, he is a visiting professor at the New York University College of Dentistry. In November 2006, he established The PLASTINARIUM, a plastination laboratory in Guben, Germany. Set to be the world's leading plastination research, development and preparation facility, it will also promote the cause of public anatomy by granting access to the general public to watch the preparation of permanently preserved, anatomical human and animal specimens. The PLASTINARIUM is a natural extension of Dr. von Hagens' thirty year career as an anatomist and advocate of public health and public anatomy.

Definitions

In discussions on the ethical justification of utilising human specimens, varying ways of understanding certain terms have frequently been the cause of misunderstandings. This list of definitions should aid in preventing such misunderstandings in the future.

Anatomy art

Aesthetically instructive presentation of bodily interiors.

Anatomical cadaver

Preserved corpse that is anatomically dissected and is buried upon completion of dissection.

Corpse

A deceased human body, which will decompose and for which a funeral will be prepared. In contrast to an anatomical specimen, it is the object of personal grief or human sympathy.

Dignity

Personal right to humane treatment guaranteed in the German constitution. It is subject to moral standards, which may vary in accordance with social progress and development.

Dissection

Removing anatomical structures and/or making them visible.

Ethics

Principles and norms that are generally valid in leading one's life, derived from an individual's responsibility towards others.

Funeral

Burial or cremation of a corpse.

Gestalt plastinate

Aesthetic, instructive whole-body specimen positioned in a life-like pose.

Inner individuality

Anatomical individuality of bodily interiors, which have been made visible through plastination.

Morals

System of ethical norms and standards of behaviour based on tradition, social conventions and religion that sets the rules for interpersonal conduct for a given time frame.

Mummy

Preserved human body, whose human form is essentially complete in the assembly of its parts and whose death goes back several generations; it is no longer an object of human grief.

Plastinate

Specimen of a human or animal, whose cells have been infused and hardened with reactive plastics.

Plastination

Method for the preservation of putrefiable biological specimens. The structural elements of the specimens are fixated, dehydrated (preferably with acetone), and under vacuum conditions are saturated with reactive polymers such as silicone rubber. Subsequently, the specimens are hardened (cured).

Plastination craftsmanship

Skilled craftsmanship in producing high-quality, aesthetic and instructive plastinated specimens.

Privilege of viewing bodies

Privilege of physicians, medical students and other representatives of the medical professions to view the insides of bodies. This privilege evolved with the development of medical science. The freedom to make use of this privilege by interested laypersons gained through the Enlightenment at the beginning of the modern era was lost when the anatomical theaters of the Renaissance were transformed into dissection halls for students and autopsy halls for pathologists.

Relics

Human remains, preferably individual bones, but also personal objects of deceased religious authorities, e.g., saints.

Reverence

A feeling of profound awe and tactful respect shown towards the dead.

Robbing the dead

Stealing the personal effects of deceased persons.

Specimen

Demonstration exhibit for research and instructional purposes, existing either as a decomposable, fresh specimen or as a preserved, permanent specimen.

Whole-body plastinate

Deceased human body, whose human form is essentially complete in the assembly of its parts and whose identity remains anonymous; it is no longer an object of human grief and has been plastinated.

Whole-body specimen

Deceased human body, whose human form is essentially complete in the assembly of its parts and has been preserved; it is no longer an object of human grief and its identity remains anonymous. It will be converted into one or more permanent anatomical specimens.

Angelina Whalley

The Human Body – Anatomy and Function

Just like all of the plants and animals that exist today, man is the offspring of primordial, single-cell organisms – the result of more than 3.5 billion years of continuing evolution. And just like all higher organisms, every human individual develops from one single cell, a fertilized egg. When grown to maturity, we consist of approximately 60 billion cells of immense variety. Nevertheless, they form a unity of a manageable number of various organic systems that cooperate in an orderly fashion in order to perform all of our complex bodily functions.

Using plastinated specimens that have been permanently and durably preserved, the structures of the human body and their functions will be explained according to the outline below.

The pictures in the following chapters show a selection of plastinates in all BODY WORLDS exhibitions. Moreover, some additional specimens are shown, which are not displayed in the exhibitions.

- The Locomotive System
- The Nervous System
- The Respiratory System
- The Cardiovascular System
- The Digestive System
- The Urinary Tract
- The Reproductive Organs
- Foetal Development
- Whole-Body Plastinates

Angelina Whalley is the creative and conceptual designer of Gunther von Hagens' BODY WORLDS exhibition, and has been the Director of the Institute for Plastination in Heidelberg since 1997. She began her medical studies at Freie Universität in Berlin and then transferred to the University of Heidelberg, where she completed her doctorate with an experimental dissertation on kidney physiology at the Physiological Institute in 1986. She also obtained her license to practice medicine in the same year. She did scientific research at the Institute of Anatomy for three years, inter alia in the plastination laboratory, as well as two years at the Institute of Pathology of the University of Heidelberg. Together with Gunther von Hagens, René Maschke and Wilhelm Kriz, she published *Schnittanatomie des Menschlichen Gehirns* (Steinkopff, Darmstadt 1990), and she established definitions for the terms used in Walter Hoffmann-Axtheim's *Lexikon der Zahnmedizin* (Quintissenz, Berlin 1993) from general pathology. Since 1993, she has also been the Director of BIODUR® Products, a company that markets plastination formulas and auxiliaries to more than 400 medical schools and universities worldwide.

1. | THE **LOCOMOTIVE** SYSTEM

The human body is composed
of various organ systems working together
in an orderly fashion to form a unified whole
and to perform the functions of life.
The body's movements, including both
stationary and forward motion,
constitute a significant portion
of these functions.
Movements are made possible
by what is known as the locomotive system
which consists of the bones,
muscles, and joints.

The Skeleton – The Internal Framework

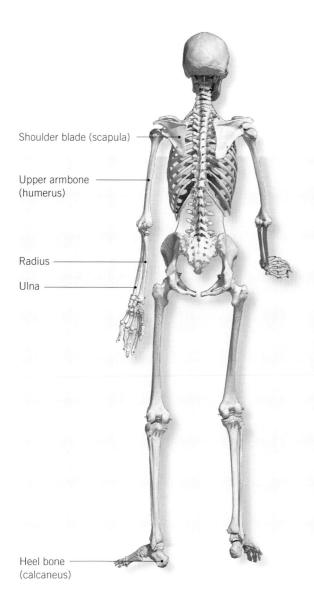

Shoulder blade (scapula)

Upper armbone
(humerus)

Radius

Ulna

Heel bone
(calcaneus)

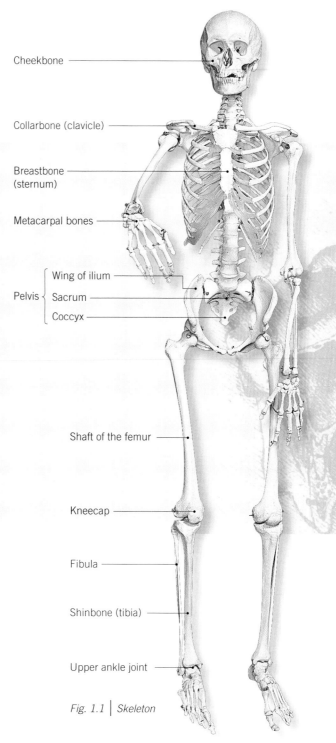

Cheekbone

Collarbone (clavicle)

Breastbone
(sternum)

Metacarpal bones

Pelvis
  Wing of ilium
  Sacrum
  Coccyx

Shaft of the femur

Kneecap

Fibula

Shinbone (tibia)

Upper ankle joint

Fig. 1.1 │ *Skeleton*

All the bones together make up the skeleton.
It has over 200 bones and 100 moveable joints.
The skeleton gives us shape,
provides stability, and allows mobility.
The skeletal muscles are attached to the skeleton,
creating a system of mechanical levers
that convert muscular action into movement.
Bones have also several other vital tasks.
They protect delicate internal organs
and store mineral salts needed for metabolism.
The bone marrow inside the bones
produces the blood cells.
The main blood cell production sites
are in flat bones, such as the breastbone,
ribs, shoulder blades, and pelvis.

Joints

The point at which two bones meet
is called a joint or articulation.
Most joints are mobile, allowing the bones to move.
Some joints only move a little, such as the vertebrae.
A few joints are fixed – for example the skull bone plates
held by fibrous connective tissue.

The shape of joints corresponds to the respective type and scope of movement required.
Their names are derived from their similarity to technical, articulated connections, such as:
• hinge joints, as in the fingers, knees, elbows, and toes. They allow only bending and straightening movements.
• Ball-and-socket joints, such as the shoulder and hip joints, allow backward, forward, sideways, and rotating movements.
• Pivot joints, such as the neck joints, allow limited rotating movements.

The articular surfaces of the bones are covered with cartilage to reduce the friction of movement.

Most joints are stabilised by tough bands of connective tissue, the ligaments. External ligaments attach to the bone on either side of the joint, forming a fibrous capsule that completely encases the joint.
The capsules contain synovial fluid. This helps lubricate the joints and cushions the impact of movement.
Most joints are synovial joints.

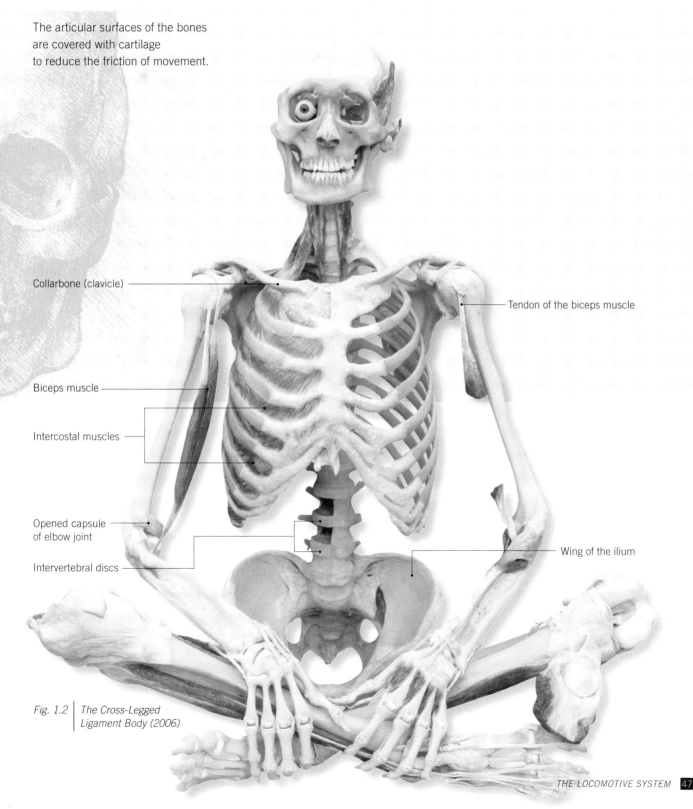

Collarbone (clavicle)

Tendon of the biceps muscle

Biceps muscle

Intercostal muscles

Opened capsule of elbow joint

Intervertebral discs

Wing of the ilium

Fig. 1.2 | The Cross-Legged Ligament Body (2006)

Joints

Shoulder Joint

The shoulder joint is a ball-and-socket joint.
It connects the upper armbone (humerus)
to the shoulder blade (scapula)
and has the greatest movement of any joint.

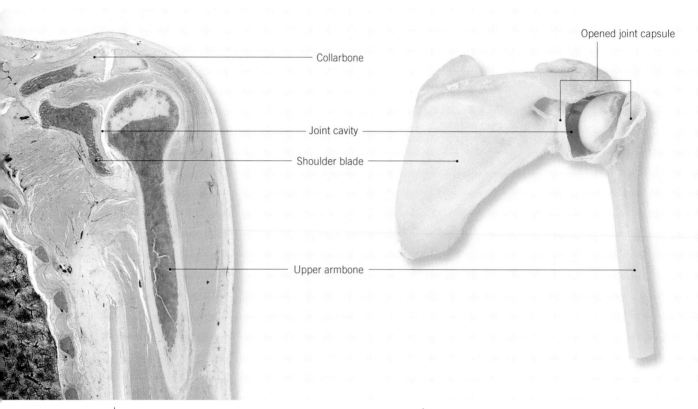

Fig. 1.3 | Femoral slice of a shoulder joint

Fig. 1.4 | The shoulder joint (seen here from behind)

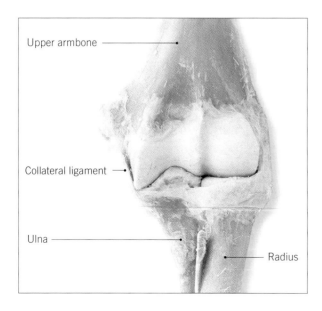

Elbow Joint

The elbow comprises three bones:
the humerus, the radius, and the ulna.
This allows three kinds of forearm movements:
flexing, extending, and turning.

If we knock the humerus –
the 'funny bone' at the elbow –
it produces an unpleasant tingling sensation,
shooting all the way down the arm.
This feeling is caused by the ulnar nerve
which is close to the skin surface there.

Fig. 1.5 | Elbow joint, viewed from the front

Hands and Feet

Hands and feet are similar in their skeletal design.
The human hand has 27 bones,
controlled by 37 skeletal muscles.
They allow for a wide variety of movement
with exceptionally fine motor functions
and a powerful gripping action.
In particular, it is the ability to bring the tips
of the thumb and the fingers together
that gives human hands their unique dexterity.

Feet and toes are crucial for walking upright.
They bear and distribute body weight
when we walk or run.
They also help the body keep its balance.
Each foot has 26 bones and over 100 ligaments.
Some of the 33 foot muscles
actually originate in the lower leg.

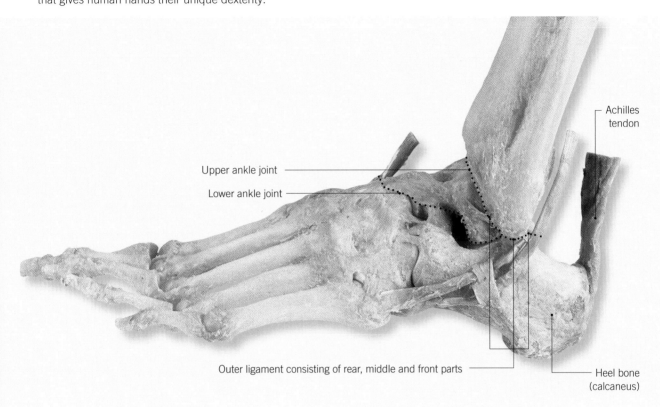

Achilles tendon

Upper ankle joint

Lower ankle joint

Outer ligament consisting of rear, middle and front parts

Heel bone (calcaneus)

Fig. 1.6 | *Dissection of foot showing ligamentous structures*

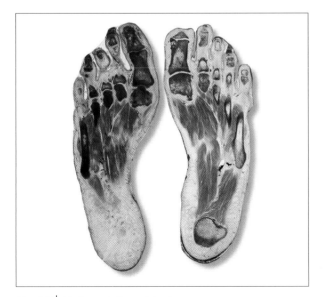

Fig. 1.7 | *Horizontal slices of the feet*

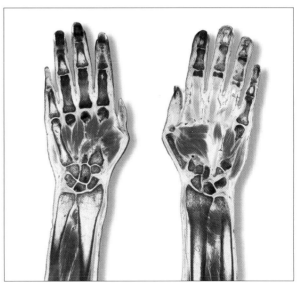

Fig. 1.8 | *Frontal slices of the hands*

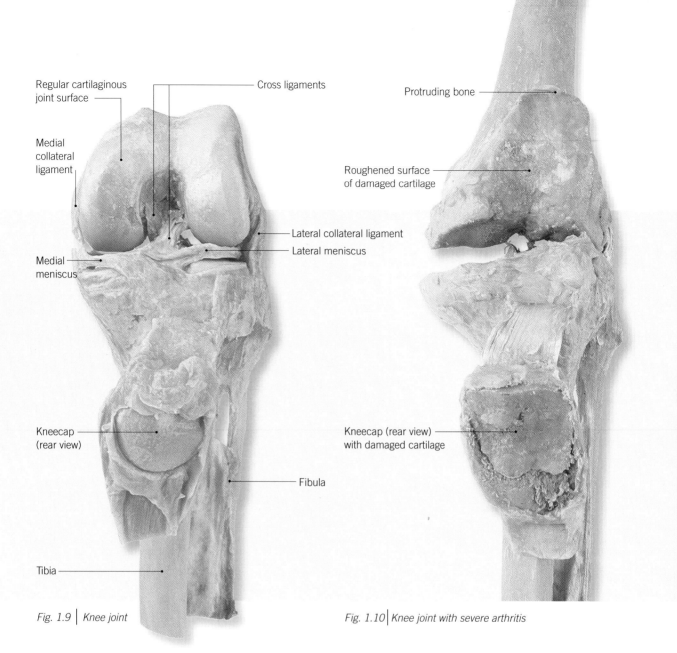

Regular cartilaginous joint surface

Cross ligaments

Medial collateral ligament

Lateral collateral ligament

Lateral meniscus

Medial meniscus

Kneecap (rear view)

Fibula

Tibia

Fig. 1.9 | Knee joint

Protruding bone

Roughened surface of damaged cartilage

Kneecap (rear view) with damaged cartilage

Fig. 1.10 | Knee joint with severe arthritis

Knee Joint

The knee has to be extremely stable.
It bears the greatest load of any joint.
It joins the thigh bone and tibia –
the weight-bearing bone in the lower leg.
One part of the knee joint is the kneecap.
This is held in a sheath of tendons.
To be stable, the knee needs 13 muscles
plus collateral and cross ligaments.
The knee joint bones are not a perfect fit.
To fill the gap, they have two
crescent-shaped cartilage wedges (menisci).

Arthritis

Since the knee has to support our body weight,
it suffers severe wear and tear over a lifetime.

The damage may cause chronic pain,
and the knee may even become inflammatory.
In a diseased or worn joint,
the cartilage loses its elasticity.
It becomes brittle and splinters,
and may even be destroyed completely.
Such cartilage damage is called arthritis.
In very advanced arthritis,
also the bones may begin to wear down,
leading to protruding bone growths.
It mostly affects patients over 50 years of age
and is more common in people who are overweight.
Weight loss tends to reduce the symptoms
associated with knee or hip arthritis.
There is also a genetic predisposition
of this condition.

Hip Joint

The hip joins the torso and legs
via the pelvic bones.
The pelvis is a flexible ring
formed by three major bones:
the two hipbones and the rear sacrum bone.
Thanks to this ring structure,
the legs can handle the torso's weight.

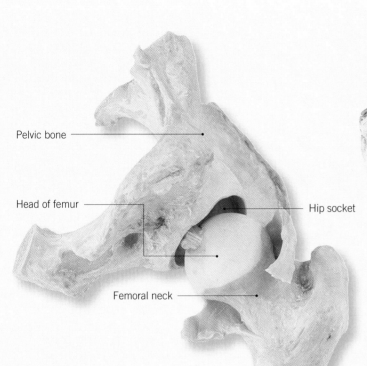

Pelvic bone

Head of femur

Hip socket

Femoral neck

Fig. 1.11 | Hip joint

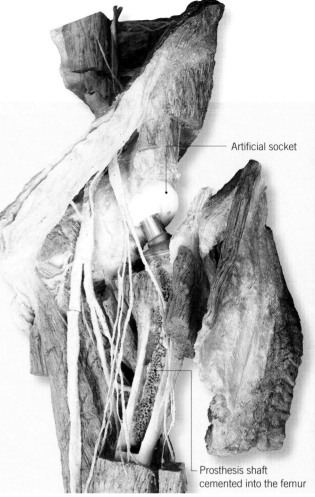

Artificial socket

Prosthesis shaft
cemented into the femur

Fig. 1.12 | Artificial hip joint

The hip sockets are recessed into the pelvis
and cover over half of the thighbone head.
The hip is a ball-and-socket joint
just like the shoulder,
except here motion is restricted
in favour of greater stability.

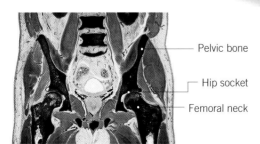

Pelvic bone

Hip socket

Femoral neck

Fig. 1.13 | Frontal slice of the pelvis

Artificial Hip Joint

A hip replacement may be necessary
if a bone becomes severely worn (arthritis),
if the neck of the femur becomes fractured
or if any other change takes place in the hip
that significantly limits its function.
Artificial hips mimic both the spherical shape
of the head of the femur as well as the angle
at which the neck of the femur
is inclined in a natural joint.

Its long stainless steel shaft is cemented
into the bone marrow canal of the femur.
The joint socket is made of Teflon.

The Skull

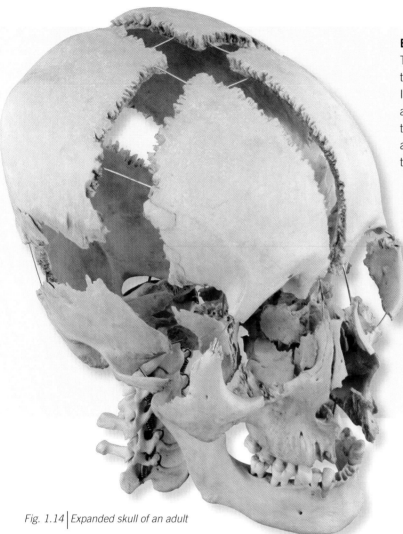

Fig. 1.14 | *Expanded skull of an adult*

Bones of the Skull

The skull's most important role is
to enclose and protect the brain.
It also gives shape to the head and face
and houses the main sensory organs:
the eyes, nose, tongue,
and, at the base of the cranium,
the inner ears.

The bone plates of a newborn baby's skull
are linked by cartilage bridges.
This allows the bone plates
to overlap slightly like shingles
when passing through the narrow birth canal.
During childhood, the separated bones
yield to facilitate growth of the skull and brain.
By adulthood, all the bones are fused together.

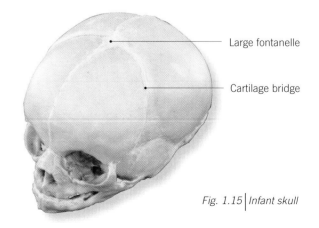

Large fontanelle

Cartilage bridge

Fig. 1.15 | *Infant skull*

Hearing

Ossicles

The ossicles of the middle ear
are the smallest bones in the body.
They are named after their shapes:
the hammer (malleus), the anvil (incus)
and the stirrup (stapes).

The ossicles form a bony chain behind the eardrum
at the end of the external auditory canal
and transmit sound to the inner ear.
The ossicles and the ear drum form the middle ear.

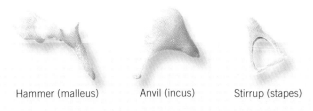

Hammer (malleus)   Anvil (incus)   Stirrup (stapes)

Fig. 1.16 | *Auditory ossicles*

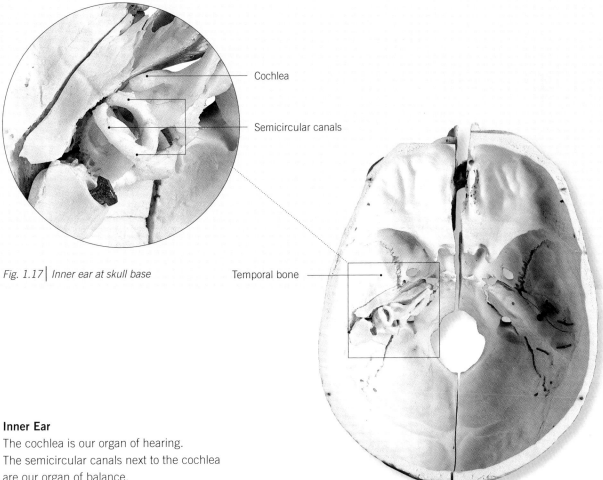

Cochlea

Semicircular canals

Fig. 1.17 | *Inner ear at skull base*

Temporal bone

Fig. 1.18 | *Skull base with inner ear dissected*

Inner Ear

The cochlea is our organ of hearing.
The semicircular canals next to the cochlea
are our organ of balance.
Both systems make up the inner ear.
They are embedded in the temporal bones
at the base of the skull.

The cochlea is full of liquid.
When sound waves travel down the auditory canal
the liquid vibrates, stimulating special sensory cells.
These cells convert the vibrations
into electrochemical messages.

The data are then carried along the auditory nerve
to the brain where the signals are interpreted.

The semicircular canals have a similar system
to convert head and body movements
into signals interpreted by the brain.

Bone Structure and Growth

Although the skeleton of an adult
weighs only about 7-9 kilograms (15-20 pounds),
it is stronger than reinforced concrete.
By comparison, steel rods of the same size
would probably weigh 4 to 5 times as much.
This is due to the structure of the bones.

Our bones are usually made of two parts:
a hard, compact outer layer
and spongy cancellous bone inside.
The structure of cancellous bone is designed
to cope with forces of pressure and contraction.
So bones can remain lightweight,
yet have considerable stability.

The soft, spongy tissue
produces the cellular components of blood:
white cells, red cells, and platelets.
It is also the most radiation sensitive tissue
of the body.

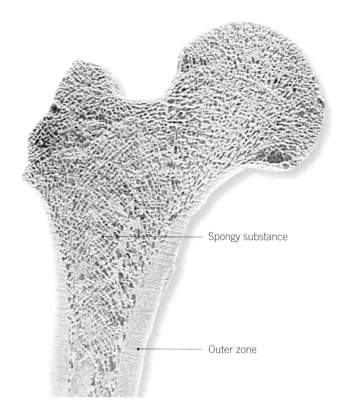

— Spongy substance

— Outer zone

Fig. 1.19 | *Adult thighbone (femur), longitudinally cut*

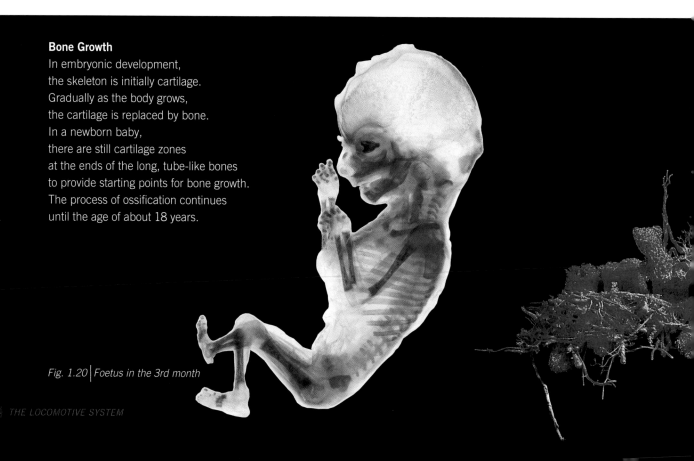

Bone Growth

In embryonic development,
the skeleton is initially cartilage.
Gradually as the body grows,
the cartilage is replaced by bone.
In a newborn baby,
there are still cartilage zones
at the ends of the long, tube-like bones
to provide starting points for bone growth.
The process of ossification continues
until the age of about 18 years.

Fig. 1.20 | *Foetus in the 3rd month*

Bone is made up of living cells,
as well as protein, mineral salts, and water.
The bone cells are constantly regenerating.
Specialised bone cells create new bone,
while other cells remove older ones.

Osteoporosis

As people age, bone tissue renewal slows down.
By the age of 70, most people's skeletons
have become about a third thinner and lighter
than they were at the age of 40.
This loss of bone density is called osteoporosis.
It makes bones more fragile and likely to break.
Such osteoporotic fractures typically occur
in the hip, spine, and wrist.

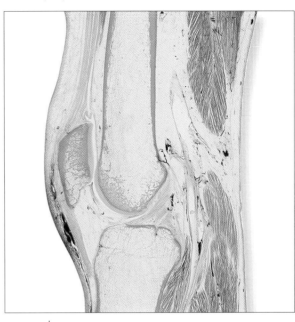

Femur

Kneecap

Tibia

Fig. 1.21 | *Longitudinal slice of knee joint with normal bone structure*

Fig. 1.22 | *Longitudinal slice of knee joint with osteoporosis*

Blood Supply of the Bone

Bone has a rich vascular supply,
receiving 10-20% of the cardiac output.

The blood supply varies
with different types of bones,
but blood vessels are especially rich
in areas that contain red bone marrow.

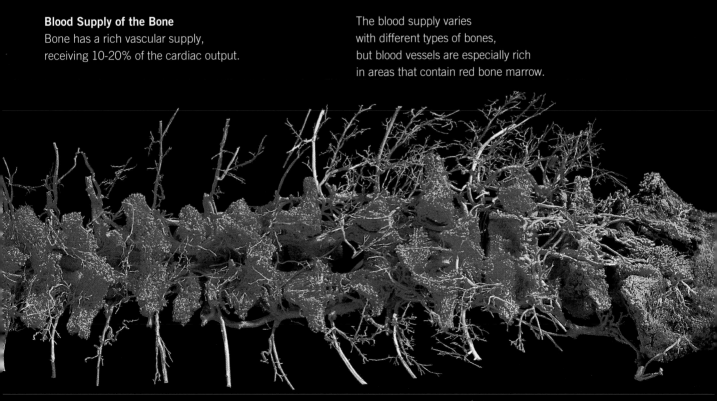

Fig. 1.23 | *Blood vessel configuration of the spine*

Bone Disorders

Bones may be deformed for several reasons:
genetic or metabolic disorders,
improperly healed bones, inflammation,
or poor load distribution.

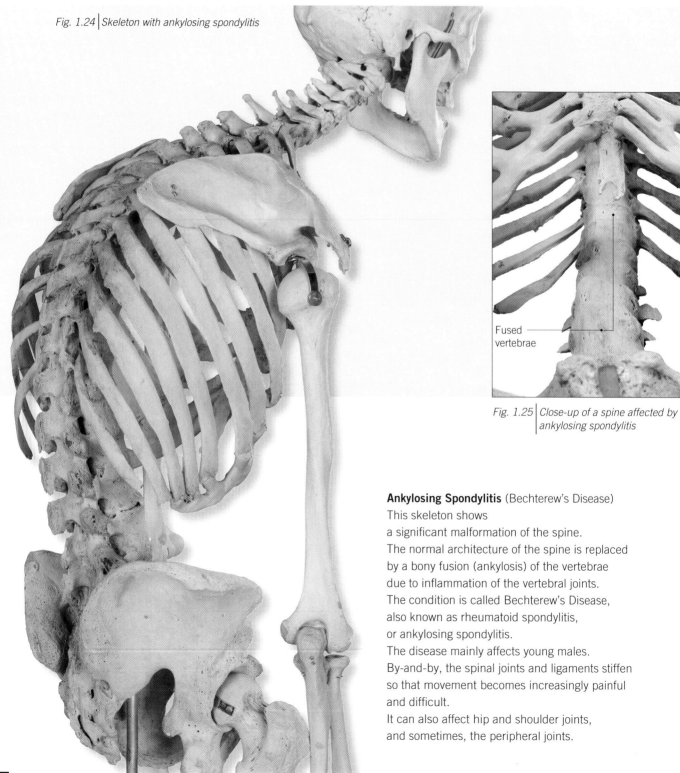

Fig. 1.24 | Skeleton with ankylosing spondylitis

Fused
vertebrae

Fig. 1.25 | Close-up of a spine affected by
ankylosing spondylitis

Ankylosing Spondylitis (Bechterew's Disease)
This skeleton shows
a significant malformation of the spine.
The normal architecture of the spine is replaced
by a bony fusion (ankylosis) of the vertebrae
due to inflammation of the vertebral joints.
The condition is called Bechterew's Disease,
also known as rheumatoid spondylitis,
or ankylosing spondylitis.
The disease mainly affects young males.
By-and-by, the spinal joints and ligaments stiffen
so that movement becomes increasingly painful
and difficult.
It can also affect hip and shoulder joints,
and sometimes, the peripheral joints.

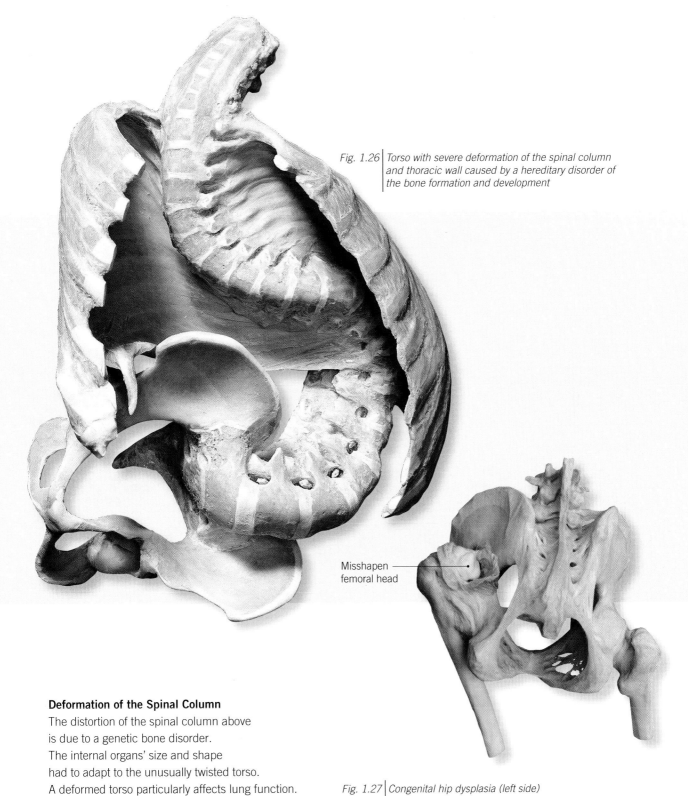

Fig. 1.26 | *Torso with severe deformation of the spinal column and thoracic wall caused by a hereditary disorder of the bone formation and development*

Misshapen femoral head

Fig. 1.27 | *Congenital hip dysplasia (left side)*

Deformation of the Spinal Column

The distortion of the spinal column above
is due to a genetic bone disorder.
The internal organs' size and shape
had to adapt to the unusually twisted torso.
A deformed torso particularly affects lung function.

Congenital Hip Dysplasia

This left hip joint in Fig. 1.27
shows a severe abnormal formation
known as congenital hip dysplasia.
The femoral head is not deeply and tightly held
by the socket of the hip bone (acetabulum).
Instead of being tightly fit,
it is loose and dislocated.

Also the femoral head and acetabulum
are not smooth and round but are misshapen,
causing abnormal wear and tear
and friction within the joint as it moves.
A congenital hip dysplasia
is already present at birth.
Genetic factors may play a role in this disorder.

Bone Repair

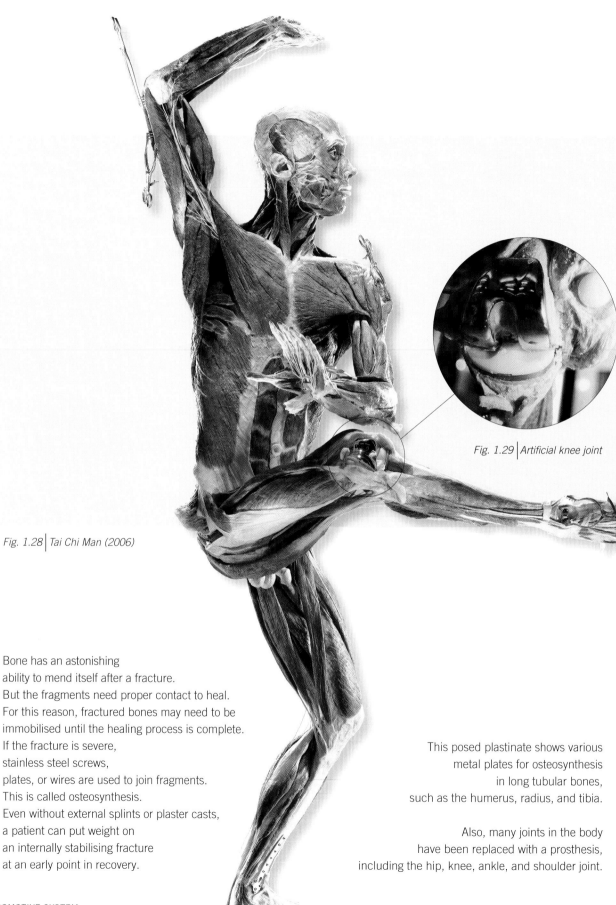

Fig. 1.28 | Tai Chi Man (2006)

Fig. 1.29 | Artificial knee joint

Bone has an astonishing
ability to mend itself after a fracture.
But the fragments need proper contact to heal.
For this reason, fractured bones may need to be
immobilised until the healing process is complete.
If the fracture is severe,
stainless steel screws,
plates, or wires are used to join fragments.
This is called osteosynthesis.
Even without external splints or plaster casts,
a patient can put weight on
an internally stabilising fracture
at an early point in recovery.

This posed plastinate shows various
metal plates for osteosynthesis
in long tubular bones,
such as the humerus, radius, and tibia.

Also, many joints in the body
have been replaced with a prosthesis,
including the hip, knee, ankle, and shoulder joint.

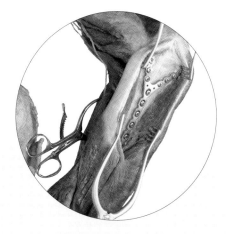

Fig. 1.30 | Osteosynthesis with metal plates

In complicated bone fractures,
an external fixation might become necessary.
This is accomplished by placing pins or screws
into the bone on both sides of the fracture.
The pins are then secured together
outside the skin with clamps and rods.
The clamps and rods are known as the "external frame".

Fig. 1.31 | External wrist fixation

Muscle System

A muscle is a biological flexor.
It functions in that its fibres contract
to become shorter.
There are three types of muscles.
They each perform different roles and
have different structures:

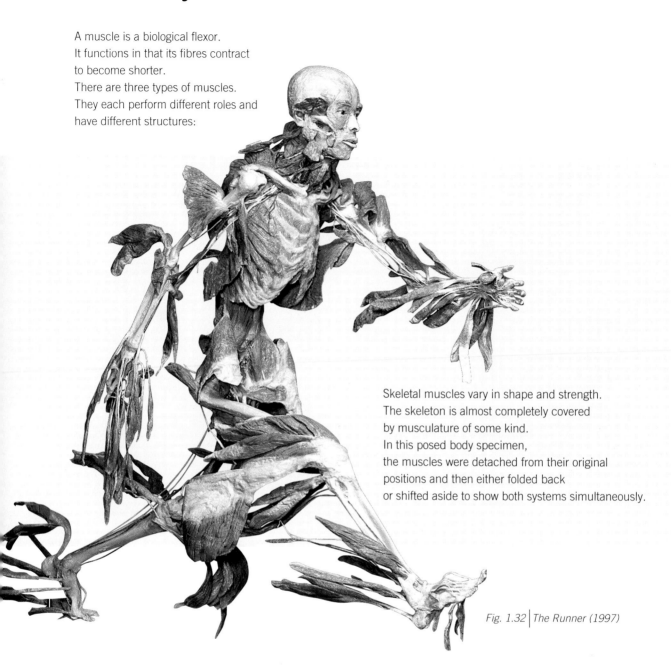

Skeletal muscles vary in shape and strength.
The skeleton is almost completely covered
by musculature of some kind.
In this posed body specimen,
the muscles were detached from their original
positions and then either folded back
or shifted aside to show both systems simultaneously.

Fig. 1.32 | *The Runner (1997)*

a) Skeletal muscles perform voluntary movements.
They can contract quickly, but only for a short time.

b) Smooth muscles perform unconscious actions,
such as propelling food along the digestive tract.
They contract slowly but can continue in a state
of contraction for long periods.

c) Cardiac muscles are involuntarily controlled.
They contract rhythmically and continuously
in order to pump blood around the whole body.

A typical muscle stretches from one bone to another,
crossing a joint.
They are attached to bones with tendons
which are made of connective fibres.

Muscles are usually arranged
in pairs with opposing functions.
The biceps, for instance, flexes the elbow,
while the triceps does just the opposite
and serves to extend the elbow.
When the biceps contracts,
the triceps inhibits any excessive movement.
This makes our movements fluid and controlled.

Muscle movement requires signals
from the brain and nerves.
When we want to move something,
the brain sends electrical signals
down nerve pathways to the muscles.
When the signals arrive,
the filaments in the muscle fibres
respond by contracting.
This moves the bones relative to one another.

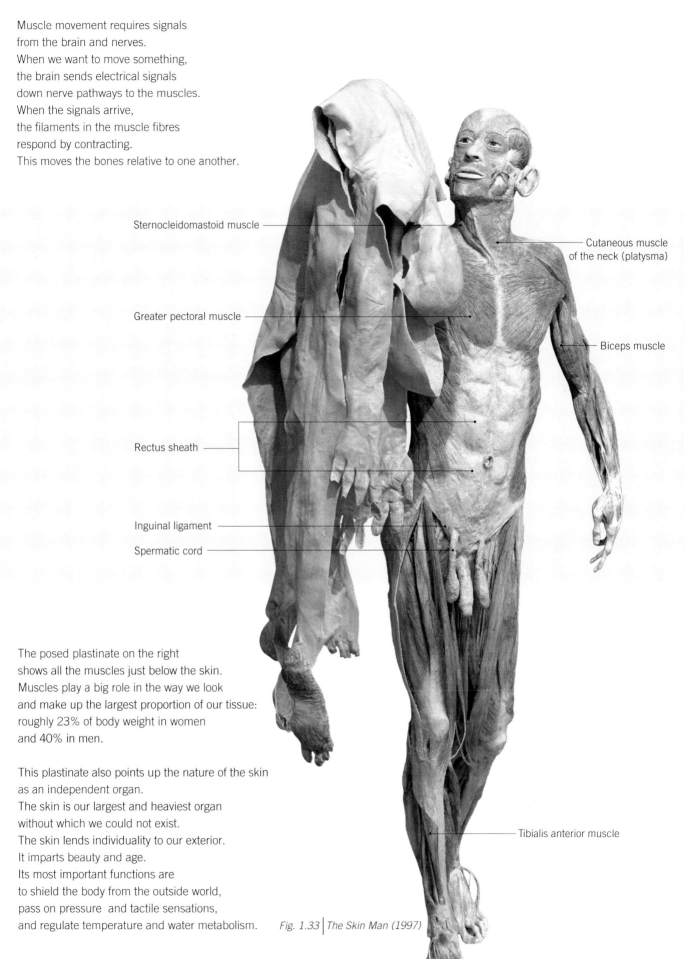

Sternocleidomastoid muscle

Cutaneous muscle
of the neck (platysma)

Greater pectoral muscle

Biceps muscle

Rectus sheath

Inguinal ligament

Spermatic cord

Tibialis anterior muscle

The posed plastinate on the right
shows all the muscles just below the skin.
Muscles play a big role in the way we look
and make up the largest proportion of our tissue:
roughly 23% of body weight in women
and 40% in men.

This plastinate also points up the nature of the skin
as an independent organ.
The skin is our largest and heaviest organ
without which we could not exist.
The skin lends individuality to our exterior.
It imparts beauty and age.
Its most important functions are
to shield the body from the outside world,
pass on pressure and tactile sensations,
and regulate temperature and water metabolism.

Fig. 1.33 | *The Skin Man (1997)*

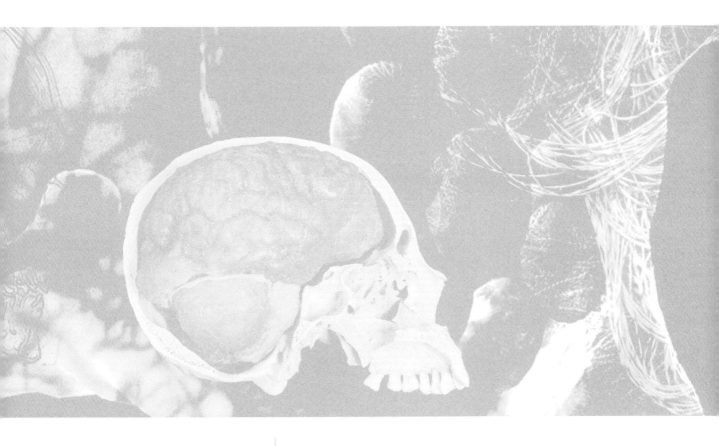

2. | THE NERVOUS SYSTEM

Without a central communication system
with connections that encompass
an entire country from one end to the other,
a modern nation would soon become ungovernable.
It is the same with the human body and its nervous system.
The nervous system regulates
hundreds of activities simultaneously.
It monitors and controls almost all bodily processes,
ranging from automatic functions
of which we are largely unconscious,
such as breathing and digestion,
to complex activities that involve thought and learning.
It is also the source of our consciousness, intelligence,
and creativity, and allows us
to communicate and experience emotions.

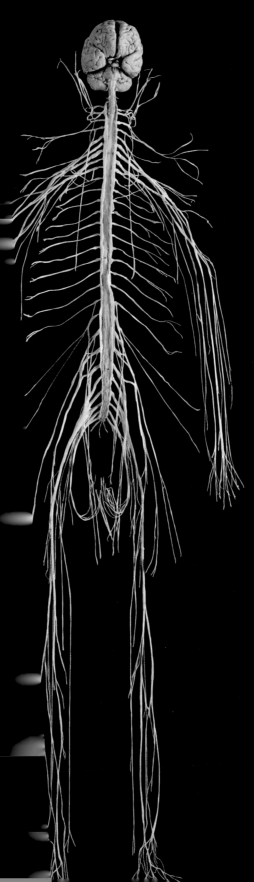

The nervous system can be divided into two parts:
a) The central nervous systems,
composed of the brain and the spinal cord.
It regulates bodily activities by
processing and coordinating nerve signals.

b) The peripheral nervous system
is made up of all the nerves that emanate
from the central nervous system and
branch out throughout the body.
They transmit the signals
between the central nervous system
and the rest of the body.

The basic units are nerve cells.
When parts of the body communicate,
they use weak electrical signals
emitted by the nerve cells.
These signals can travel at up to 400 km/h (250 mph).

The peripheral nerves originate directly
from either the brain or spinal cord
and become increasingly fine as they branch out
into the peripheral regions of the body.
Here, only the main peripheral nerve branches are shown.

Fig. 2.1 | Isolated central and peripheral nervous system

The Brain

The brain is the body's command centre.
It processes sensory information,
coordinates most movement and thinking,
and allows us to feel, remember, and communicate.

The skull bones protect the brain,
rather like a shell around a walnut.
As humans evolved, the cerebrum,
formed by the two cerebral hemispheres,
gradually grew and expanded.
This is where voluntary action is coordinated.
To grow within the restricted skull space,
the surface became convoluted and furrowed.
The furrows hide roughly two thirds
of the brain's surface.
Spread out flat, the cerebral cortex
would be approximately 1.5 sq. metres (16 sq. feet).

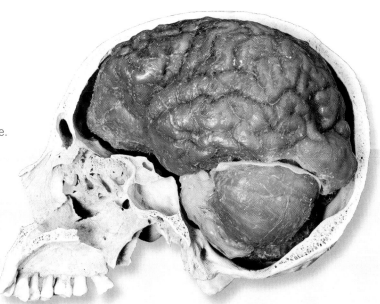

Fig. 2.2 | *Brain in half skull*

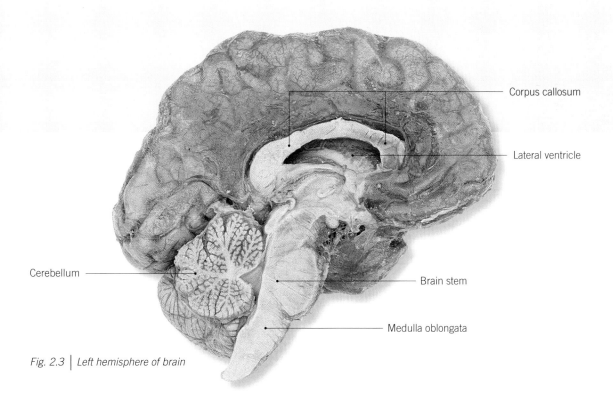

Corpus callosum

Lateral ventricle

Cerebellum

Brain stem

Medulla oblongata

Fig. 2.3 | *Left hemisphere of brain*

The cerebrum is the largest part of the brain.
A groove runs down its convex shape,
dividing it into two cerebral hemispheres.
At its bottom, the corpus callosum is visible.
It joins both cerebral hemispheres.

Much of the inter-hemispheric communication
in the brain is conducted across the corpus callosum.
Beneath that are the brain stem and cerebellum.
The brain is connected to the spinal cord
by the medulla oblongata.

Inside the Brain

Both the brain and the spinal cord contain areas of grey and white matter; as can best be seen in a cross section.

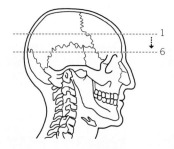

The outermost layer of the cerebrum (cortex) and a group of nuclei deep in the hemispheres (basal ganglia) are composed of densely packed nerve cells (neurons). They are referred to as grey matter. Due to the polymers used for Plastination, the grey matter appears brownish. In grey matter, nerve impulses are processed.

The cerebral cortex plays a key role in memory, attention, perceptual awareness, thought, language, and consciousness.

The basal ganglia pre-process millions of nerve signals going into or out of the cortex. They also send signals on to the relevant brain "centres" for further analysis. Among other functions, they help coordinate movement.

White matter consists of nerve fibres. They interconnect the different regions of the central nervous system and transmit the nerve impulses.

Fig. 2.4 | *Series of horizontal brain slices*

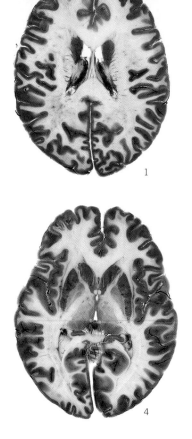

1

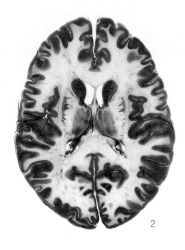

4

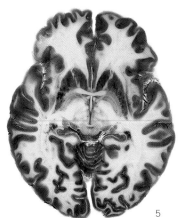

5

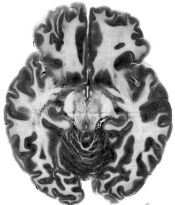

3

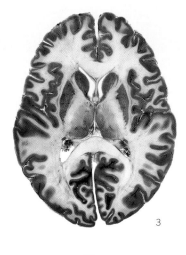

6

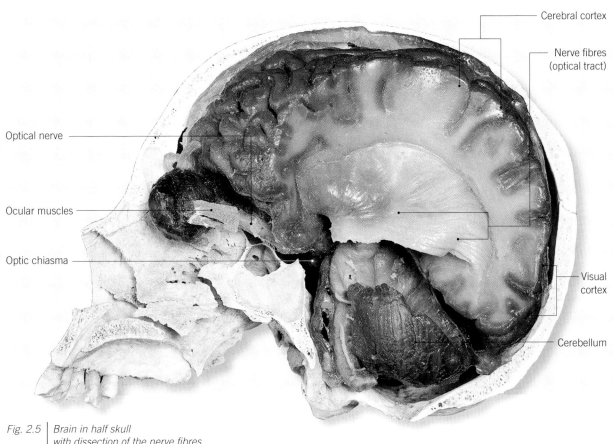

Cerebral cortex

Nerve fibres
(optical tract)

Optical nerve

Ocular muscles

Optic chiasma

Visual
cortex

Cerebellum

Fig. 2.5 | Brain in half skull
with dissection of the nerve fibres

In the brain specimen shown above,
the optic nerve fibres are exposed
that run from the eyes to the visual cortex
at the back of the brain.
Visual information is received via the retina of each eye.
This information passes down the two optic nerves,
which meet at a junction called the optic chiasma.

Here, half of the nerve fibres from each eye
cross to the other side of the brain.
The fibres continue along the optic tract
all the way up to the visual cortex.
Here, the brain integrates the signals
into a composite colour image.

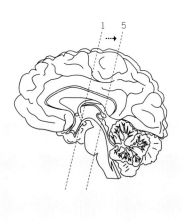

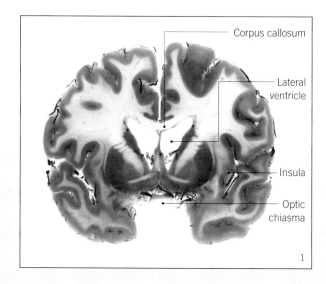

Corpus callosum

Lateral ventricle

Insula

Optic chiasma

1

Fig. 2.6 | Series of frontal brain slices

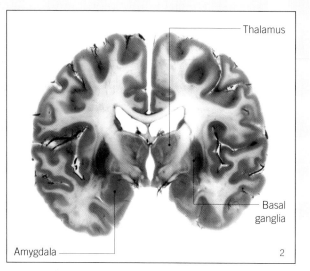

Thalamus

Basal ganglia

Amygdala

2

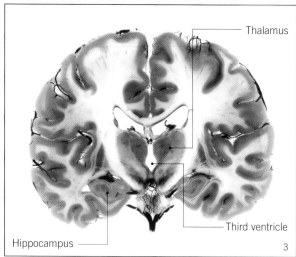

Thalamus

Third ventricle

Hippocampus

3

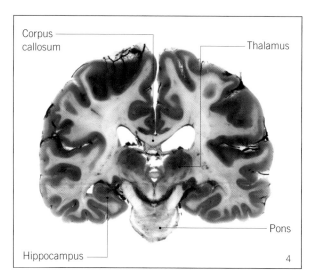

Corpus callosum

Thalamus

Pons

Hippocampus

4

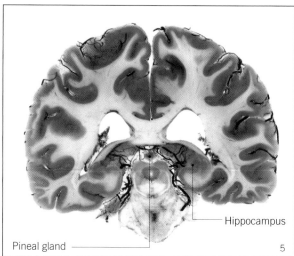

Pineal gland

Hippocampus

5

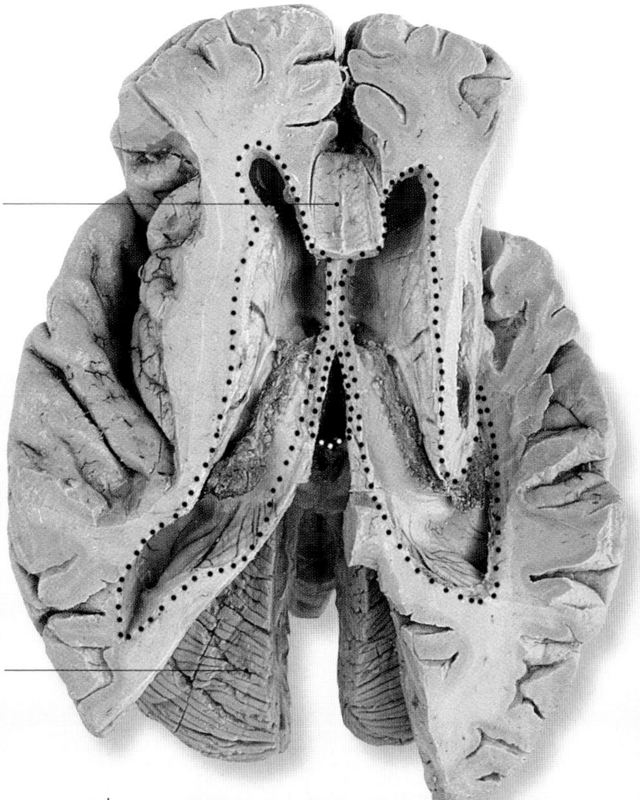

Brain Ventricles

The brain has four interlinked cavities called ventricles.
Fluid circulates within these ventricles.
Among other functions,
the fluid serves as an internal shock absorber.

Corpus callosum

Cerebellum

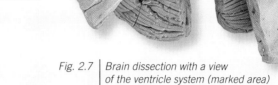

Fig. 2.7 | Brain dissection with a view
of the ventricle system (marked area)

Distended ventricle

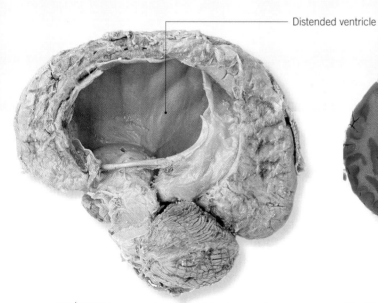

Fig. 2.8 | Right brain hemisphere with hydrocephalus

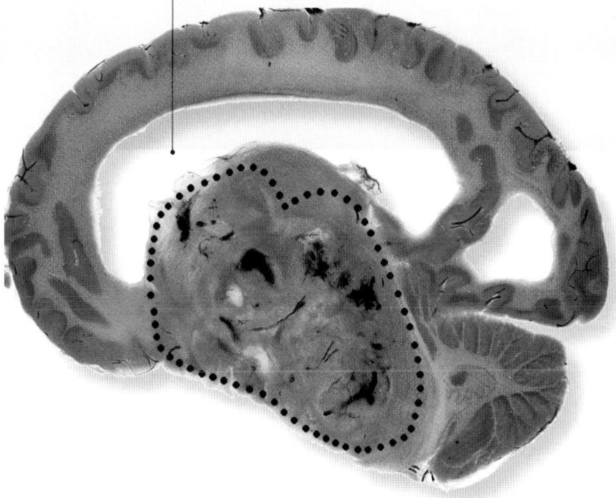

Fig. 2.9 | Brain slice with brain stem tumour (marked area)
and hydrocephalus

Hydrocephalus

When the flow within the ventricles is blocked,
the amount of fluid will increase.
This causes the ventricles to expand,
thereby compressing and damaging brain tissue.
This condition is also known as "water on the brain".
It can be caused by tumour growth,
inflammation, or congenital malformation.

The malignant tumour growth shown in Fig. 2.9
has taken over a large portion of the brain stem,
putting pressure on and blocking the ventricles.

The Diseased Brain

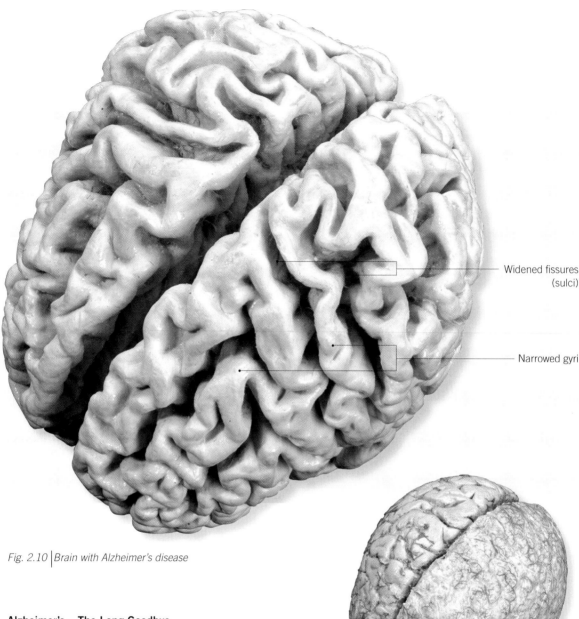

Widened fissures
(sulci)

Narrowed gyri

Fig. 2.10 | *Brain with Alzheimer's disease*

Fig. 2.11 | *Normal brain. In the left hemisphere,*
the meninges (pia mater) are left intact.

Alzheimer's – The Long Goodbye

Alzheimer's disease is a progressive
and fatal brain disorder.
Brain cells are irreversibly destroyed,
causing the cerebral cortex to atrophy.
The physical effects of the disease are evident
in the significant narrowing of the cortex area.

Alzheimer's is not a natural part of aging
but a disease more common with age.
Gradually, short-term memory fades.
The person becomes increasingly disoriented
as other cognitive functions begin to fail,
and memory is almost entirely lost.

One in 10 people over 60 suffers from Alzheimer's.
With an ageing world population,
estimates predict 14 million Alzheimer patients
in the USA alone by the year 2050.
There is no cure for Alzheimer's yet,
but various drugs can alleviate some symptoms.

Blood Supply to the Brain

The brain is only 2% of our total body weight
but needs 20% of our blood supply.
If the blood flow to the brain is interrupted
for only 10 seconds, we lose consciousness.
If it is interrupted for longer than 10 seconds,
we can suffer severe brain tissue damage.

Fig. 2.12 | Brain vessel configuration
of the brain

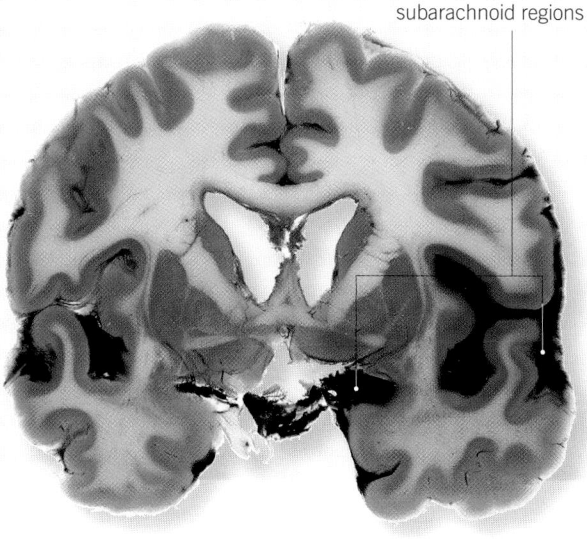

Blood in the
subarachnoid regions

Fig. 2.13 | Brain slice with a haemorrhage in the brain stem

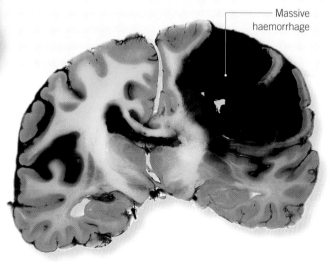

Massive
haemorrhage

Fig. 2.14 | Brain with a massive haemorrhage following a stroke

Stroke

In a stroke, an artery to the brain is blocked
or blood leaks from a ruptured blood vessel.
Both can seriously damage brain tissue.
The symptoms of a stroke develop rapidly
and depend on the size and location
of the affected area.
They can include severe disabilities, such as
numbness, paralysis, slurred speech, and sudden death.

Damages on the brain blood vessels
are often due to high blood pressure.
But long before it creates a health emergency,
hypertension often takes a subtle toll
on mental faculties.
It can reduce attention, learning, memory,
and decision-making skills.

The Autonomic Nervous System

This plastinate shows all the major nerves.
The spinal cord down our backbone
is like a main cable joining body and brain.

Many nerves around the spine
belong to the autonomic nervous system (ANS).
The ANS automatically regulates bodily functions,
including circulation, respiration, and digestion.

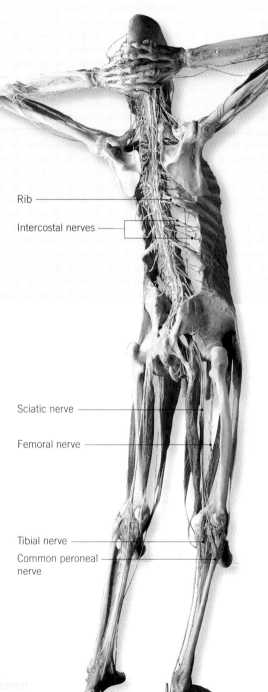

Rib

Intercostal nerves

Sciatic nerve

Femoral nerve

Tibial nerve

Common peroneal
nerve

There are two types of autonomic nerves:
sympathetic and parasympathetic.
They have opposing effects
and are not under conscious control.

The sympathetic nervous system stimulates the body
for action and prepares it at times of stress.
For example, it increases the rate and strength
of the heartbeat, dilates the bronchial tubes,
and releases glucose from the liver.

The parasympathetic nervous system, also called vagus,
influences the organs to maintain energy
or to relax and restore energy.
The vagus nerve is for instance stimulated
by the sight, smell, and taste of food.
It increases stomach acid secretion
and triggers peristalsis, pushing the food
through the digestive tract.
In the cardiovascular system, the vagus nerve
decreases the rate and strength of the heartbeat.

Fig. 2.15 | *Man at Leisure (2002)*

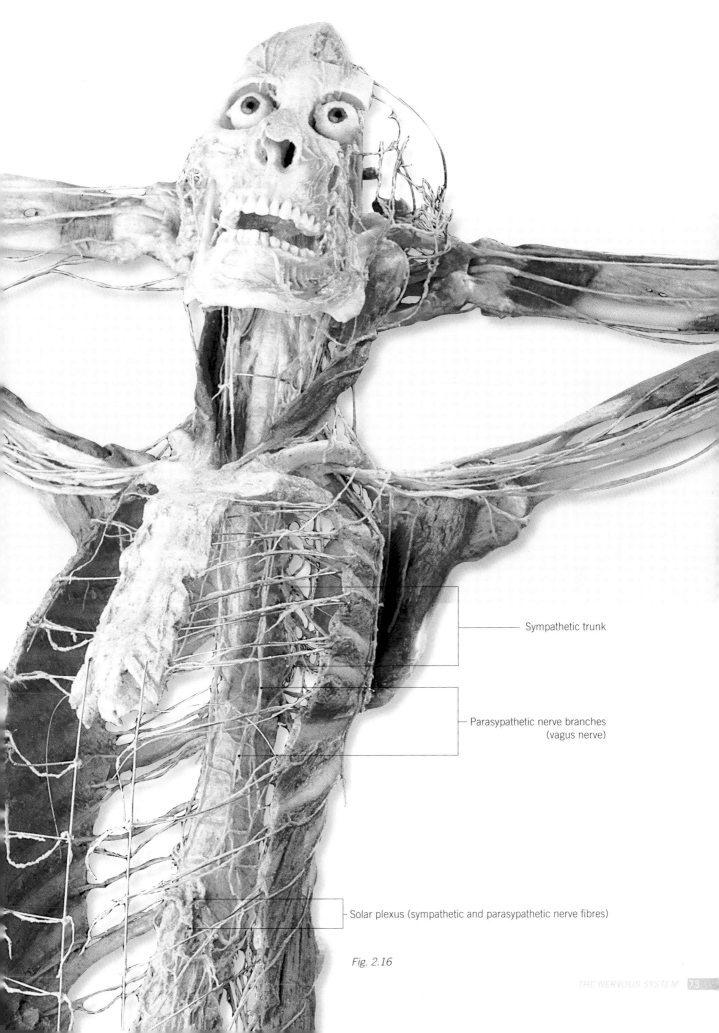

Sympathetic trunk

Parasypathetic nerve branches
(vagus nerve)

Solar plexus (sympathetic and parasypathetic nerve fibres)

Fig. 2.16

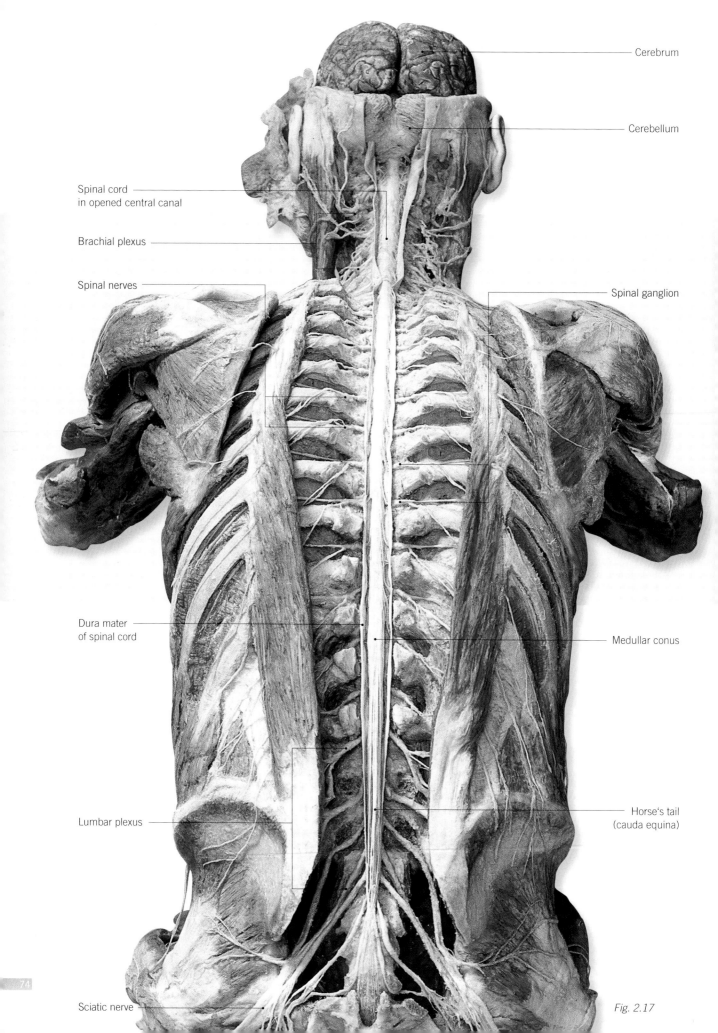

Cerebrum

Cerebellum

Spinal cord
in opened central canal

Brachial plexus

Spinal nerves

Spinal ganglion

Dura mater
of spinal cord

Medullar conus

Lumbar plexus

Horse's tail
(cauda equina)

Sciatic nerve

Fig. 2.17

The Chess Player

This posed plastinate has been given
the posture of a person deep in thought
to illustrate how nerve fibres run throughout
the entire human organism.
The pose emphasises the special character
of this plastinate – its anatomical identity.

The brain is visible in the opened skull.
From there, the spinal cord extends down
through the spinal column
that is open towards the back.
From between the vertebrae,
31 pairs of spinal nerves
connect the spinal cord to the rest of the body.

Fig. 2.18 | The Chess Player (1997)

The bundle of nerves at the base of the spine
is the cauda equina – the "horse's tail".
The two sciatic nerves run from the lower spine
behind the hip joint down the leg.
They are the largest and
longest nerves in the body.

Fig. 2.19 | Dissection of the facial nerves
(Trigeminal nerve; arrow)

3. | THE **RESPIRATORY** SYSTEM

Human life requires a continuous supply of oxygen,
which we extract from the air.
Without this element, most of the body's cells
would not be able to survive more than a few minutes.
Oxygen is indispensable for cell metabolism,
a process that transforms nutrients into energy
to keep the body functioning.

Getting Air into the Lungs

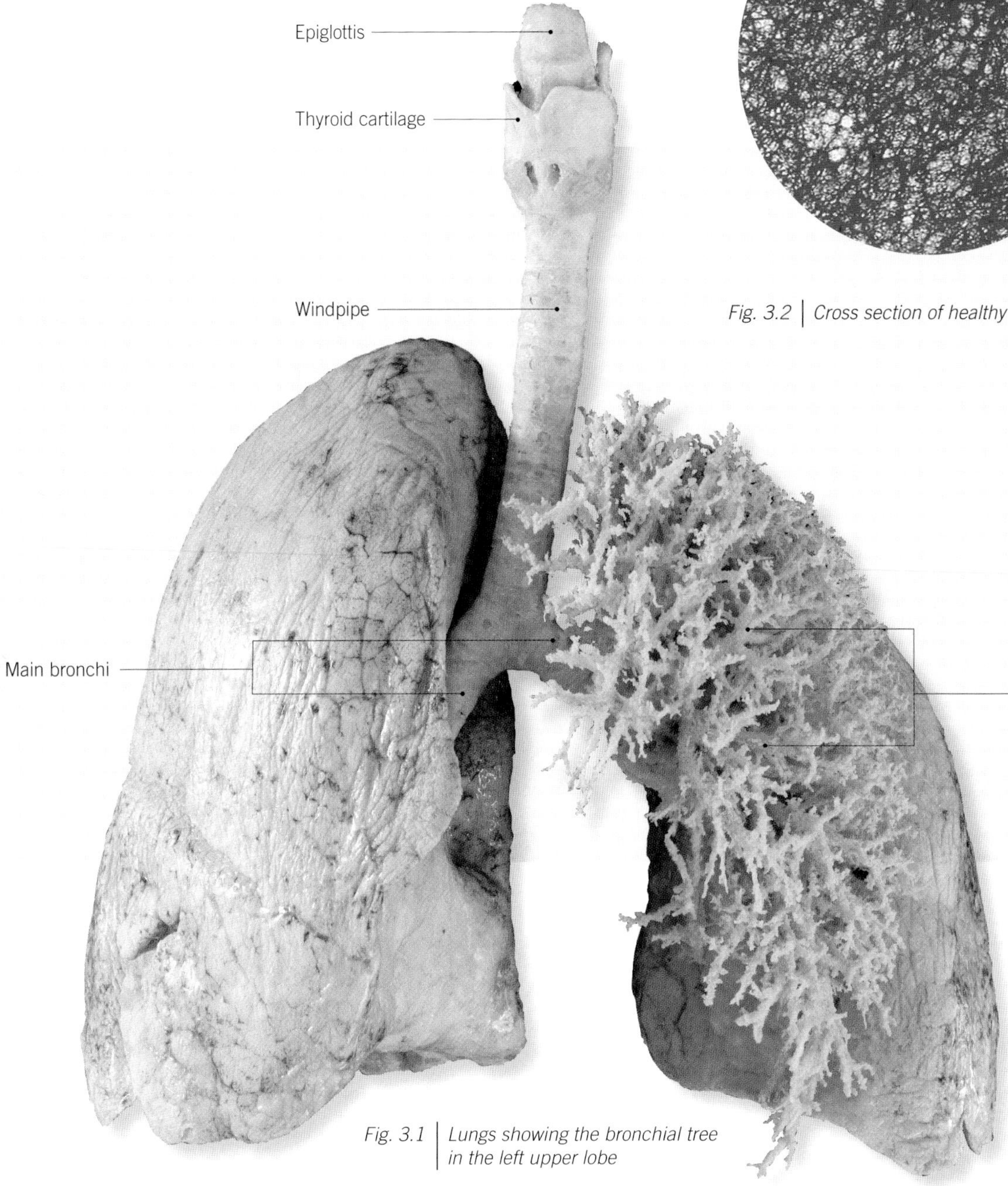

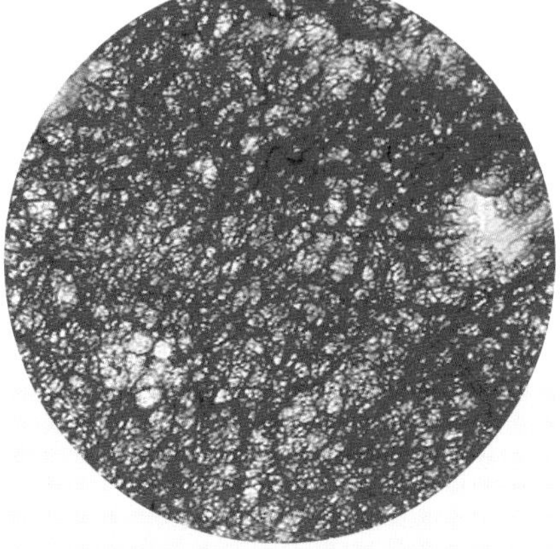

Fig. 3.2 | Cross section of healthy lung tissue

Epiglottis

Thyroid cartilage

Windpipe

Main bronchi

Bronchi

Fig. 3.1 | Lungs showing the bronchial tree in the left upper lobe

The lungs absorb oxygen from the air
and pass it on to the blood.
Every minute, about 5-6 litres (11 to 13 pints)
of air pass into the lungs.
To reach the lungs,
the air first passes the nose and mouth,
and then the larynx and windpipe.
The windpipe divides into two major bronchi,
one leading to each lung.

Rather like the branches of a tree,
the bronchi subdivide into ever smaller parts,
as shown in the upper lobe of the left lung here.

The windpipe and bronchi
contain supporting cartilage
so they stay rigid and open at all times,
no matter how much the air pressure fluctuates.

The bronchial passages in the lungs
lead into clusters of tiny air sacs (alveoli)
that give the lungs a sponge-like appearance.
This can best be seen
in an enlarged cross section of lung tissue.
Each alveolus is surrounded

by a network of capillaries,
where oxygen and carbon dioxide are exchanged.
Each lung contains 300 to 450 million alveoli.
Spread out flat, they would cover
between 80 and 120 sq. metres
(860 and 1,300 sq. feet).

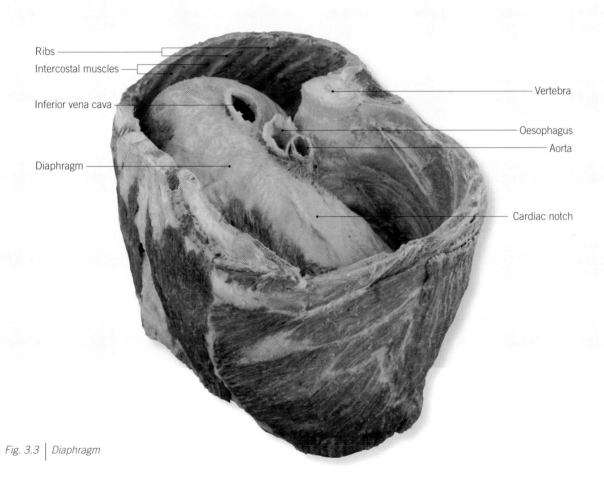

Ribs

Intercostal muscles

Inferior vena cava

Diaphragm

Vertebra

Oesophagus

Aorta

Cardiac notch

Fig. 3.3 | *Diaphragm*

When we breathe in,
muscles work to expand the chest.
The primary respiratory muscle is the diaphragm.
This is a thin dome-shaped muscular partition
that separates the chest from the abdomen.
When its muscle fibres contract,
the diaphragm drops
and the thoracic cavity enlarges.
The intercostal muscles between the ribs
additionally enlarge the thoracic cavity
by pulling the chest up and out.
As the lungs expand, the air flows in.

To exhale, the diaphragm and intercostal muscles
simply relax and return to their resting position.

Although we can influence our breathing,
it is usually controlled subconsciously
by the respiratory centre in the brain.
If the spinal cord is severely injured,
breaking the nervous system link
between the brain and the muscles,
the person dies unless artificially ventilated.

Taking a Breath

As air flows from the nose into the windpipe, it first passes over the nasal conchae. Their fine hairs filter dust and bacteria, while the mucous membrane heats and moistens the inhaled air. Our smell receptors are located at the top of the nasal cavity.

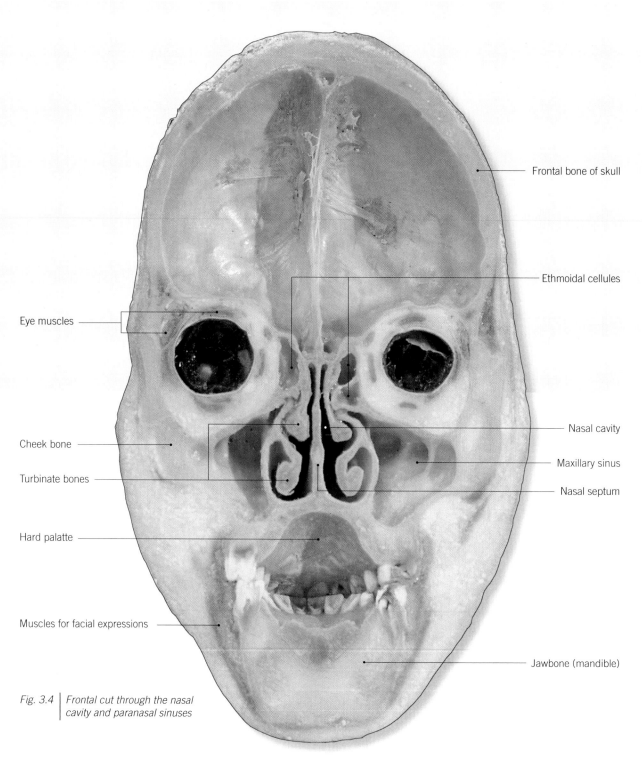

Frontal bone of skull

Ethmoidal cellules

Eye muscles

Nasal cavity

Cheek bone

Maxillary sinus

Turbinate bones

Nasal septum

Hard palatte

Muscles for facial expressions

Jawbone (mandible)

Fig. 3.4 | *Frontal cut through the nasal cavity and paranasal sinuses*

Producing Sounds

Breathing exchanges oxygen and carbon dioxide
and also allows us to produce sounds.
The key organ for sound is the larynx,
located between the oral cavity and the windpipe.

The upper part of the larynx is the epiglottis.
When we swallow, this cartilage flap
covers the windpipe entrance,
directing food and liquid into the oesophagus.
The vocal cords are in the middle of the larynx,
adjusted by a series of delicate muscles,
allowing us to modulate our voice.

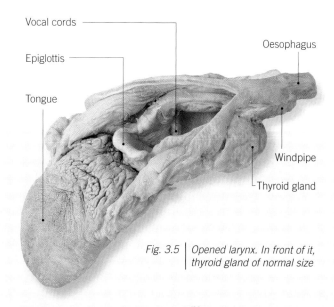

Vocal cords — Oesophagus
Epiglottis —
Tongue — Windpipe
Thyroid gland

Fig. 3.5 | Opened larynx. In front of it, thyroid gland of normal size

Epiglottis — Hyoid bone
Vestibule of the larynx —
Thyroid catilage
Arytenoid muscles —
Windpipe (trachea) —

Fig. 3.6 | Larynx, rear view

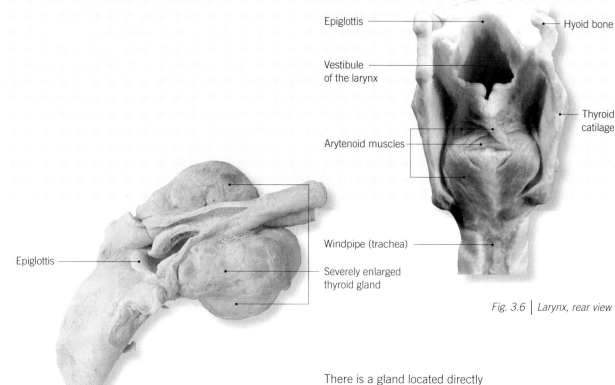

Epiglottis — Severely enlarged thyroid gland

Fig. 3.7 | Enlarged thyroid gland (goiter)

There is a gland located directly
in front of the windpipe below the larynx, the thyroid.
The thyroid produces hormones
that regulate metabolic functions
and the body's level of activity.
It can significantly enlarge and cause the neck to swell,
a condition known as goiter.
If the swelling is very severe,
it can constrict the trachea and impair breathing.
Goiters can have different causes,
including iodine deficiency.

The Diseased Lung

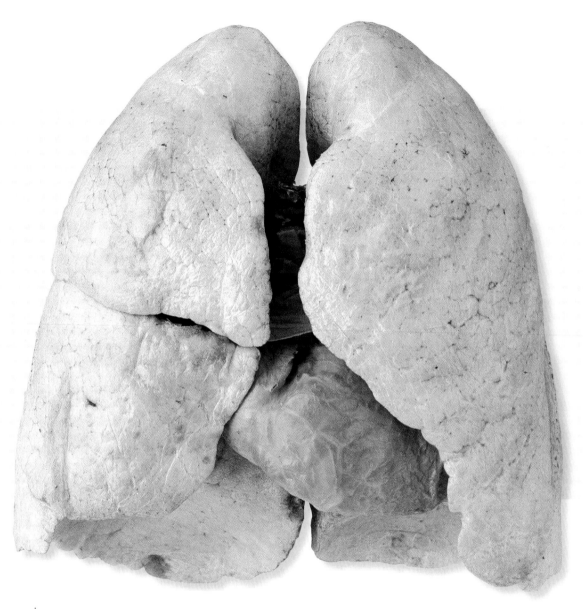

Fig. 3.8 | *Non-smoker's lungs. The heart is in between the two lungs*

The heart is surrounded by the lungs.
Since the heart is located left of centre,
the left lung is slightly smaller than the right.
The lungs have horizontal and diagonal fissures
dividing them into individual lobes:
three on the right and two on the left.

When we breathe in,
we also inhale fine particles of dust,
that form deposits in the lung tissue.
These deposits usually disappear in time.
As we grow older, though,
the lung often exhibits small surface marks
similar to those on this lung.

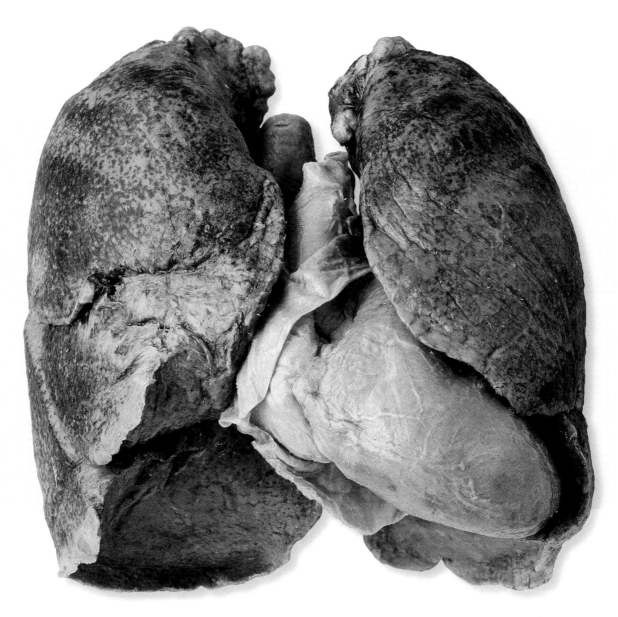

Fig. 3.9 | Smoker's lungs

Tar and soot particles from cigarette smoke
form deposits in the pulmonary tissue.
The deposits turn the lung black.
Just 20 cigarettes a day
produce an annual 150 millilitres (5 fl. ounces) of tar.
That is about the volume of a full coffee cup.

When smoking a cigarette, it only takes about 8 seconds
for the nicotine to reach the brain.
Breathing speeds up, the arteries narrow,
blood pressure and heart rate rapidly increase,
and the central nervous system is stimulated.

Nicotine raises the levels
of a neurotransmitter called dopamine
in brain areas linked to pleasure and reward.
This effect of nicotine may explain
why many people find it so hard to stop smoking.

After quitting smoking, the tar will gradually decompose
and the lungs will recover –
even after many years of smoking.
Also smoking related health risks can greatly be reduced.

Lung Cancer

Smoking negatively affects the body
in different ways and can shorten a person's life
by an average of five years.
One of the dangers of long-term smoking
is the development of lung cancer.

Lung cancer is 20 times more common
in smokers than non-smokers
and is the most common cause of death in men.
It is the most lethal malignant tumour worldwide,
causing up to 3 million deaths annually.

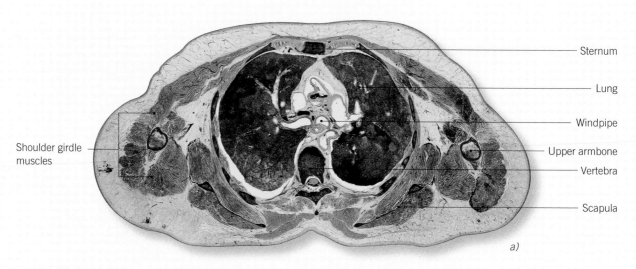

Sternum

Lung

Windpipe

Shoulder girdle
muscles

Upper armbone

Vertebra

Scapula

a)

Fig. 3.10 | Cross sections of the thoracic cavity with
a) a non-smoker's lungs and
b) a smoker's lungs

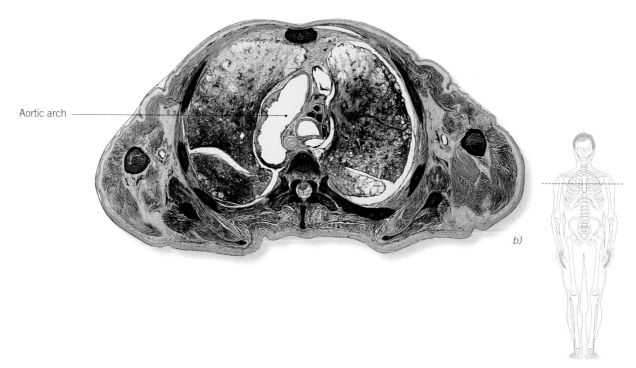

Aortic arch

b)

Most lung cancers originate
from the bronchial walls.
Thus, they are also called bronchial carcinoma.
The bronchi get in direct contact
with our immediate environment
and inhaled carcinogens such as tobacco smoke.

This can directly affect the bronchial walls
and contribute to local tumour growth.

In the lungs shown in Fig. 3.12 a solid tumour originating
from the bronchial wall is considerably narrowing the air
passage to the right lung.

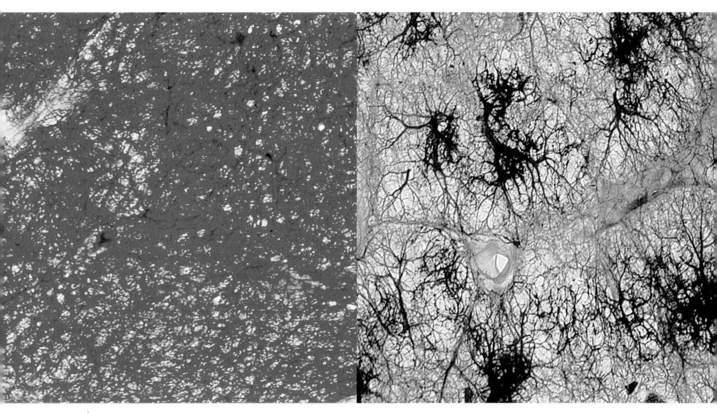

Fig. 3.11 | *Enlargements of sections of lung tissue taken from a non smoker (left) and a smoker (right)*

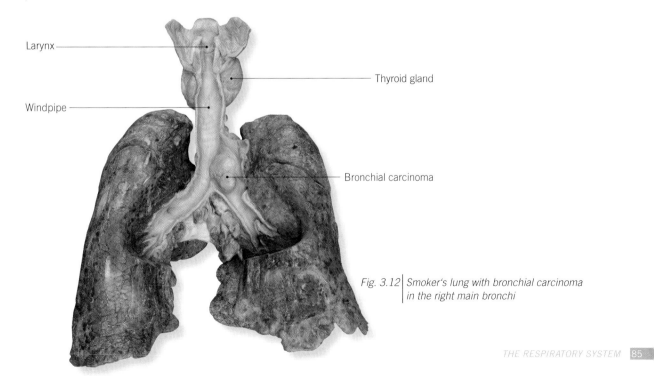

Larynx

Thyroid gland

Windpipe

Bronchial carcinoma

Fig. 3.12 | *Smoker's lung with bronchial carcinoma
in the right main bronchi*

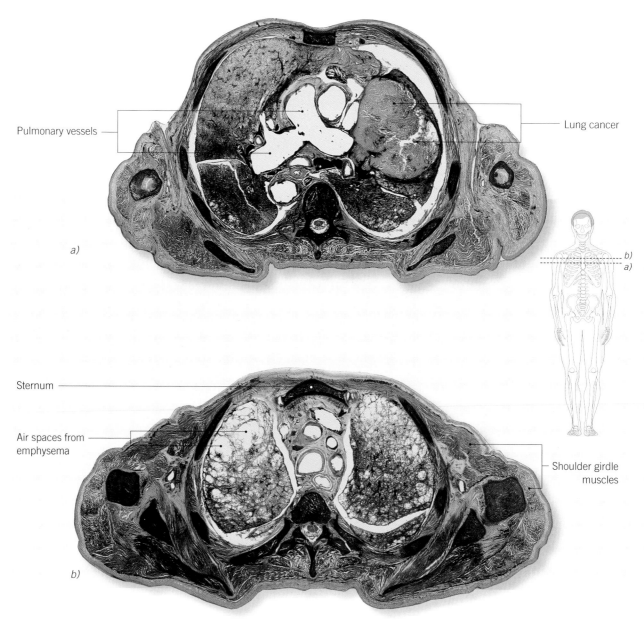

Pulmonary vessels —

— Lung cancer

a)

b)
a)

Sternum —

Air spaces from
emphysema

— Shoulder girdle
muscles

b)

Fig. 3.13 | Cross sections of the thoracic cavity with a) a smoker's lungs with lung cancer and
b) a smoker's lungs and emphysema

Lung Emphysema

Another danger of long-term smoking
is the development of emphysema.
Emphysema is a relatively common disease.
It doesn't develop suddenly
but comes on very gradually.
Air sacs in the lungs are irreversibly destroyed,
leaving behind cavities in the lung tissue.
These cavities reduce the lung surface available
for the exchange of oxygen and carbon dioxide,
causing shortness of breath.
Many older people naturally experience

increasing lung emphysema.
In many cases today, however,
emphysema is the result of years of smoking.
Lung emphysema also puts a strain
on the right side of the heart:
The more lung tissue is destroyed
the smaller the capillary bed of the lungs gets.
This eventually raises the vascular resistance
and pulmonary artery pressure,
'overloading' the right ventricle.
If left untreated, the person may suffer
right-sided heart failure.

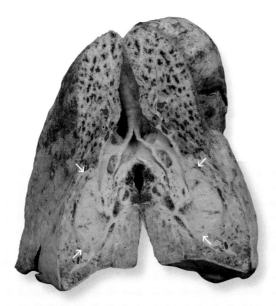

Fig. 3.14 | *Smoker's lungs with lung cancer.*
The solid, whitish looking tumour has invaded almost the complete lower lobe.

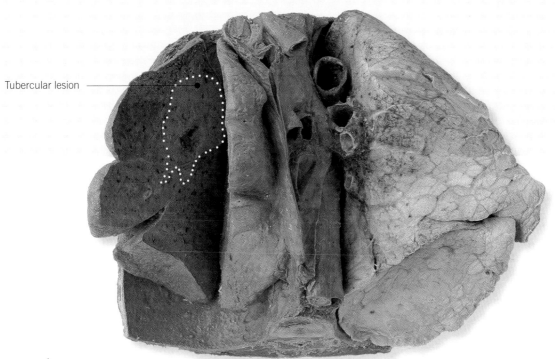

Tubercular lesion ————

Fig. 3.15 | *Lungs with tubercular lesion*

Tuberculosis

In principle, tuberculosis bacilli
could attack any organ.
Primarily, though, they infect the lungs.
Tuberculosis is characterised by
an inflammatory lesion with a cavern.

This is thickened tissue collapsed at centre.
Tuberculosis may also affect other organs,
such as the brain.
When it takes the form of meningitis,
it is a life-threatening condition.

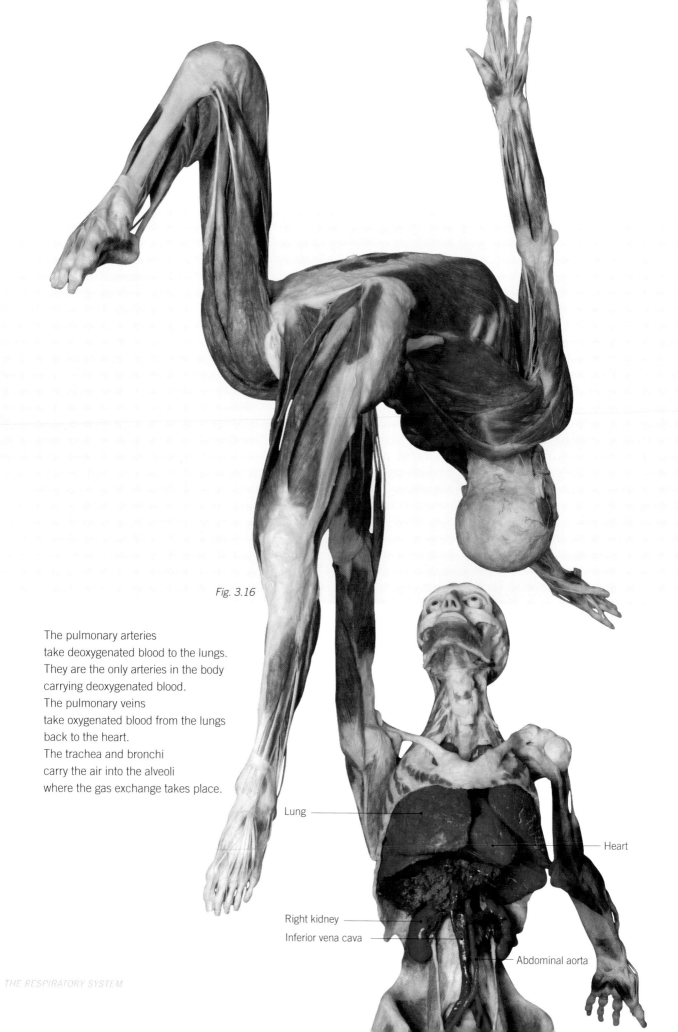

Fig. 3.16

The pulmonary arteries
take deoxygenated blood to the lungs.
They are the only arteries in the body
carrying deoxygenated blood.
The pulmonary veins
take oxygenated blood from the lungs
back to the heart.
The trachea and bronchi
carry the air into the alveoli
where the gas exchange takes place.

Lung

Heart

Right kidney

Inferior vena cava

Abdominal aorta

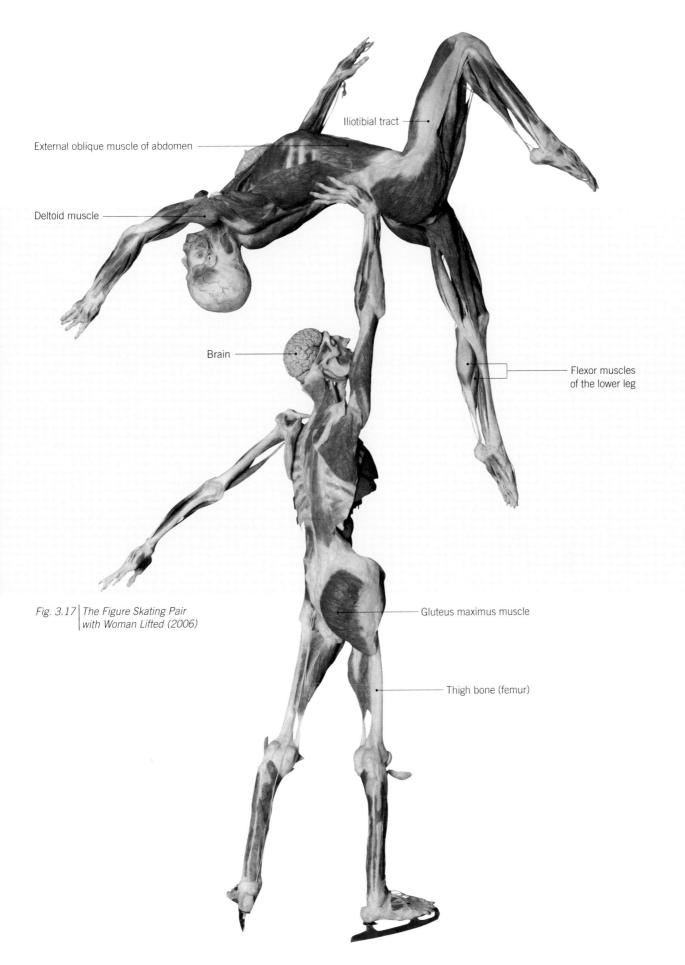

External oblique muscle of abdomen

Iliotibial tract

Deltoid muscle

Brain

Flexor muscles
of the lower leg

Fig. 3.17 | *The Figure Skating Pair
with Woman Lifted (2006)*

Gluteus maximus muscle

Thigh bone (femur)

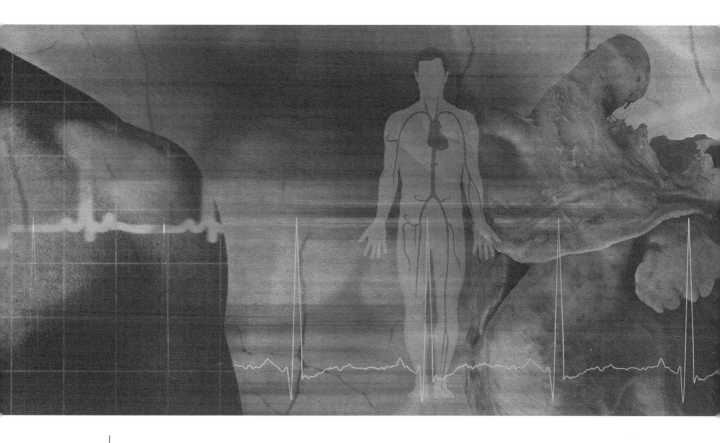

4. | THE **CARDIOVASCULAR** SYSTEM

The cardiovascular system is an
organism's major transport system.
Not only does it distribute nutrients,
oxygen and hormones to individual regions of the body;
it also collects metabolic by-products
which are then eliminated.
The heart is the engine of this system,
and the dense network of blood vessels
form the transport routes.

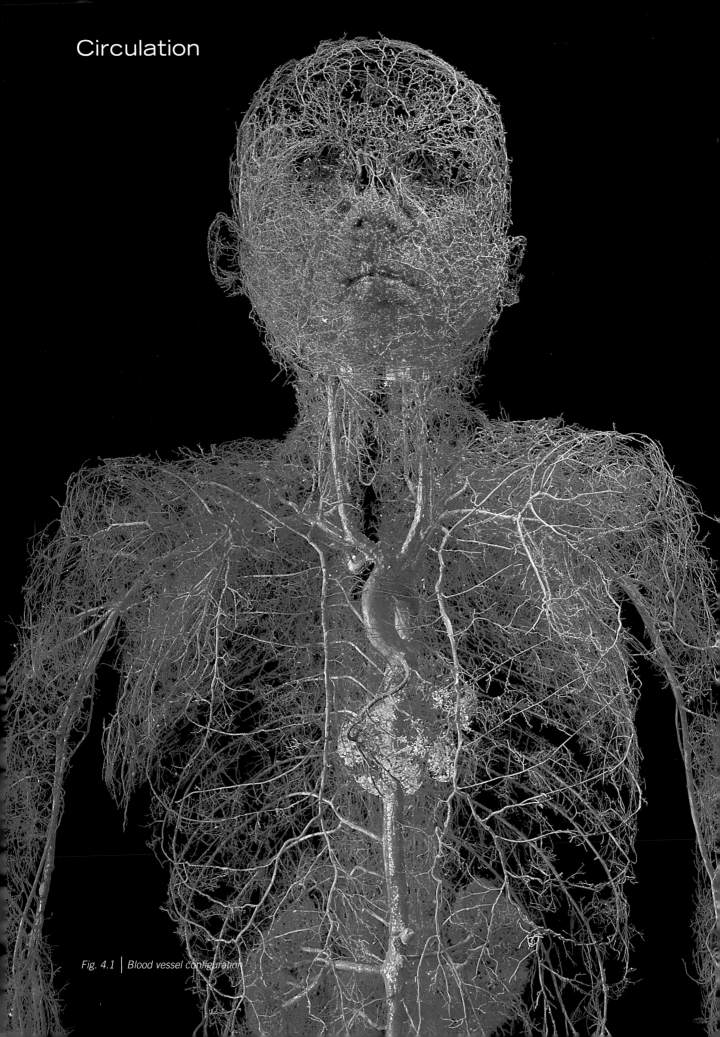

Circulation

Fig. 4.1 | Blood vessel configuration

Generally speaking, the vessels represent
major highways that distribute blood to the body.
They taper down more and more
as they pass into the organs and tissue
to form an intricate network
of minute, hair-like vessels called capillaries.
It is here that the interchange of nutrients,
oxygen, and other substances takes place
between the blood and tissue cells.

The dense network of arteries, veins,
and capillaries that carry blood
to and from the heart
is more than 96,500 kilometres (60,000 miles) long.
Laid end to end,
the cardiovascular network
of an average adult would wrap
around the earth more than twice.

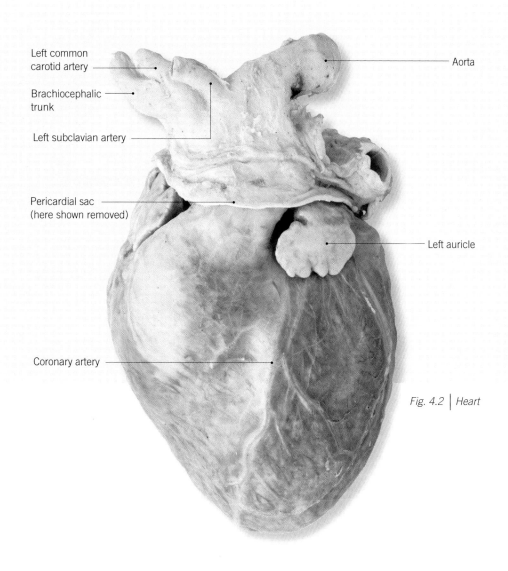

Left common carotid artery

Brachiocephalic trunk

Left subclavian artery

Pericardial sac (here shown removed)

Aorta

Left auricle

Coronary artery

Fig. 4.2 | Heart

The heart is the engine of the cardiovascular system.
The hollow, muscular organ
constantly pumps blood around the body.
Its muscle fibres run spirally
so that it can contract the chambers on all sides.
The size of the heart is roughly that of our fist
and weighs approximately 300 grams (11 ounces).

At rest, the heart has about 70 beats per minute
and pumps about 75 millilitres (3 ounces) of blood
through the body with each beat.
This adds up to about 1 million barrels of blood
during an average lifetime of around 75 years.
That is enough to fill more than 3 super tankers.

The Body's Pump

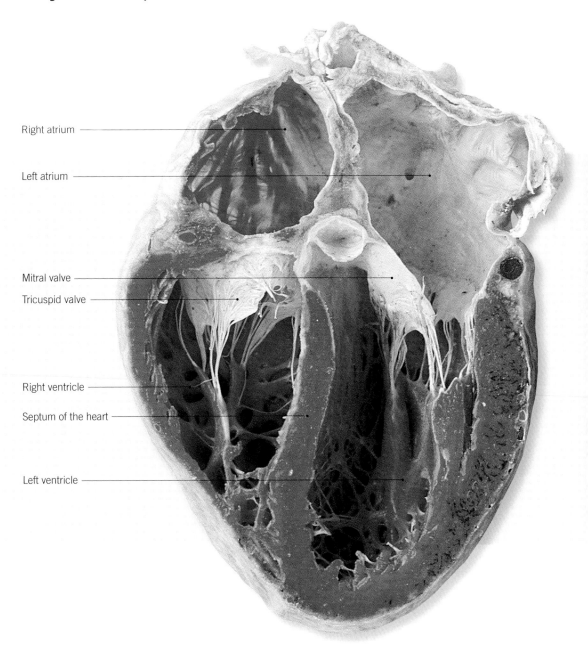

Right atrium

Left atrium

Mitral valve

Tricuspid valve

Right ventricle

Septum of the heart

Left ventricle

Each side of the heart
has an atrium for incoming blood
and a ventricle to pump blood out.
The left ventricle of the heart distributes
the oxygen-rich blood from the lungs
to all the body's cells.
Here, oxygen and nutrients are exchanged for waste
through the web-like beds of capillaries.
The oxygen-poor blood drains through veins
back to the right heart
and from here to the lungs for replenishment.

To get enough oxygen to all of the body's organs,
all of our blood must pass through the lungs
and around the body at least once a minute.

The gas exchange is incredibly fast.
The blood in the capillaries of the lungs
comes into contact with air
for only about 0.75 seconds
but is fully oxygenated after about
a third of this time.

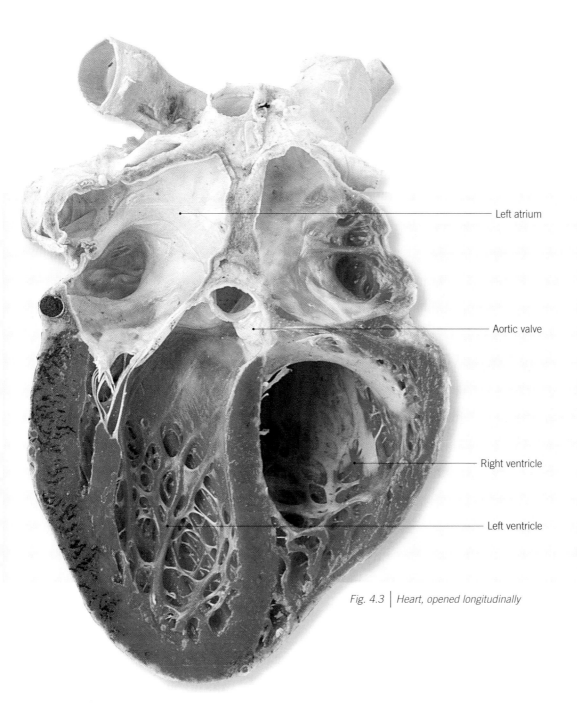

Left atrium

Aortic valve

Right ventricle

Left ventricle

Fig. 4.3 | Heart, opened longitudinally

The heartbeat is regulated
by special muscle fibres in the heart walls.
These fibres are not visible to the naked eye.

The rhythm of our heart accompanies us
throughout our lives, without a moment's rest.
The sound – lub-dub, lub-dub, lub-dub – is created
by the four heart valves as they direct blood flow
through the heart's four chambers.

The closing of the two valves
between the atria and the ventricles –
mitral and tricuspid – creates the first part
of the heartbeat, the lub.
The second part of the heart beating – dub –
is the closing of the aortic and pulmonary valves
that separate the ventricles from the arteries.

If the valves do not close properly and leak,
the sound will be muffled.

Controlling Blood Flow

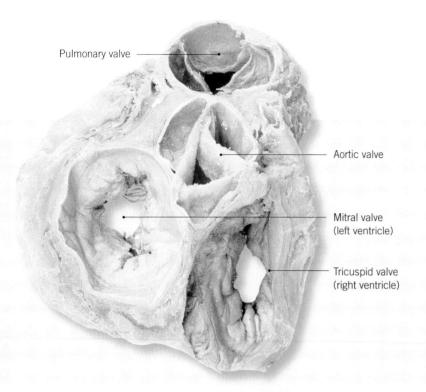

Pulmonary valve

Aortic valve

Mitral valve
(left ventricle)

Tricuspid valve
(right ventricle)

Heart Valves
Blood flow between the atria and ventricles
is controlled by one-way valves.
These are flaps of fibrous tissue, called cusps.
As the ventricles begin to contract,
the pressure inside the ventricles rises
and slams the cusps tightly shut.
There are also valves at the openings
to the aorta and pulmonary arteries
to prevent backflow.
The heart in Fig. 4.4 is dissected
to show all four valves viewed from above.

Fig. 4.4 │ *View of the cardiac valves from above*

Aortic Valve Infection (Endocarditis)
The endocardium is the heart's inner lining.
Endocarditis is an inflammation
of the lining and the heart valves.
After the infection has healed,
permanent scars and growths
may remain on the valve, as shown in Fig. 4.5.
These scars impair the heart's function:
If a valve fails to work properly,
the heart needs greater pressure
to pump the same volume of blood.
If an endocarditis is bacterial,
it can lead to serious complications,
including heart or kidney failure.

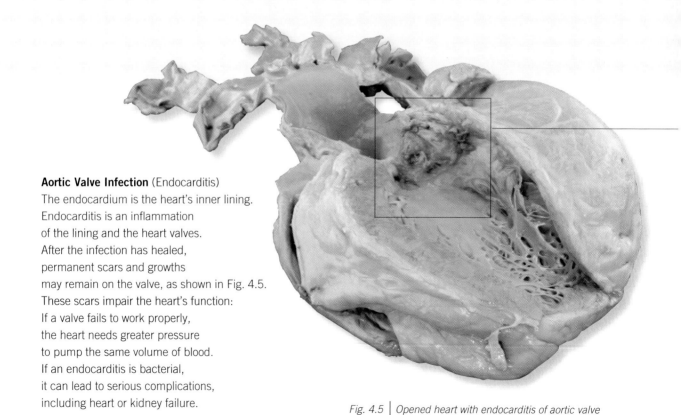

Fig. 4.5 │ *Opened heart with endocarditis of aortic valve*

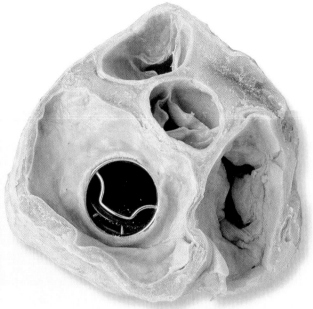

Fig. 4.6 | Cardiac valves from above with mitral valve prosthesis

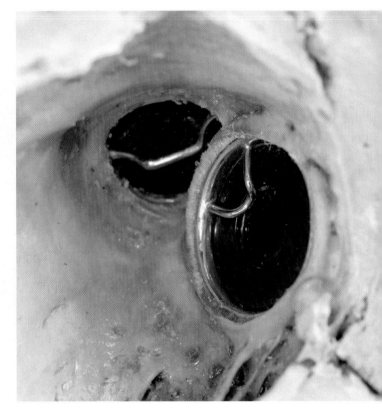

Fig. 4.7 | Heart with mitral and aortic valve prosthesis

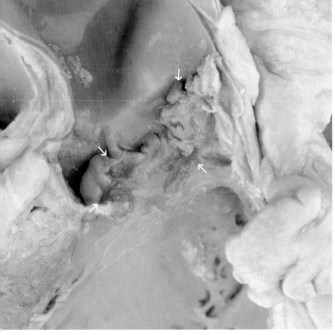

Artificial Valves

Bacterial or rheumatic infections (endocarditis)
can deform the heart valves so much
that they can no longer open sufficiently
or close properly.
In severe cases, the affected valves
have to be replaced with artificial ones.
Above, both the aortic semilunar valve (the valve
between the left ventricle and the aorta)
and the mitral valve (the valve separating
the left atrium and the left ventricle)
are replaced with prostheses.

Fig. 4.8 | Close-up of aortic valve with endocarditis

Blood Supply of the Heart

The cardiac muscle has its own blood vessels
to supply it with oxygen and nutrients.
They are called coronary arteries.
Two main arteries branch from the aorta
and subdivide into smaller blood vessels
that penetrate the heart muscle.

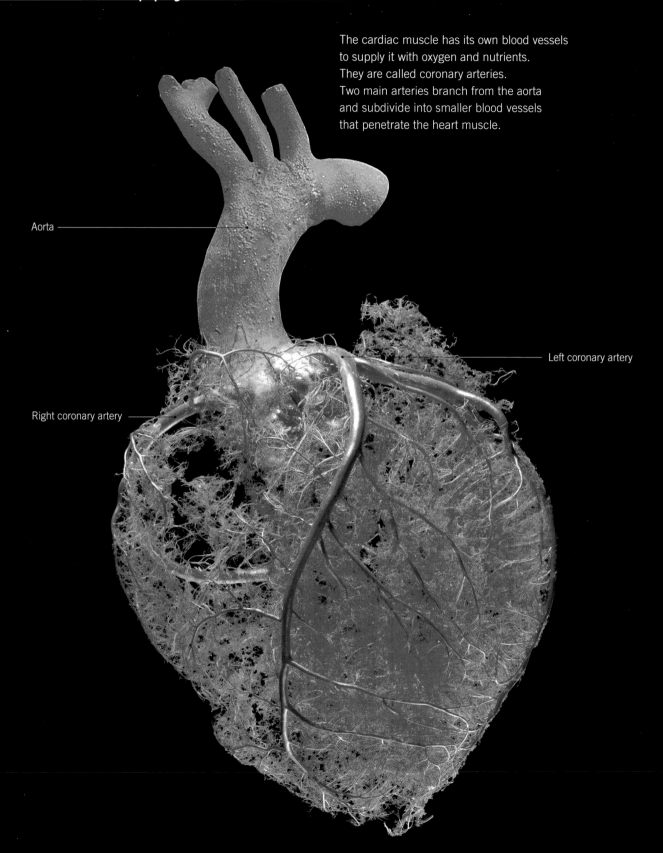

Aorta

Left coronary artery

Right coronary artery

Fig. 4.9 | *Configuration of the coronary arteries*

Coronary Artery Disease

In a diseased artery,
a fatty substance called plaque
forms on the arterial walls.
The plaque may gradually become
a bulge that obstructs blood flow.

When a coronary artery is affected,
it causes angina with symptoms, such as
chest pains and shortness of breath.

Heart Infarct

When the blood flow in a coronary artery is interrupted,
the muscle cells it supplies die.
This condition is known as heart attack.
If only a small section of the heart is affected,
it can continue to pump blood through the body,
and the person will survive the heart attack.
But the heart functions will be weakened.
Gradually, a white scar of connective tissue
will replace the dead cells.
The heart wall is then
significantly thinner in the affected area.

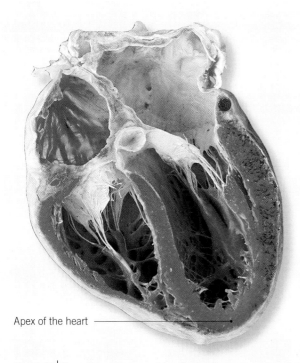

Apex of the heart

Fig. 4.10 | Normal heart, opened longitudinally

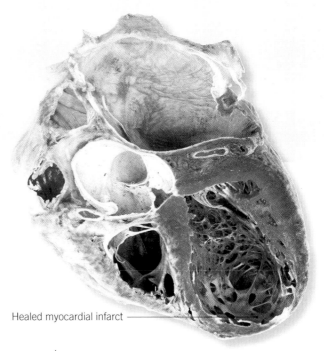

Healed myocardial infarct

Fig. 4.11 | Old, healed infarct in the apex of the heart

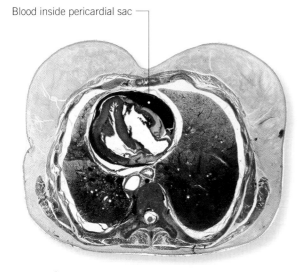

Blood inside pericardial sac

*Fig. 4.12 | Cross-section of the thoracic cavity
with pericardial tamponade*

A heart attack can also be so severe
that the cardiac wall tears.
Blood then flows into the pericardium,
compressing the heart from outside.
This condition is called 'pericardial tamponade'
and is usually fatal within minutes.

Heart Hypertrophy

All muscles increase with exercise
and so do our heart muscles.
An athlete's heart can even weigh
over 500 grams (18 ounces).

However, the heart also enlarges under strain,
for example, high blood pressure,
defects in the heart wall,
or faulty heart valves.
The massive hypertrophy shown here,
the heart weighs 800 grams (1.7 pounds),
was due to a heart muscle disease.

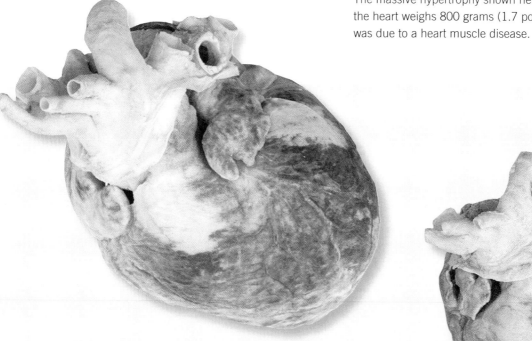

Fig. 4.13 | *Cardiac hypertrophy in comparison with a normal heart*

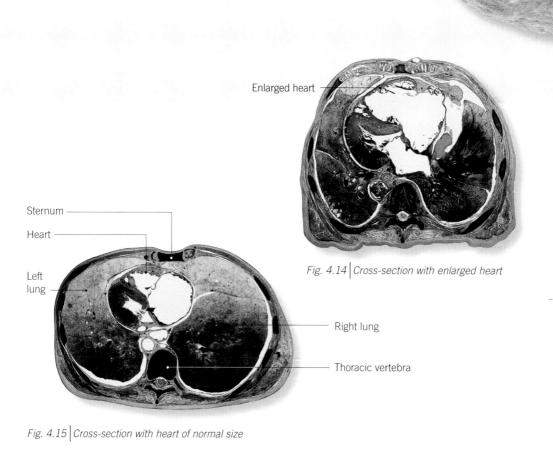

Enlarged heart

Fig. 4.14 | *Cross-section with enlarged heart*

Sternum

Heart

Left
lung

Right lung

Thoracic vertebra

Fig. 4.15 | *Cross-section with heart of normal size*

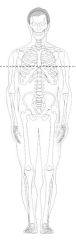

Blood Vessel Configurations

Blood vessel configurations are perfect samples
of the inner profiles of blood vessels.
Here, only the main arterial branches are shown.
If also the capillaries were injected,
the arterial network would look so dense
that one could not look through.

The vessels are first injected
with a dyed plastic.
By the time the plastic has cured,
it has taken the shape of the vessels.
The surrounding soft tissue
can then be removed mechanically
and chemically with the aid of ferments.

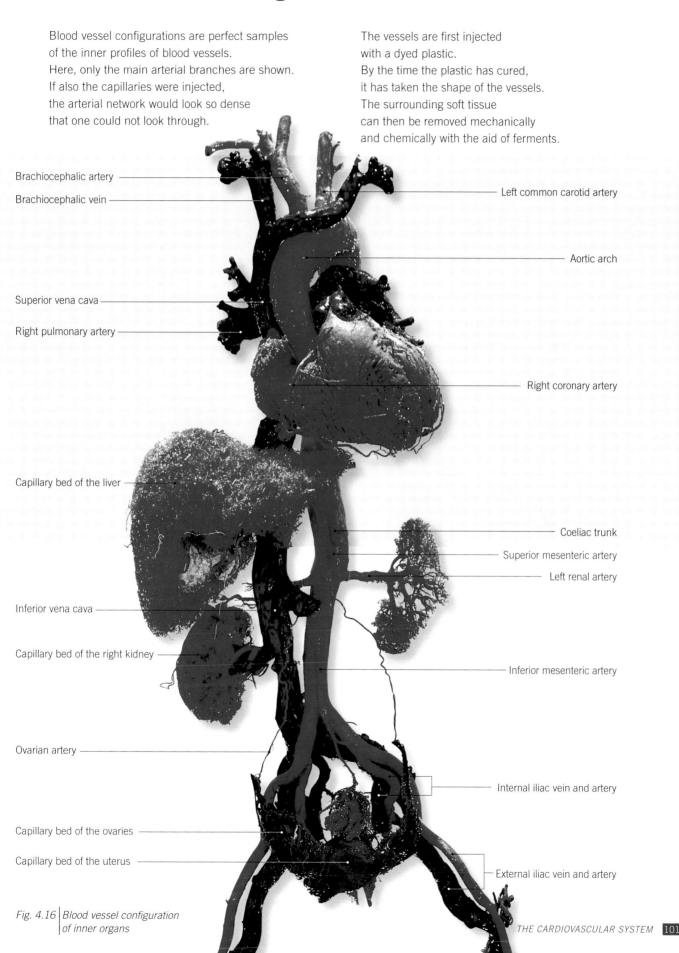

Brachiocephalic artery

Brachiocephalic vein

Left common carotid artery

Superior vena cava

Aortic arch

Right pulmonary artery

Right coronary artery

Capillary bed of the liver

Coeliac trunk

Superior mesenteric artery

Left renal artery

Inferior vena cava

Capillary bed of the right kidney

Inferior mesenteric artery

Ovarian artery

Internal iliac vein and artery

Capillary bed of the ovaries

Capillary bed of the uterus

External iliac vein and artery

Fig. 4.16 | *Blood vessel configuration
of inner organs*

Arteries

Fig. 4.17 | Inner lining of a healthy aorta

Fig. 4.18 | Inner lining of aortas with varying degrees of hardening of the arteries (arteriosclerosis)

Arteries have a thin layer of muscles
in their walls, helping the heart pump the blood.
When the heart beats, the artery expands
as it fills with blood.
When the heart relaxes, the artery contracts,
exerting a force that is strong enough
to push the blood along.
This rhythm between the heart and the artery
constitutes our pulse.

The aorta is the largest artery in the body.
It is almost as thick as a garden hose.
Capillaries, on the other hand,
are so thin that it takes ten of them
to equal the thickness of a human hair.

The interior wall of a young, healthy artery
is completely smooth as is the aorta shown above.
To guarantee the blood supply to our organs,
our bodies monitor and regulate
the blood pressure in the arteries.
If arterial pressure is too low,
not enough blood reaches the body tissue.
If pressure is too high,
it could damage blood vessels and organs.
Responses are controlled by the
autonomous nervous system within seconds.

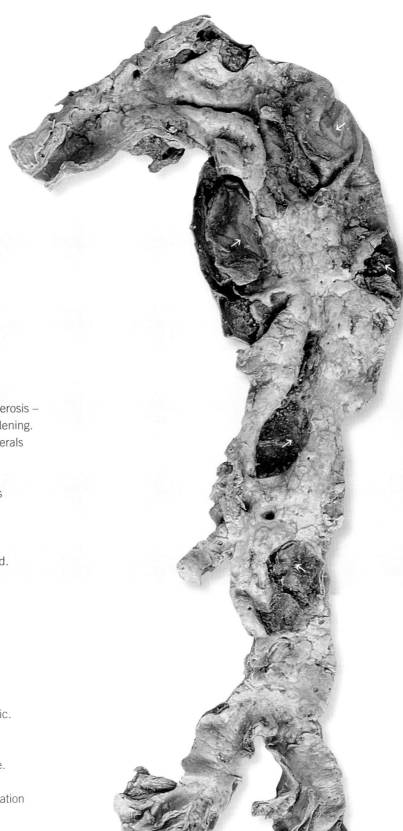

Arteriosclerosis

The aortas on the left show arteriosclerosis –
the process of arteries gradually hardening.
This is due to fats, proteins, and minerals
deposited on the blood vessel walls.
As the disease progresses,
the internal walls of the blood vessels
start to deteriorate and form ulcers.
Blood clots collect on the ulcers,
narrowing the arteries even more,
until they become completely clogged.

Aorta with Aneurysm

Normally blood vessel walls are elastic.
If wall segments become hard,
they develop weak points
that dilate under high blood pressure.
As in the opened aorta on the right,
the dilated areas interfere with circulation
and cause blood to clot.
Since these "pouches" (aneurysms)
usually have thin and weak walls,
high blood pressure can rupture them.
The result is severe, often fatal, haemorrhaging.
Large quantities of coagulated blood
can clearly be seen here in the aneurysms
of the arterial wall.

Fig. 4.19 | *Aneurysms in the aorta, filled with blood clots.*

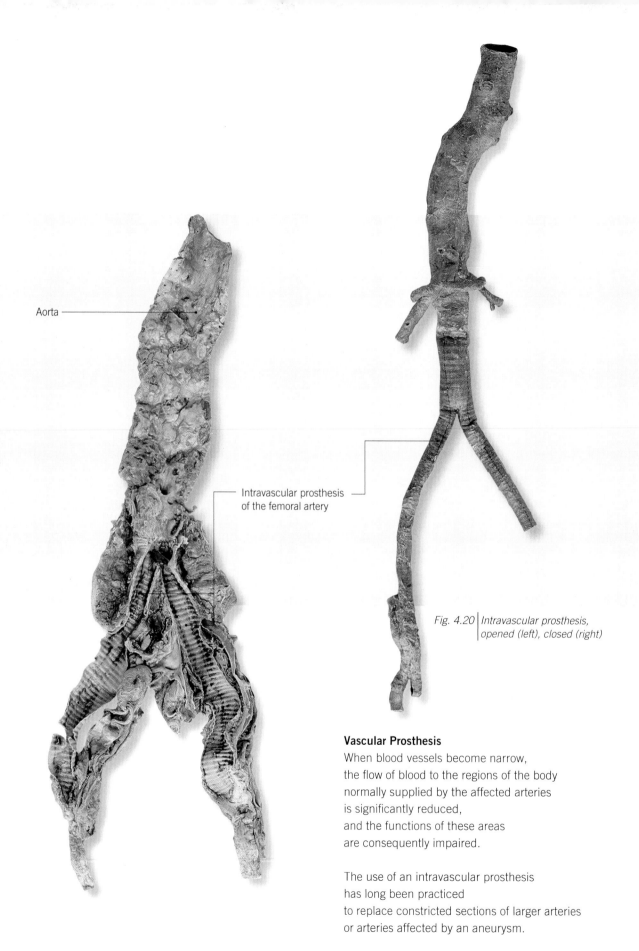

Aorta

Intravascular prosthesis
of the femoral artery

Fig. 4.20 | Intravascular prosthesis,
opened (left), closed (right)

Vascular Prosthesis

When blood vessels become narrow,
the flow of blood to the regions of the body
normally supplied by the affected arteries
is significantly reduced,
and the functions of these areas
are consequently impaired.

The use of an intravascular prosthesis
has long been practiced
to replace constricted sections of larger arteries
or arteries affected by an aneurysm.

Blood

Blood consists of a pale liquid called plasma
in which billions of red and white blood cells
and platelets float.
Red blood cells are by far the most numerous.
They transport oxygen and carry away carbon dioxide.

A red blood cell can circumnavigate the entire body
in less than 20 seconds.
The colourless white cells are part of the body's
built-in defence mechanisms.
Platelets are involved in blood clotting.

Together, these three kinds of blood cells make
45% of the blood tissue (55% is plasma).

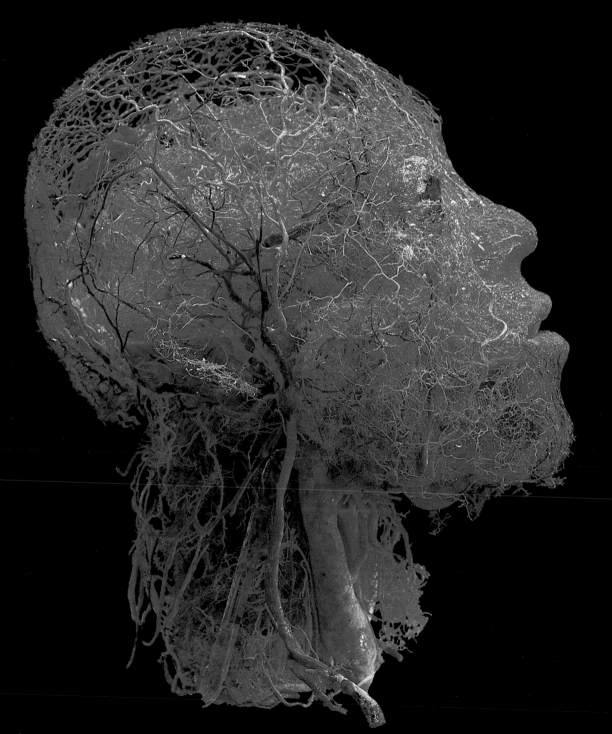

Fig. 4.21│Blood vessel configuration of the head

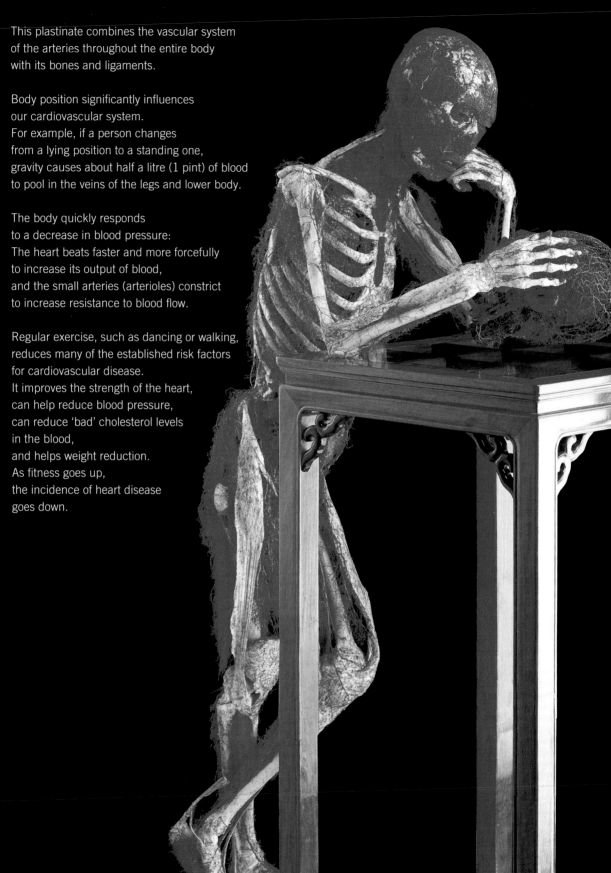

This plastinate combines the vascular system
of the arteries throughout the entire body
with its bones and ligaments.

Body position significantly influences
our cardiovascular system.
For example, if a person changes
from a lying position to a standing one,
gravity causes about half a litre (1 pint) of blood
to pool in the veins of the legs and lower body.

The body quickly responds
to a decrease in blood pressure:
The heart beats faster and more forcefully
to increase its output of blood,
and the small arteries (arterioles) constrict
to increase resistance to blood flow.

Regular exercise, such as dancing or walking,
reduces many of the established risk factors
for cardiovascular disease.
It improves the strength of the heart,
can help reduce blood pressure,
can reduce 'bad' cholesterol levels
in the blood,
and helps weight reduction.
As fitness goes up,
the incidence of heart disease
goes down.

Fig. 4.22 | The Thinker (2002)

Spleen

Old blood cells are broken down by the spleen.
Consisting of lymphatic tissue,
the spleen also plays a key role in the body's immune system.
The spleen is roughly 12 centimetres (5 inches) long
and weighs about 85-130 grams (3-5 ounces).
It is located on the left of the upper abdomen,
right next to the stomach and pancreas.

Fig. 4.23 | *Normal spleen*

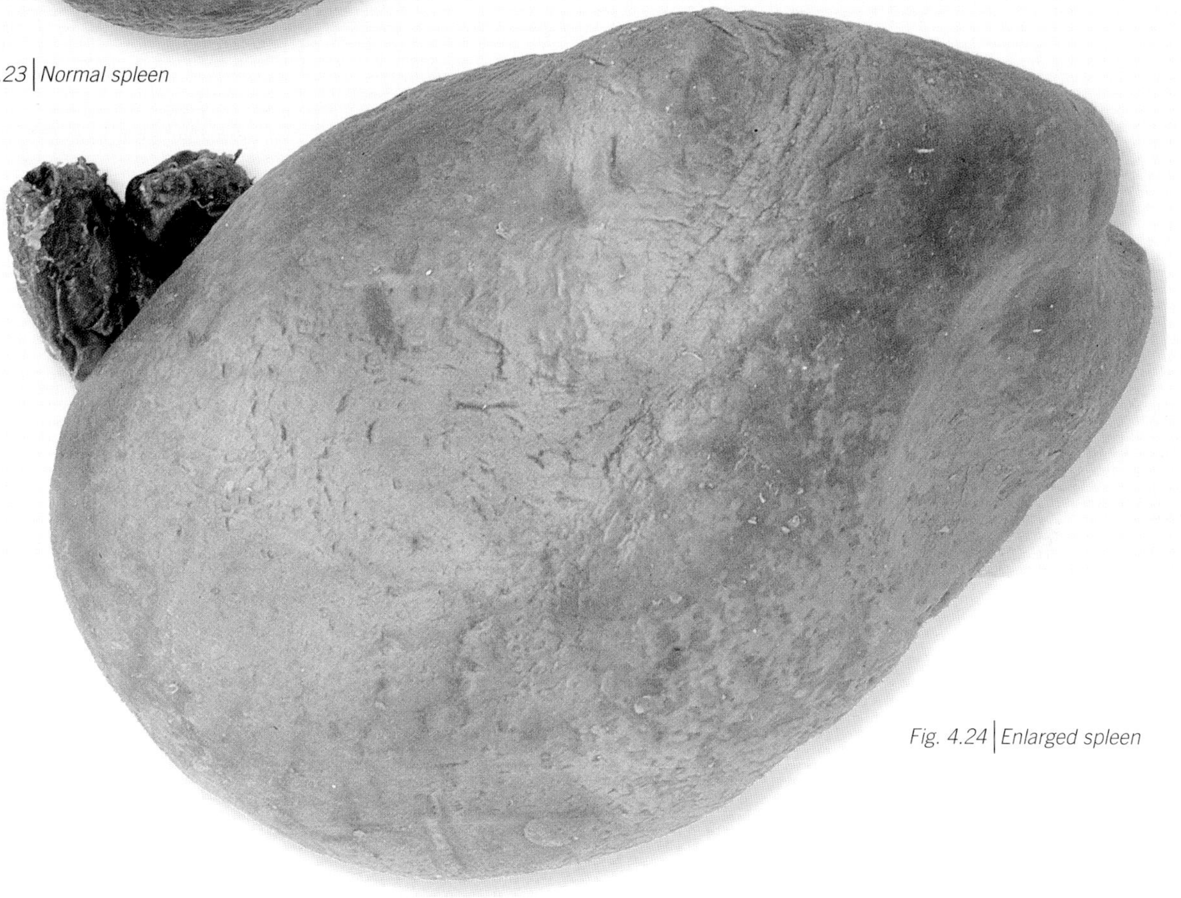

Fig. 4.24 | *Enlarged spleen*

Enlarged Spleen due to Leukaemia

Leukaemia is a malignant disease
of the bone marrow and blood.
It leads to the production of large numbers
of non-functioning white blood cells
which must be broken down in the spleen.
To cope with this enormous strain,
the spleen enlarges.
In very extreme cases,
an affected spleen can weigh up to 9 kilograms
(20 pounds).

5. | THE **DIGESTIVE** SYSTEM

All of the organs of the human body
require an uninterrupted supply of energy
if they are to perform their functions properly.
Once they have been processed chemically,
the nutrients present in food and absorbed
through the digestive tract provide the
organism with the energy that it requires.
The organs of the digestive tract break down
food both mechanically and chemically
in a way that allows the nutrients to pass into
the blood, where they can be transported to
each individual cell.

Fuelling the Body

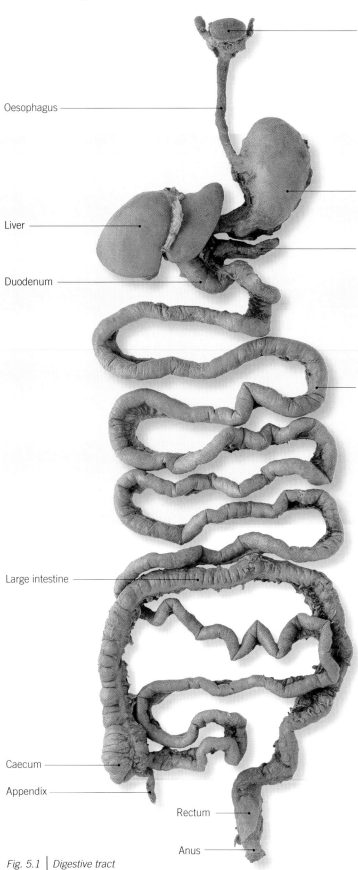

Tongue

Oesophagus

Stomach

Liver

Pancreas

Duodenum

Small intestine

Large intestine

Caecum

Appendix

Rectum

Anus

Fig. 5.1 | *Digestive tract*

The Organs of the Digestive System
The digestive tract is like a long tube –
roughly 9 metres (30 feet) in length.
Food is first coarsely broken down in the mouth,
then passes through the oesophagus
and into the stomach.
Gradually, it is fed into the duodenum
where digestive enzymes
from the liver and pancreas are added.
The small intestine is a main site of digestion,
where nutrient molecules are absorbed
into the bloodstream.
Indigestible food particles
pass into the large intestine
where water is extracted.
They are then excreted through the rectum.
The entire digestive process
takes up to 20 hours.

The organs are tightly packed
in the abdominal cavity.
They are enclosed in the peritoneum,
the sheet of body tissue that lines the abdomen.
The peritoneum also produces a mucous fluid,
a lubricant to enable the organs to move.

The stomach and intestinal tract muscles
move the food by peristalsis,
a rhythmic, wave-like muscle movement.
Peristalsis is involuntary.
It can be stimulated by food
or even the smell of food,
or, if necessary, by medication.

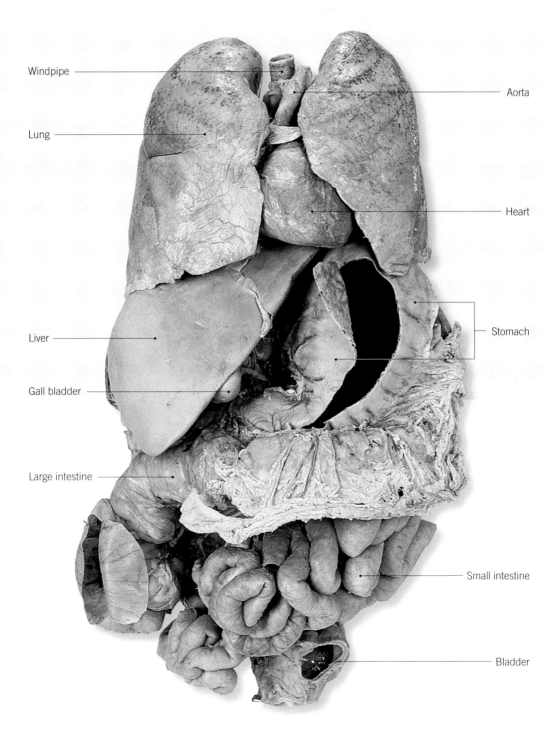

Windpipe

Aorta

Lung

Heart

Liver

Stomach

Gall bladder

Large intestine

Small intestine

Bladder

Fig. 5.2 | *Thoracic and abdominal organs in their natural relationships and positions*

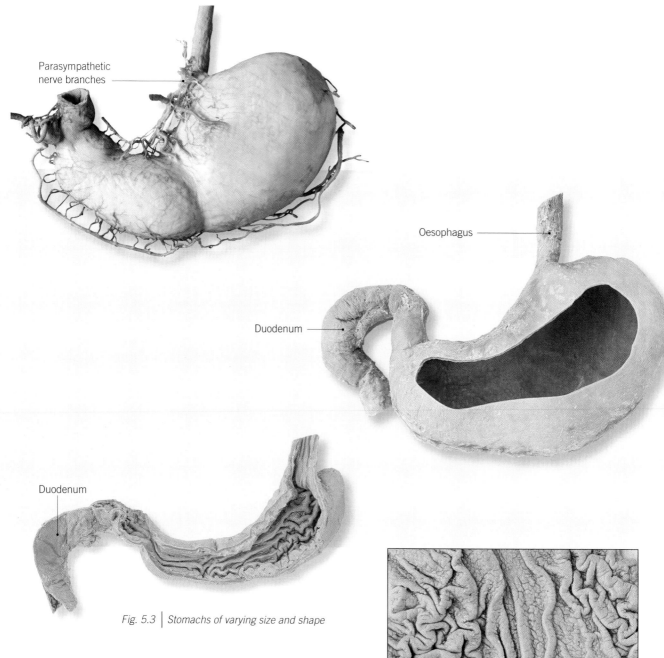

Parasympathetic
nerve branches

Oesophagus

Duodenum

Duodenum

Fig. 5.3 | Stomachs of varying size and shape

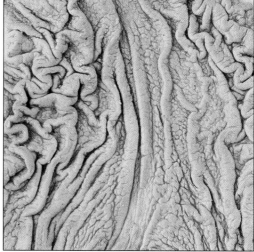

Fig. 5.4 | Mucous membrane of stomach lining

Stomach

The stomach is a hollow, muscular organ,
capable of holding 2-3 litres (4-6 pints).
It stores food and initiates
chemical and mechanical digestion,
slowly releasing its contents into the intestines.
The stomach's size, shape, and position
depend on the amount of food in it,
the position of the body,
and the person's age and eating habits.
The stomach's inner wall is lined
with a furrowed mucous membrane.
It has roughly 5 million glands,
secreting around 2 litres (2 quarts)
of gastric juices each day.

The juices mainly contain
hydrochloric acid and enzymes
that break food down into proteins.
The glands also secrete a type of mucus
to stop the stomach from digesting itself.

Fig. 5.5 | *Inflammation of the mucous membrane with dot-like signs of bleeding*

Fig. 5.6 | *Stomach ulcer*

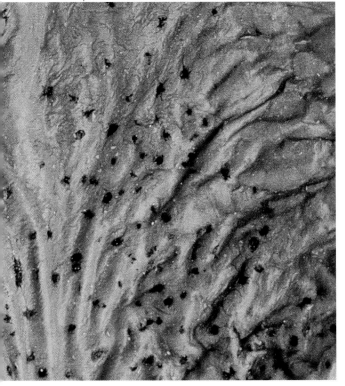

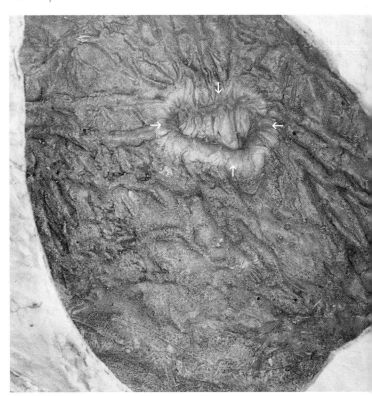

Stomach and Duodenal Ulcers

The opened stomachs in Fig. 5.6 and 5.7
have circular lesions at their inner lining,
a stomach and duodenal ulcer, respectively.
Overproduction of hydrochloric acid
can damage the lining of the stomach
and especially that of the duodenum.
Ulcers readily form if this condition exists
concurrently with a bacterial infection,
particularly that of Helicobacter pylori.
Ulcers can cause symptoms of indigestion,
including severe pain.
They can usually be treated with medicines
but, if left untreated,
can lead to serious complications,
including bleeding or perforation of the stomach.

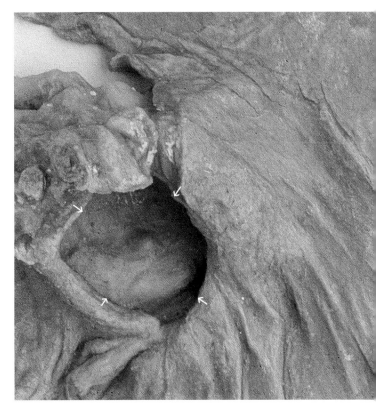

Fig. 5.7 | *Duodenal ulcer*

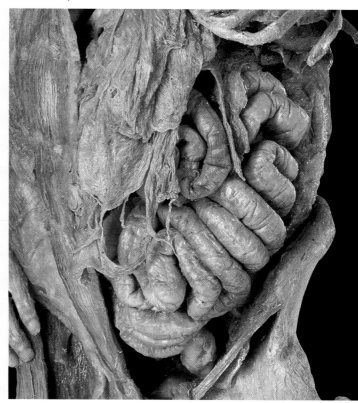

Small Intestine

Most digestion occurs in the small intestine.
Nutrients are chemically broken down
and released into the bloodstream.
To increase the area for absorbing nutrients,
the small intestine has ring-shaped folds
and a dense network of finger-shaped villi,
each 1 millimetre (0.04 inches) in length.
The villi cells also form tiny projections,
rather like the bristles of a microscopic brush.
Each projection is only 1 1/2 thousandth of a millimetre
(60 micro inches) long.
If laid out, 3 metres (10 feet) of small intestine
would expand to 120-150 sq. metres
(1,300-1,600 sq. feet).

The small intestine absorbs almost all nutrients
into the blood stream.
To accomplish this,
the small intestine's lining is equipped with
an extraordinarily fine network of blood vessels.
After a meal, blood supply
to the intestines increases considerably.
The absorbed nutrients flow to the liver
via the portal vein for further processing.

Fig. 5.10 | *Blood vessel configuration of intestines*

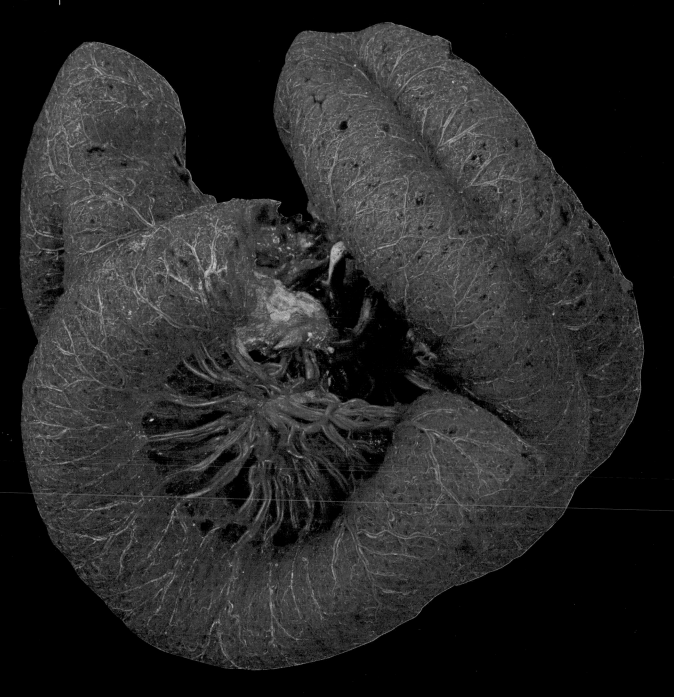

Fig. 5.11 | *Caecum with appendix*

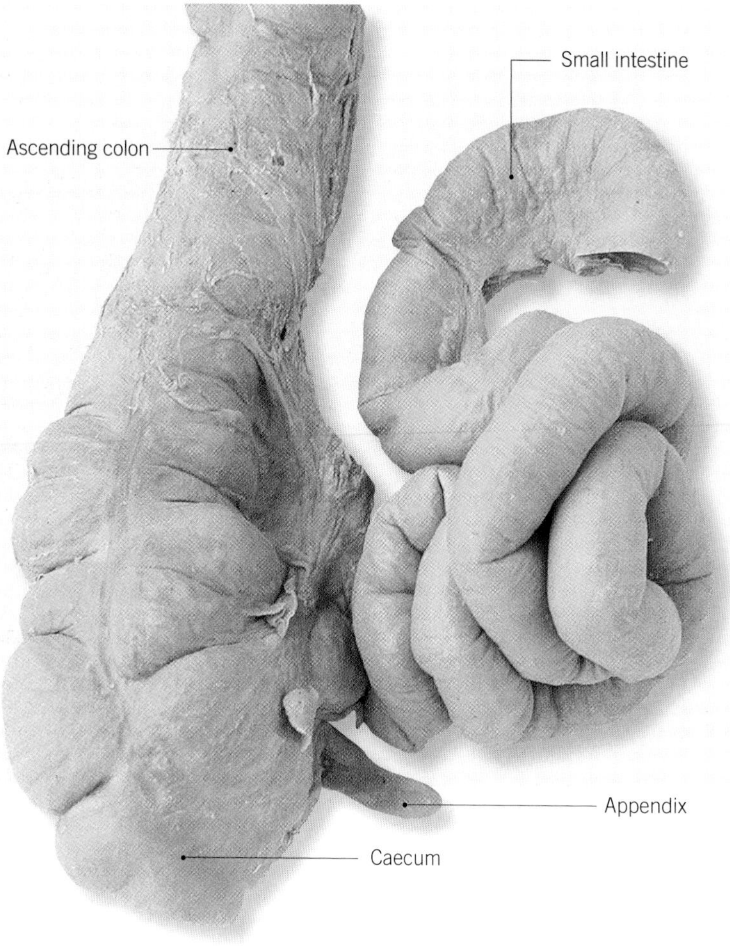

Fig. 5.12 | *Section of large intestine*

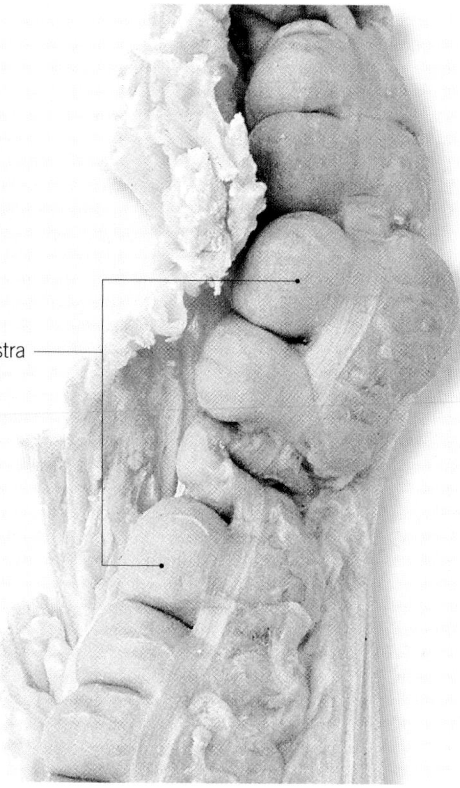

Ascending colon

Small intestine

Haustra

Appendix

Caecum

Large Intestine (Colon)

Indigestible material from the small intestine
is released to the large intestine.
There, water is absorbed
to thicken the waste products.
It also absorbs vitamins
that are produced by billions of bacteria
in the colon.
The large intestine appears segmented
due to its various "pouches" (haustra).

The caecum, the first part of the large intestine,
is on the right-hand side of the lower abdomen.
Attached to the caecum is the appendix.
It varies from 1.5-20 centimetres (0.6-8 inches) in length
and 0.5-2 centimetres (0.2-0.8 inches) in thickness.
It does not fulfill any essential function
and may be an evolutionary leftover.
Its position in the abdominal cavity also varies.
Removal of the appendix due to appendicitis
is one of the most common surgical procedures.

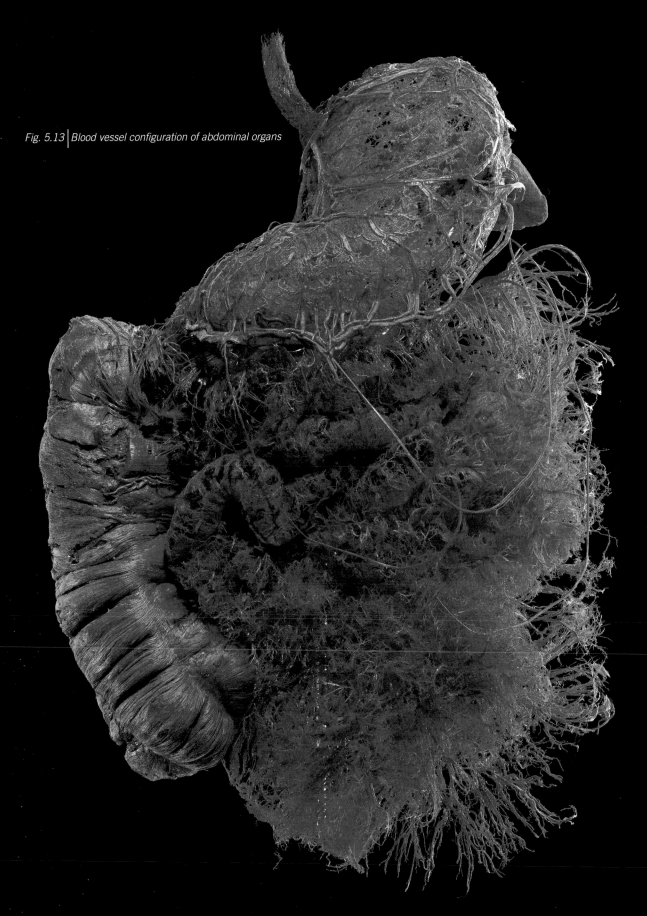

Fig. 5.13 | Blood vessel configuration of abdominal organs

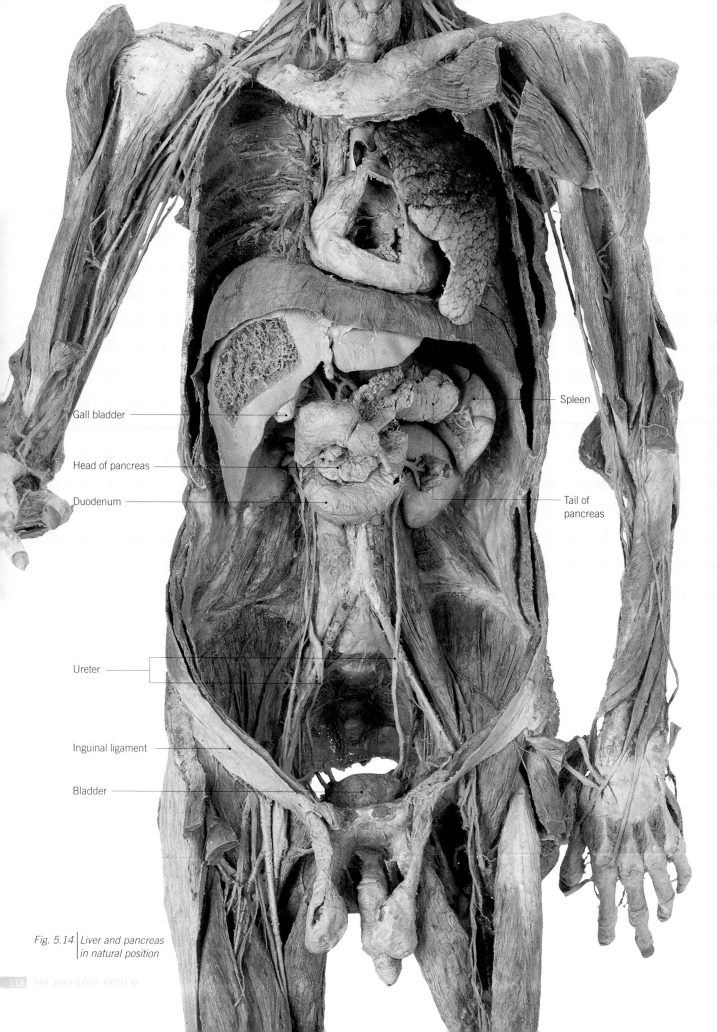

Gall bladder

Head of pancreas

Duodenum

Ureter

Inguinal ligament

Bladder

Spleen

Tail of
pancreas

Fig. 5.14 | Liver and pancreas
in natural position

Digestive Juices

Pancreas

The pancreas produces a powerful juice that
breaks down fat, proteins, and carbohydrates.
The juice is released into the duodenum
in response to the arrival of food
in the digestive tract.

The pancreas also secretes two hormones,
insulin and glucagon,
directly into the bloodstream.
These regulate the sugar levels in the blood.
If the pancreas does not produce enough insulin,
sugar levels in the body rise uncontrollably.
This condition is known as diabetes mellitus.
It causes damage to the heart and blood vessels.

The pancreas is located across the back of the abdomen,
behind the stomach.
The right side, called the head,
is the widest part of the organ
and lies in the curve of the duodenum –
the first section of the small intestine.
The tapered left side extends slightly upward,
called the body of the pancreas,
and ends near the spleen, called the tail.

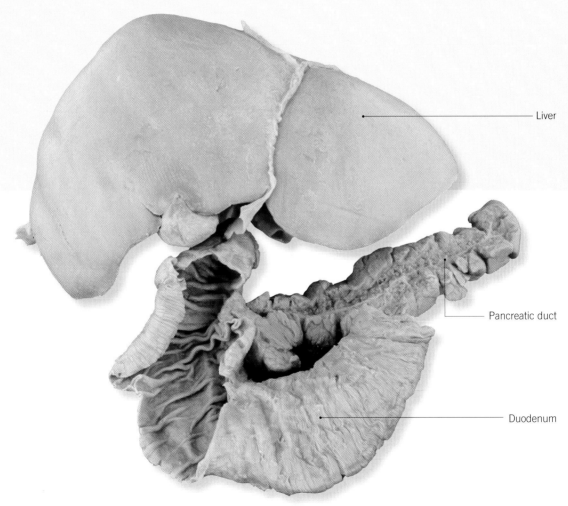

Liver

Pancreatic duct

Duodenum

Fig. 5.15 │ *Liver, pancreas, and duodenum in their natural relationships*

The Liver

The liver is the largest organ in the body.
On average, it weighs approx. 1.5 kilograms (3.3 pounds).
Its key function is to metabolise
carbohydrates, fats (lipids), and proteins.
It also absorbs toxic substances from the blood,
transforming them into harmless waste products.

Every minute, about 1.5 litres (1.6 quarts) of blood
flow through the liver.
Most of it comes from the digestive tract.
The digested nutrients are delivered to the liver
for further processing or storage.

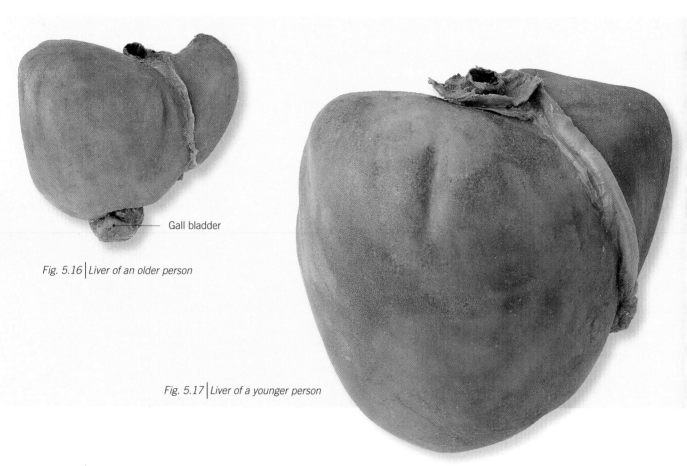

Gall bladder

Fig. 5.16 | *Liver of an older person*

Fig. 5.17 | *Liver of a younger person*

Fig. 5.18 | *Cross-section through the upper abdomen*

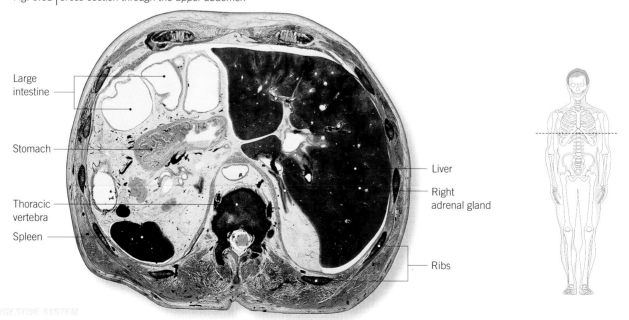

Large
intestine

Stomach

Thoracic
vertebra

Spleen

Liver

Right
adrenal gland

Ribs

In a body slice taken from the upper abdomen (Fig. 5.18)
one can see that the liver takes up nearly all
of the upper right abdomen.
The dark-reddish colour of the liver and spleen
is due to the rich blood flow through them.
The spleen is much smaller,
and is located in the upper left abdomen.

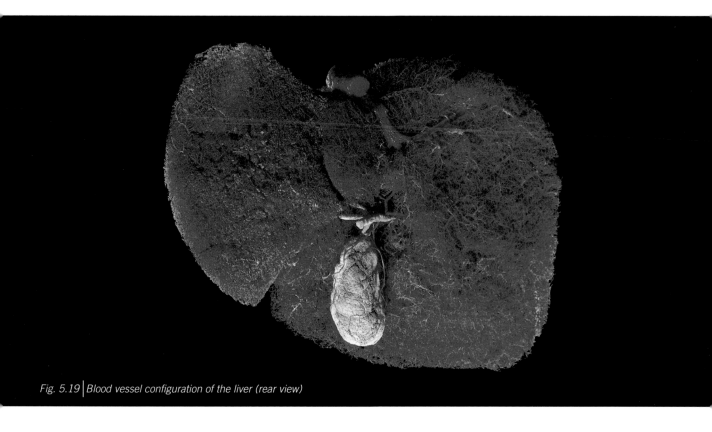

Fig. 5.19 | Blood vessel configuration of the liver (rear view)

Liver cells also produce bile –
0.7-1.2 litres (3-5 cups) each day.
The bile is stored in the gall bladder.
If no digestion is taking place,
the bile is stored temporarily,
in thickened form, in the gall bladder (above in yellow).

If it has an unbalanced chemical composition,
bile can harden into gallstones.
Gallstones can be as small as a grain of sand,
or as large as a golf ball.
They cause inflammation and discomfort,
with symptoms similar to indigestion,
especially after a fatty meal.
If a stone becomes lodged in the bile duct,
it will cause severe pain.

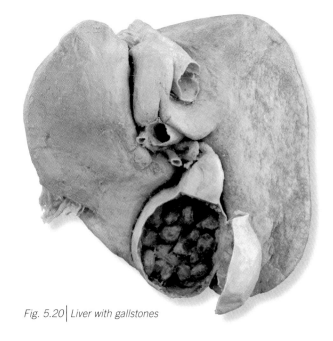

Fig. 5.20 | Liver with gallstones

The Diseased Liver

Fatty Liver

The liver also breaks down and detoxifies alcohol.
Excessive drinking causes fat to accumulate in liver cells.
As a result, the liver enlarges and turns yellowish.
But refraining from alcohol abuse, it can recover.

Fatty liver may also be associated with diabetes mellitus,
high blood triglycerides, and other metabolic abnormalities.
Just consuming a high-fat diet does not result in fatty liver.

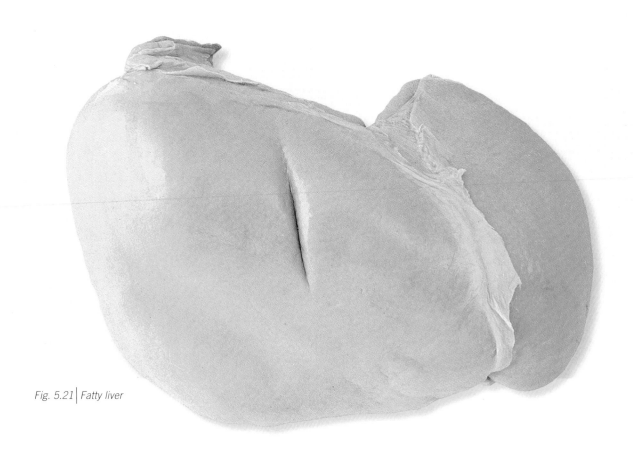

Fig. 5.21 | *Fatty liver*

Fig. 5.22 | *Liver slices with metastases (←)*

Liver Metastases

Due to its rich blood supply,
the liver is frequently affected by tumour metastases.
When a tumour invades the circulatory system,
individual cells may break off the main tumour
and enter the bloodstream.
They may then stick in the capillary network
of other organs as if trapped in a filter
and grow into new tumours.
They mostly appear as light-coloured lumps.

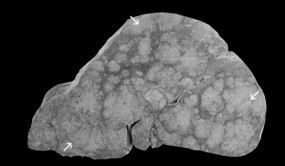

Fig. 5.23 | *Whole liver and liver slice with cirrhosis*

Shrunken Liver (Cirrhosis)

Frequent, heavy consumption of alcohol can cause permanent liver damage. Here, connective tissue scars spread like a net through the entire organ and have replaced the dead liver cells. Functioning cells in the shrunken liver form small islands or nodules, visible both on the surface and on a slice of the liver. As the disease becomes more advanced, liver functions become increasingly restricted.

Fig. 5.24 | *Liver with metastases*

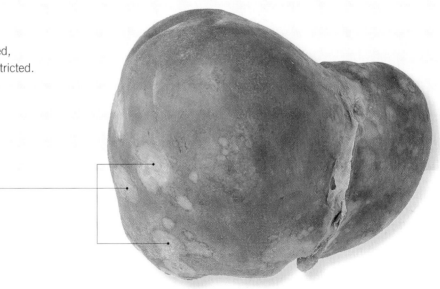

Metastases

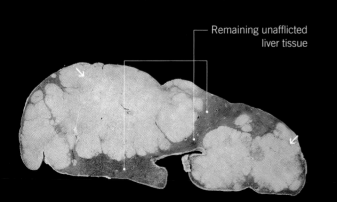

Remaining unafflicted
liver tissue

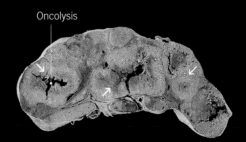

Oncolysis

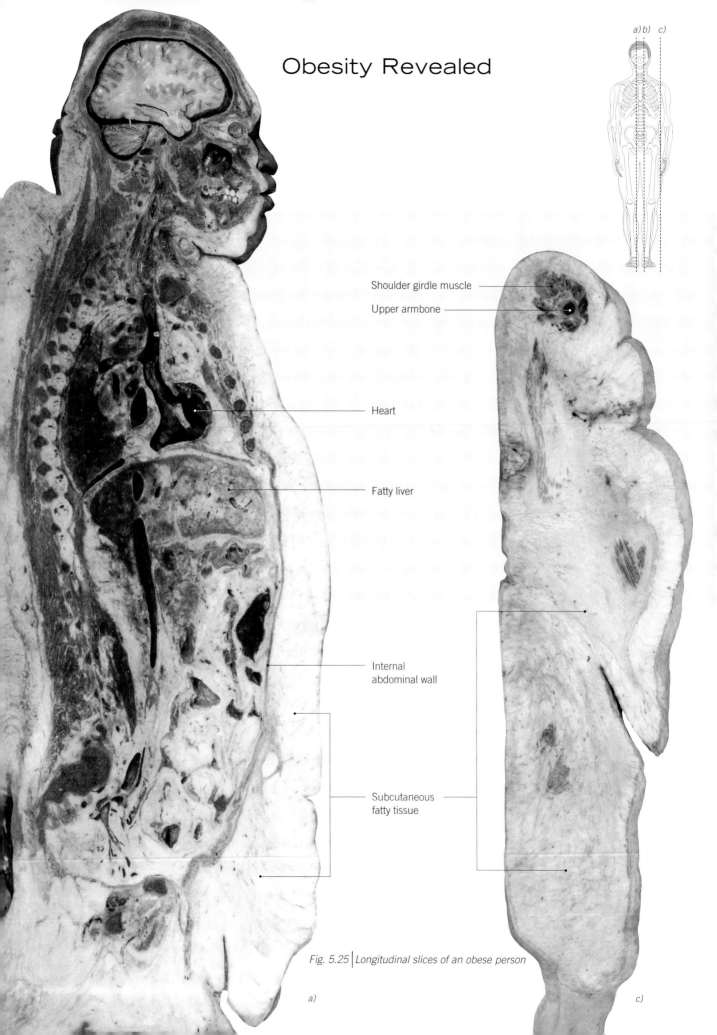

Obesity Revealed

Shoulder girdle muscle

Upper armbone

Heart

Fatty liver

Internal
abdominal wall

Subcutaneous
fatty tissue

Fig. 5.25 | *Longitudinal slices of an obese person*

a)

c)

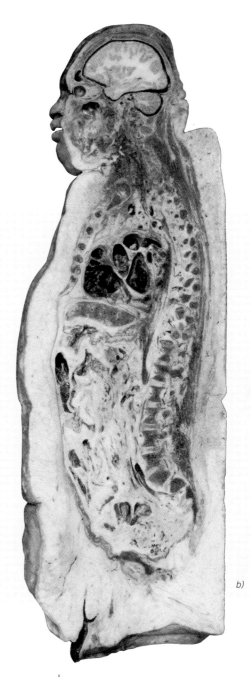

Fig. 5.26 | *Longitudinal slice of a normal person*

Fig. 5.27 | *Longitudinal slice of an obese person*

The longitudinal body slices in Fig. 5.25 and 5.27
show a severe degree of obesity.
Obesity means having too much body fat.
Here, the subcutaneous fatty tissue
is notably thickened.
But also the fat inside the abdominal cavity
is considerably increased.
This person's weight was about 136 kilograms
(300 pounds).

Obesity occurs over time
when we eat more calories than we need.
The balance between calories-in and calories-out

differs for each person.
Factors that might tip the balance
include the genetic makeup, overeating,
eating high-fat foods and not being physically active.

Being obese increases the risk
for chronic diseases
such as diabetes, high blood pressure,
arthritis, stroke, and some forms of cancer.
It especially puts a strain on the heart.
This obese man's heart is enlarged.
He died from a heart malfunction
when he was only about 50 years old.

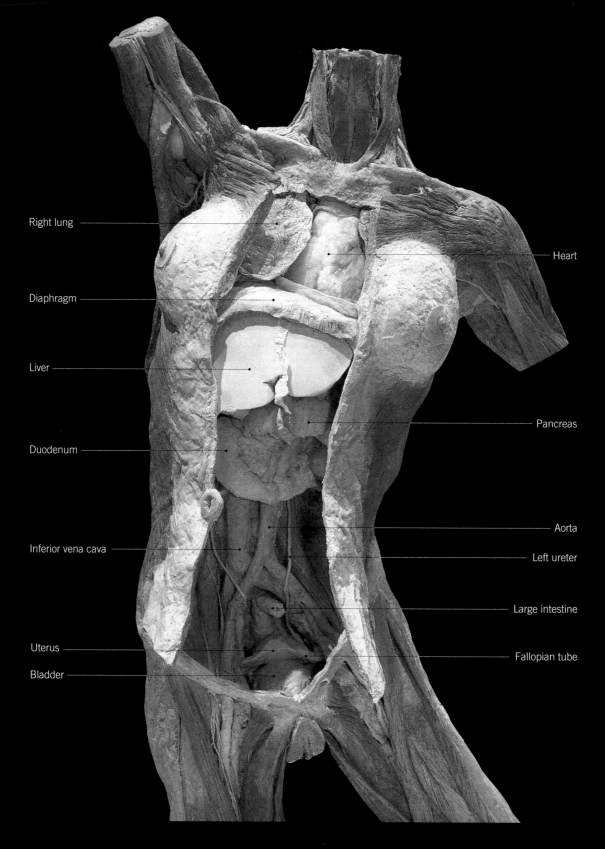

Right lung

Heart

Diaphragm

Liver

Duodenum

Pancreas

Inferior vena cava

Aorta

Left ureter

Large intestine

Uterus

Fallopian tube

Bladder

Female Torso (1999)

This opened torso shows the internal organs of the chest
and abdominal cavities in their proper positions.
The stomach as well as the large and small
intestines have been almost completely removed
to permit a view of the organs
located between the abdominal cavity
and the wall of the back, known as the retroperitoneum.

These include the ureters, the aorta and the lower vena cava,
as well as the pancreas and the duodenum.
In the small pelvic cavity,
the bladder can be seen, and behind it,
the uterus, which is inclined forward
with the Fallopian tubes emerging from the sides.
The large intestine extends downward behind the uterus.

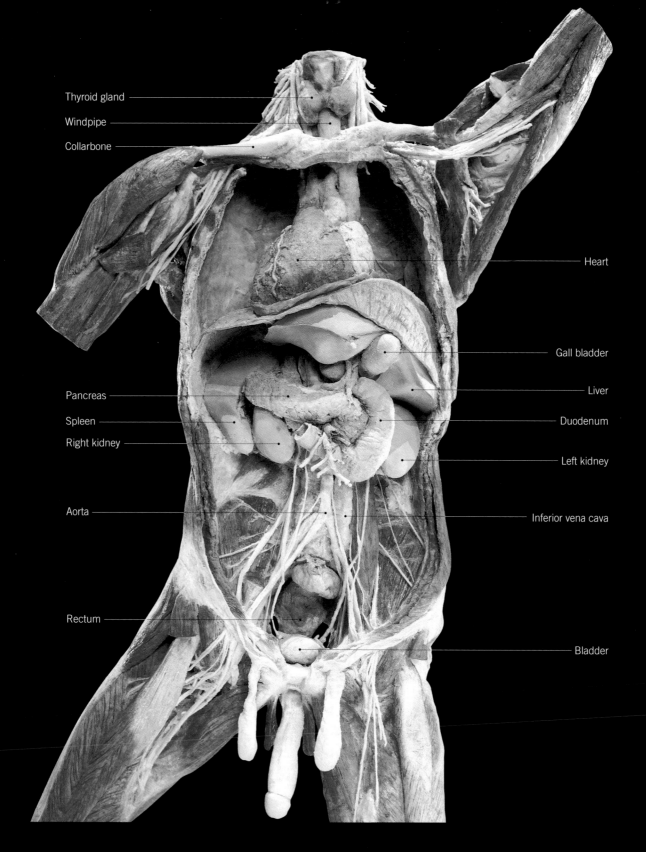

Thyroid gland

Windpipe

Collarbone

Heart

Gall bladder

Liver

Pancreas

Spleen

Duodenum

Right kidney

Left kidney

Aorta

Inferior vena cava

Rectum

Bladder

Male Torso with Situs Inversus (1999)

This torso displays a rare anatomical variation, known as situs inversus.

Here the organs of the chest and abdominal cavities are transposed through the sagittal plane, showing a reversed mirror-image: the apex of the heart points to the right instead of the left; the liver is on the left side of the body while the spleen is on the right; and the pancreas extends from left to right across the spinal column instead of vice versa. This anatomical variation does not cause any disorders. The incidence of this phenomenon is about 1 in 25,000. The bladder can be seen in front of the rectum in the small pelvic cavity.

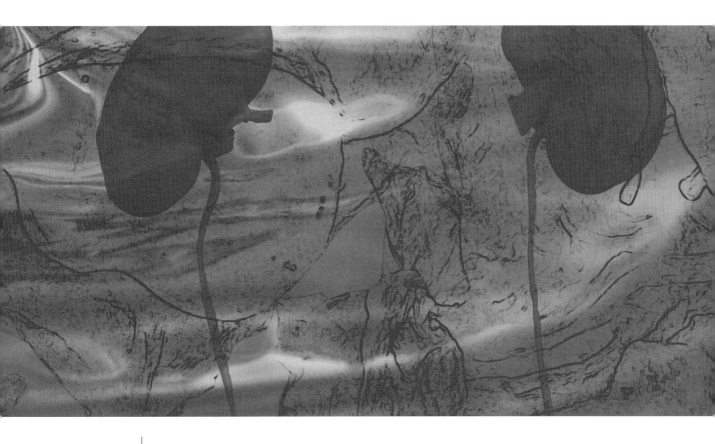

6. | THE **URINARY** TRACT

Like any organism,
the complex human body also produces waste.
Part of these waste products are discharged through urine.
In addition, the kidneys constantly filter
dissolved waste products and water out of the blood.

Filtering Waste

Urinary Tract

The kidneys filter water-soluble waste products
from the blood and expel them in the urine.
The urine first collects in the renal pelvis
which is a part of the ureter in the kidney.
Then the urine flows down the ureters
into the bladder, where it is stored.
Finally, it leaves the body via the urethra.

The male urethra runs from the bladder,
through the prostate gland,
to the tip of the penis.

The female urinary tract is in the lesser pelvis
near the reproductive organs.
The uterus and its adjoining structures
are directly behind the bladder.
When the bladder fills with urine,
the uterus becomes increasingly upright
so that it is visible in ultrasound imaging.

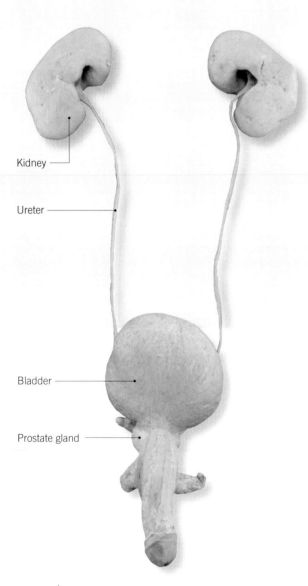

Kidney

Ureter

Bladder

Prostate gland

Fig. 6.1 | *Male urinary tract*

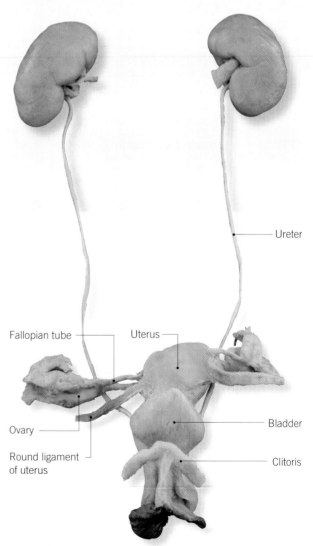

Ureter

Fallopian tube

Uterus

Ovary

Bladder

Round ligament
of uterus

Clitoris

Fig. 6.2 | *Female urinary tract*

Fig. 6.3 | *Kidney*   *Fig. 6.4* | *Longitudinal section through the kidney*

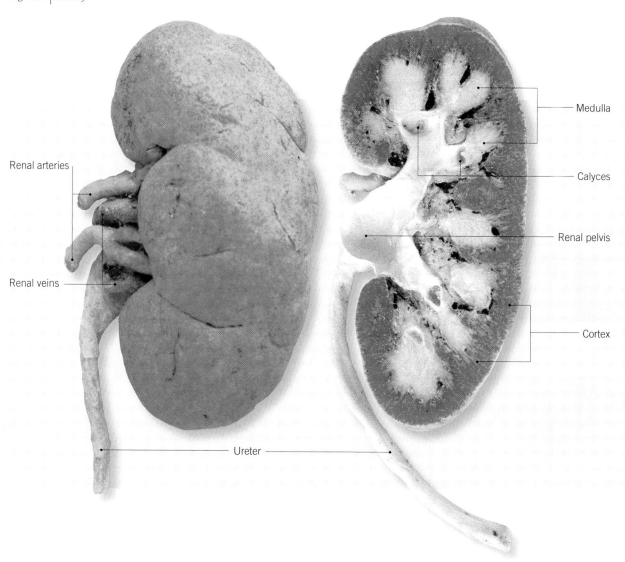

Medulla

Calyces

Renal arteries

Renal veins

Renal pelvis

Cortex

Ureter

Kidneys

The kidneys are two bean-shaped organs,
each weighing 115-200 grams (4-7 ounces).
They are located on either side of the spine.
They are set in the renal bed, the perinephrium,
held in a thick layer of fatty tissue,
and protected by the ribcage.

A section through the kidney exposes the cortex,
where the blood is filtered,
and the inner medulla,
the white, cone-shaped blocks of tissue,
where the urine is concentrated.
The medulla's fine collection structures
open into cup-like calyces.
From there, the urine empties into the renal pelvis.

The body's entire volume of blood
flows through the kidneys
around 15 times each hour.
The blood is filtered by the renal corpuscles
and their fine clusters
of blood vessels (glomeruli).

Kidneys play a major role
in the regulation of blood pressure
by keeping the body fluids balanced.
Extra fluid in the body
increases the amount of fluid
in the blood vessels
and raises the blood pressure.

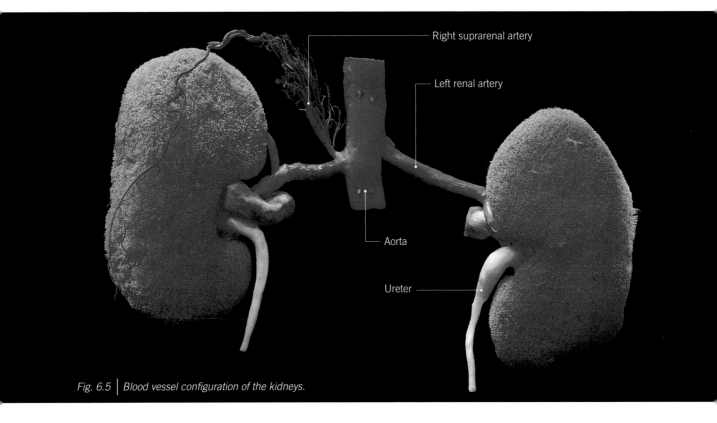

Right suprarenal artery

Left renal artery

Aorta

Ureter

Fig. 6.5 | *Blood vessel configuration of the kidneys.*

Adrenal Glands

Kidneys have a triangular-shaped gland on top.
These are the adrenal glands.
They are supplied with blood via the suprarenal artery.
The adrenal glands are part of the endocrine system.
They influence energy use and stress response
through the synthesis of hormones,
including cortisol and adrenaline.
In stressful situations,
the released adrenaline speeds our heartbeat,
thereby increasing circulation,
and recirculates stored glucose,
which provides a sudden burst
of energy and strength.

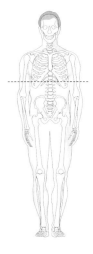

Fig. 6.6 | *Cross-section of kidney, detail*

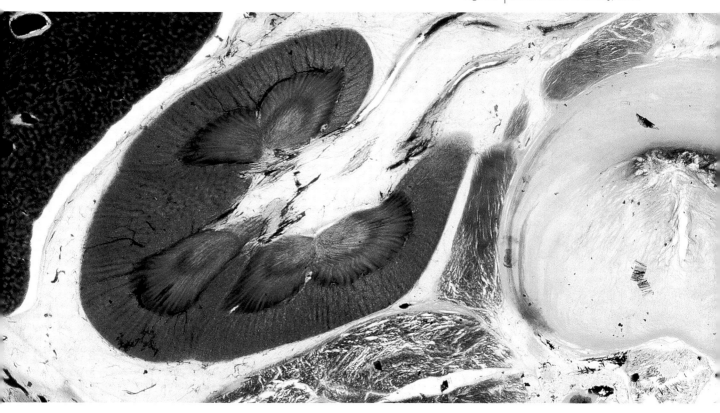

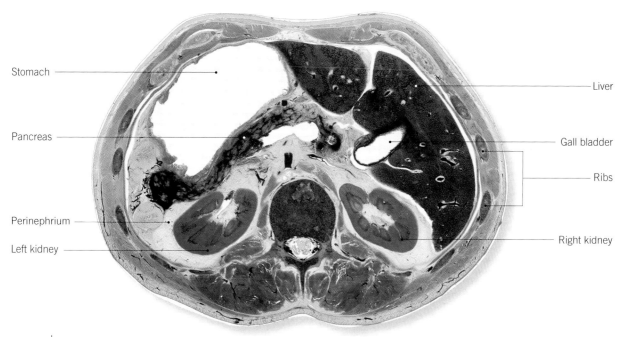

Stomach

Pancreas

Perinephrium

Left kidney

Liver

Gall bladder

Ribs

Right kidney

Fig. 6.7 | *Cross-section through the upper abdomen*

The Diseased Kidney

Kidney Cysts

Around one in ten people have kidney cysts,
fluid-filled, sac-like cavities.
Generally they do not cause any problems
and are often only detected by chance,
e.g., during ultrasound of the abdomen.

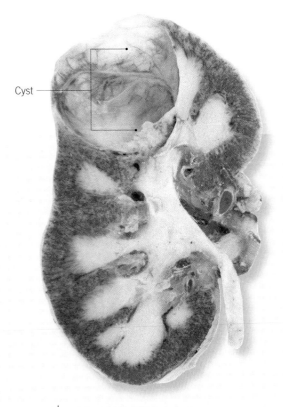

Cyst

Fig. 6.8 | *Kidney with single cyst*

Shrunken Kidney

Chronic infections in the kidneys
destroy kidney tissue,
causing scars and organ shrinkage.
This restricts the kidneys' ability to function.

Fig. 6.9 | *Shrunken kidney caused by chronic infectious processes*

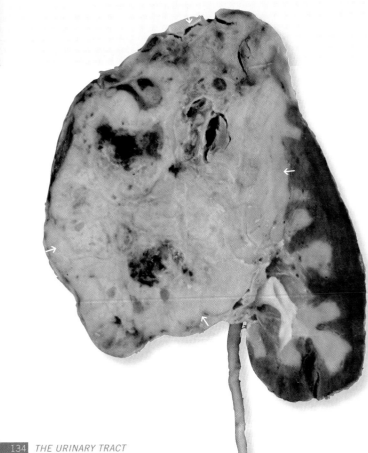

Kidney Cancer (Hypernephroma)

In adults, the most common type of kidney cancer
is renal cell carcinoma, which begins in the cells
that line the small tubes within our kidneys.
If the tumour invades the renal pelvis,
blood will be visible in the urine.

Fig. 6.10 | *Kidney with tumour*

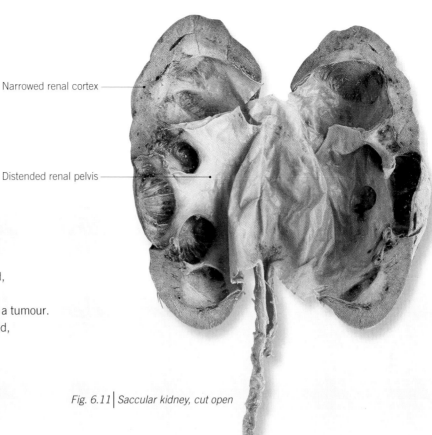

Narrowed renal cortex ———

Distended renal pelvis ———

Saccular Kidney (Hydronephrosis)
The internal diameter of ureters
is less than 3 millimetres (0.1 inch).
Therefore they can easily be blocked,
for example by a kidney stone
or by external compression, such as a tumour.
As urine is constantly being produced,
such blockage causes it to back up
in the renal pelvis,
which in turn makes it distend
and stretch the kidney tissue.

Fig. 6.11 │ *Saccular kidney, cut open*

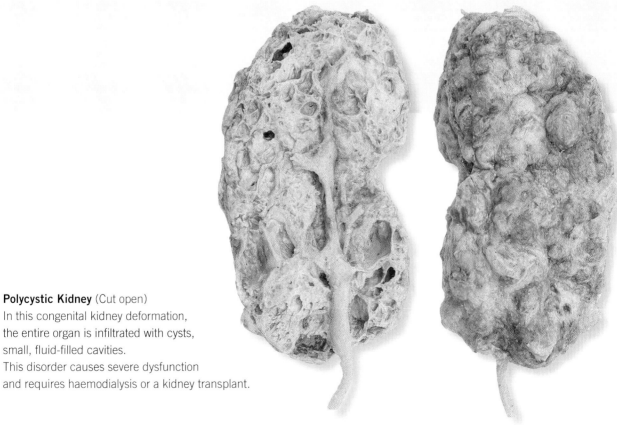

Polycystic Kidney (Cut open)
In this congenital kidney deformation,
the entire organ is infiltrated with cysts,
small, fluid-filled cavities.
This disorder causes severe dysfunction
and requires haemodialysis or a kidney transplant.

Fig. 6.12 │ *Polycystic kidney, a) longitudinal section*   *b) surface*

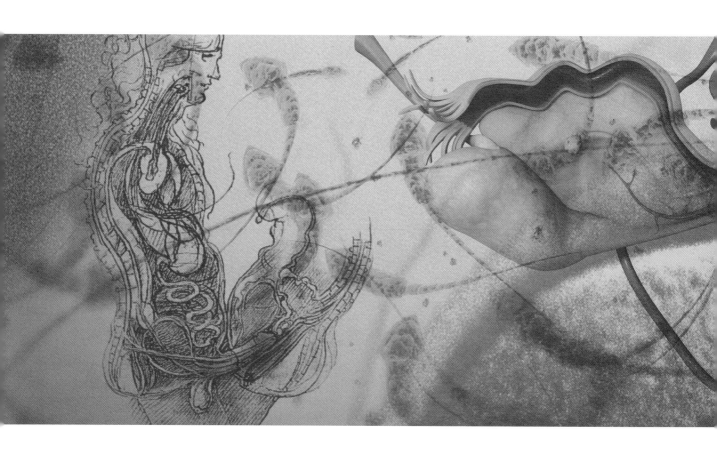

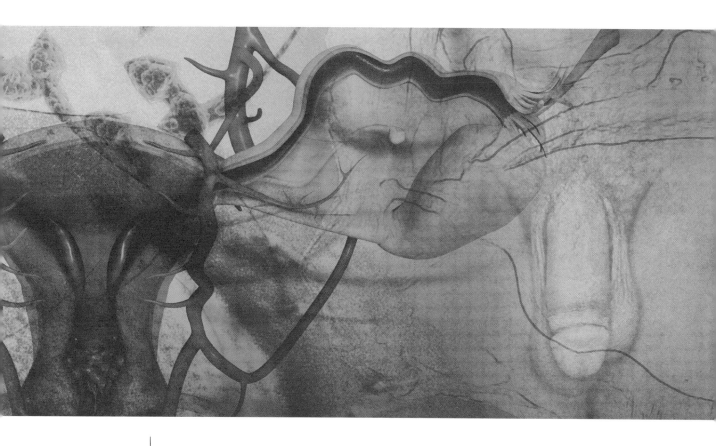

7. | THE **REPRODUCTIVE** ORGANS

The external male and female genitals
mark the end of the urinary system.
The invisible internal genitals
are the true reproductive organs,
where eggs and sperm are produced.
Reproduction is an essential aspect of life.
New life is created when a male sperm
fertilises a female egg.

Male Reproduction

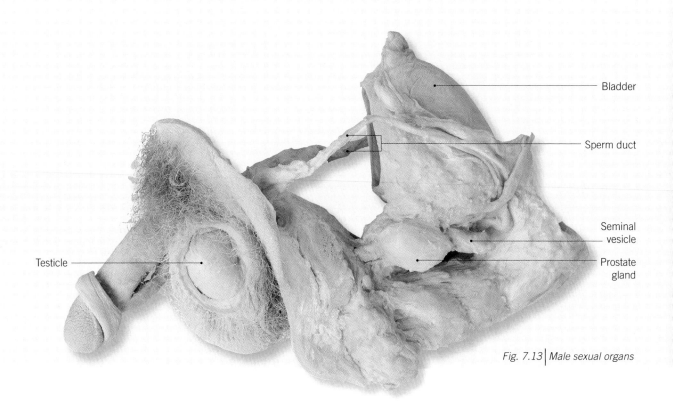

Bladder

Sperm duct

Seminal vesicle

Prostate gland

Testicle

Fig. 7.13 | Male sexual organs

Male Reproductive Organs
The penis and the scrotum
are the visible male reproductive organs.
The scrotum contains two egg-shaped testes
and the epididymides, tubes to transport sperm.
Male reproductive organs also include
the seminal vesicles in the body,

the prostate gland, and the sperm duct,
as well as other connecting tubes.
The cascade of hormones in sexual arousal
is controlled by the hypothalamus,
located in the centre of the brain.

Testes

The testes are roughly the size of walnuts.
In their thousands of finely coiled tubes,
the seminiferous tubules,
about 300 million sperm mature every day.
Sperm are stored in the epididymides –
tubes that envelope the testes like a hood.

During orgasm, rhythmic contractions
pump the sperm through the vas deferens.
Where the vas deferens joins the urethra,
the fluids from the prostate gland
and the seminal vesicles mix with the sperm.
Rhythmic contractions of the urethral muscles
ejaculate the sperm.

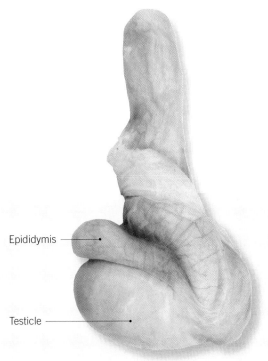

Epididymis

Testicle

Fig. 7.14 | *Testicle with epididymis*

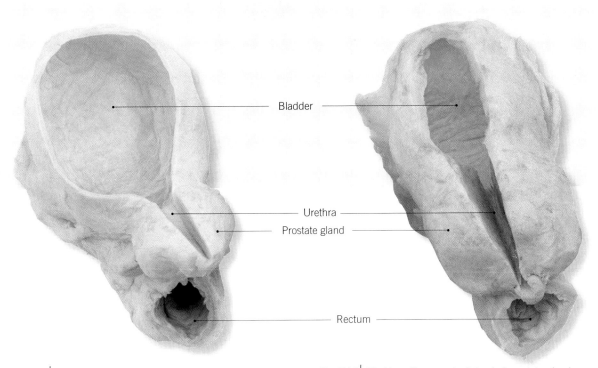

Bladder

Urethra
Prostate gland

Rectum

Fig. 7.15 | *Bladder with prostate gland*

Fig. 7.16 | *Bladder with severely distended prostate gland*

Prostate Gland

The prostate is directly below the bladder
and surrounds the urethra.
At ejaculation, the prostate's secretions
are mixed with semen
to facilitate the movement of the sperm.

Prostate Gland Enlargement

With advancing age,
the prostate gland tends to distend,
narrowing the urethra
and partially blocking the urine flow.
This condition is also known as benign prostatic
hyperplasia.

Female Reproduction

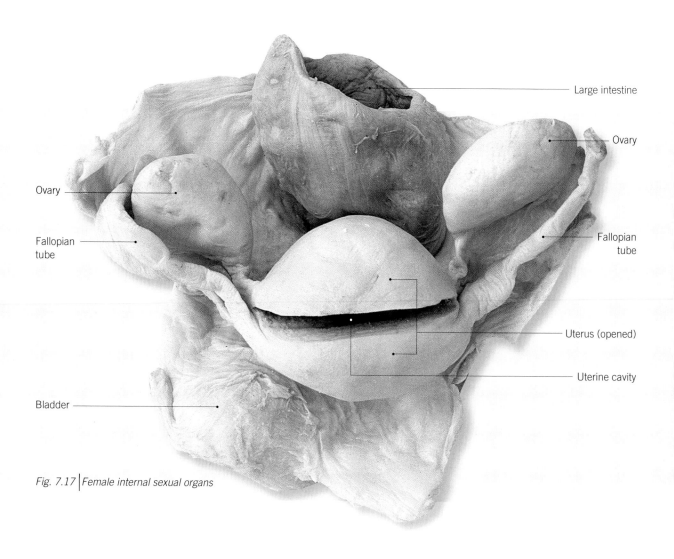

Large intestine

Ovary

Ovary

Fallopian tube

Fallopian tube

Uterus (opened)

Uterine cavity

Bladder

Fig. 7.17 | Female internal sexual organs

Female Reproductive Organs

The female reproductive organs
are largely within the body:
the two ovaries and Fallopian tubes,
the uterus, and the vagina.
The released eggs from the ovaries
pass down the Fallopian tubes into the uterus
where the fertilised egg can develop.

The external female genitals
are collectively referred to as the vulva.
The labia minora are the inner lips of the vulva.
They consist of thin stretches of tissue
within the labia majora that fold and protect
the vagina, urethra, and clitoris.
The opening to the urethra
is just below the clitoris.
It is not related to sex or reproduction
but is instead the passage for urine.

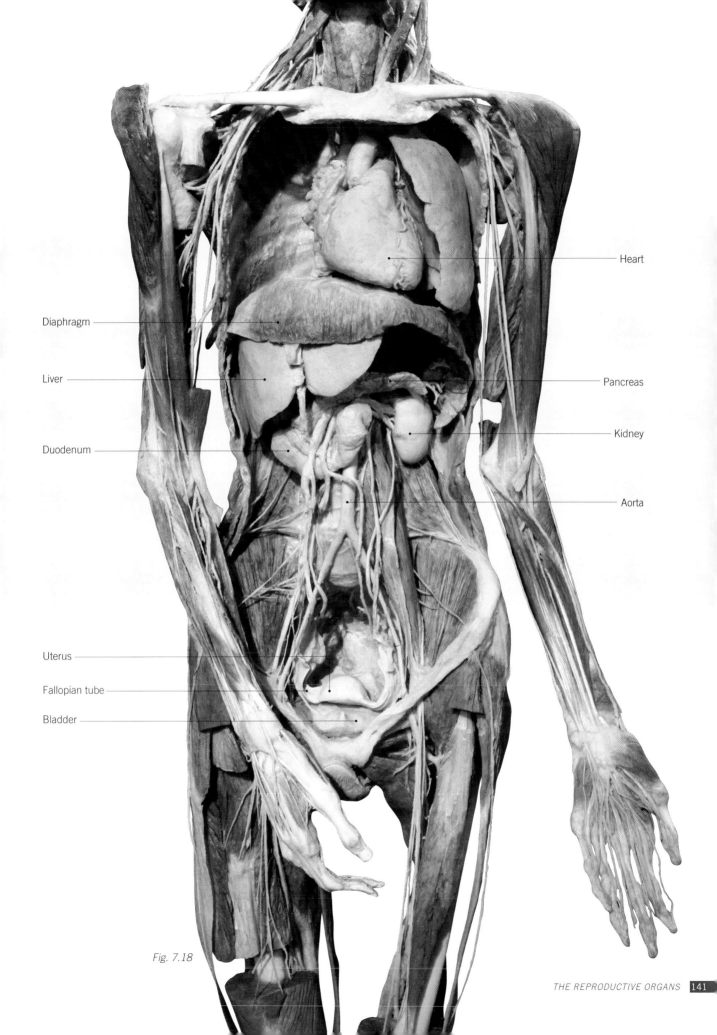

Heart

Diaphragm

Liver

Pancreas

Kidney

Duodenum

Aorta

Uterus

Fallopian tube

Bladder

Fig. 7.18

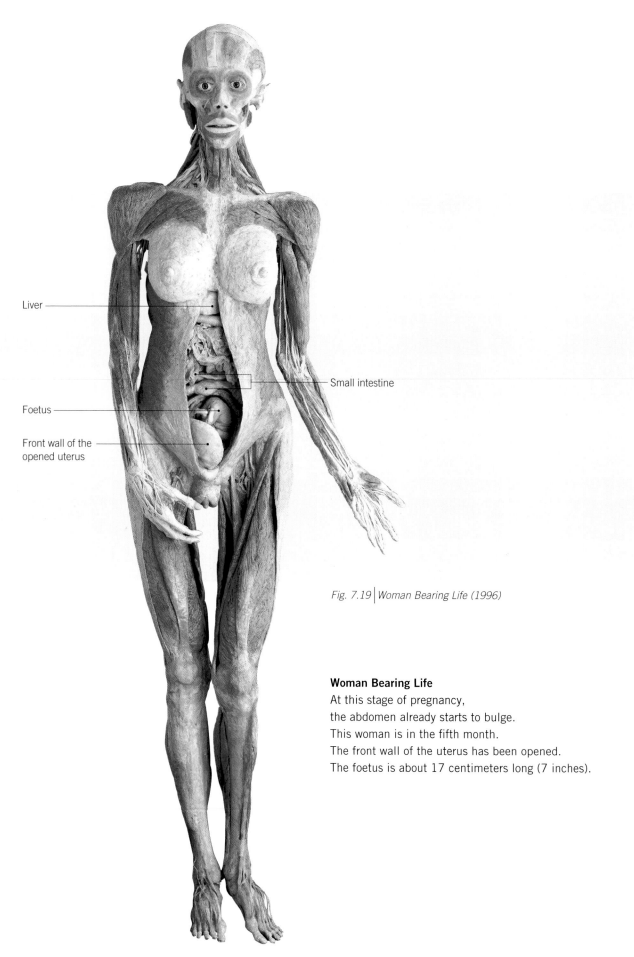

Liver

Small intestine

Foetus

Front wall of the
opened uterus

Fig. 7.19 | Woman Bearing Life (1996)

Woman Bearing Life
At this stage of pregnancy,
the abdomen already starts to bulge.
This woman is in the fifth month.
The front wall of the uterus has been opened.
The foetus is about 17 centimeters long (7 inches).

Myomas

Myomas are uterine fibroid tumours.
Since the wall of the uterus is muscle,
myomas are also made of muscle tissue.
Here, the uterine walls are covered
with numerous myomas.
Myomas are benign.

However, they can cause discomfort,
menstrual disorders,
or complications during pregnancy.

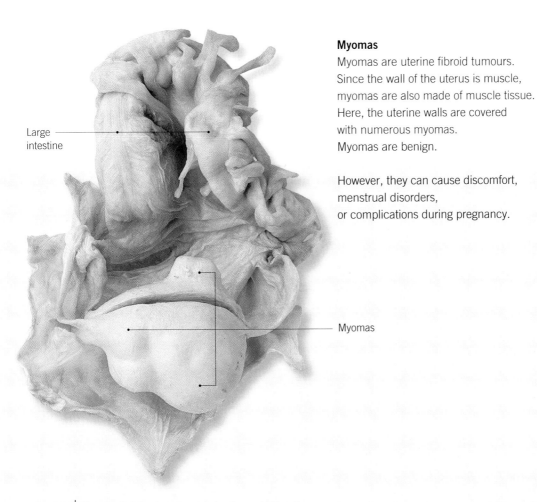

Large intestine

Myomas

Fig. 7.20 | *Myomas (benign tumours made of muscle fibres) on the uterus*

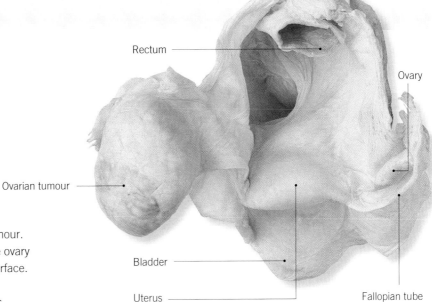

Rectum

Ovary

Ovarian tumour

Bladder

Uterus

Fallopian tube

Ovarian Tumour

Here, the right ovary has ovarian tumour.
The tumour growth has enlarged the ovary
and given it an irregularly shaped surface.
Many ovarian tumours are benign.
However, malignant ovarian tumours
are very fast growing
and can pass from early to advanced stages
within just twelve months.

Fig. 7.21 | *Ovarian tumour*

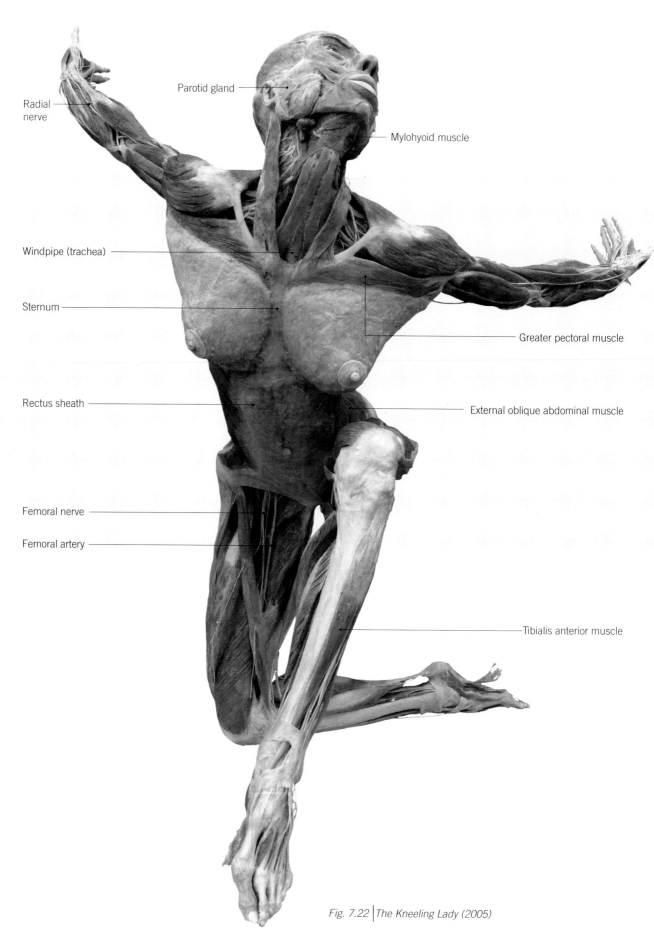

Radial nerve

Parotid gland

Mylohyoid muscle

Windpipe (trachea)

Sternum

Greater pectoral muscle

Rectus sheath

External oblique abdominal muscle

Femoral nerve

Femoral artery

Tibialis anterior muscle

Fig. 7.22 | *The Kneeling Lady (2005)*

Fig. 7.23 | *Longitudinal slice through a female breast*

Fig. 7.24 | *Longitudinal slice through a female breast*
with breast cancer (marked area)

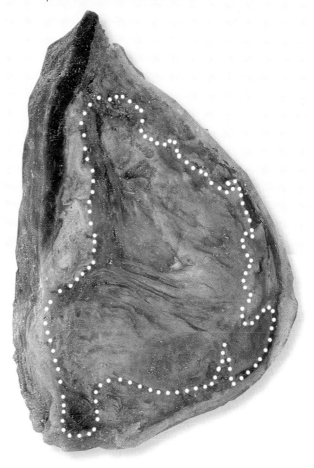

Mammary Glands

The mammary glands produce milk
to feed the young and are part of
a woman's external sexual organs.

They consist largely of fatty tissue,
permeated by milk glands and
a glandular duct network so fine,
it is hardly visible to the naked eye.
Small milk ducts empty
into ever-larger collection ducts
that finally find an outlet at the nipple.
During pregnancy, the body releases hormones
which increase the number of milk glands
and glandular ducts significantly.

Breast Cancer (Mammary Carcinoma)
Breast cancer is the most common cancer in women.
This longitudinal slice shows a female breast
almost completely infiltrated
by the hard tissue of breast cancer.

8. | PRENATAL DEVELOPMENT

The first period of human life
takes place invisibly in the mother's body.
A single cell, or zygote, is formed
when the father's sperm fertilises the mother's egg.
It carries its own unique set of chromosomes
that determine the characteristics and traits
of the conceived human being.
The zygote is hardworking and tireless.
One hour after conception,
it begins to divide and multiply.
Eight hours after conception,
the zygote has already formed 1,000 cells.
With humans, pregnancy lasts an
average of 266 days.

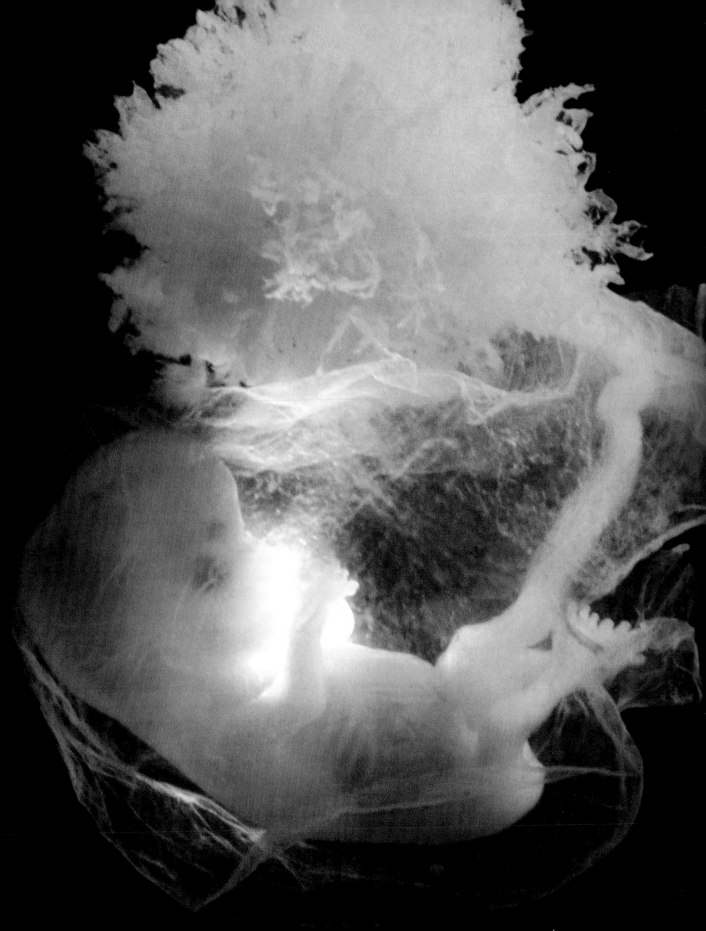

Fig. 8.1 | Embryo in the 8th week

A Human Takes Shape

Fig. 8.2 | *Developmental stages from the fourth to the eighth week of pregnancy. During the first eight weeks of pregnancy, the developing organism is called an embryo. During this time, all organs are formed.*

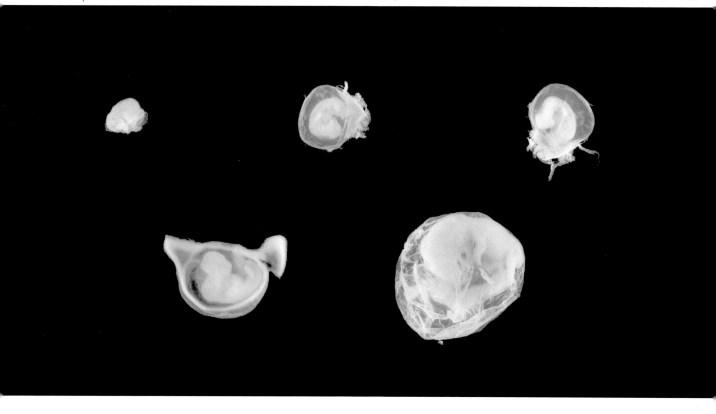

Embryonic Development

When the fertilised egg
travels down the Fallopian tubes,
it divides several times before
embedding itself in the lining of the uterus.
There the cells continue to divide.
Soon the cells start to specialise,
creating different tissues and organs.
After only four weeks,
an embryo already has a heart and eyes.
It also has four buds,
the start of its arms and legs.
After eight weeks,
organ differentiation is largely completed.

Foetal Development

The developing child is called a foetus
after the ninth week of pregnancy.
This is a phase of growth and organ maturation.
By the fourth month,
the liver and pancreas are developed,
together with the intestines and kidneys.
Hair and nails begin to grow.

In the fifth month,
the nervous system starts to mature,
and the mother can feel the foetus move.
After the seventh month,
the foetus could survive a premature birth.
In the last two months,
the foetus mainly gains in size and weight.

13th Week of Pregnancy	*17th Week of Pregnancy*	*19th Week of Pregnancy*

Fig. 8.3

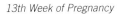

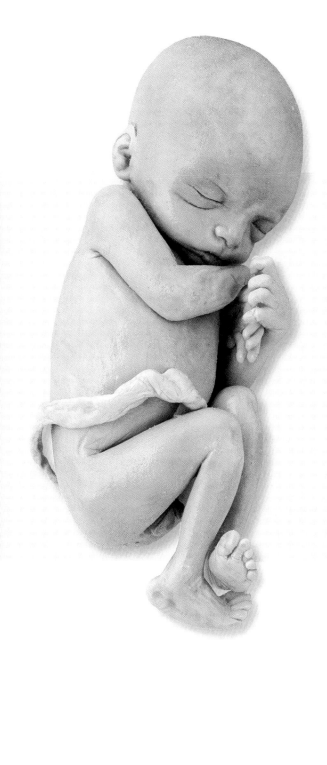

23rd Week of Pregnancy

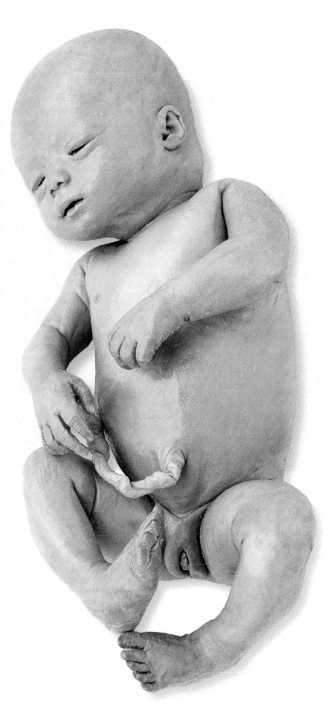

32nd Week of Pregnancy

The First Weeks

Roughly 30 hours after fertilisation,
a tiny human egg begins to divide
into two identical daughter cells.
These cells keep dividing
and form a cluster of cells, the blastocyst,
which migrates down the Fallopian tube.

It settles in the uterus as an embryo
on the sixth day after fertilisation.
Pregnancy will last about 260 days from that point.

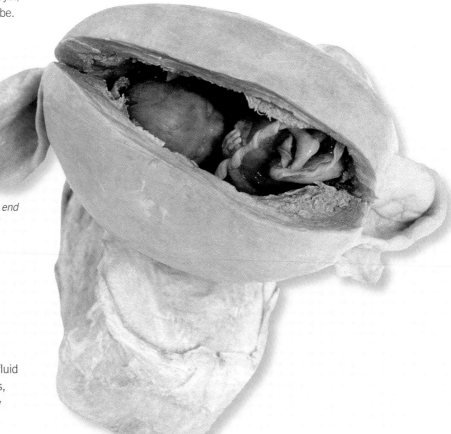

Fig. 8.4 | *Foetus inside the uterus at the end of the 3rd month of pregnancy*

The embryo, suspended in amniotic fluid
and surrounded by foetal membranes,
is linked to the maternal blood supply
via the umbilical cord and placenta.

During the first four weeks,
the embryo is roughly 4 millimetres (0.15 inches) long.
It will grow to 3 centimetres (1.2 inches)
and weigh 4 grams (0.1 ounce)
by the end of the eight week.
All of the organs will be in place by the end
of this period, after which the developing child
is referred to as a foetus.
The length and weight of the foetus
then begins to increase significantly,
as it proceeds through further stages of development.

Week 13 to 14

Coordinated movements will begin,
although the mother is not yet able to feel them.
The relatively large head will straighten up,
the lower extremities are already well developed,
and the toenails will begin to grow.

Week 15 to 16

The foetus is now 15 centimetres (6 inches) long
and can weigh up to 200 gram (7 ounces).
Its gender can be detected via ultrasound,
and its skeleton will show up clearly on x-rays.
Its body becomes more proportioned.
Foetal blood begins to develop in the liver.
Ovaries have already developed in female foetuses.

Week 17 to 18

Fetal growth has slowed;
the weight of the foetus has increased to 300 grams
(10.5 ounces).
The skin is still thin,
because the (white) subcutaneous fatty tissues
have not yet developed.
However, brown fatty tissues have begun to form,
allowing the small organism to produce its own heat.
The uterus has developed in female foetuses.
Mothers can feel the foetus move from this point on.

Week 19 to 20

Toward the end of this phase,
the foetus will be 28 centimetres (11 inches) long
and weigh up to 450 grams (1 pound).
The body and head of the foetus are now covered
with fine hair which contains little pigment.

Week 21 to 24

The foetus begins to gain weight more rapidly again,
and its proportions resemble more of a baby.
The fingernails will start to grow,
and the skin is still red and wrinkled.
The lungs are capable of breathing,
if insufficiently, because there is not yet
any coordination between them and the nervous system.
This lack of coordination could cause
more or less severe damage to the brain,
if the baby is born at this stage.

Week 25 to 28

The lungs are now fully capable of breathing,
which means that the foetus is capable of living
outside the womb.

During week 26, the eyes can open,
and subcutaneous fatty tissue
has given the body a more rounded shape.
Until this point, the spleen has been producing blood;
during week 28, bone marrow takes over this function.
The foetus weighs more than 1,300 grams (2.8 pounds).

Week 29 to 32

The foetus' body will grow to over 42 centimetres (16.5 inches),
and its weight increases to 1.5 to 2.1 kilograms
(3.3 to 4.2 pounds).
The fingernails grow to the tips of the fingers,
and the skin will now be pink and smooth.
The eyes respond to light by means of the pupillary reflex,
and the hands respond to stimulus with a "grasping" reflex.
Infants born during week 33 will usually survive.

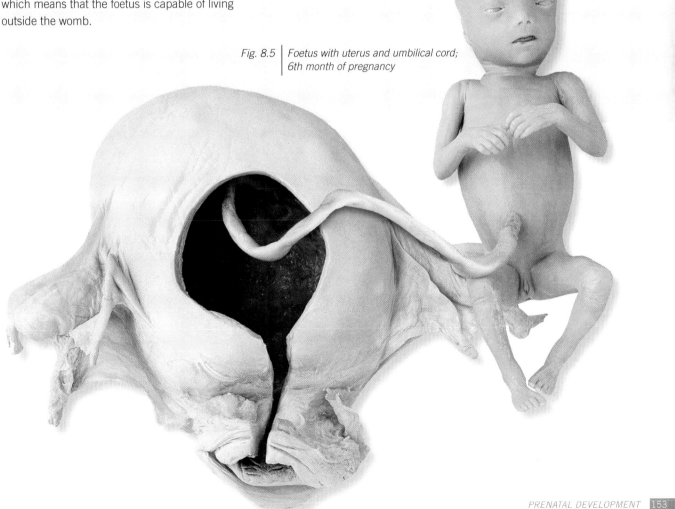

Fig. 8.5 | Foetus with uterus and umbilical cord;
6th month of pregnancy

Nourishing the Foetus

Placenta

The placenta exists only during pregnancy.
During the first ten weeks of pregnancy,
it develops at the point
where the fertilised egg embeds itself
in the lining of the uterus.

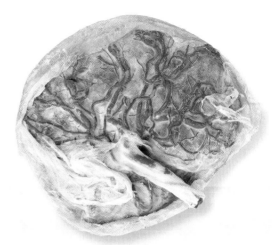

Fig. 8.6 | Placenta. On the surface of the foetal side, the arteries and veins of the umbilical cord vessels branch out

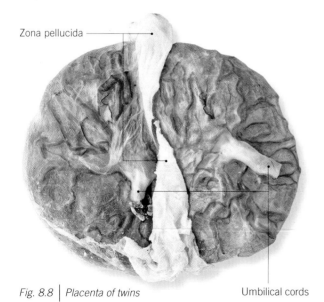

Fig. 8.7 | Placenta. The uterine side shows the dense vascular bed, in which the exchange of nourishment and oxygen takes place.

The placenta is connected to the foetus
via the umbilical cord
and provides it with nourishment.
The blood vessels of the umbilical cord
branch out on the surface of the foetal side.
The foetus' heart pumps blood
through the umbilical cord artery
to the vascular bed of the placenta.
This is bathed in the mother's blood
from the lining of the uterus.
Here, substances, such as oxygen and nutrients,
as well as waste and CO_2, are exchanged.
This exchange can then occur
without mixing the mother's and child's blood.
Oxygen- and nutrient-enriched blood
flows back to the foetus via the umbilical vein.

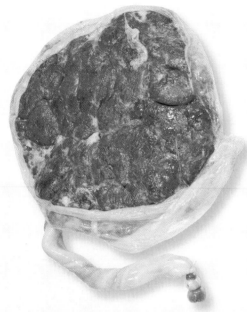

Zona pellucida

Fig. 8.8 | Placenta of twins

Umbilical cords

Placenta of Twins

Twins are conceived
when a fertilised egg divides into two embryos
or two fertilised eggs develop simultaneously.
In the first case,
the twins share the same genetic code
and are identical or monozygotic twins.
They are always of the same sex.
In the second case,
the twins are fraternal or dizygotic twins.
They are genetically as similar or different
as any other non-identical siblings.
Identical twins can either share one placenta
or have seperate ones.
Non-identical twins always have seperate placentas.

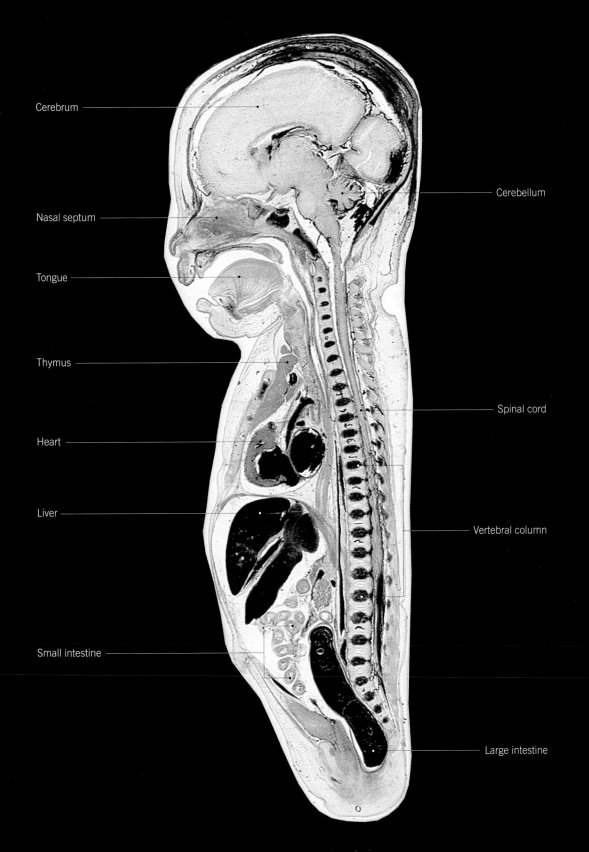

Cerebrum

Cerebellum

Nasal septum

Tongue

Thymus

Spinal cord

Heart

Liver

Vertebral column

Small intestine

Large intestine

Longitudinal Slice of a Foetus in the 7th Month

The position of the various organs
already corresponds to those in an adult body.

Fig. 8.9

Congenital Deformities

Congenital deformities can either be the result
of pathological factors
or abnormal development of the foetus
caused by damage form external sources,
such as alcohol or drug abuse of the mother
or from infectious diseases.

From the third to the eighth week of pregnancy,
embryos are especially susceptible to such influences.
During this time the rate of cell division is particularly high
and organ differentiation is in progress.
Abnormal development of individual cells
can lead to malformation of the entire organism.

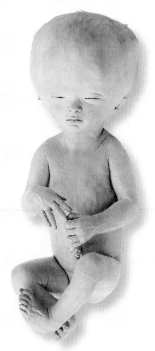

Fig. 8.10 | New-born child with hydrocephalus

Fig. 8.11 | Conjoined twins

Hydrocephalus

Congenital hydrocephalus is caused
by an imbalance between the brain's production
of cerebrospinal fluid
and the body's ability to distribute or absorb it properly.
In foetuses and small children
it causes the entire skull to expand.
The reason for this is that the cranial sutures
have not yet become ossified
because of anticipated cranial growth;
they thus give way to the increased internal pressure.
This condition is also known as "water on the brain".
The excess fluid can increase pressure in the baby's brain,
possibly resulting in brain damage
and loss of mental and physical abilities.

Conjoined Twins

Conjoined twins originate from a single fertilised egg.
Malformations of this type occur
when individual cells or tissues fail to divide completely
during the first two months of pregnancy.
The foetuses then share either the skin alone
or internal organs.
Chances of survival and operability depend on
the extent to which shared organs are critical for survival.

The best known conjoined twins were
Eng and Chang Bunker, born in Siam in 1811,
hence the name Siamese twins.

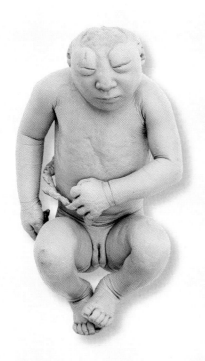

Fig. 8.12 | Foetus with anencephaly

Fig. 8.13 | Foetus with chest and abdominal defects

Anencephaly

Anencephaly is a congenital birth defect
in which the top of the skull is missing
and degenerated tissue is all that is left
where the brain should be.
It occurs in about one out of 1,000 pregnancies.
If ultrasound images indicate such a serious defect,
it can be confirmed early via amniocentesis.
Life expectancy for a baby with anencephaly after birth
is just a few hours, sometimes a few days at most.

Chest and Abdominal Wall Defect

Abdominal wall defects occur
when a child's abdomen does not develop fully
while in the womb.
This causes the intestine to develop outside the abdomen.
In this case, also the heart protrudes from the body.

Chest and abdominal wall defects are very rare.
It is not exactly known what causes them.

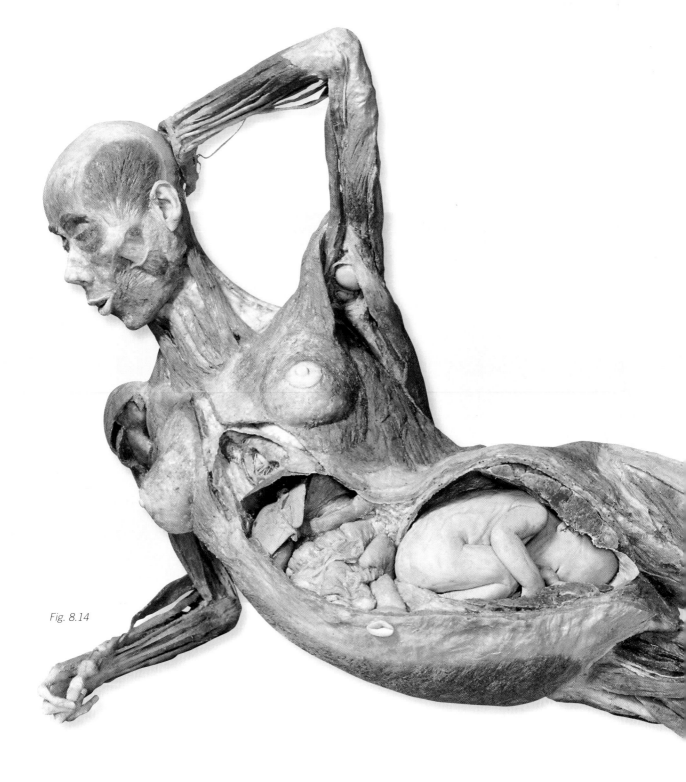

Fig. 8.14

Reclining Pregnant Woman
(1999)

The foetus and the placenta
can be seen in the opened uterus
which has been cut through at its front wall.
The child already measures 28 centimetres (11 inches)
and is pressing the abdominal organs
of the mother upwards.

The mother's liver can be seen
under the right arch of her rib cage
while the opened stomach is under the left one.
Below these are horizontal parts of the large intestine
and loops of the small intestines.

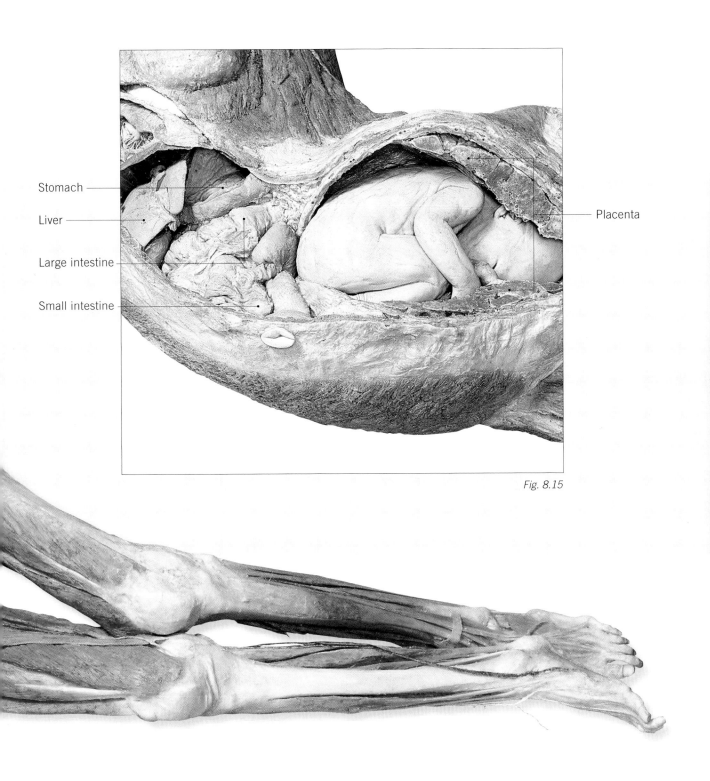

Stomach

Liver

Large intestine

Small intestine

Placenta

Fig. 8.15

9. | **WHOLE-BODY** PLASTINATES

Andreas Vesalius (1514 to 1564),
personal physician to Emperor Charles V
and King Philip II of Spain,
was the first to assemble a complete skeleton.
Since then such internal bony structures
of the human organism have served
as instructional and visual models.
At that time, it was not possible
to obtain a corpse complete with flesh,
much less to be able to erect it.
The soft tissue would have quickly putrefied
or it would have dried out as in mummies, at best.

As a consequence,
we have only inherited depictions of the
discoveriesed by the founding fathers of anatomy
during their dissections,
which were occasionally executed in pictures
according to their perceptions.

Creating durable whole-body plastinates
and positioning them in lifelike poses
was first made possible by plastination
in the early 1990s.
The old Latin proverb of anatomy,
"Hic gaudet mors succurrere vitae"
(Here Death enjoys standing by Life),
can thus be realised in its truest sense.

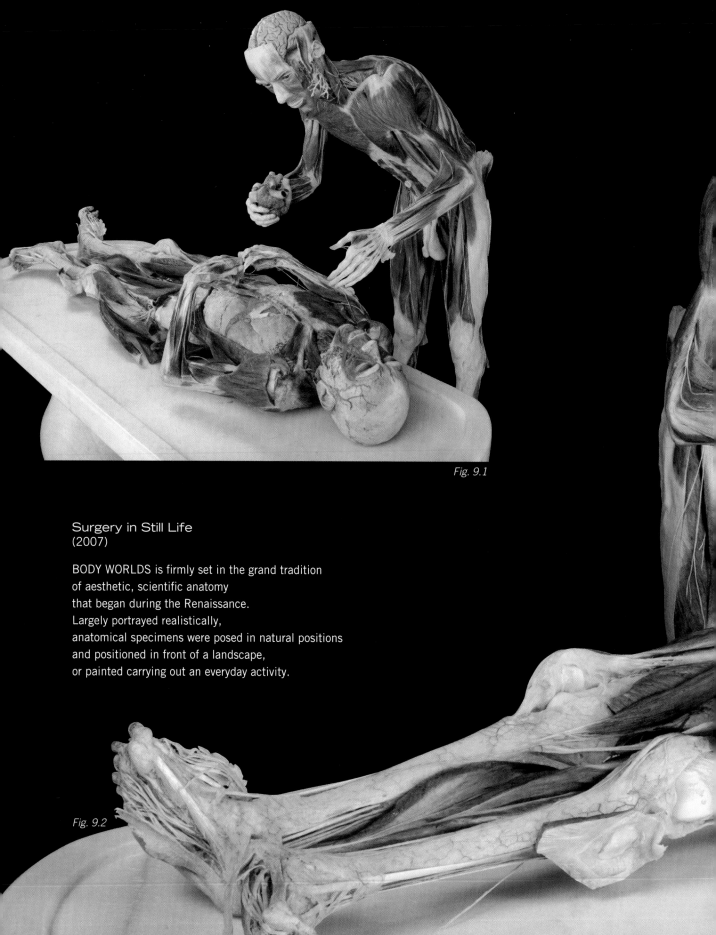

Fig. 9.1

Surgery in Still Life
(2007)

BODY WORLDS is firmly set in the grand tradition
of aesthetic, scientific anatomy
that began during the Renaissance.
Largely portrayed realistically,
anatomical specimens were posed in natural positions
and positioned in front of a landscape,
or painted carrying out an everyday activity.

Fig. 9.2

This plastinate refers to
Rembrandt's famous painting
'The Anatomy Lesson of Dr. Nicolaes Tulp'
which shows the Dutch surgeon and mayor of Amsterdam
dissecting the forearm of a corpse.
The outstretched body underwent open-heart surgery
during its lifetime.
The breastbone still contains wires
that are typically used in surgery
to re-close the chest.
The standing specimen shows
especially detailed pathways of all the nerves,
which emanate from the spinal cord.
They travel like telephone lines
from the spinal cord up to the fingertips
and down to the toes.

Fig. 9.3

The Badminton Player
(2007)

Plastination allows for completely new kinds
of anatomical dissections,
such as dissection by expansion.
Here, like in an exploded view,
anatomical structures are opened up
and shifted apart.
This creates artificial spaces,
allowing all organs in the body to be viewed,
even if they overlap or cover one another.
Extended bodies are made possible
only with plastination,
since it gives the tissue the necessary stability.

In this posed plastinate,
the body shell as well as the limbs
were split frontally along functional structures
and then pulled apart.
For example, in the left upper arm,
the extensor muscles that stretch out the arm
were left with the front part,
whereas the flexor muscles bending the arm
were left with the rear part.
In the middle is the spine
together with all internal organs.

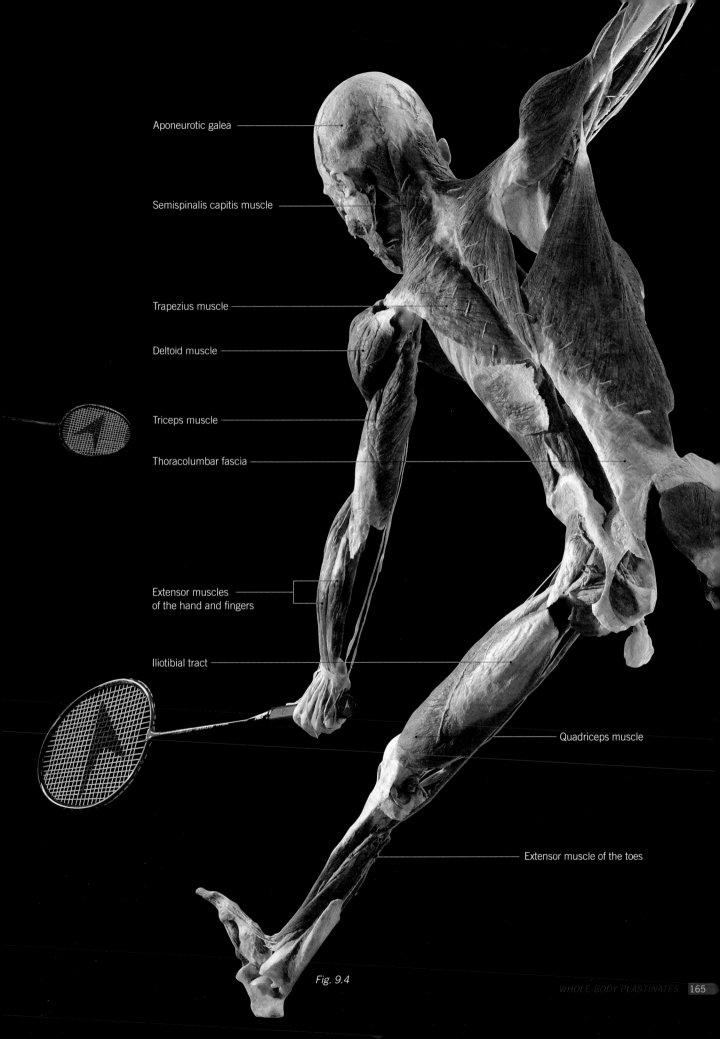

Aponeurotic galea

Semispinalis capitis muscle

Trapezius muscle

Deltoid muscle

Triceps muscle

Thoracolumbar fascia

Extensor muscles
of the hand and fingers

Iliotibial tract

Quadriceps muscle

Extensor muscle of the toes

Fig. 9.4

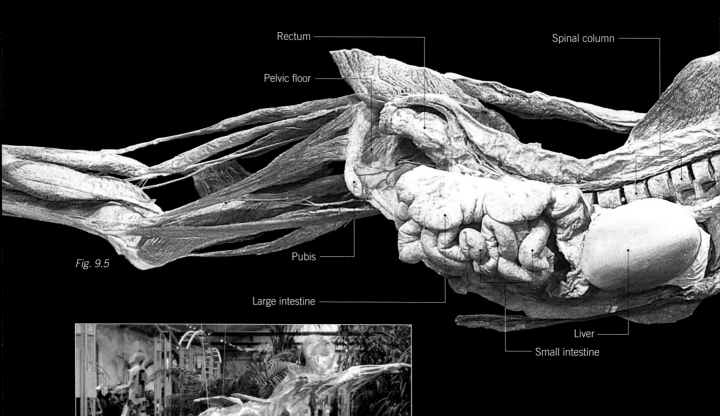

Rectum

Pelvic floor

Spinal column

Fig. 9.5

Pubis

Large intestine

Liver

Small intestine

Fig. 9.6

The Swimmer
(2001)

The body shell has been laterally separated
into two halves.
However, the inner organs
have been left in their original positions
either in the left or right body half.
On the corresponding side and opposite each organ,
cavities indicate the position, form, and size
of the organs that have been removed.

The vertebrae can thus be seen in the left half,
with the oesophagus in front,
and the liver and the intestines
in the abdominal cavity.
The inter-vertebral discs can be seen
in the right half,
as well as the uterus with the ovaries
and Fallopian tubes in the pelvic cavity.

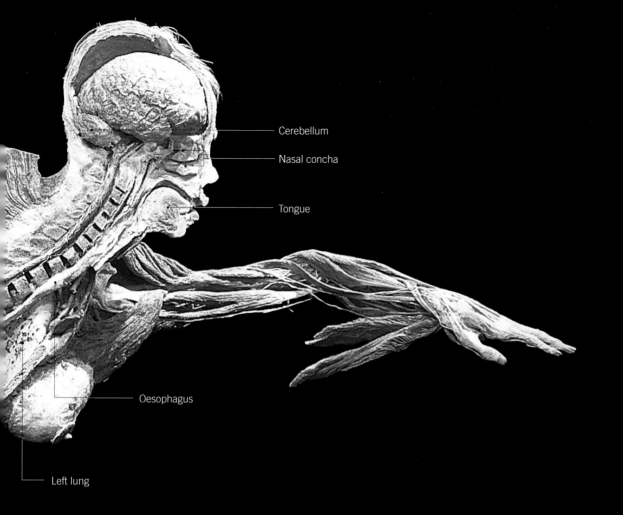

Cerebellum

Nasal concha

Tongue

Oesophagus

Left lung

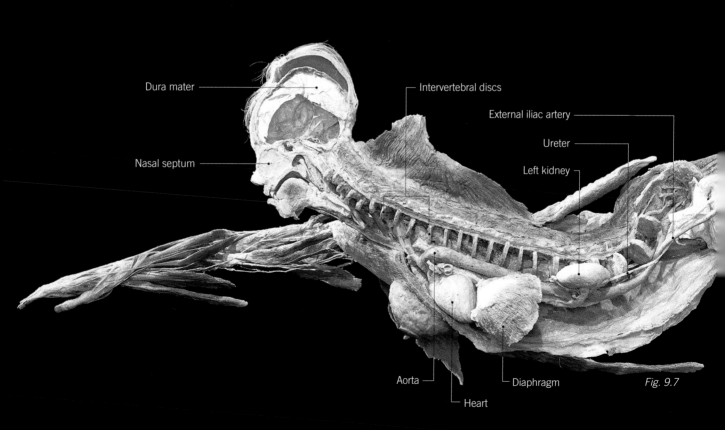

Dura mater

Nasal septum

Intervertebral discs

External iliac artery

Ureter

Left kidney

Aorta

Heart

Diaphragm

Fig. 9.7

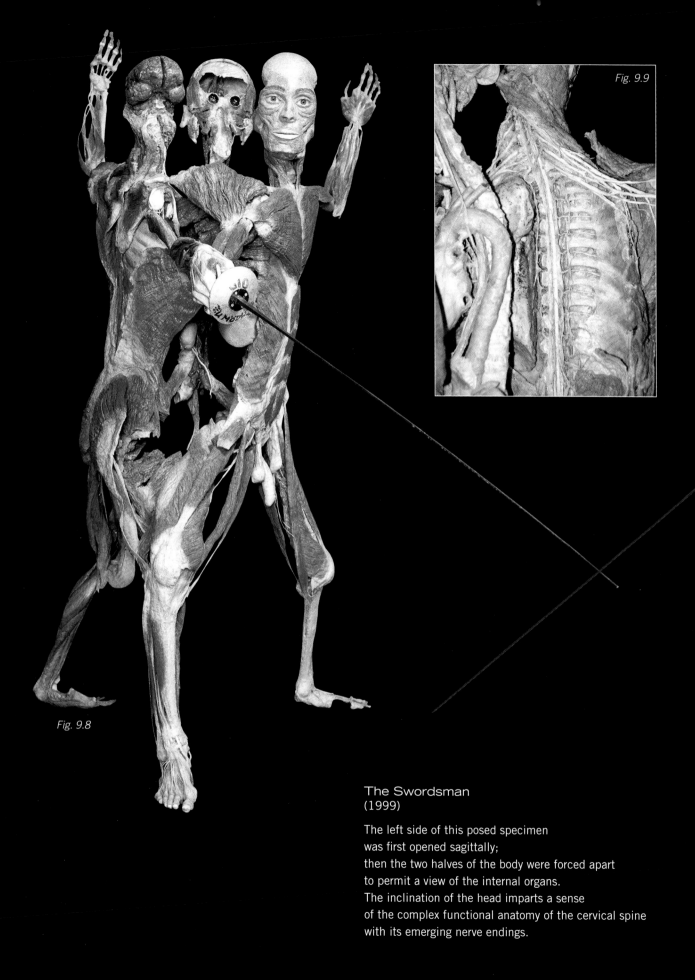

Fig. 9.8

Fig. 9.9

The Swordsman
(1999)

The left side of this posed specimen
was first opened sagittally;
then the two halves of the body were forced apart
to permit a view of the internal organs.
The inclination of the head imparts a sense
of the complex functional anatomy of the cervical spine
with its emerging nerve endings.

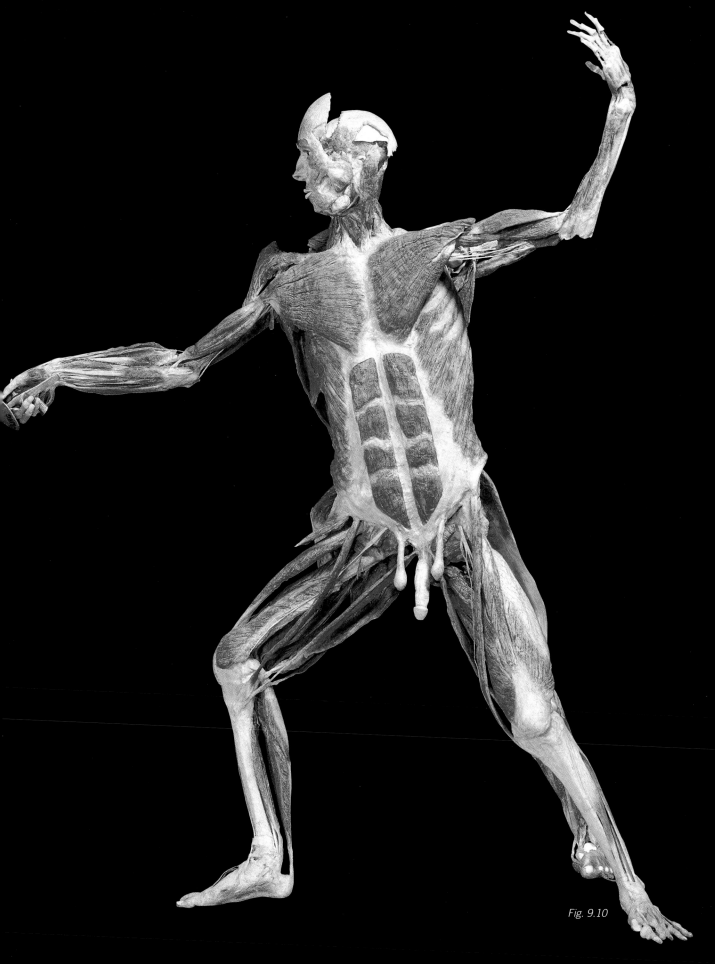

Fig. 9.10

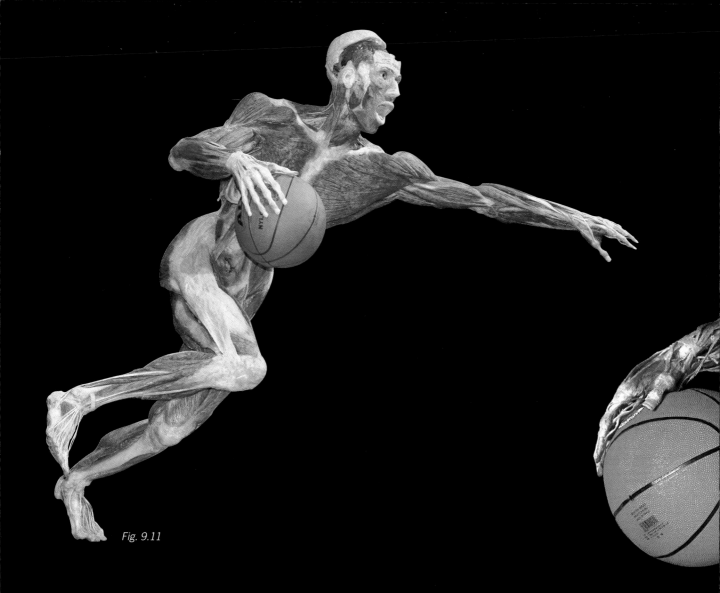

Fig. 9.11

The Basketball Player
(2002)

The Basketball Player plastinate
demonstrates the skin modelling muscles
of our body in a very dynamic posture.
The skull has been opened to reveal the brain.
The intestines have been removed
in order to show the large back muscles
at the rear of the abdominal cavity.
The urinary bladder rests
at the bottom of the small pelvis.

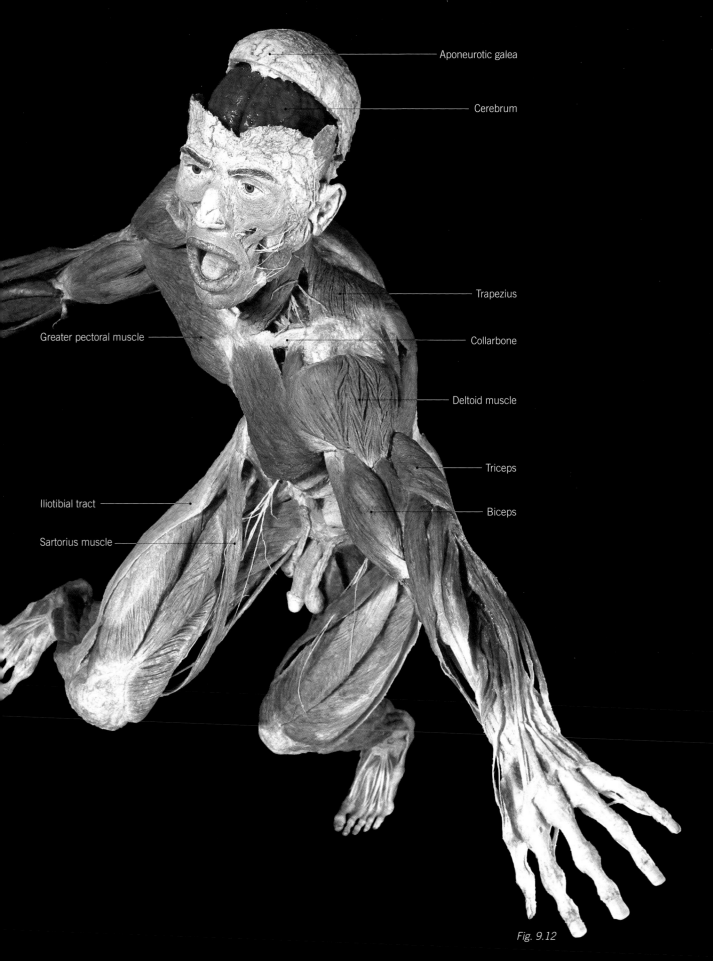

Aponeurotic galea

Cerebrum

Trapezius

Greater pectoral muscle

Collarbone

Deltoid muscle

Triceps

Iliotibial tract

Biceps

Sartorius muscle

Fig. 9.12

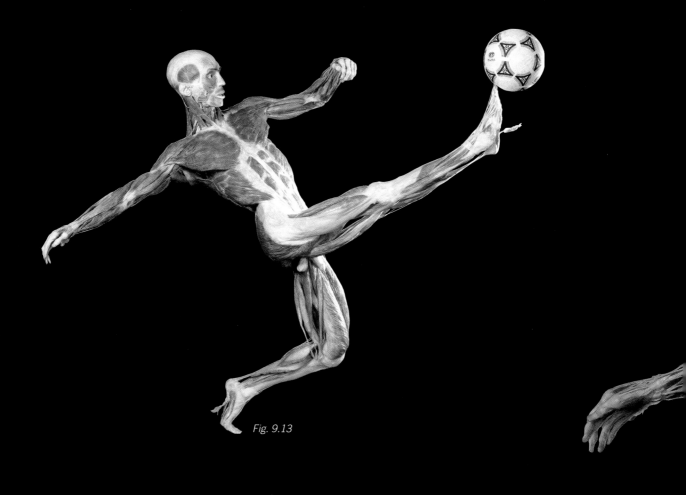

Fig. 9.13

The Soccer Player
(2005)

Skeletal muscles make up
almost half the weight of our body.
We use these muscles when we sit, stand, or move.
The skeletal muscles vary in shape and strength.
The muscles that surround the spine
are the most powerful ones.
They give us posture.
This plastinate shows the interplay
between surface and intermediate muscles
when they work together in movement.

Fig. 9.14

Fig. 9.15

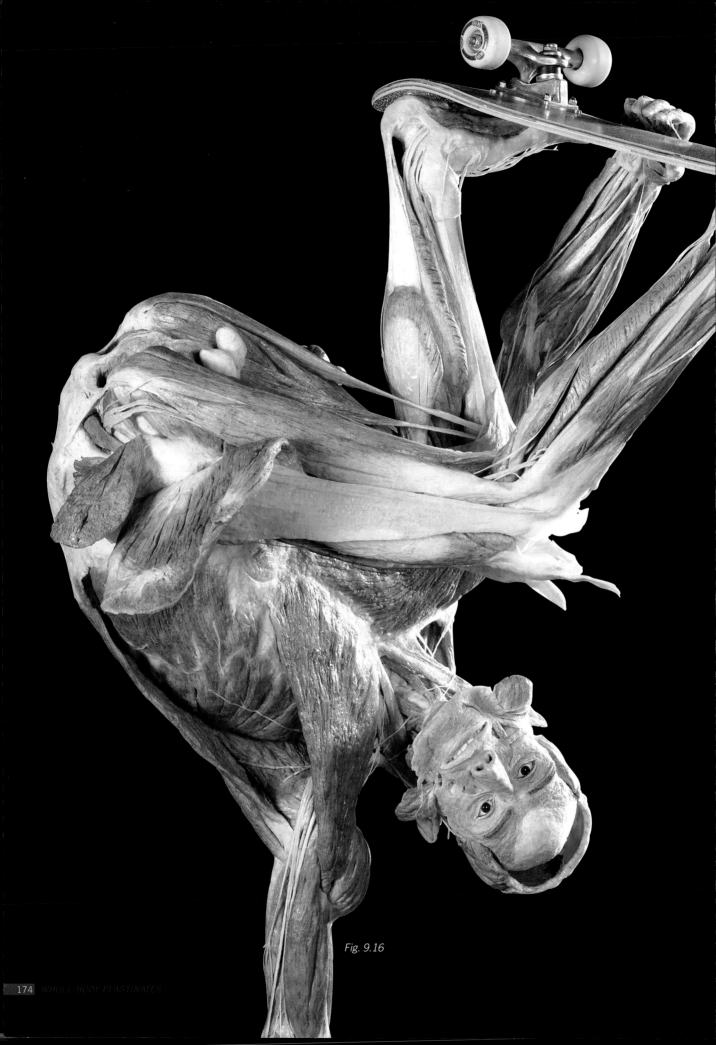

Fig. 9.16

The Skateboarder
(2005)

This skateboarder's upside-down trick offers
an insight into the anatomy of the buttocks.
The buttocks comprise three gluteal muscles.
The largest – the gluteus maximus
is one of the body's strongest muscles.
Here, the muscles are flapped back
to reveal the thick band of the sciatic nerve
running underneath past the sitting bone of the pelvis.
Skateboarding is demanding on the knee joints.
Here, the kneecaps have been lifted.
The knee joint is a hinge joint
and, like most joints in the body,
contains a lubricating fluid called synovial fluid.
Since the knee supports much of the body weight,
obesity may make knee osteoarthritis more likely.

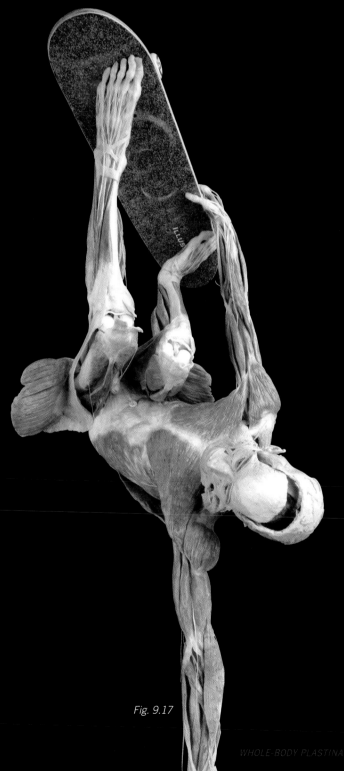

Fig. 9.17

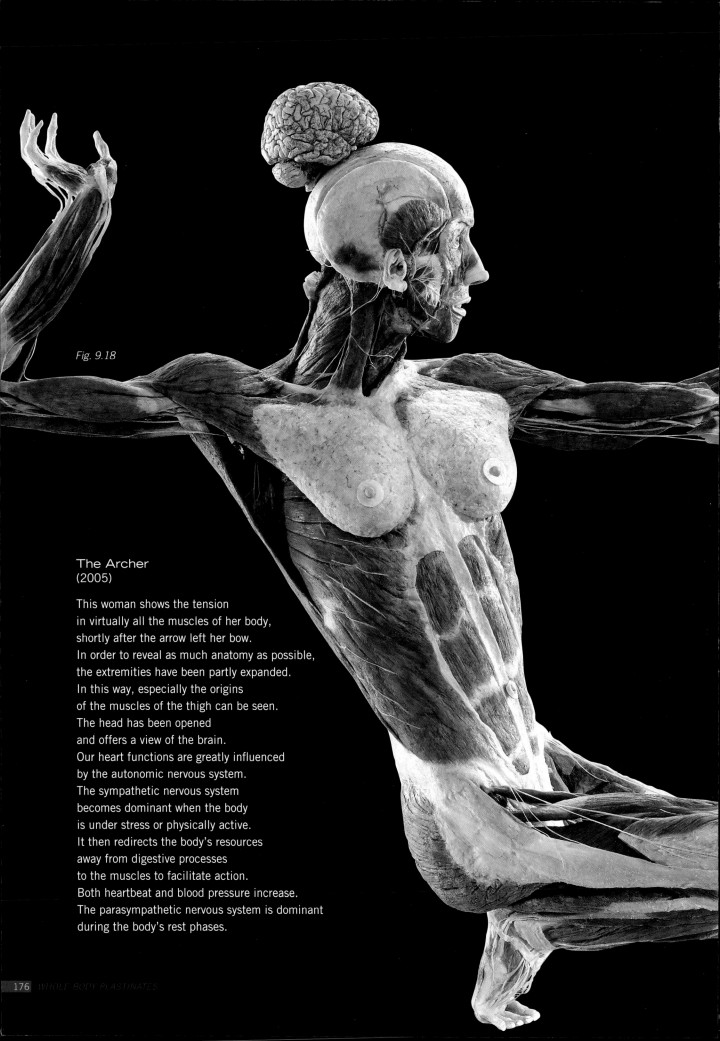

Fig. 9.18

The Archer
(2005)

This woman shows the tension
in virtually all the muscles of her body,
shortly after the arrow left her bow.
In order to reveal as much anatomy as possible,
the extremities have been partly expanded.
In this way, especially the origins
of the muscles of the thigh can be seen.
The head has been opened
and offers a view of the brain.
Our heart functions are greatly influenced
by the autonomic nervous system.
The sympathetic nervous system
becomes dominant when the body
is under stress or physically active.
It then redirects the body's resources
away from digestive processes
to the muscles to facilitate action.
Both heartbeat and blood pressure increase.
The parasympathetic nervous system is dominant
during the body's rest phases.

Fig. 9.19

Fig. 9.20

The Juxtaposed Couple
(2006)

The juxtaposed plastinates embody
the relationship between the heart and the brain,
both physiological and physical.
The relationship between the two organs,
though still not fully explored,
is best explained by injuries and disease.

The skull, and thoracic and abdominal cavities
are opened from behind.
The brain rests on top of the occipital bone,
which in turn sits at the top
of the vertebral column.
The woman's lung is represented
by a cast of the bronchi (white)
and the large lung vessels (red).
In the male body, the lungs can be seen
with the heart resting on the diaphragm,
our primary respiratory muscle.

The brain with its cool logic,
and the heart with its volatility,
act alone as well as in concert – juxtaposed –
to make up our essential selves.
But the heart alone is viewed as the vessel
of love and malice, compassion and cruelty,
good and evil.

Fig. 9.21

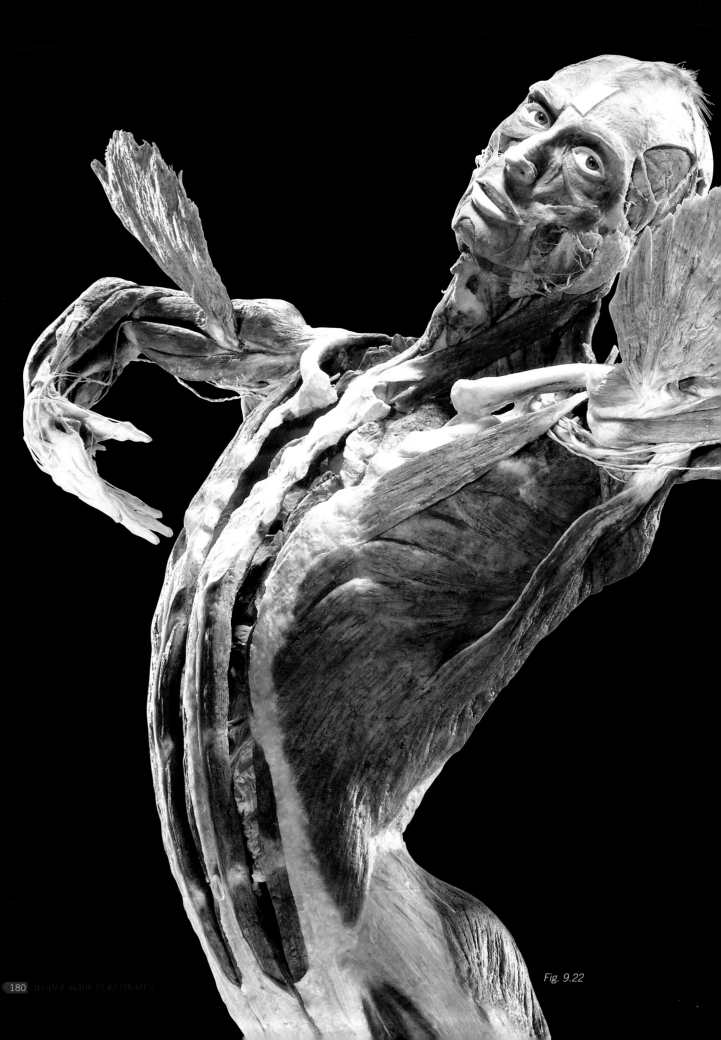

Fig. 9.22

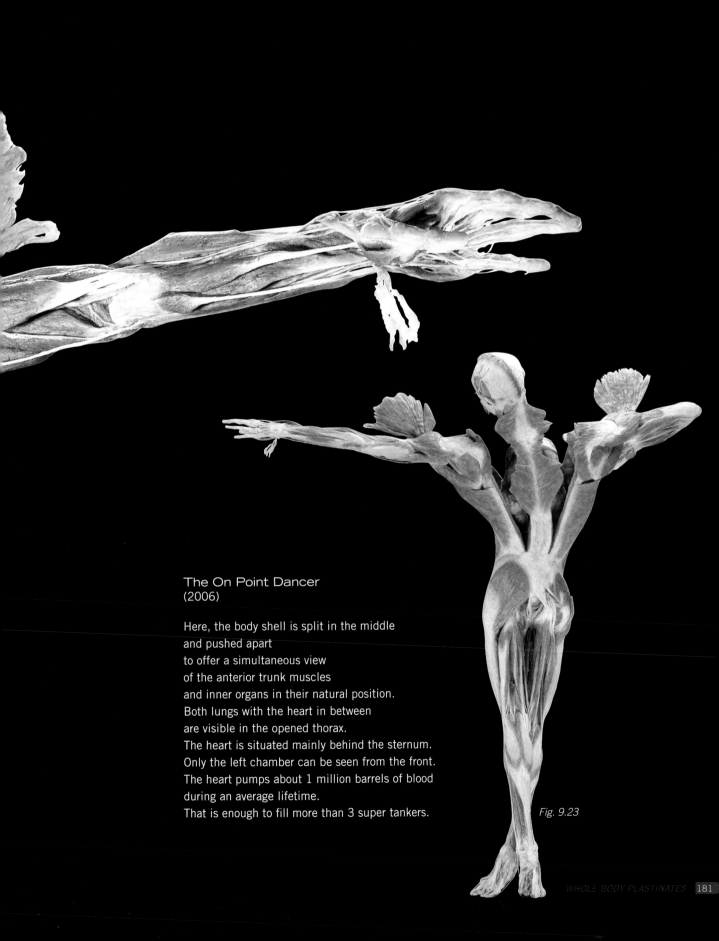

The On Point Dancer
(2006)

Here, the body shell is split in the middle
and pushed apart
to offer a simultaneous view
of the anterior trunk muscles
and inner organs in their natural position.
Both lungs with the heart in between
are visible in the opened thorax.
The heart is situated mainly behind the sternum.
Only the left chamber can be seen from the front.
The heart pumps about 1 million barrels of blood
during an average lifetime.
That is enough to fill more than 3 super tankers.

Fig. 9.23

Limber Gymnast with Organs
(2006)

While balancing on three wooden balls
with outstretched legs, this plastinate
presents his internal organs
with lungs, heart, liver, and intestinal tract.
Those organs were taken out from behind.
The spine is flipped up,
offering a view into the thoracic
and abdominal cavities.

The ability to maintain balance
depends on information that the brain receives
from the eyes,
the muscles and joints,
and the vestibular organs in the inner ears.
All three of these sources send information
in form of nerve impulses
from sensory receptors to our brain.
Our body's posture is largely maintained
by reflexive, involuntary control.

Fig. 9.24

Fig. 9.25

The Ponderer
(2005)

This sitting specimen shows the spinal cord
and the detailed pathways of nerves branching off it.
The spinal cord and brain
comprise the central nervous system.
This system controls and integrates body functions.
Because it is so crucial, it is very well protected.
It is embedded in three tough sheets
of connective tissue, called meningues.
The spinal cord is also enclosed in the backbone.
From between the vertebrae,
31 pairs of spinal nerves
connect the spinal cord to the rest of the body.
The bundle of nerves at the base of the spine
is the cauda equina – the 'horse's tail'.
The two sciatic nerves run from the lower spine
behind the hip joint down the leg.
They are the largest and longest nerves in the body.

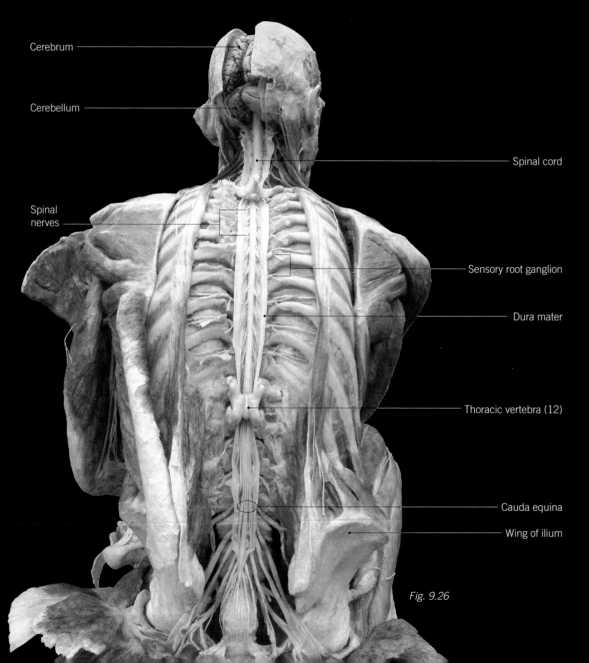

Cerebrum

Cerebellum

Spinal cord

Spinal nerves

Sensory root ganglion

Dura mater

Thoracic vertebra (12)

Cauda equina

Wing of ilium

Fig. 9.26

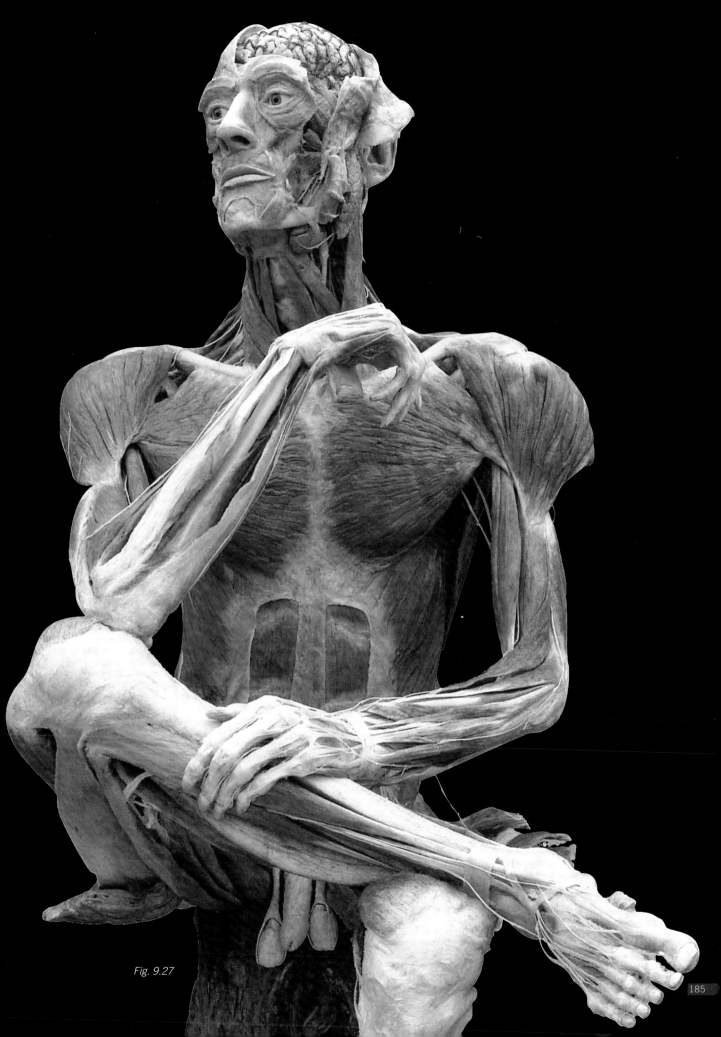

Fig. 9.27

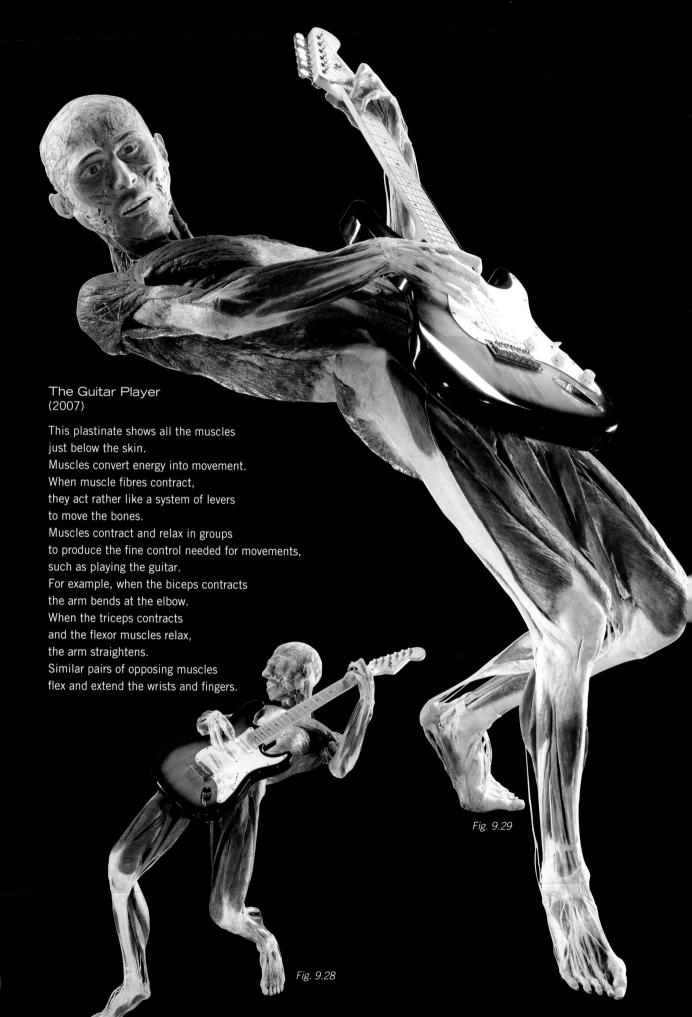

The Guitar Player
(2007)

This plastinate shows all the muscles
just below the skin.
Muscles convert energy into movement.
When muscle fibres contract,
they act rather like a system of levers
to move the bones.
Muscles contract and relax in groups
to produce the fine control needed for movements,
such as playing the guitar.
For example, when the biceps contracts
the arm bends at the elbow.
When the triceps contracts
and the flexor muscles relax,
the arm straightens.
Similar pairs of opposing muscles
flex and extend the wrists and fingers.

Fig. 9.29

Fig. 9.28

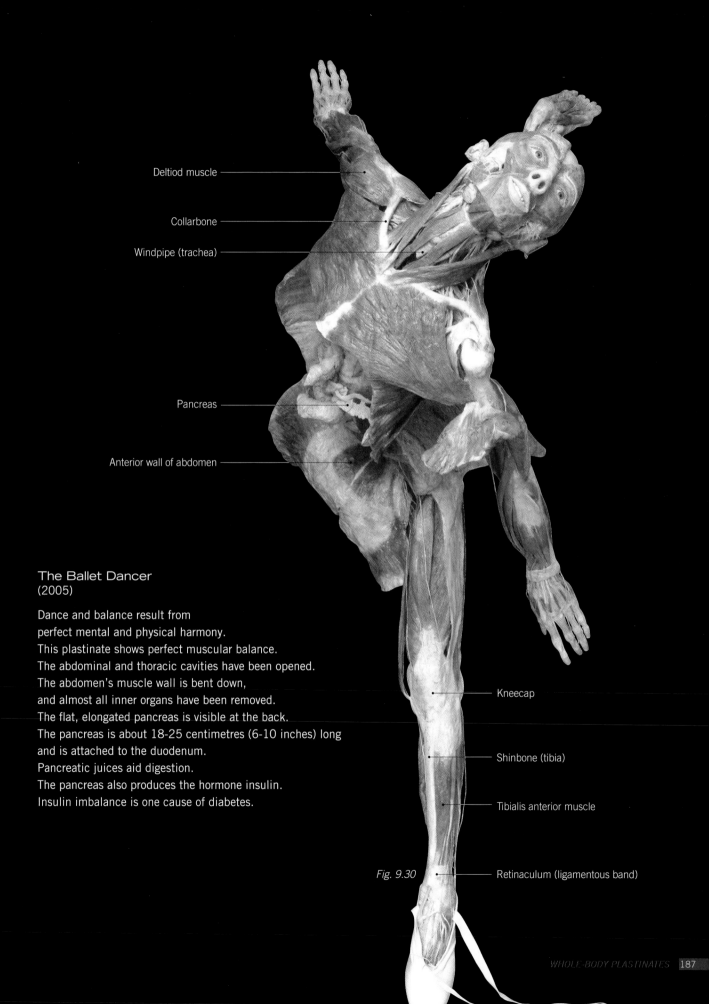

Deltiod muscle

Collarbone

Windpipe (trachea)

Pancreas

Anterior wall of abdomen

The Ballet Dancer
(2005)

Dance and balance result from
perfect mental and physical harmony.
This plastinate shows perfect muscular balance.
The abdominal and thoracic cavities have been opened.
The abdomen's muscle wall is bent down,
and almost all inner organs have been removed.
The flat, elongated pancreas is visible at the back.
The pancreas is about 18-25 centimetres (6-10 inches) long
and is attached to the duodenum.
Pancreatic juices aid digestion.
The pancreas also produces the hormone insulin.
Insulin imbalance is one cause of diabetes.

Kneecap

Shinbone (tibia)

Tibialis anterior muscle

Fig. 9.30

Retinaculum (ligamentous band)

The Jumping Dancer
(2005)

This particular preparation
enables the simultaneous view
of muscles from the front
and inner organs from the back.
The rear body wall together with the brain
were flipped down to present
the central nervous system,
composed of brain and spinal cord,
and the thoracic and abdominal inner organs.
This arrangement enables us
to view the inner side of the neck,
thorax, abdomen, and pelvis upside down
on the back of the specimen.

Fig. 9.31

Also the thoracic and abdominal cavities
with lungs, kidney, and intestines
can clearly be seen.
Especially noticeable is the diaphragm,
a thin muscle plate
which, as the 'breathing muscle'
divides the thoracic cavity
with the heart and lungs
from the abdominal cavity
with the liver, intestines, and kidneys.
A small anatomical highlight of this specimen
are the exposure of the round heads
of the femoral bones from behind.

Fig. 9.32

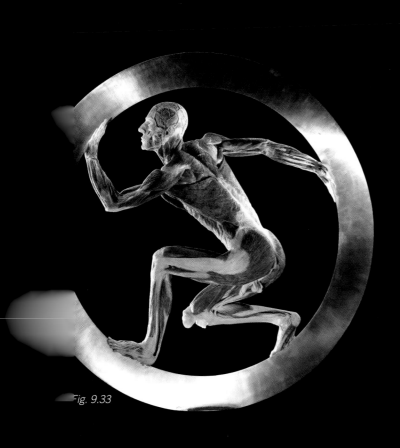

Fig. 9.33

The Wave Roller
(2007)

With his dynamic pose and ease of balance,
the wave-rider glides his steel wheel
elegantly down the waterfall.
His posture highlights his tensed muscles
and the tendon-like aponeuroses.
Aponeuroses are membranes
with a whitish-silvery colour.
They separate muscles from each other
and are made of the same taut connective tissue
as the round tendons of spindle-shaped muscles.
The largest aponeuroses protectively cover
the torso and the inner organs.
The large dorsal lumbar aponeurosis –
the lumbodorsal fascia –
is the tendon-like continuation
of the broad back muscles.
It also serves as an elastic connective tissue
for the muscles and tendons underneath.
This soft connective tissue is called fascia.
A network of fascia is found throughout the body
and surrounds the muscles.
The aponeurosis of a muscle
can also be the fascia for
other muscles lying deeper underneath.

Fig. 9.34

Fig. 9.35

The Hurdler
(2005)

This plastinate shows the interplay
between surface and intermediate muscles.

A muscle can only shorten.
When we move, different muscles act on
opposite sides of a joint, pulling it in the
different directions in which it can move.
For example, the biceps flexes the elbow,
while the triceps at the back of our arm
does the opposite and extends the elbow.
When the biceps contracts,
balancing activity in the triceps
inhibits excessive movement.
This makes our movements fluid and controlled.

Any increase in energy expenditure
requires rapid adjustments in blood flow
that affect the entire cardiovascular system.
During extensive muscle activity,
such as running and cycling at maximum intensity,
muscle blood flow accounts for 80-85%
of the total cardiac output.

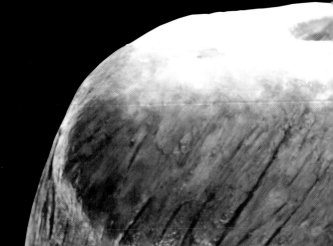

Fig. 9.36

The High Jumper
(2006)

Complex movement, as in sports,
require not only strength and skill
but also the precise coordination
of the brain and the muscles.
This plastinate shows the muscles
of a high jumper in functional pose.
His arms have been extended away from the body
to open the view on the anatomy of the arm pit.
The important vessels and nerves
supplying the arm
can thus be seen.
The inner organs in their natural positions
have been made visible by folding back
the walls of abdomen and chest.

Fig. 9.38

Fig. 9.37

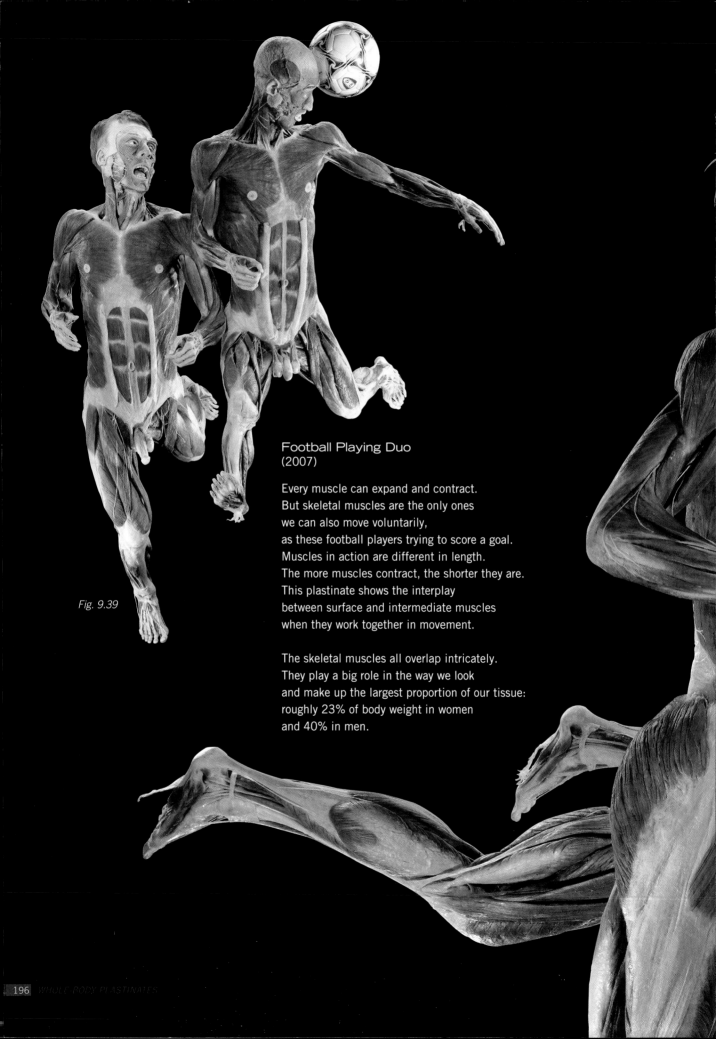

Football Playing Duo
(2007)

Every muscle can expand and contract.
But skeletal muscles are the only ones
we can also move voluntarily,
as these football players trying to score a goal.
Muscles in action are different in length.
The more muscles contract, the shorter they are.
This plastinate shows the interplay
between surface and intermediate muscles
when they work together in movement.

The skeletal muscles all overlap intricately.
They play a big role in the way we look
and make up the largest proportion of our tissue:
roughly 23% of body weight in women
and 40% in men.

Fig. 9.39

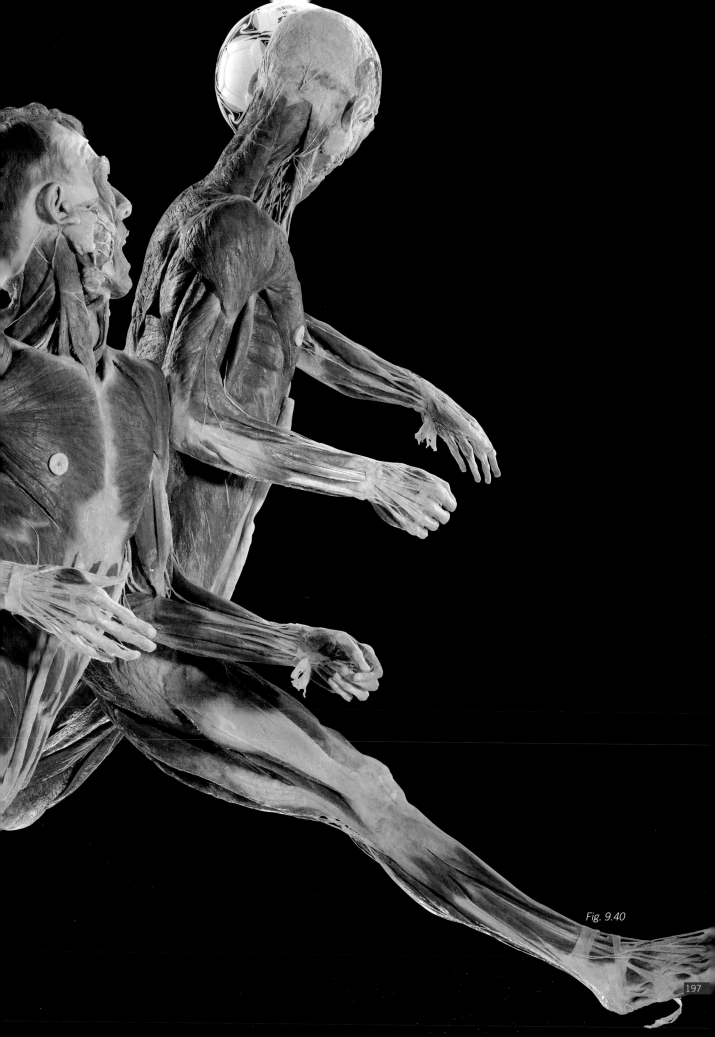

Fig. 9.40

The Football Gladiators
(2007)

Muscles are usually arranged in pairs
with opposing functions.
For example, the quadriceps muscle,
the big bulky muscle on the front of the thigh,
allows us to straighten the knee.
The hamstring muscle on the back of the thigh
allows us to bend the knee.
The combination of all the skeletal muscles
allows us a huge variety of movements,
including walking, running, smiling, writing,
or playing football.

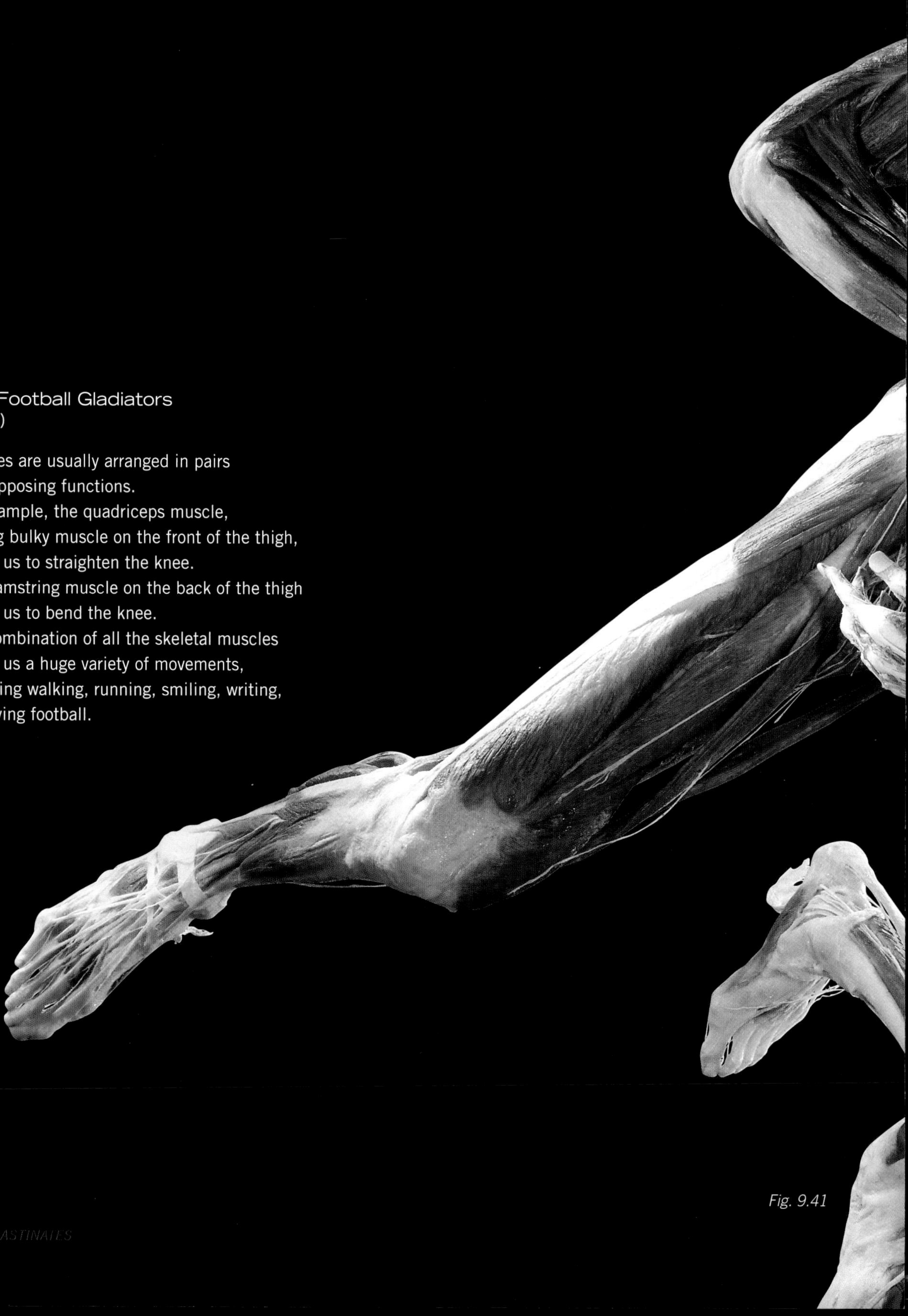

Fig. 9.41

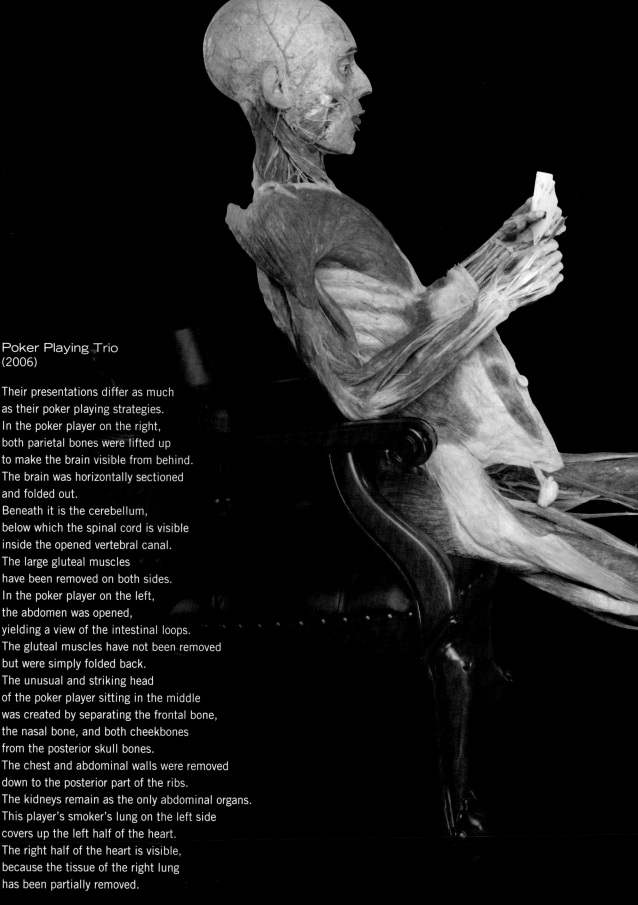

Poker Playing Trio
(2006)

Their presentations differ as much
as their poker playing strategies.
In the poker player on the right,
both parietal bones were lifted up
to make the brain visible from behind.
The brain was horizontally sectioned
and folded out.
Beneath it is the cerebellum,
below which the spinal cord is visible
inside the opened vertebral canal.
The large gluteal muscles
have been removed on both sides.
In the poker player on the left,
the abdomen was opened,
yielding a view of the intestinal loops.
The gluteal muscles have not been removed
but were simply folded back.
The unusual and striking head
of the poker player sitting in the middle
was created by separating the frontal bone,
the nasal bone, and both cheekbones
from the posterior skull bones.
The chest and abdominal walls were removed
down to the posterior part of the ribs.
The kidneys remain as the only abdominal organs.
This player's smoker's lung on the left side
covers up the left half of the heart.
The right half of the heart is visible,
because the tissue of the right lung
has been partially removed.

Fig. 9.42
This Trio played a round of poker in the James Bond movie, "Casino Royale".

Fig. 9.43

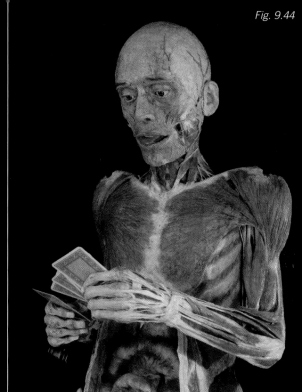

Fig. 9.44

Fig. 9.45

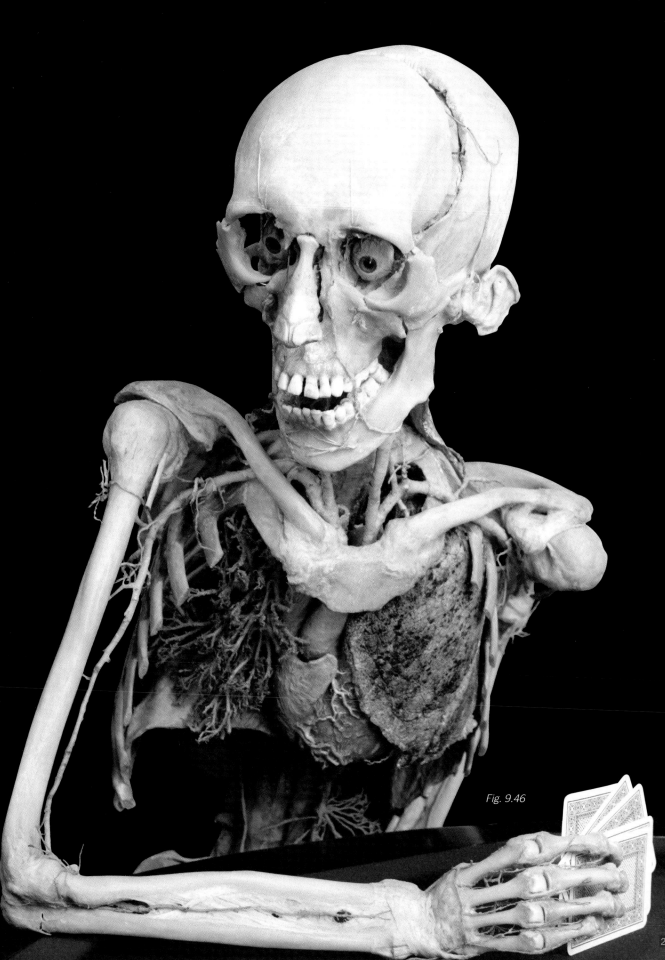

Fig. 9.46

Fig. 9.47

The Rearing Horse with Rider
(2000)

Both the human and the horse
share a very similar anatomical arrangement
in the form, position, and microscopic structures
of their organs and muscles.
However, there are major differences in the proportions.
Compared to the horse, human musculature is rather puny,
while on the other hand, the larger human brain
results in significantly higher intelligence.

In humans, the humeri (long bones of the arm)
and thighbones are relatively long,
while the hands and feet are relatively short.
In horses, the bones of the fore and hind limbs
are by contrast relatively short and closer to the trunk.
However, the cannon bones, fetlocks,
pasterns, and hoofs are relatively long,
and the number of phalanges of the toes is reduced
so that the joints of the limbs have different positions.

Fig. 9.48

Gorilla
2003

Primates are mammals that most resemble humans
in their anatomy and behaviour.
This lowland gorilla weighs 200 kilograms (441 pounds),
is 1.85 metres (6.1 feet) tall,
measures 1.55 metres (5.1 feet) around the chest
and 2.4 metres (7.9 feet) from fingertip to fingertip
with its arms outstretched.
Female gorillas are shorter (1.3 metres/4.3 feet)
and only weigh half as much.
Gorillas generally walk on all fours.
Standing upright is straining for them
because of the slight curvature of their spine.
Compared to humans,
they have a deeper and broader chest,
wider jaws, and significantly longer bones
in the forearms, metacarpi, and fingers.
When standing, their arms extend down
beyond their knees.
Like other apes, gorillas do not have a tail.
The thumbs and big toes can be used
opposite the fingers and toes
for grasping or climbing.
The gorilla's internal organ structure displays
the long intestines typical of herbivores.
Gorillas spend 50% of their waking hours feeding,
aided by their powerful chewing muscles.

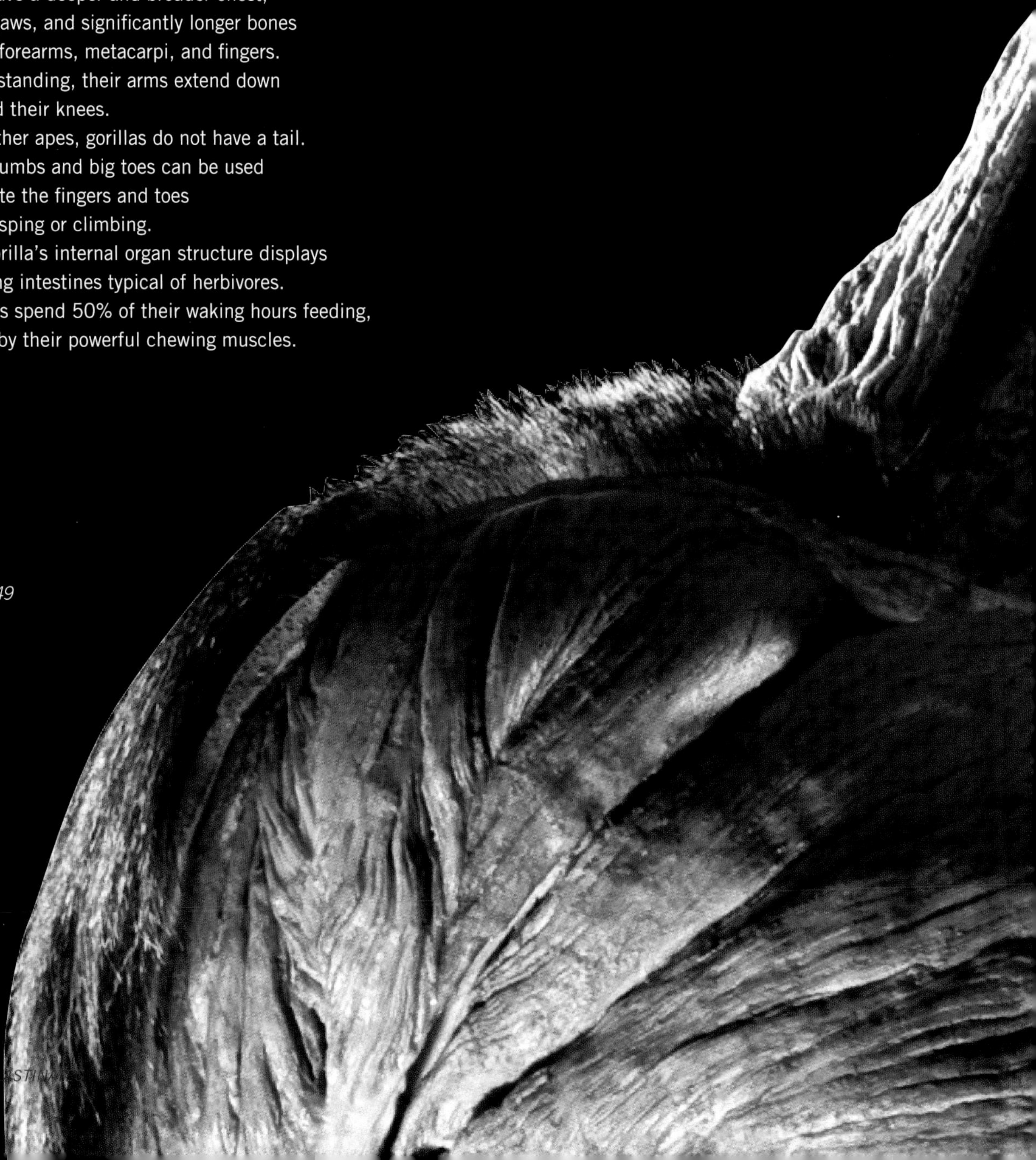

Fig. 9.49

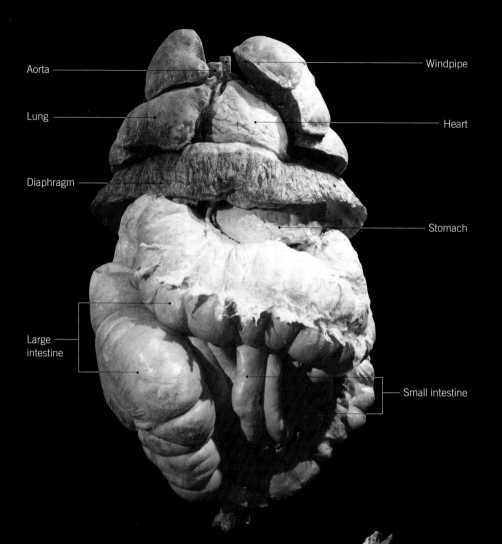

Aorta

Lung

Diaphragm

Windpipe

Heart

Stomach

Large
intestine

Small intestine

Fig. 9.50 | *Internal organs of the Gorilla.*

Fig. 9.51

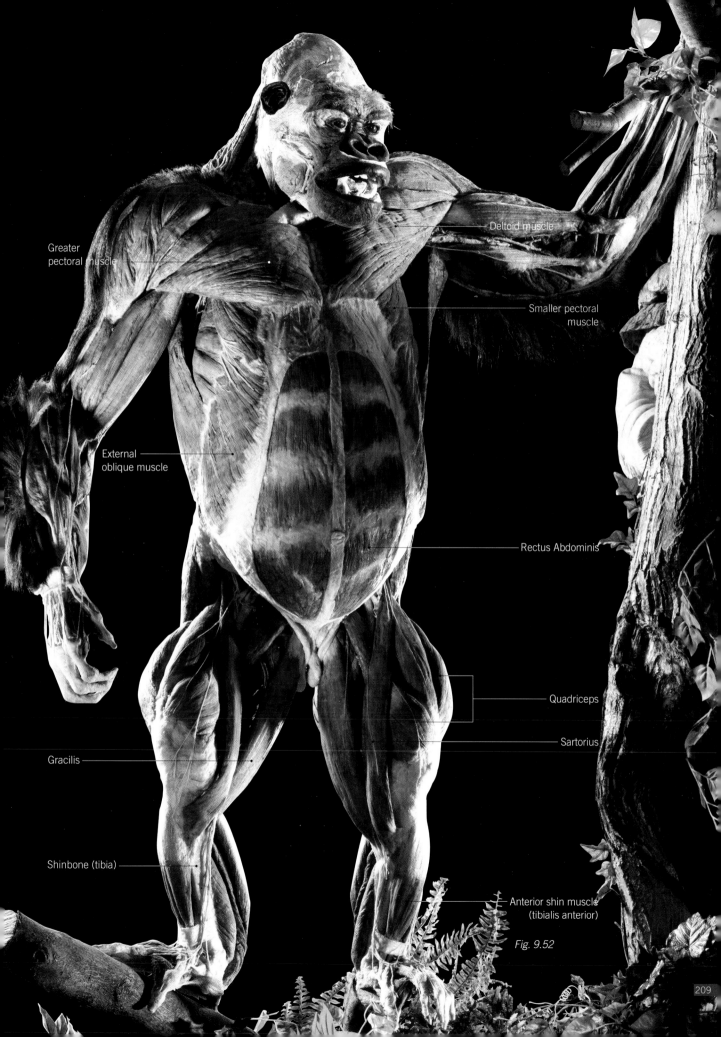

Deltoid muscle

Greater
pectoral muscle

Smaller pectoral
muscle

External
oblique muscle

Rectus Abdominis

Quadriceps

Sartorius

Gracilis

Shinbone (tibia)

Anterior shin muscle
(tibialis anterior)

Fig. 9.52

209

Gunther von Hagens

On Gruesome Corpses,
Gestalt Plastinates* and Mandatory Interment

Grim and Gruesome Corpses in Anatomy

"A dissection hall full of cadavers is no Garden of Eden [...] From time immemorial, it has been the cause of revulsion for delicate nerves, and with few exceptions the brief duration of such anatomists can be easily understood when spent in such rooms. That they become desensitised after a certain period of time can not offset the harmfulness involved and will show that people can learn to live with nearly anything when the spirit of research guides them even to such sources of truth."

Anatomist Anton Hyrtl wrote this in 1860 at a time when he and his colleagues had to fetch their cadavers from the gallows and to dissect them publicly.[1] Because decomposition proceeded very fast during the summer, public dissections could only be performed during the cold months. The discovery of formaldehyde at the end of the 19th century proved to be a major breakthrough in mitigating the unpleasantness of anatomical training. Since then, it has been used to preserve cadavers. It stops decomposition. It also permits anatomical cadavers to be dissected regardless of the season and over several months. Nevertheless, anatomical cadavers have retained a certain bloodcurdling aura, and thus give rise to an emotional revulsion. Their psychological impact on students is critical. Hence, in 1984, Herbert Lippert, an anatomist in Hanover, described anatomical cadavers as "dehumanising" in the Deutsches Ärzteblatt.[2] As they monopolise anatomical instruction, they are "too little oriented to the living." Cadavers "accustom students not to expect any expression of feelings from patients." They "are gradually viewed not as human beings but only as problems. [...] Despite all of the officially professed respect due to body donors, most students could not imagine that a member of their families could donate his or her body for anatomical study."

What makes anatomical cadavers so unpalatable? The fact that they are dead cannot be the reason. Gestalt plastinates are just as dead as anatomical cadavers, and yet every day about five people who attend the BODY WORLDS exhibition sign up as body donors for plastination. Conversely, in my 20 years as a university anatomist, I have never once experienced that a student or colleague became a body donor for anatomical study. Consequently, there must be a fundamental difference in the way both anatomical cadavers and gestalt plastinates in the Körperwelten exhibition are perceived.

*Gestalt Plastinate: Aesthetic, instructive wholy-body specimen positioned in a life-like pose.

The reason for this is not difficult to understand. Observers cannot identify with the "grim and gruesome corpses" in dissection halls. Bloated, discolored and surrounded by the caustic odor of formaldehyde, they are the unpleasant but necessary evil of practical anatomy. Students, many of whom are holding a scalpel in their hands for the first time, are totally out of their element in a dissection class. In the brief time available to them, a "massacred specimen" is all too often the result. These student depredations on corpses together with increasing desiccation as well as the accompanying brown or black discolouration all contribute to making anatomical cadavers generally "grim and gruesome." The reason that they are nevertheless of vital importance for anatomical training is to be found in their authenticity. Even the best pictures or models cannot replace the original just as viewing a picture of a landscape or a computer animation cannot give a realistic idea of a forest. Authentic anatomical specimens make bodily interiors 'graspable' in both senses of the word.

New Possibilities for Specimens through Plastination

Plastinates are authentic anatomical specimens. They are permanently preserved because the fluids and soluble fats in their tissue have been replaced initially with ice-cold acetone and subsequently with plastic in a vacuum. The reactive plastics used in this process, such as silicone rubber or epoxy resin, harden after infusion. As a consequence, plastinates remain dry, odourless and accurate in detail down to the microscopic level. They can be pliable, rigid or even transparent.[3] This has made them the most natural and best-preserved specimens since the beginning of anatomy.

By hardening the plastic in such specimens, the tissue becomes thoroughly solidified so that not only the bones, but also the muscles and other soft tissue can take over supporting functions. In this way, anatomically preserved bodies cannot just be positioned upright, as has only been possible with skeletons, but in a whole variety of new and innovative forms for presenting dissected specimens as well. Hence, through plastination, it has first become possible, for example, to present the muscular system in an upright pose, completely independent of its own skeleton; without the hardened plastic, the muscles would simply collapse.

As such bodies are placed in a particular pose, I call them gestalt plastinates. The nature of the pose must be strategically planned; here the theme determines the pose as form follows function. In planning such poses, I distinguish between anatomically correct positioning, motion posing and fragmentation of a body.

Poses

Whole-body plastinates that have been infused with silicone but have not yet been hardened are still pliable and are a kind of 'pre-specimen,' which will become a durable specimen only after the silicone hardens. However, hardening cannot take place immediately after the specimen has been removed from the silicone tank because at that point it is initially a crumpled heap of matter. In this situation, we are virtually compelled to shape it in some way, even if this is only an upright pose. Moreover, all of the dissected structures, every organ, every nerve and every vessel must be correctly positioned anatomically before the plastic hardens, thereby permanently 'freezing' the respective pose. One wrong angle of even one of the eight vessels emanating directly from the heart and this one mistake could overshadow the plastinator and his work well beyond his lifetime. A whole-body plastinate requires ap-

proximately 1,000 pins, foam pads and supporting wires until each structure has been fixed and hardened in an anatomically correct position. This is painstaking, demanding work.

With the first whole-body plastinates, I oriented the respective poses according to the anatomical structures to be displayed, without regard for the overall appeal of the total design. As a result, the specimens either appeared rigid as lifeless mannequins or they looked unnaturally distorted or even grotesque when, for example, the lower leg was twisted for a better view of the sole of the foot or the head was tilted back to afford a better look at the lower jaw and throat regions. It was obvious that the instructional value of anatomical exhibits would be significantly enhanced by the overall aesthetic impact of gestalt plastinates. Just as the appeal of a picture is determined by its frame and vice versa, poses and instructiveness interact with each other in gestalt plastinates. For special anatomical themes, some bodily poses are more suitable than others are. Each pose, each bodily posture, possesses its own specific instructional potential. Hence, exhibits of artificial shoulder, elbow, hip and knee joints concretely call for the respective joints to be appropriately bent. As shown

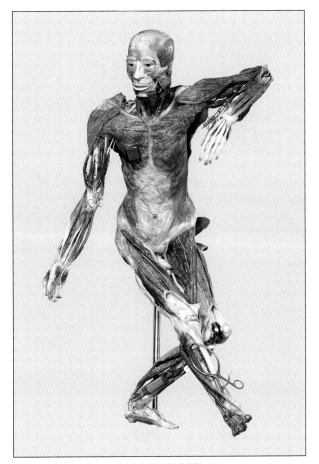 

Fig. 1: The Orthopaedic Body (1997)

in Figure 1, these bent joints can be harmoniously displayed in the pose of a dancer.

It was the anatomical artists of the Renaissance who were the first to reduce the distance between anatomised cadavers and the living, by imparting poses of motion to whole-body specimens. This can be seen in many depictions; there are also several dry specimens from a later period, unfortunately largely in pitiful condition.[4] The lifelike poses of these musclemen have endowed these specimens with the illusion of life, which tends to suppress any thoughts of corpses and mourning or even to neutralise these ideas. The illusion of movement suggested when viewing specimens positioned in lifelike poses is based on unconscious memories of visual images of motion. Such specimens are animated by poses of motion in the imagination of viewers. This succeeds especially when typical aspects of movements are magnified or even exaggerated. With *The Runner*, this means concretely that the length of the stride has to be exaggerated to a fantastic degree. Generally speaking, this is the same technique as that used by sculptors to bring life to a kinetic sculpture hewn out of a block of marble. The lifelike poses of gestalt plastinates are so similar to the living that viewers can actually recognise and even feel their own corporeality and can identify with it.

Gestalt plastinates are not objects of mourning; they are instructional specimens. Mourning would interfere with learning; our thoughts would digress. Consequently, I have attempted to make gestalt plastinates appear as lifelike as possible. Freed of the stigma of revulsion, such vital, holistic anatomy thus becomes feasible, with which viewers can be fascinated by its authenticity.

It is just this holistic, lifelike presentation that does not let viewers forget that each gestalt plastinate represents a unique and individual life. Each gestalt plastinate is an anatomical treasure, unique down to the microscopic, indeed down to the genetic and thus the molecular levels. Hence, the design efforts of a plastinator actually affirm his intention to upgrade the value of the human body. The ethical reservation that with gestalt plastinates "the human corpse [...] is degraded to an object" is thus refuted.[5]

The illusion of bringing life to a body can be reinforced through a striking facial dissection, an emotional pose, typical lifelike details such as accessories, clothing, tools or by creating spaces familiar to viewers, like workplaces or the natural environment. The idea of functionality in the imagination serves the illusion of motion. When a gestalt plastinate 'is playing chess' or 'is riding,' death is brought closer to life in a kind of humorous fashion. "It would be hard to imagine whole-body plastinates without that special humour (the pose, as one of the few hate-filled visitors to the exhibition claimed as the main reason for his rejection of it), with which von Hagens has quite obviously succeeded in transforming the energy of the threat emanating from repression into zestfulness, without letting either desire or inhibition penetrate the consciousness [...]."[6]

Fragmented Gestalt Plastinates

Traditional anatomical dissection is based on removal. The insides of the body are successively laid bare, layer by layer, 'dissecting by removal' as it is typically called. First the skin is removed, then the muscles, followed by the organs, until only the bones and ligaments are left. Therein lies the weakness of this method of dissection, as by the end of the course, students have often forgotten which parts were removed at the beginning. Such 'leftover' dissections are even more incomprehensible for laypersons.

Conversely, in architectural and engineering studies, it is common to present complex, three-dimensional situations in so-called 'exploded views' that leave nothing out but instead show the structures separately by displacing the individual components spatially while retaining their proper relationships to the whole. By means of their displacement, an insight into the structure is made possible, which aids in understanding the compact three-dimensionality.

When I opened an anatomical atlas for the first time, I was surprised that I was led picture by picture into the depths of the body in large strides, but the intermediate structures that could have given me a three-dimensional understanding were nowhere to be seen. As a student, I learned that the missing pieces consisted mainly of fat and connective tissue that had landed on the dissection-room floor. The so-called 'exploded skull,' which permits a view into the complex bone structure of the cranium by means of a spatial displacement of the individual bones, has been the only exploded specimen in anatomy departments until now. This is understandable as a certain hardness is needed for fragmentation that was not possible with soft tissue prior to the discovery of plastination. Fragmented whole-body specimens can be folded open, expanded horizontally and longitudinally, turned into 'drawer bodies,' and of course 'exploded' to show their inner workings. For this purpose, bodily fragments are expanded, are opened as bodily 'doors' or are pulled out like drawers. Insights are gained by spatially moving certain components without removing any organs or body parts. In this way, views of the inside of the body can be gained that have remained unseen until now. Fragmented gestalt plastinates succeed when the arrangement virtually prompts viewers perforce to reconstruct the exploded bodily fragments in their original positions, in other words to close the body in the mind's eye. It thus brings about a mental animation of the fragmented gestalt plastinate in the eye of the beholder, which can even serve to enhance its impressiveness.

Mental, spatially opened dissections are the parents of practical fragmentation and expansion. They are the forms of creative thinking that challenges my imagination most intensively, which I first began to master after 15 years of dissection work. For the first few years, I taught anatomy with pictures, just as I had got to know them in anatomy atlases and in dissection courses. When I was teaching anatomy, these pictures helpfully came to mind. In my imagination then, the human body resembled more a stick figure than the genuine, densely structured insides of the body. My knowledge of anatomy gained more depth after the invention of slice plastinates and the daily anatomical occupation with plastinate body slices. My idea of the body's insides became more compact because 1/8-inch-thick slices permitted me continually to observe how structures spread throughout the body, which ones are above and below them, which ones are to the right and to the left, which ones are in front and behind. A contributing factor to solidifying my anatomical conception was the fact that I called upon students in seminars over a number of years to think themselves randomly into the various bodily structures, to shoot imaginary arrows in all directions within these spaces and to describe exactly the anatomical paths that were followed. In establishing new views of bodily interiors, it is usually more helpful not to look at anatomical pictures to see what they show, but to analyse what they do not show. Why, for example, is the eustachian tube never shown from below? Why is the gluteal musculature never shown from above? In the meantime, I have been aided in such considerations by a database comprising 20,000 anatomical pictures ranging over five centuries, which I am constantly expanding.

When the approximately 5,000 definable structures of the body's interior had become so familiar to me as people's own bodily surfaces are to them, I no longer needed any pictures to know where exactly these structures were to be found deep below the exterior. Just as anyone can walk through his or her own apartment in the mind's eye, I thus began to 'wander' through the human body mentally. Unlike apartments, in bodies everything is tightly packed, structure to structure, without any spaces in between. As a consequence, I do not mentally move between anatomical structures, but inside of them. I wend my way through organs, bones and muscles and slide down nerves, as if I were moving around in a basement storeroom crammed with sacks of potatoes and peas and the electric wiring in between. The burlap used to enclose such foodstuffs corresponds to the connective tissue covering the organs, muscles and nerve tracts in the body. Now I only have to observe the surrounding area carefully and to blot out the adjoining organs in my mind in order to permit completely new bodily landscapes to evolve. These are then mentally exposed by removing, displacing or separating the structures located in front of them. The pancreas can thus be made visible either by removing the stomach that blocks it or by shifting the stomach upwards or by cutting it in two and moving it laterally to both sides. When exposing structures with such invasive thinking, I always have the choice of dividing them either geometrically by cutting or functionally in accordance with their natural surface relief.

However, there are not only instructional interfaces inside the body itself; they can also be imagined from the outside towards the inside. These can be mentally expanded into fissures. Structures that are of interest can, if necessary, be imagined from their more instructive sides and finally these fissures are displayed as aesthetically appealing showrooms of bodily interiors. Gestalt plastinates conceived in this way must be considered and reconsidered again and again, like a chess game in which one or both players has his or their back to the board so that the moves have to be announced while the constellations of pieces formed in the mind's eye are constantly changing with each move. The moves also get better and better the more often they can be reconsidered and, if necessary, can be altered mentally. In doing so, the position of the pieces can be optimised through isolated movements in front of the mind's eye. The faster I can successively perform these movements in all three directions in front of my mind's eye, the easier it is to choose alternatives and to make decisions about which one of the bodily images thus imagined comes closest to my objective.

I call fragmented gestalt plastinates of the whole body 'exploded specimens.' To a particular degree, they aid the understanding of laypersons looking into such specimens, who need the totality of the body in order to comprehend it. The unusual body forms resulting from fragmentation are in fact a necessary consequence, but are not the object of my artistic efforts. Creative impulses are foreign to today's macroscopic anatomy, which is entirely devoted to students' instruction and research. However, it is just not possible at all to get a cadaver soaked in formaldehyde to stand up straight and to remain in a given position. It is thus understandable that when professional anatomists occasionally criticise certain bodily specimens in the BODY WORLDS exhibition "that are not to be justified by a single didactic principle," they are breaking with visual anatomical patterns that have obtained for decades.[7] The reactions of visitors to the BODY WORLDS exhibition have shown that the type of representation that creates interspaces without removing organs or other bodily parts is superior to traditional dissections in imparting holistic anatomical knowledge.

Examples of Specimens

The Runner

The *Runner* is the first and only anatomical whole-body specimen worldwide, in which both the skeleton and the muscles are all visible at the same time. For this purpose, the muscles were detached at their fleshy origins on the respective bones largely located near the torso, and were then either folded back or laterally shifted in groups. For an unobstructed all-around view, it was necessary to lead the extremities away from the torso, e.g., either towards the front or back. This inevitably resulted in the positioning of the *Runner*.

If certain "associations with Baron Frankenstein" are awakened here,[8] for me this is an indication of the realisation suggested to me by Bazon Brock that varying ways of thinking can all lead to the same creative results.[9] Consequently, the *Runner* has been evaluated in varying ways. Opinions on this specimen range from a "unique synergistic view of the loco-motive system, especially for physiotherapists"[10]; "a specter right out of a chamber of horrors: [...] It is naked and what's more: [...] Pieces of flesh are hanging downwards [...]"[11]; to "Mercury, the messenger of the gods, on a swing."[12]

Reclining Pregnant Woman (Fig. 2)

It was difficult to position this gestalt plastinate: the body should not be made to appear lifeless and should permit an optimum view of the foetus in the uterus, while at the same time showing proper respect for this double tragedy. The physical discomfort of an advanced state of pregnancy made the reclining pose obvious. In this connection, this pose, in which the body is lying upright on its side, has aided in pro-viding the desired lifelikeness as well as the necessary ten-sion. The head has been tilted to the side with the eyes closed, i.e., consciously away from the viewer, and the hand of the free arm has been laid on the back of the head, as with a headache. In this way, the body language of this pose fundamentally differs from a lascivious provocation, in which the head would be coquettishly thrown back and the eyes would be enticingly trained on the viewer.

Two opinions that show very different ways of seeing things should be quoted at this point: "I cannot get the image of the pregnant woman out of my head. I am the mother of four children. However, I have first truly understood the miracle of pregnancy while in front of this woman's body."[13] Con-versely: "A plastinated pregnant woman in a pin-up pose strikes Kerstin as not being in very good taste."[14]

Examples of Expansion

The 'exploded skull' is the only example of an expanded dis-section known to traditional anatomy. In producing this spec-imen, all of the individual skull bones that have been pre-viously separated are shown as a kind of anatomical 'big bang' as if they were about to scatter in all directions. This principle, when applied to the entire body, led to *The Ex-ploded Body (Fig. 3)*. The next consideration was not to ex-pand the bodily fragments in all directions at the same time, but selectively in one of the possible directions. With bod-ies expanded longitudinally, expansion was upwards *(Fig. 4)*, with the *Organ Man* it was lateral *(Fig. 5)* and with the *Swordsman* it was towards the front and rear.

The Swordsman (Fig. 6)

Of the three gestalt plastinates expanded in a particular di-rection, the *Swordsman* has been made the most lifelike with its typical positioning. In order to facilitate the viewers' abil-ity to return the fragments to their original positions in the mind's eye, the right knee and elbow joints serve as pivots to open the front and back halves of the body. Dissection of a third layer of organs including the spinal column, kid-neys, heart and the insides of the head was dictated by the

didactic attempt to display the organs as separately as pos-sible, while at the same time showing the spinal cord from the front with the peripheral nerves emerging from it, es-pecially those of the arms and legs.

The Lassoer (Fig. 7)

With the *Lassoer*, several expansion techniques were com-bined with one another. To turn the head left, it was not sim-ply rotated, but was opened to offer a view inside of it. For this purpose, the head was opened with two cuts running parallel to the nose. The resulting fragments were then fanned out like an accordion. The view into the torso was made possible by swinging out the three segments of the torso. To make it easier for viewers to close it up again in the mind's eye, a strip of tissue from the chest and ab-dominal walls was left in place, as was a lower left-hand sec-tion of the torso. In order to show the large number of fin-ger and foot muscles with their marionette-like tendons, the tendons of both forearms and of the right lower leg were sep-arated from their attachments and then together with the venters of the muscles were twisted laterally in such a way that the elbow joints and the one knee joint could serve as pivots. The superficial and deeper muscles of the right thigh have been made simultaneously visible by separating the for-mer from their origins at the hip. This integrated superficial and deep dissection has been combined with a lateral shift of the left leg so that both the head of the femur that has been removed from the hip socket and the hipbone (ac-etabulum) itself can be viewed.

The Drawer Body (Fig. 8)

Traditional anatomical representations have given a false im-pression of the compactness of bodily interiors and close spatial relationships of the individual structures to one an-other. The interior of the body is a tightly packed, functional system of adjacent organs without fissures and interspaces. *The Drawer Body* presents just this compactness in the human body. In order not to be reminded of figures creat-ed by Dali, I have refrained from dissecting too many draw-ers, namely for the chest organs, the upper and lower ab-domen as well as the small pelvic cavity with the reproductive

Fig. 2: Reclining Pregnant Woman (1999)

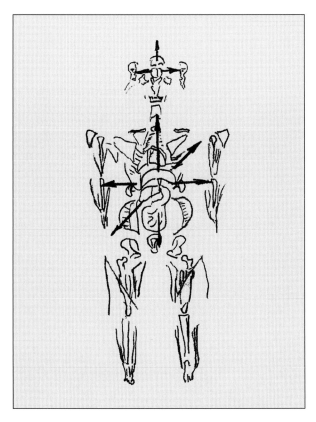

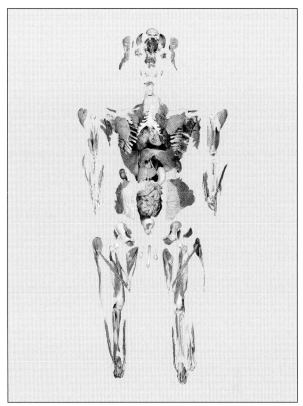

Fig. 3: The Exploded Body (1997)

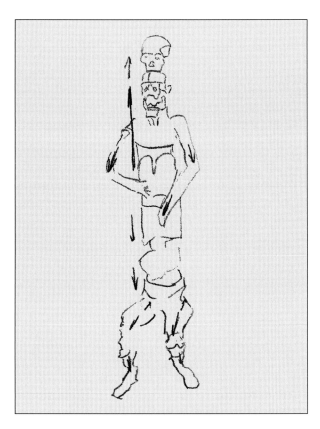

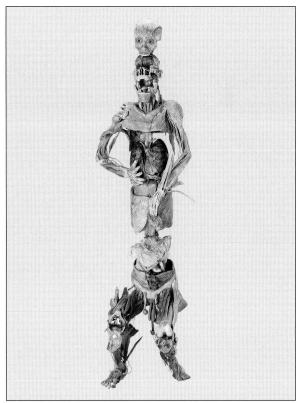

Fig. 4: The Longitudinally Expanded Body (1996)

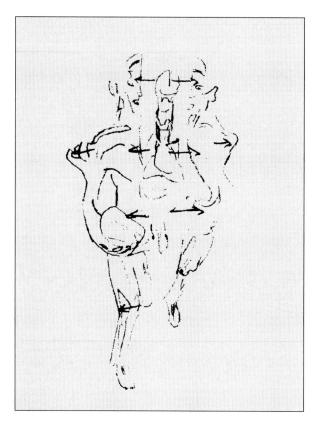

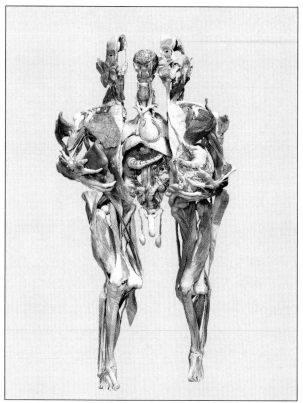

Fig. 5: The Organ Man (2000)

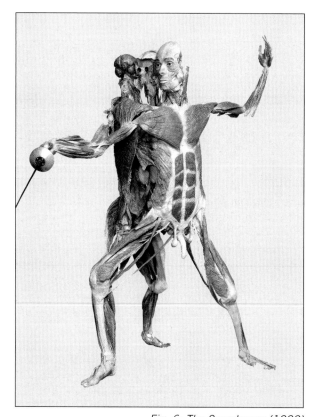

Fig. 6: The Swordsman (1999)

organs, although in my opinion this would be the most understandable way of presenting them. Instead, I have concentrated on one large window that contains two bodily doors to permit a more detailed view: one for the heart and another one for the glandular cavity, which I have combined with an opening in the stomach.

Lifelike Ambience

One of the essential design principles of the BODY WORLDS exhibition has been based on the conviction that a lifelike and attractive setting, e.g., one enlivened with plants and objects from daily life, would facilitate dealing with human specimens. As it is the anatomy of living human beings that interests us, it should be imparted in an environment which is familiar to visitors and in which they can feel comfortable. Just as the artists of the Renaissance placed their anatomical figures in lively landscapes adorned with plants and animals, I like to put the gestalt plastinates back into the living world from which they came. The gestalt plastinate posed as a *Chess Player* has been given a chess board, while the *Swordsman* wields a foil. Other gestalt plastinates have been placed in a garden setting complete with a brook. Lippert referred to the negative effects and atmosphere in the dissecting halls common at most universities. He wrote that ca-

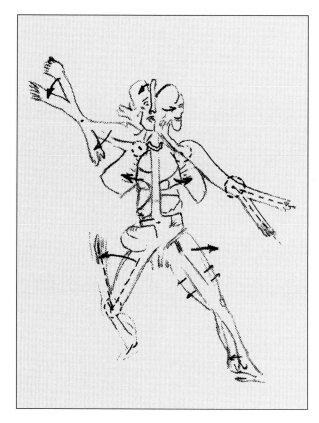

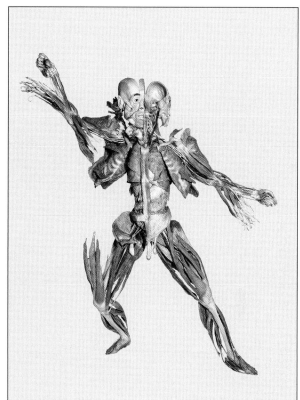

davers used for anatomical study were presented to students in an environment "that caused fear to arise instead of confidence." Students would thus become so accustomed to working in such an uninviting, sterile environment "that they would no longer be able to understand the shock of patients reacting to hospital facilities" (Lippert, cf. Ref. 2).

Creative and Aesthetic Anatomy

Anatomical artists of the Renaissance drew the human body just as they perceived it. In order to make clear the candid presentation of reality – an autopsy, i.e. seeing for oneself – they included light and shadow in their studies of dissections. They even painted a fly shown sitting on the cadaver in order to indicate the moment of viewing. Viewers were supposed to be able to rely on these pictures; nothing was generalised. The schematisation of anatomical drawings developed later. The anatomical artists preferred to draw musclemen in aesthetic and lively poses, frozen, so to speak, between life and decomposition. They were more interested in dissected bodies as form and relief than in the details of their insides. As the anatomical artists began to die off, dissection lost its creative and aesthetic components. Today creative anatomy is only practiced in such clinical areas as reconstructive surgery (e.g., of the face) and aesthetic surgery (also known as plastic surgery).

In the criticism quoted here that "dissections are not just carried out – as alleged – according to objective criteria [...], but in light of the effects,"[15] I see scant regard for the surroundings in which knowledge is imparted. An aesthetic anatomy atlas, endowed with an emotionally positive ambience, instead of an abhorrently disgusting book, a richly coloured gestalt plastinate instead of a grisly cadaver, will all help to make anatomy an emotionally positive experience. Why have schoolbooks and museums become so much better today than they were 20 years ago? Because they concentrate on presenting effects, colourful pictures and small stories that are easy to remember. Pedagogical research has proven that that which is presented in an emotionally positive way can be learned faster and is easier to remember. I gladly make use of effects when they facilitate learning. The church recognised this much earlier than pedagogical science. Whatever was supposed to stick in people's minds was gold-plated, optically refined in every imaginable way as well as put in monstrance's and publicly displayed, e.g., canonised relics of skeletons that were carried through Cologne during Corpus Christi processions.

What is the ethical-moral difference between the glass eye of a gestalt plastinate and the glass eye used in a reconstructive facial operation or between a gesture of movement in a gestalt plastinate and a breast enlargement in a living person. There is no reason not to let gestalt plastinates have the same things that we as the living take for granted. How-

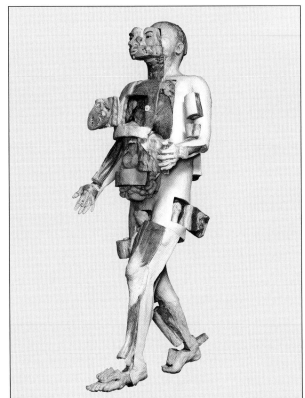

Fig. 8: The Drawer Body (1999)

ever, a plastination laboratory is not a beauty salon for bodily interiors as the plastination process when professionally applied only prevents cadavers from being turned into the usual gruesome anatomical apparitions. This becomes readily apparent on the one hand when we view aesthetic, transparent body slices that do not require any type of colouration,[16] while on the other hand when we see deformed foetuses that in no way have any aesthetic appeal on which to feast the eyes.

Design parameters rooted in us cannot be abandoned in reconstructing or positioning specimens if a gestalt plastinate is to be perceived as a whole. Apparently the design potential of our bodies is limited—beyond the given anatomical structure—by deeply rooted constraints about ourselves. Although I can create interspaces to facilitate viewing at will, nevertheless my imagination is subject to very limited tolerances should the body be regarded as a whole. It seems important for the symmetry of the design to be unblemished. An improperly positioned eye, a shoulder that has been removed, a missing extremity can degrade the design and make the body appear chopped up.

Gestalt and fragmented plastinates, made possible by solidifying soft tissue and organs, are capable of imparting the feeling that they are authentic representatives of very individual human lives better than the traditional, partial dissections or individual specimens preserved in formaldehyde or supine cadavers could ever do. This complies with my ob-

jective of making the physical body accessible without the gruesome aspects, which has never been seen in this way by human eyes before and which will positively amaze viewers acquiring knowledge in such an aesthetic-instructive manner that they will find the design compelling just because it is convincingly aesthetic and instructive but not morally offensive.

The Beauty of Bodily Interiors

Is the human body generally attractive? To answer this question, let us first turn to depictions of bodily exteriors in art history: Without doubt, the depictions and sculptures of the Renaissance in the 15th century only showed the beauty of the body. In contrast, the Expressionists of the 20th century also presented suffering and fragile, emaciated, sickly bodies. Neither group, neither the artists of the Renaissance nor the Expressionists, depicted the untruth. Both sides of the body, the attractive and the less attractive, are real – here a perfect, strapping body, there an old and feeble body or even a mutilated one. Both sides are also shown in the BODY WORLDS exhibition – here aesthetically posed plastinates, there severely deformed foetuses.

Sensitivity to the beauty of bodily exteriors has been acquired evolutionarily. In doing so, only those bodily attributes were able to gain acceptance as criteria for beauty that signaled health and vitality (bodily symmetry, muscle volume, smooth, soft skin, etc.) and that showed promise of being successfully passed on to the coming generations as each person's own genes. Conversely, evolution has not developed any visual preferences for non-visible bodily interiors; they can only be experienced indirectly (for example, exhalation, perspiration or excrement). Consequently, viewers do not find a diseased heart or a cirrhotic liver any less attractive than healthy organs. Pathologists can even rave about 'groovy' cancerous metastases in the liver. However, unpleasant visual appearances and indirect attributes of bodily exteriors can be so revolting that all we can do is flee.

In light of varying aesthetic assessments of bodily exteriors and interiors, aesthetic presentation of gestalt plastinates can be achieved by avoiding physical revulsion (no missing teeth, no empty eye sockets, no excrement, no offensive odours, etc.) and by taking general aesthetic principles into consideration, which are subject to our perceptions:

Designing aesthetic gestalt plastinates aids in overcoming taboos that are hostile to the body. It permits us to satisfy our deep curiosity about our own persons and to open our hearts to ourselves. Our bodies can thus undergo a change in meaning: from a grisly unknown quantity to an intimate main attraction of creation.

Culture and Bodies

The Aristotelian philosophy on the dualism of body and soul found its way into Christianity via the Roman Catholic world. As a consequence, the Christian religion at the same time became the most amicable of all towards anatomy. Modern anatomy was thus able to become established in Italy, the land of anatomy-friendly popes. Scholars of the Enlightenment learned to devote themselves to the body in a selectively anatomical way, free of any mystique or grief.

At the beginning of the 3rd millennium, technical progress has made it possible for us to gain new ways of viewing the human body thanks to internal imaging processes developed for medical purposes, such as computerised axial tomography (CAT), magnetic resonance processes or 3D ultrasound used with living human bodies. Whether the interiors of our bodies are made visible by means of the density distribution of our bodily fluids or body temperatures, we can experience our bodies in a new and visually different way each time.

With the aid of computerised image processing, it has become possible to manipulate such body-related data artificially. High-performance, three-dimensional computer-graphics software now allows us to create new bodily images in cyberspace that are capable of evoking emotional responses from viewers. In addition to this ability to be experienced graphically, plastination also permits us to make bodily interiors authentically perceptible in 3D. There are no new possibilities for depicting the body that are truly fascinating; it is only the body itself that is fascinating. Skeletons and mummies have now been joined by a new representative of post-mortem physical existence, namely gestalt plastinates. Body donors have bequeathed these bodies to future generations of their own free will as a kind of 'anatomical cultural heritage.' In this connection, a plastinator has assumed the role of a designer.

The debate surrounding the BODY WORLDS exhibition, and especially the gestalt plastinates shown therein, has been conducted very emotionally; nevertheless, it affects the culturally acquired appreciation of our physical being. The way in which we deal with our bodies has been culturally shaped by our traditions. How much nudity and how many bodily interiors can be shown publicly have been regulated and placed under taboo. It affects our cultural identity based on group acceptance. From totally veiled women in strict Islamic countries to uninhibited nudity during Carnival in Rio de Janeiro, we can find all of the nuances involved in dealing with naked skin. In Sudan a disputed nudity border in fact separates the veiled Islamic North from the more liberal, naked black-African South. Naturally, dealing with naked skin and with bodily interiors also differs accordingly. Because gestalt plastinates serve educational purposes, they may be more nude than naked skin, since in most cultures nudity is only acceptable in art and in medicine.

Whether nudity is placed under taboo is not only dependent on the location, but also on the purpose in mind. The public will generally be more apt to concede a nudity show to artists of nude paintings than to someone attending a striptease show. It is no different when physically showing bodily interiors. Medical students may look at bodily interiors. Artists may not necessarily be given this right, while laypersons will have to justify why they should not be considered voyeurs: "It is probably that weird, creepy feeling, a kind of voyeurism, that drives people in droves to the BODY WORLDS exhibition, this sensationalism, when a corpse stares into space."[17]

The cultural significance of plastination is threefold:

1. For the first time, people have been dispensing with traditional burials for the sake of educating the public about anatomy.
2. Showing attractive bodily interiors has made it possible to emancipate the body. Bodily interiors are no longer repressed by the immediate effects on our consciousness of the body. We can thus develop anatomical pride in our bodies. Numerous comments made by visitors to the exhibition have documented this: "I now understand myself better and am full of admiration for my body." "I am the mother of five children. Today I have better understood the life that I was able to give my children." "I stand in awe of the Creator, intend to stop smoking and to do more for and with my wonderful body. What a pity that I hadn't seen this much earlier."[18]

Gunther von Hagens and his plastination team positioning the mega plastinate "The Rearing Horse with Rider" (2000)

Characteristics	Beauty	Ugliness
Clarity	Clear, precise dissections	Offensive, imprecise dissections
Dynamics and functions	Lifelike poses, flexed muscles	Deathlike poses, motionlessness
Human forms	Preserved, perfect forms, sustained symmetry	Fragmentation of the body, mutilation, deformation
Harmonious distribution	Harmonious windows in the body	Disharmonious bodily openings
Dimensions and forms	Proportional structures	Disproportional structures
Frequency of presentation	Rare and surprising	Frequent, conventional, commonplace
Colours	Colourful	Grey and monotone
Odours	Odourless	Stinking, pungent
Blood	Solid or removed	Dripping

Tab. 1: Perceptions of the human body

3. With gestalt plastinates, death takes on a new dimension. It gains a certain proximity to reality, which imbues the image of death with a particular reconciliation. Comment of a body donor: "Since seeing the BODY WORLDS exhibition, I can await my death with absolute calmness."

A surprisingly large number of visitors to the BODY WORLDS exhibition – i.e., surprising for commentators from our society at large, the media, church representatives, anatomical professionals and politicians – has shown through high acceptance ratings that laypersons do not always fulfill prognostications about their anticipated interests.[19] It is just this fact that means democratisation for anatomy.

Five hundred years ago, anatomical artists bolted a skeleton together for the first time and made it a permanent part of society. Now at the turn of a new millennium, we are again experiencing the resurrection of excoriated bodies as gestalt plastinates. Plastination is thus able to satisfy the desire for immortality, which until now has been monopolised by the church, in a way that is commensurate with our times. Christian burial is quasi a tacit, accepted body donation for Christian funeral services. However, these rites emphasise the spirit and disregard the body. Although donating bodies for plastination will return meaning to the body, we still fear the death of the body, but do not fear the death of the soul.

We experience and exercise the daily death of the soul every time we go to sleep; we tend to repress the death of the body. However, the valuable and unique body that we groom and care for each day does not suddenly have to become something useless after death. Speaking from the standpoint of depth psychology, Susanne Sarial commented that "by walking a tightrope along the abyss of projections, von Hagens has succeeded in relaxing the repression mechanisms through the unexpected humour and the aesthetics of his specimens to such an extent that a small connecting tunnel is created to our primal sexual curiosity and to the closely-related, general cognitive interest and narcissism involved, which is uniquely our own."[20] This narcissism acts in two ways: On the one hand, in the narcissistic satisfaction that we will not someday simply disappear into thin air, but instead will achieve a certain immortality through plastination. On the other hand, this narcissistic satisfaction acts in a way that grants the body every imaginable form of attention and implies the thought of aesthetically designing the body according to our own values […] the body is not just a 'container of disgusting fluids,' not the Devil's playground for sins of the flesh, as propagated by Christianity, but a 'stylised cultural happening.'"[21] Redesigning the body through plastination strengthens this narcissism, which is diametrically opposed to the 'memento mori' of the Church and its teaching on "dust to dust."[22] In a period of redefining the value of the body, which is bound up with greater esteem, donating bodies for plastination seems to be a response to Christian negation of the body, which is no longer in tune with the times – a response that considers the body less as a "sack of maggots" (Luther) than as a marvel of creation.

Gestalt Plastinates between Art and Science

The public debate on the artful character of gestalt plastinates has demonstrated their communicative function, which has turned them into a cultural happening. These gestalt plastinates do not serve any artistic purpose; however, they can certainly comply with artistic criteria. Like works of art, well-executed gestalt plastinates possess aesthetic appeal and emotional worth. This is expressed, inter alia, in that half of all visitors have also come to the exhibition because of its aesthetic appeal. Nearly one-third of the visitors have assessed the exhibition as an art show.[23]

Here I personally accept the aspect of *Könnenskunst* (skilled art)[24] everywhere and have coined the term BODY WORLDS to preclude any misunderstandings. I define this as the aesthetic-instructive presentation of bodily interiors. Presentation is meant both in the sense of exhibiting art and of demonstrating artistic craftsmanship. The aesthetic-dynamic designs made possible for the body by plastination for anatomical purposes permits an emotionally experiential and visual anatomy instead of conventional academic and textbook anatomy. In addition to BODY WORLDS the term 'designing anatomy' suggests itself here; its results are gestalt plastinates. The aesthetic value of specimens is enhanced by the design of the respective plastinate and its ambience, just as a monstrance enhances the religious impact of a relic. The objective of designing anatomy is to impart anatomical-functional insights and thus does not transform anatomical specimens into objects of art. Hence, I do not produce chandeliers out of human bones[25] or make an arrangement of brains and testicles in order to designate it as a "masculine medallion."[26] I do not carve cauliflower out of brains and do not transform a penis with testicles into a revolver. As art and beauty are in the eyes of the beholders, gestalt plastinates are not turned into objects of art by my supposed "disposition as an artist." I am an inventor; for me the creativity of an artist is even more disciplined than the more objective thinking of a scientist. My model is an inventor like Edison, who realised his inventions during his lifetime and achieved financial success with them.

Gestalt plastinates are also not turned into art by my supposed outward appearance as an artist, which is often assumed because of my hat.[27] Like artists, inventors are individualists. And so were the anatomists of the Renaissance, when they wore hats while lecturing or dissecting within the circle of their colleagues. After I had familiarised myself with the works of Josef Beuys, I could say that we had much in common and neither of us was 'old hat.' The reason is that he is a model for me both because of his unconventional thinking and his efforts to conduct a regular discourse with laypersons about his work and theses. The difference between us lies in the fact that he sought the favour of laypersons but won the approval of intellectuals, while I have courted the favour of professional colleagues but have actually only gained the approval of laypersons.

What Is a Corpse

Given that the debate about when life begins and ends, and thus when a body begins and stops living, has been largely concluded, the definition of a living human being would not appear to be controversial. Yet as recently as 200 years ago, the beginning and end of a human life could only be established by observing a person's first and last breath. More precise definitions did not become available until our understanding of medicine began to grow. With the invention of the microscope, for instance, we could pinpoint the beginning of human life as the point at which an ovum is fertilised, and with the discovery of the circulatory system came the conviction that life ended when the heart stopped beating. Still more insight was provided by the inventions of electrocardiography (EKG) and electroencephalography (EEG), which can be used to detect electricity in the heart and brain and display this information in graphic form. Since then, a lack of any electrical activity in the heart and brain have marked the dividing line between life and death. From this time onward, a dead human body has been referred to as a corpse in casual speech. Developments in artificial respiration and in heart-lung machines have renewed the debate surrounding the end of life because these technologies have allowed the heart to continue beating even after brain death and have kept the rest of the organism 'alive' through artificial means. Brain death is now considered the critical factor in determining the 'true' time of death and is also used as a basis for organ transplants.

Conversely, in light of the recent controversy surrounding the legality of the BODY WORLDS exhibition, the question "What is a corpse?" would appear to be in need of further clarification. The *Kulturkampf* in the media has really been quite dramatic, revolving around the questions "morbid or educational?", "anatomical exhibition or illegal cemetery?", "bloodcurdling corpses or plastination?" The controversy surrounding the BODY WORLDS exhibition in Cologne came to a head when representatives of the Lutheran Church of Cologne demanded that municipal authorities prohibit the exhibition.[28] At the root of this public dispute are widely disparate views of what a corpse really is. The passions unleashed by this controversy have been further inflamed by the lack of uniformity in the use of various terms. The words 'corpse,' 'cadaver,' 'the deceased' and 'body,' for instance, are used as synonyms, although their distinctions should really be clearly defined (see below).

General encyclopedias, such as *Brockhaus* and *Meyer*, define a corpse as "the body of a human being after death" and "the human body after death."[29] A corpse is thus defined by the point at which its existence begins as such, i.e., at the moment of death. The *Deutsche Rechtslexikon* attempts a definition based on human form: "A corpse is body, recognisable in its entirety, of a human being who has died or was born dead (not miscarried). Its legal classification is disputed."[30] Both approaches, however, fail to answer the question "When does a corpse cease to be a corpse?" Until now this has not been a relevant question because the transformation from corpse to dust or ashes, whether in the grave or in the crematorium, has not been a visible process.

Jürgen Gaedke provides the most extensive definition of a corpse, describing it in terms of the end of its existence: "A cadaver is a lifeless human body until such time as the relationship between its individual components is eliminated either by the natural process of decomposition or by another equivalent method of destruction (such as cremation). This also includes human bodies that have been dissected for scientific purposes, provided there exists the intent of interring individual parts together in the traditional manner." [31]

What is striking about this definition is that Gaedke uses the term 'cadaver' and limits the definition by emphasising 'decomposition' and the 'intent' to inter. According to this, gestalt plastinates should not be viewed as corpses subject to burial because they neither decompose nor [must they be] are they buried. Nevertheless, this definition and its application to plastinates are not clear enough to distinguish satisfactorily between bodies that decompose and the various forms of non-decomposing corpses. What is needed is a system for comparing and contrasting the various forms of a corpse's existence.

In the following I have attempted to organise the terms generally used in this context, emphasise their unique qualities and summaries the results in a diagram (see Figure 1).

All Corpses Are Bodies, But not All Bodies Are Corpses

When using the term 'bodies,' it is important to draw an existential difference between a 'corpse,' which exists in reality, and the 'deceased,' which does not. How else, as Wetz astutely observes, could we refer to the "corpse of the deceased?" [32] The term 'corpse' describes the dead, lifeless body; conversely, the term 'deceased' conjures up an image of the formerly living individual, who continues to exist in the memory of the survivors. A special category of bodies is represented by brain-dead organ donors, whose corpses are used for transplants and are by definition dead due to the irreversible loss of brain function (brain death). The remaining organs, however, are artificially kept 'alive' until they are extracted for transplants.

For the purpose of creating a system for categorising the various forms of post-mortem corporeal existence, I shall use the term 'corpse' exclusively, for the sake of clarity. I have classified corpses according to their relative permanence, which reflects their material composition, or, to be more precise, the amounts of water and preservatives that they contain. This results in three major classifications of corpses, namely the corpse itself (a corpse in a state of decomposition), wet cadavers and dry cadavers.

1. A corpse is a dead human body that will decompose and/or dry out and shrink when exposed to the air. A corpse is generally buried and is a dead body in a legal sense. When used colloquially, the term 'dead body' generally refers to a corpse as defined here. Corpses are necessarily of interest to the authorities, as decomposition makes corpses a potential source of disease. For this reason, lawmakers have required that corpses be buried within 36 to 96 hours. [33] Because the identity of a corpse is generally known, and there are usually friends and family, they are typically designated as corpses to be mourned, i.e., as objects of individual grief and individual human pathos. An unclaimed body is an anonymous corpse whose identity is not known. This category also includes waterlogged corpses. Corpses not only serve as objects of mourning: pathological and/or medical dissection of corpses is also useful for determining the legal cause of death of the individual.

2. Wet cadavers have been preserved in fluid and consequently do not decompose, although they will dry out when exposed to air, shrinking significantly and turning brown or black. In order to preserve these cadavers, they must be protected from drying out and shrinking, either by keeping them wet (i.e. in liquid or in an atmosphere of at least 100% humidity) or preserved using a process that dries them without shrinkage. Because preservation renders them non-infectious, they do not generally represent a health problem to the authorities. Wet cadavers include those used for anatomical study and what are known as 'bog bodies.' Because they are exposed to the air when dissected by students, cadavers used for anatomical study tend to exhibit significant signs of drying out and shrinkage within three to four months, even if kept meticulously moist. After use in the dissection lab, these cadavers are generally buried. To supplement their museums, anatomical institutes typically transform entire cadavers or parts of cadavers into permanent specimens or skeletons. Bog bodies are preserved by the tannic acid found in bogs and must likewise be stored under moist conditions to prevent massive shrinkage. The identity of these corpses is not generally known because they usually are already hundreds of years old by the time they are found. A special class of wet cadavers is glacier bodies (such as 'Ötzi'). Decomposition of these corpses has been arrested not by chemical processes, but rather by permafrost. A frozen body is subject to a continuous, albeit slow drying process (whereby moisture is lost due to sublimation), and as a result will either be a wet or a dry cadaver, depending on the amount of time it remains frozen. If a frozen body thaws prematurely, those parts of it that have not been dried out will be subject to decomposition.

3. Finally we have what are known as 'dry cadavers,' which, due to continuous dehydration, neither decompose nor shrink significantly. Artificial dry cadavers are filled with preservatives or other materials such as natural resins

that prevent moisture from entering the body and introducing bacteria. Mummies are typical examples of dry cadavers. The mortal remains of the pharaohs were worshipped as visible, physical manifestations of the hereafter. Today, as relics from a former time, mummies remind us of our own mortality.

For a better overview see Table 2, which summarises the most important criteria described above.

The above classification scheme organises corpses according to the degree to which they decompose, which, in turn, is dictated by their physical state and/or the manner in which they are preserved. In this light, plastinates and skeletons would have to be classified as dry cadavers. Both retain the recognisable form of the human body; both are preserved in a dry state and do not decompose. The dehydration process leaves no visible signs of shrinkage in either one. All three representatives of this category are incomplete: mummies lack internal organs, plastinates generally lack skin and skeletons lack muscles, organs and skin. Skeletons can, accordingly, be viewed as bone skeletons, mummies as combined skin and bone skeletons (without organs) and plastinates as combined organ, muscle and bone skeletons (without skin).

Figure 2 classifies human body parts, organs and tissue remains as fresh, dead and preserved specimens. This chart provides an overview of the wide variety of permanent anatomical specimens.

Should Plastinates Be Buried?

Church leaders were not the only ones calling for mandatory burial of plastinates – lawyers were as well. According to Thiele, "state burial regulations expressly require across-the-board, mandatory burial," especially if both "corpses used for anatomical study" as well as "severed body parts" are subject to mandatory burial.[34] Such legal requirements are "based on considerations of custom and the ethical treatment of deceased individuals as dictated by local culture." The "exempt status accorded to corpses used for anatomical study … merely postpones obligatory burial."

In the *Rheinische Merkur*, von Campenhausen argues, "that Germany legally mandates the burial of all corpses without exception is an expression of human custom and of respect for the dignity of the deceased even after death." In the case of corpses used for anatomy, "burial is merely postponed. The same is true for organ transplants, where the donated organ is later buried with the recipient of that organ. There are no exceptions to the legal requirement of dignified burial."[35]

Ernst Benda makes three arguments against the BODY WORLDS exhibition: 1) by invoking mandatory burial, 2) by citing the provision stated in article 13 of the Burial Reg-

ulations of Baden-Württemberg ("Corpses may not be put on public display") and 3) by summarising as follows: "Transforming a corpse into a permanent exhibition piece is prohibited by law…" The responsibility for the error, he feels, lies "where the transformation process took place," i.e., at the Institute of Plastination.[36]

Plastination has now existed for 23 years, and this is the first time that anyone has demanded that plastinates be buried. This demand would presumably never have arisen were it not for the fact that the BODY WORLDS exhibition shows entire bodies that have been dissected and plastinated. Mandatory burial, however, makes very little sense given that burial has never been demanded for the permanent anatomical specimens on display in countless museums. Permanent displays of human specimens have been shown in public anatomical collections throughout Europe ever since the Renaissance; such exhibits are regularly expanded with new specimens. In Germany, for instance, we have the Museum of Pathology and Anatomy in the Charité (the Virchow Museum) in Berlin; Austria has the Federal Museum of Pathology and Anatomy in the Vienna *Narrenturm*; and Switzerland has the Anatomical Museum of Basel.

Most of Europe's anatomical museums are located in Italy, where public anatomy was established during the Renaissance at the anatomical theatres of Padua and Bologna. These include the Museum of Veterinary Medicine, Pathology and Teratology in Ozzano (Emilia), the *Museo di Antropologia Criminale* in Turin, the *Museo di Anatomia Patologica* in Rome, the *Museo di Anatomia e Istologia Patologica* in Bologna, the *Museo del Istituto di Anatomia Umana e Patologia* in Pavia, the *Museo Anatomico* in Modena and the *Museo Anatomico* in Naples. Some of these museums also include entire dissected bodies in their anatomical collections. Have the critics overlooked these? Or should these specimens be judged differently due to their age and historical significance?

It is also striking that it is not anatomists who are demanding that plastinates be buried, but rather a handful of lawyers and theologians who are unfamiliar with both the complex reality of anatomical dissection *(Figure 2)* as well as anatomical practices around the world. If the demand for burial is psychologically rooted in the use of entire bodies for exhibits, then the following questions would be justified and are not meant at all cynically: How large may an anatomical specimen be before it is no longer considered a corpse and thus subject to mandatory burial? If the corpse were perhaps quartered or cut into sections, its components physically separated and, for instance, shipped in separate crates, would it no longer be considered a corpse? How many body parts would have to be separated? How many tissue groups (skin, muscles, organs or entire extremities) would have to be dissected and removed? The example of a dismembered corpse has taught us that a corpse does not necessarily have to be contiguous. A murderer cannot argue that there is no corpse, and thus no victim, because he dismembered it. This means

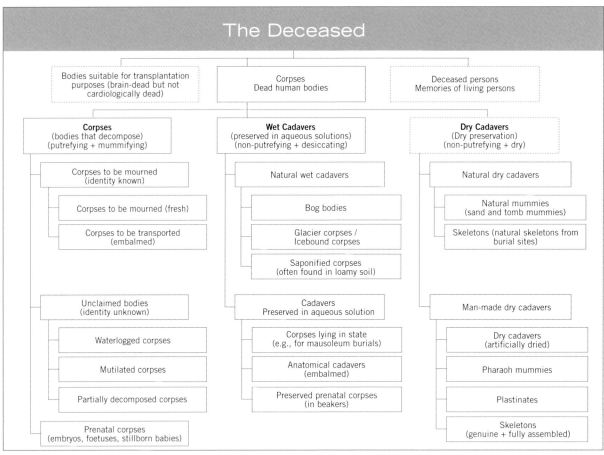

Fig. 1: The deceased, cadavers and corpses (© Gunther von Hagens)

that the criterion that a body be complete cannot be an appropriate one for evaluating plastinates. More important is the distinction between corpses or body parts that can decompose and permanently preserved specimens that cannot, regardless of the degree of completeness. This places the focus of the dispute not on the issue of whether plastinates are corpses, but rather on the question of how to handle corpses and body parts.

Characteristics of Plastinates

The intention of the following discussion is to elaborate on the characteristic qualities of plastinates as compared to other corpses. To aid in this discussion, I will classify these qualities into the following categories: the purpose for which the plastinate is intended, how it is administered and the qualitative changes that have taken place. The purpose of a plastinate can be deduced from the reasons for which a corpse has been donated: to further research, instruction and public education. The administrative act consists of accepting the corpse for plastination, which includes both receipt of the signed donation form as well as ensuring anonymity. The qualitative change involved be-

gins with the first step in the plastination process, i.e., in transforming the corpse into a pre-plastinate. This is done by injecting the necessary chemicals into the vascular system, followed (in the case of cross-sectional plastination) by freezing and impregnating the specimen with polymer. The transformation from pre-plastination to plastination (both for whole-body and partial specimens) is accomplished by curing the polymer in each cell within the specimen. Creating anonymity is important for disassociating the corpse from the specimen because this is the only way of ensuring that the plastinate will not be an object of reverence. In other words, anonymity ends the feeling of individual, emotional attachment to the deceased. The anonymity of plastinates also makes sense because it is in line with anatomical traditions and distinguishes plastinates from corpses to be mourned as well as from mummies and relics of known individuals. For this reason, non-anonymous plastinates must be exceptions to the rule and must be thoroughly justified. It goes without saying that each human specimen continues to have human qualities. That also means that plastinates may only be used in accordance with the last will and testament of the donor, i.e., exclusively for the purposes of research, instruction and public education. Plastinates that can no longer be used

Quality of Corpses	Cadavers	Wet Cadavers	Dry Cadavers
Decomposing	+	-	-
Desiccating	+	+	-
Water content	+	+	-
Preservatives	-	+	+
Whole-body specimens	Corpses to be mourned Unclaimed bodies	Bog bodies, Glacier corpses, Anatomical cadavers	Mummies, Skeletons, Gestalt plastinates
Partial-body specimens	Decomposing body parts	Dissections preserved in aqueous solution	Relics Plastinated organs

Tab. 2: Criteria for distinguishing corpses

are disposed of appropriately, i.e., they are cremated separately and not included with household waste – just as any other human remains would be.

Intended Purposes

Because of the purpose intended for a plastinate, we can perform procedures on it that would not be possible on a corpse intended for mourning. Dismemberment, for instance, is only possible because a plastinate is intended for anatomical study. In his definition of a corpse, Gaedke addresses the subject of intended purpose as follows: "A cadaver is a lifeless human body …, provided there exists the intent of interring individual parts together in the traditional manner."[37] Regarding those individuals who determine how to dispose of a body, he writes, "The survivors of the deceased are generally those who exercise the right of disposition… This right of disposition may also carry with it the authority to photograph or even dissect the corpse."[38] Whole-body religious artifacts such as the mummies of Capuchin monks and the ornaments fashioned from bones that adorn certain churches serve a ritualistic purpose that precludes burial. The state's respect for this purpose is what has allowed these relics to survive in crypts and churches to this day, whereas the purpose of mummies and relics used to serve ritualistic purposes today largely revolves around tourism. A publicly displayed plastinate serves the purpose of public education. As recently as one hundred years ago, processions of relics drew hundreds of thousands of people to Cologne; plastinates are now doing the same thing. They are a modern way of combining curiosity with a thirst for knowledge and the desire for a deeper understanding of the shocks to which the flesh is heir.

Consent of the Individual Donors and the Survivors

Acquiring the consent of individuals to use their corpses for the purposes of research, instruction and public education is a development that did not arise until the past few decades. In the late Middle Ages, when the science of anatomy was in its infancy, anatomical studies were preferably performed on the corpses of executed criminals. Unclaimed corpses were later used for anatomical instruction. This practice was codified in the Prussian directives of 1889, which stated that unclaimed corpses were to be taken to institutes of anatomy. Most institutes of anatomy in Germany were still operating according to this regulation as recently as the 1980s. The moral standard underlying this regulation is the conviction that anatomical study was no less honorable than burial. In addition, this legislation was also based on the conviction that the state was obliged to offset the shortage of corpses that could be used for the purposes of research, education and training. In the early years of scientific anatomical study, this shortage had led to grave robbing and even murder.[39] After 1945, an additional regulation went into effect in Germany, allowing individuals to establish in their wills whether their bodies could be used for anatomical study after their deaths. This made it possible for institutes of anatomy to meet their needs for corpses largely through voluntary donations. Contrary to the conviction of many laymen, no one has ever been paid to donate their bodies to anatomical science. When death benefits in Germany sank from DM 7,500 to DM 2,100 today, the number of "testamentary donors" rose so sharply and so suddenly that donations specified in last wills and testaments became the sole source of corpses for anatomical institutes. Since that time, in fact, these institutes have generally been covering their annual demand for donated corpses within the first few months of each year and do not accept donations for the remainder of the year. As a result of this development, the consent of the individual for using his or her corpse for anatomical study is often required in

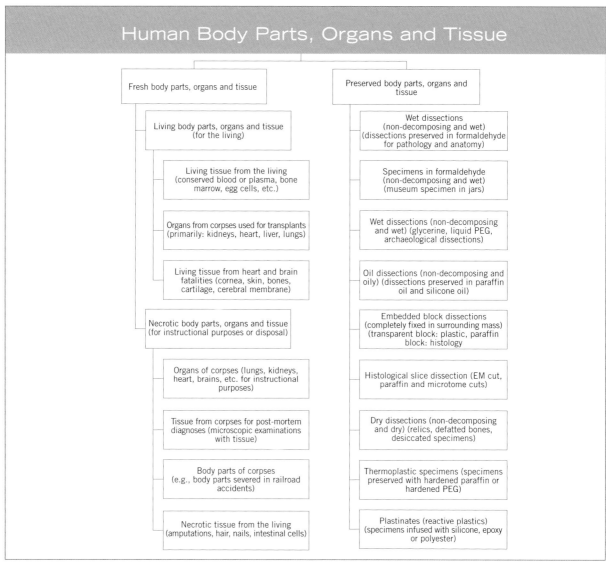

Human Body Parts, Organs and Tissue

- Fresh body parts, organs and tissue
  - Living body parts, organs and tissue (for the living)
    - Living tissue from the living (conserved blood or plasma, bone marrow, egg cells, etc.)
    - Organs from corpses used for transplants (primarily: kidneys, heart, liver, lungs)
    - Living tissue from heart and brain fatalities (cornea, skin, bones, cartilage, cerebral membrane)
  - Necrotic body parts, organs and tissue (for instructional purposes or disposal)
    - Organs of corpses (lungs, kidneys, heart, brains, etc. for instructional purposes)
    - Tissue from corpses for post-mortem diagnoses (microscopic examinations with tissue)
    - Body parts of corpses (e.g., body parts severed in railroad accidents)
    - Necrotic tissue from the living (amputations, hair, nails, intestinal cells)
- Preserved body parts, organs and tissue
  - Wet dissections (non-decomposing and wet) (dissections preserved in formaldehyde for pathology and anatomy)
  - Specimens in formaldehyde (non-decomposing and wet) (museum specimen in jars)
  - Wet dissections (non-decomposing and wet) (glycerine, liquid PEG, archaeological dissections)
  - Oil dissections (non-decomposing and oily) (dissections preserved in paraffin oil and silicone oil)
  - Embedded block dissections (completely fixed in surrounding mass) (transparent block: plastic, paraffin block: histology
  - Histological slice dissection (EM cut, paraffin and microtome cuts)
  - Dry dissections (non-decomposing and dry) (relics, defatted bones, desiccated specimens)
  - Thermoplastic specimens (specimens preserved with hardened paraffin or hardened PEG)
  - Plastinates (reactive plastics) (specimens infused with silicone, epoxy or polyester)

Fig. 2: Taxonomy of human body parts, organs and tissue

Germany, even though it is not legally mandated. Introducing a formal donation policy for plastination reflects the conviction that the values of a democratic society, i.e., that individuals have as much discretion over the use of their bodies as possible, dictate that a public exhibition can only be based on a conscious decision on the part of donors.

In practice, the general requirement that the use of a corpse be determined by a conscious decision on the part of the individual has not been applied uniformly. Unlike dissections carried out for the purpose of anatomical study, autopsies, for instance, do not require any consent from either the deceased or his or her survivors; in fact, objections raised by these individuals have no effect whatsoever. After nearly every fatal traffic accident, for instance, the district attorney's office orders an autopsy to determine who was at fault in the accident. No one takes offence to this practice. The permanent specimens on display at anatomical museums stem almost exclusively from individuals who were never asked for their consent.

On the other hand, both the right to a burial as well as morally or legally mandated burials do, in fact, apply to mummies, skeletons, bone fragments and even the smallest anatomical specimens if they have inherent moral or religious meaning. In cultures where burial is dictated by religion, all that is required to create unifying, collective mourning among members of that society is a shared sense of connectedness to the discovered mortal remains (mostly bones) of their ancestors.

An example of this is the enforceable right of burial claimed by the native inhabitants of the United States and Australia. The US Congress passed two laws in 1989/90 (the "National Museum of the American Indian Act" and the "Native American Grave Protection and Repatriation Act") stipulating that the anonymous remains of Native American ancestors must be turned over to Indian groups for burial upon reasonable application. The "Aboriginal and Torres Strait Islander Heritage Protection Law" was passed in 1987 in the Australian state of Victoria, granting aboriginal peoples the right to have the bones discovered at archaeological sites repatriated – a right that led to the reburial of fossilised skeletal remains that were up to ten thousand years old.[40] There is also an example of this in Germany: In 1989, German television's Channel 3 (SWF) showed a short film about the National Socialist origins of histological specimens at German universities.[41] The administration at the University of Heidelberg disposed of the problem "in a manner suitable to corpses": The glass slides were crushed and buried in the Heidelberg cemetery. This example demonstrates that the size of the tissue sample and the manner of preservation does not necessarily have any effect on burial decisions, even if the amount of tissue involved is only one-fiftieth the size of a drop of blood and 70% of it consists of the plastic with which it is saturated between the two slides. Conversely, there is no burial requirement for the hundreds of thousands of anonymous skeletons found in secondary schools, theatres, crypts and private collections around the world. The same is true of the mummies of pharaohs and of corpses preserved in glaciers ('Ötzi').

Anonymity

Because students are expected to be interested in anatomical structures and not in the fate of the deceased, anonymity has had a long tradition in the study of anatomy. Anonymity neutralises the individual, emotional bonds to the deceased and underscores the change in meaning of a corpse from an object of mourning to one of study. Lippert questions this practice when he writes, "The corpse is a tool for training students in all aspects of dehumanisation because the patient is just a number with no name or feelings. … Its only need is for a little moisture … Early on in the course, the students bombard the instructor with questions about the corpse's origins, his or her occupation and medical history. This personal interest fades away over the course of the semester. The corpse becomes an object that students can use to earn academic credit."[42]

When evaluating the pros and cons, I would be in favour of providing anatomy students with information relevant to the physical state of the corpse, such as the age and cause of death. For plastinates, however, there are serious reasons for consistency when it comes to maintaining anonymity. On the one hand, anonymity provides an additional means of disassociating the plastinate from the corpse. On the other hand, it eliminates any legal problems that might result from the survivors' permanent rights of disposition. Experience has shown, unfortunately, that wills stipulating an individual's desire to donate his or her body for anatomical study often unleash family conflicts, some of which have occasionally even made it to court. As a result, revealing the identity of a plastinate will always remain an exception to the rule.

Tradition and Dignity

Religious sentiments and concepts of morality, tradition and dignity have played a crucial role in shaping the way in which we handle corpses, and have given rise to a wide variety of burial rites in individual societies. In Tibet, for instance, religious conviction mandates that corpses be fed to vultures, and in India the ashes of the deceased are scattered in the Ganges. Gaedke considers this issue as follows: "All rights of disposition of the deceased are subject to the limitations stipulated in article 138 of the German Civil Code (BGB), in which neither the views of the deceased nor those of the survivors are sufficient in their own right for settling issues of human rights and human dignity, i.e., for determining whether the use of a corpse violates standards of reverence or moral codes. Disposal of a corpse must instead represent an objective violation of moral codes or standards of reverence."[43] In other words, applying traditional moral concepts requires a majority consensus within society.

What this means for the BODY WORLDS exhibition is that the debate about human dignity and displaying plastinates in public cannot be separated from the traditions and moral convictions of the general populace. Particularly in a democracy, citizens should indeed have the right to contribute to a decision regarding what is and what is not considered dignified, and what can and cannot be displayed – especially when these considerations do not limit the rights of others. For me, the dignity of the deceased, which has been debated again and again in the context of the BODY WORLDS exhibition, is a sense of traditional values that resides in the mind of the mourner. It is not an inherent aspect of the decaying corpse, the urn full of ashes or a plastinate. As such, the visible corpse is, sociologically speaking, a 'souvenir of mourning' that keeps the memory alive but that gradually loses meaning as the corpse decomposes; if embalmed it becomes an 'icon of mourning' (as in the cases of Lenin's and Mao's tombs). Benda also indicates that the corpse itself has nothing to do with dignity when he argues that "even a dead human being retains his or her dignity. It is not, however, the body that deserves respect, but rather that which, depending upon one's religious convictions, is not mortal and has been released from the body."[44] Benda thus denies the dignity of the body, conferring dignity instead upon the soul of the deceased, which is certainly an alternative for those who believe in the existence of the soul.

Legal Recognition of Mandatory Burial

The right to burial is not a Federal issue in Germany; this means that the Institute for Plastination in Heidelberg is subject to the burial laws of the state of Baden-Württemberg.[45] All of the paragraphs in which the word 'corpse' is used, however, make it very clear that the law is referring only to corpses that decompose, i.e. 'cadavers' to be either buried or used for anatomical study. A 'corpse in a legal sense' is therefore a cadaver.

Article 27 of the Burial Regulations of Baden-Württemberg states that "all corpses must be taken to a public morgue, if available, within 36 hours of death, but not before a death certificate has been issued," and article 37 states that "every corpse must be buried." As discussed above, the unclear definition of a corpse makes it impossible to classify a plastinate as a corpse. This is also reflected in the practices associated with human corpses around the world, which require mandatory burial only for those corpses that fit the above definition of 'cadaver' and not for all corpses. If this were not the case, there would be no publicly accessible mausoleums and museums would not be able to display mummies, skeletal remains, corpses that have been preserved in moors or corpses that have been artificially preserved. The argument that corpses used for anatomical study are subject to mandatory, albeit delayed, burial[46] is irrelevant in this context, because the length of the delay has not been defined and has been applied arbitrarily depending on a given corpse's usefulness; in other words, the amount of time that plastinates may be exhibited does not have to be limited. Burial laws do not regulate wet cadavers, such as those found in moors and glaciers, any more than they do dry cadavers, i.e., mummies, skeletons and plastinates. If dry cadavers were corpses as defined by law, then skeletons and mummies would be subject to the same regulations as cadavers (corpses slated for burial), i.e., they would need proper documentation when transported across international borders and would have to be sealed in zinc coffins. Similarly, burial laws have no provisions for pathological and medical dissections; these are regulated by individual state laws. Small corpses (such as embryos and foetuses) and partial specimens of the human body are subject only to laws governing perishable specimens. Accordingly, article 30.2 of the Burial Regulations of Baden-Württemberg states as follows: "Severed body parts and miscarried fetuses not intended for burial are to be disposed of in a hygienic manner and in accordance with traditional sensitivities."

Violations of the law are addressed in article 49 of the Burial Regulations, but this does not apply to permanent specimens. Here the law states that "Anyone who intentionally or negligently disposes of or denies burial to a corpse shall be held in violation of the law." Yet just as burial laws do not regulate the disposal of permanent specimens, they likewise do not prohibit the process of converting corpses or body parts that would otherwise decompose into permanently preserved specimens. There are therefore no governmental regulations prohibiting the process of converting a corpse into a wet or dry cadaver. This has made it possible to convert corpses into skeletons for the past four hundred years. Just as corpses converted into skeletons are not subject to burial requirements, mandatory burial likewise does not apply to corpses made into plastinates.

Transformation from a Corpse to a Plastinate

In summary, a donated body is converted from a corpse to a dry cadaver following the death of the donor. By the time that a corpse must be buried by law, it has already been transformed into a pre-plastinate by eliminating the risk of decomposition, by establishing the intended purpose of the plastinate and by ensuring the anonymity of the donor. At this point the corpse has lost all of those properties that would ordinarily make it subject to mandatory burial. The specimen can no longer decompose once it has been preserved by the plastination process. Initial preservation is complete within 8 to 24 hours of receiving the corpse. Dissection and the subsequent plastination process take between two weeks and a year; they are complete, i.e., the pre-plastinate is transformed into a plastinate, after the polymer within the specimen (roughly 70% polymer) has cured.

For mandatory burial to be waived, it is critical that the dead human body no longer be capable of decomposing and thus of spreading disease, that the intended purpose of the specimen be anatomical study and public education (as is the case for whole-body specimens displayed in museums) and that the donor remain anonymous.

Customs Regulations

In conclusion, I would like to say a few words about applicable customs regulations for shipping human anatomical specimens, including plastinates, across international borders. Contrary to claims in a few sensationalist reports in the media[47] such shipments are subject to clear and unmistakable regulations. Plastinates are "items in anatomical collections," and as such are shipped under Customs Classification Code 97050000.[48] This customs code encompasses "zoological, botanical, mineralogical or anatomical collections or items in such collections." Because customs law has not yet been thoroughly internationalised, a case may well arise in that a plastinate may be shipped in Germany as an item in an anatomical collection, and in Mexico as a 'medical specimen' (used for organs intended for transplantation). Shipping plastinated specimens abroad has also at times meant providing explanations, describing "items in an anatomical collection," for instance, as "human and animal specimens in the broadest sense; not intended for human consumption." Customs technicalities in other countries have also at times required that plastinates be described as 'human by-products' (used to describe human ashes), and 'medications' in the broadest sense (used for stored blood, even though plastinates have been preserved as solid, permanent specimens).

Some argue that preserved, whole-body specimens must be declared as corpses so that they can be regulated with appropriate documentation, thereby ensuring that the specimens do not become the victims of foul play.[49] This argument would appear out of touch with reality. The state never checks to make sure that corpses have really been buried, nor is there any need for this. Murderers, after all, are concerned with getting rid of corpses, not with keeping them, and preserving the bodies would certainly not serve this end. There are no known cases where bodies have been disposed of by preserving them for the purpose of anatomical study.

References

[1] Joseph Hyrtl: "Handbuch der praktischen Zergliederungskunst" ["Handbook of Practical Dissection"], 1860.

[2] Herbert Lippert, Anatomist in Hanover: "Die Inhumanität der Medizin und die Anatomie" ["The Inhumanity of Medicine and Anatomy"], Deutsches Ärzteblatt, issues 36–39, vol. 81, 1984.

[3] Gunther v. Hagens: German Patent: No. 27 10 147 (1978); US Patents: Nos. 4,205,059 (1981), 4,244,992 (1981), 4,278,701 (1982), 9,320,157, inter alia; G. v. H., K. Tiedemann, W. Kriz: "The Current Potential of Plastination", review article, Anat Embryol (1987) 175: pp. 411–421.

[4] KÖRPERWELTEN exhibition catalogue, 9th printing, 2000, p. 15, Figs. 8 & 9: Two ca. 200 year-old anatomical, whole-body specimens.

[5] U. Bleyl, "Und was wir sind, das werdet ihr sein. Zur Würde und Unantastbarkeit der plastinierten Toten." ["And what we are, you will also be – On the dignity and inviolability of plastinated corpses"], editorial in: Der Pathologe, 19, (1998), pp. 171–175.

[6] S. Sarial, "KÖRPERWELTEN – Ein Ausstellungserfolg aus psychoanalytischer Sicht" ["A successful exhibition from a psycho-analytical standpoint"], Zeitschrift für Klassische Psychoanalyse, 16 (1998), 1.

[7] Mitteilungen der Anatomischen Gesellschaft [Announcements of the Anatomical Society]: 2, 98, Institute for Anatomy at the Medical University of Lübeck (publ.), 23538 Lübeck

[8] H. Eggebrecht: "Mehr als Haut und Knochen" ["More than just skin and bones"], Märkische Oderzeitung, 14/2/1998.

[9] B. Brock: Symposium on the KÖRPERWELTEN exhibition, paper presented in Gürzenich, Cologne, on 8/3/200.

[10] E. J. Wormer: "Faszination Plastination" ["Fascination Plastination"], in: Orthopädie & Rheuma, 1/4/2000.

[11] U. Clewing: "Makabres Arrangement zum Anfassen" ["Macabre arrangement to be touched"], in: tageszeitung (TAZ) on 8/10/1998.

[12] A. Krzok: "... werde ich auferweckt in einem neuen Körper?" ["... will I be resurrected in a new body?"], in: Der Weg [weekly Lutheran magazine] on 14/12/97.

[13] Entry in the guest book of the KÖRPERWELTEN exhibition in Cologne, Heumarkt (12/2–31/7/2000).

[14] R. Willemsen: "Wir sind wieder wir" ["We are ourselves again"], in: Süddt. Zeitung Magazin, 9/6/2000; (Kerstin was a participant in the TV reality show Big Brother).

[15] W. Wortreng, M. Meili: "Sind die Augen wirklich echt?" ["Are the eyes really genuine?"], in: Die Weltwoche on 9/23/1999.

[16] G. von Hagens, K. Tiedemann, R. Romrell, M. Ross: Coloured Atlas of Slice Anatomy, Stuttgart, Schwer: 1991.

[17] I. Vorpahl: "Die Toten nicht der Neugier preisgeben" ["Don't let the dead become victims of curiosity"], in: Rhein-Neckar-Zeitung on 18/11/1997, quoted there: Prof. Klaus Unsicker.

[18] Entries in the guest book of the KÖRPERWELTEN exhibition.

[19] E.-D. Lantermann, "Körperwelten im Spiegel der Besucher" ["KÖRPERWELTEN as Seen by Visitors"], in: KÖRPERWELTEN exhibition catalogue, (same as Ref. 4), pp. 211–218.

[20] Sarial (same as Ref. 6).

[21] Ibid.

[22] Ibid.

[23] Cf. Lantermann (same as Ref. 19).

[24] B. Tag, Symposium on the KÖRPERWELTEN exhibition, paper presented in Gürzenich, Cologne, 8/3/200.

[25] See Ref. 4, p. 18, Fig. 16: "Tschechische Kirche mit Kronleuchter aus Knochen" ["Czech church with chandelier made of bones"].

26 M. Brendel: "Von den Heimlichkeiten der Natur" ["On the Secrets of Nature"], Berlin: 1998, p. 17, Fig. 7.

27 U. Fischer: "Wenn der Tod zum Spektakel wird" ["When Death Goes on Display"], KÖRPERWELTEN exhibition catalogue, (same as Ref. 4), pp. 233–237.

28 I. Müller-Münch: "Gruseln und Kommerz – ein Graus für die Geistlichkeit" ["Grisliness and Business – A Horror for the Clergy"], in: Frankfurter Rundschau, 1/26/2000; M. Stankowski: "Hauptsache schön:" ["Beauty is the main thing:"], in: Kölner Woche, 2/10/2000.

29 Brockhaus-Enzyklopädie [Brockhaus Encyclopaedia],19th printing, Mannheim, 1990; Meyers Enzyklopädisches Lexikon [Meyer's Encyclopaedic Lexicon], Mannheim, 1971.

30 Deutsches Rechtslexikon [German Legal Lexicon], Munich, 1992, p. 885.

31 J. Gaedke: Handbuch des Friedhofs- und Bestattungsrechts [Handbook on Cemetery and Interment Law], Cologne, Munich, 7th Printing, 1997, pp. 119–122.

32 F. J. Wetz, "Die Würde des Menschen" ["The Dignity of Man"], KÖRPERWELTEN exhibition catalogue, (same as Ref. 4), p. 246. Cf. also his article in this volume.

33 Municipal Ordinances on Cemeteries and Corpses (Interment Laws) for Baden-Württemberg (7/21/1970, 7/23/1993, 2/7/1994).

34 C. Thiele: "Plastinierte Körperwelten, Bestattungszwang und Menschwürde" ["Plastinated KÖRPERWELTEN, Mandatory Interment and the Dignity of Man"], in: Neue Zeitschrift für Verwaltungsrecht (NVwZ), 4, 2000, pp. 405-408.

35 A. von Campenhausen, "Körperwelten verletzt das deutsche Recht" ["KÖRPERWELTEN violates German law"], Rheinischer Merkur, 3/10/ 2000.

36 E. Benda: Von der Vergänglichkeit zum Plastinat. Zur »Körperwelten«-Ausstellung in Köln, in: Neue Juristische Wochenschrift (NJW), 2000, 24, pp. 1769–1771.

37 Gaedke: (same as Ref. 5).

38 Ibid.

39 J. Suttcliffe, N. Duin: "The Resurrection Men", in: A History of Medicine, New York, 1992.

40 K. Wiltschke-Schrotta: "Human remains on display – curatorial und cultural concerns", Tod und Museum. Paper presented in the Pastoralzentrum Bolzano on 6/3/2000.

41 Television broadcast: German Channel 3 (Südwest 3), 3/20/1989, Reihe Abenteuer Wissenschaft ["Science as an Adventure Series"], "Nazi Specimens–Specimens of Nazi Victims as Instructional Material…".

42 Lippert: (same as Ref. 2).

43 Gaedke: (same as Ref. 5).

44 Benda: (same as Ref. 36).

45 See Ref. 31.

46 Cf. Thiele: (same as Ref. 34).

47 Television broadcast: Channel 3SAT, 1/5/2000, "Die Leichenshow" ["The Cadaver Show"].

48 Warenverzeichnis für die Außenhandelsstatistik [List of goods for statistics on exports], 1998 Edition of the Federal Bureau of Statistics.

49 "Die Leichenshow" ["The Cadaver Show"] (same as Ref. 47).

Charleen M. Moore and C. Mackenzie Brown

Gunther von Hagens and BODY WORLDS
Part 1: The Anatomist as Prosektor and Proplastiker

Recent calls to reintegrate the sciences and humanities are challenged by the contemporary work of anatomist Gunther von Hagens and his *BODY WORLDS* exhibits of plastinated cadavers. The anatomical quest to understand our physical interior has long been in tension both with aesthetic ideals and religious sensitivities regarding the metaphysical significance of the human body. Part I of this two-part Historical Note examines tensions epitomised by Goethe's figures of the prosektor and proplastiker. The former, driven by scientific curiosity, is willing to destroy, even desecrate, the human form to obtain knowledge. The latter demurs at such mutilation of our physical body, wondrous even in death – seeking instead to rejoin what the prosektor has pulled apart, to restore human dignity. In the confrontation between prosektor and proplastiker, roles disturbingly fused in the person of von Hagens himself, questions arise regarding the authenticity of models as well as the appropriate recipients of such mediated yet intimate anatomical knowledge. Part II will focus on religious perspectives on the human body, variously interpreted as God's handiwork, habitation for the soul, and vehicle of resurrection. Consideration also is given to the role of anatomist as priest, prophet and Promethean creator, roles self-consciously embraced by von Hagens. *Anat Rec (Part B: New Anat) 276B:8–14, 2004.* © 2004 Wiley-Liss, Inc.

KEY WORDS: anatomy; art; anatomical exhibitions; medical education; education; plastination; religion

The Conflict of Two Cultures Continues

The intersection between anatomy, art and religion has frequently resulted in a conflict between different views of the human body and of what it means to be human. The anatomist historically has stood at this intersection, often striving to integrate quite disparate roles – scientist, artist/dramatist, and priest/prophet. We explore this conflict and the roles of the anatomist, using Gunther von Hagens and his *BODY WORLDS* exhibitions of plastinated cadavers as the contemporary embodiment of this controversy. Von Hagens' work challenges the recent call to reintegrate the sciences and the humanities. Proponents of such integration decry the lack of insight into human creativity on the part of those who would regard the two enterprises as tightly boundaried or opposed. Stephen Jay Gould, for example, in one of his last books, *crossing over: where art and science meet*, coauthored with the artist Rosamond Wolff Purcell, notes:

"Small minds have usually viewed Science and Art as adversarial – at least from Goethe's complaints about narrow-minded naturalists who would not take his anatomical and geological works seriously because he maintained a day job as a poet to C.P. Snow's identification and lament about two noncommunicating cultures... But the unifying modes and themes of human creativity surely transcend the admitted differences of subject matter in these two realms of greatest interest and occasional (even frequent) triumph of both heart and mind." (Gould and Purcell 2000, p. 13).

Of direct relevance to our present topic are some of the anatomical illustrations in the book, including a beautiful photograph of the original skeletons juxtaposed with wax models of craniopagus Siamese twins. Perhaps even more unsettling are the photographs in an older Gould and Purcell collaboration, *Finders, Keepers,* of Fredrik Ruysch's remarkable late 17th century preparations of infant heads, variously adorned with frilly lace, preserved as wet specimens in shimmering glass jars (Purcell and Gould 1992, 25-27).

Confined to the printed page, Gould and Purcell's integration of anatomy and art remains safely abstract. However, in the exhibit halls of Japan, Germany, Austria, Belgium, South Korea, and England where *BODY WORLDS* has appeared, such integration can be as explosive as some of the "exploded view" plastinated cadavers themselves (Fig. 1).

For human anatomy, unlike other areas of scientific investigation, both explores and proposes who and what we humans are in the most intimate of ways, using methods and means that often disturb deep-seated aesthetic, moral and religious sensitivities.

Interestingly, Goethe himself, while lamenting the separation of the two cultures, was keenly aware of the deep tension between the scientific quest for certain kinds of knowledge – specifically that of our physical interior – and the humanistic imperative to preserve human dignity. These two ideals collide in the figures of the Prosektor and the Proplastiker in Goethe's story of the young and ambivalent anatomy student Wilhelm Meister. Confronted in the dissecting room with the arm of a young woman who, despairing of love, had drowned herself, Wilhelm visualises the lovely limb encircling the neck of her lover. The image overwhelms the aspiring anatomist: "The repugnance to deform still further the splendid production of Nature was at variance with the demand which man, thirsting for knowledge, has to make on himself" (Goethe 1947, 234). A visiting Proplastiker (plastic anatomist) sees Wilhelm's hesitation and suggests an alternative to anatomical destruction: modeling in wax and other materials. The visitor explains "that building up teaches more than tearing down, joining together more than separating, making what is dead alive, more than making what is already dead still further dead." (Goethe 1947, p. 236). Taking Wilhelm aside, the Proplastiker contrasts the gruesome work of the Prosektor (dissector) with his own beautiful plastic transformations (compare Figs. 2 and 3), and reveals to Wilhelm a replica of the bony skeleton of the young woman's arm. The Proplastiker sees his art as an imitation of divine creativity – even of divine restitution. Claiming his work represents a first step "to put life again into the rattle of the dead bones," the Proplastiker refers to Ezekiel's vision of the Lord's resurrecting the dead, noting how the prophet "had first to see his valley of bones gather together and join themselves in this manner before the limbs were able to move, the arms to touch and the feet to raise themselves upright." (Goethe 1947, p. 236).

> Human anatomy, unlike other areas of scientific investigation, both explores and proposes who and what we humans are in the most intimate of ways, using methods and means that often disturb deep-seated aesthetic, moral and religious sensitivities.

In Gunther von Hagens we see a fusion of Goethe's scientific Prosektor and humanistic Proplastiker, with his various pedagogical, aesthetic and spiritual – or quasi-spiritual – agendas. As Prosektor, von Hagens is universally acknowledged as unexcelled. As Proplastiker, he is most engaging and, at the same time, most enraging. To gain insight into the controversies surrounding the creator of *BODY WORLDS*, we must first examine in historical perspective the diverse views of the human body that such a fusion brings and the tensions it generates, focusing on the interpretive viewpoints of the anatomist as scientist, artist/dramatist and priest/prophet.

Scientific Views of the Human Body – The Anatomist as Prosector

There are many ways to glean scientific knowledge about the body other than peering into dead ones – for instance, one could observe how the living body reacts to being needed or burned, as with the Chinese practices of acupuncture and moxibustion (Kuriyama 1999, p. 118; Porter

Fig. 1: Gunther von Hagens' late 20th century plastinated whole body in an "exploded-view" presentation. The intent stated by von Hagens is to show relationships between various structures of the body. This and other whole-body plastinates of von Hagens have been publicly displayed in Europe and Asia in a travelling exhibition called BODY WORLDS. Copyright: Gunther von Hagens, Institut für Plastination, Heidelberg, Germany (www.bodyworlds.com).

1997, pp. 7-8). Such practices are often sustained by and implicated in traditional notions of the body as a mirror or microcosmic reflection of cosmic forms and forces. The reasons that anatomy became the privileged mode of exploring the body in the West during and after the Renaissance are naturally complex, but the development is related at least in part to the view of the body, not as a microcosm, but as a beautifully and intricately designed machine. Thus, the Western anatomist is interested in the way the body moves and functions, its structure and parts, and the means to repair the delicate mechanisms when they no longer perform properly. It seems hardly an accident that the meticulously rendered drawings of flayed bodies and articulated skeletons found in anatomical textbooks from the Renaissance on are frequently in motion, the reanimations depicting the abilities of this incredible machine.

The basic assumption of anatomy, then, is that "the dead shall teach the living," an anonymous motto that in one form or another adorns the entrances to many anatomy laboratories in medical schools today. But who is to have access to knowledge about the internal workings of the complex machinery that is our body? In other words, to whom are the dead to teach? Only those who, by academic or professional qualifications are allowed to pass through the dissecting room doors of our teaching institutions – that is, only research scientists and future health care providers? Or is such knowledge to be given to the general public, regardless of educational qualifications and motivations?

The scientist is often portrayed as being unconcerned about the lay public's view of her work. And yet, in order to make informed decisions from voting for funding for scientific research to participating in their own health care, the general public needs to be informed about their bodies and the effects various insults can have. At the same time, few members of the general public would want to access such intimate knowledge in the traditional venue of the dissecting room. While authenticity of presentation is an important desideratum for the public, perhaps even more so is concern for a non-repelling and aesthetic presentation. Thus, in general, models have been used to disseminate knowledge to the lay audience while actual specimens have been reserved for the education of a privileged few.

For teaching future scientists and health care professionals, the use of models alone – at least until the very recent possibility of using virtual cadavers – has often been regarded as less than ideal (Aziz et al., 2002). At the same time, anatomy instructors have viewed preserved specimens as valuable adjuncts in assisting students to interpret their own dissections from Vesalius' articulated skeleton overlooking the dissecting table, down to the present use of

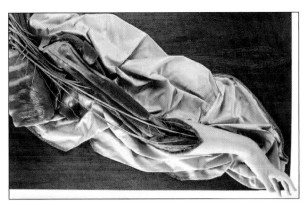

Fig. 2: Eighteenth century wax model of a woman's arm showing the magnificence of human anatomy without the horror inherent in human dissections, illustrative of the Proplastiker's "beautiful transformations." In "La Specola" Museum in Florence. Photo credit: Saulo Bambi, Museo di Storia Naturale, Sezione Zoological "La Specola."

plastinated sections of muscle and bone in the anatomy laboratories along side the whole cadaver. Development of ways to preserve soft tissues began with the early preparations of anatomists such as Frederik Ruysch (1638-1731) and Honoré Fragonard (1732-1799), using desiccation, special varnishes or injection of vessels with embalming fluids. Such specimens increasingly have come into use, providing an authenticity missing in models that tend to be idealised representations and lack the unique and anomalous features of real cadavers.

Preservation methods have reached their acme in the plastination techniques used by Gunther von Hagens. In the late 1970s, von Hagens developed a procedure for preserving whole bodies and individual organs using curable polymers. These chemicals replace the water and lipids in the body and are subsequently hardened. As von Hagens notes: "When I replace this water by a permanent polymer like silicon rubber, then there is no decay anymore. Certainly, those specimens will hold longer than the mummies from the pharaohs" (quoted on National Public Radio, *All Things Considered* 2001, p. 11).

While stopping decomposition in a most convincing manner, plastination involves such extensive chemical manipulation of the corpse that some have asked how natural or authentic such specimens are. José Van Dijck, for one, questions whether plastination provides for any more "scientific transparent truth" than any other mechanical mediation that seems, naively in her opinion, to remove "the contamination of human intervention" (van Dijck 2001, p. 117). She notes that some of the classical, eighteenth century wax models are more life-like than von Hagens' specimens. Whatever the philosophical merits of such questions, from a practical standpoint, are the plastinates sufficiently "real" to serve the pedagogical needs of the professional anatomist? And does the chemical manip-

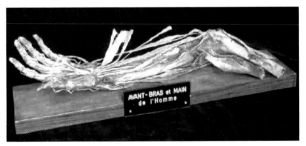

Fig. 3: Honoré Fragonard's eighteenth century dissection of a preserved arm, suggestive of the Prosektor's "gruesome works." In the musée Fragonard de l'École nationale vétérinaire d'Alfort. The arm was preserved through desiccation and a varnish coating developed by Fragonard, whose exact formula has not been discovered. Copyright: C. Degueurce, musée Fragonard, France.

ulation preserve enough of the authentic while removing the horror, smell and repugnance that is part of the dissecting room ambience to still attract and fascinate, as well as educate, the general public? A tentative answer is that they certainly are real enough to provoke the controversies that mere models would not, as well as to attract over eleven million visitors to the exhibits to date. Indeed, no other exhibition has presented the internal structure of the human body to as many individuals from the general population or even the scientific community.

One of us (CMM) saw *BODY WORLDS* while attending a scientific meeting in Vienna in 1999. First learning about von Hagens and *BODY WORLDS* when he came to her meeting to promote the exhibit, she became interested in seeing the exhibit for its educational components. Immediately striking to her while walking through the exhibit were the technically exquisite dissections. The spinal nerves of the "chess player," the whole skin dissection "carried" by one of the cadavers and the disembodied plastinated vessels of a hand were among the most impressive. The scientific information provided with the dissections illustrating the growth of a human foetus and the malformations that can occur, as well as the comparisons of healthy and diseased lungs and normal and cirrhotic livers that show the effects of smoking and drinking clearly served an educational function. Similarly, the displays of bodies showing pacemakers, hip replacements and artificial knees allowed the public to see more directly advances that have been made in medical care.

The circus element, however, that von Hagens encouraged when he escorted guests dressed as space creatures through the exhibit with TV cameras in tow, made the author uneasy with this so-called "edutainment." And yet as an anatomist/dramatist von Hagens is not dissimilar from the anatomists in the anatomical theatres of 16th century Bologna and Padua who sold admission tickets to their dissections, not only to medical and art students, but to the non-professional public as well who looked on the procedure as entertainment as much as education. In fact, on November 20, 2002, von Hagens recently reintroduced the public autopsy, dissecting an elderly male's preserved body before a London audience of five hundred people.

No other exhibition has presented the internal structure of the human body to as many individuals from the general population or even the scientific community.

The admission charge was £ 12. Unlike some other visitors to von Hagens' *BODY WORLDS* exhibit, though, the author was not particularly disturbed by the artistic poses in which many of the whole-body plastinates were presented, seeing the life-like postures as splendidly illustrating the workings of the body engaged in everyday activities. Von Hagens also follows in a long history of representing cadavers in artistic displays to help allay the sense of disgust, among whatever other motives may have been at work. While he often denies that he is an artist when arguing that his dissections have been made purely to educate, he does accept the notion that the plastinates themselves are "anatomy art" (von Hagens 2000, p. 34).

Artistic Views of the Human Body – The Anatomist as Proplastiker

According to the early 16th century anatomist Berengario de Carpi, the flayed figures like those appearing in his *Commentaria* (1521) were to assist physicians in their surgical incisions and artists in their rendering of the human body. Leonardo, Michelangelo and other artists dissected cadavers to learn the internal structure, especially the musculature and skeletal scaffolding. Such artistic representations of the human body have presupposed a conception of personhood as willful agent, making choices that muscles, especially, translate into action. As Kuriyama notes with regard to Western anatomical and artistic traditions: "Interest in the muscularity of the body was inseparable from a preoccupation with the agency of the self" (Kuriyama 1999, p. 144). Muscles are thus, par excellence, the mediating organ between the autonomous will of the person and the actions of his or her body. Renaissance anatomical artists celebrated this mediating function by displaying the flayed and dissected human body in their sketches, paintings, engravings and sculpture, not as lifeless forms, but as robust and vivid "musclemen," anticipating the Proplastiker's ideals of "making what is dead alive."

Throughout the 17-18th centuries, dissections and even dried specimens were rare, so artists (the real proplastikers) such as Zumbo, Ecolli, Susini and the Manzolinis created exceptionally realistic wax models of dissected human specimens. The models preserved the information from these dissections, and more often than not, appeared as pieces of art in themselves. Body casts from cadavers represented another way to present anatomical models in an aesthetically pleasing mode. William Hunter (1718-1783), who taught artists as well as medical students, did not actually display the body of the criminal he flayed, but instead made a cast of the smuggler recast of which now resides in the Royal Academy of Arts, London posed in the position of the Dying Gaul, a sculpture in the Capitoline Museum in Rome (Figs. 4 and 5). In the process, Hunter significantly blurred the line between anatomical and artistic goals.

Anatomy art – from sketch to sculpture – began as an imitation of body and life. In Hunter's "Smugglerius," ana-

Fig. 4: A 3rd century B.C.E. Roman copy of an earlier Greek work from Pergamon, in the Capitoline Museum, Rome. Known as The Dying Gaul, this sculpture served as a model for William Hunter's anatomy art two millennia later. Photo credit: E. Lessing, Art Resource, NY.

tomical representation imitates not just life but also art. With the development of better ways to preserve body specimens, the potential for anatomical presentation to effect a radical "reversal of art-representing-body into body-representing-art" (in the words of van Dijck, 2001, 116) was soon realised. Thus Ruysch created his fantastic dioramas made entirely of human material (Fig. 6). Honoré Fragonard, the cousin of the celebrated painter of the same name, posed one of his whole-body dissections as Samson holding the jaw of an ass (Fig. 7).

This radical reversal runs rampant in the plastinates of von Hagens. The positions of his figures "are at least as determined by artistic conventions as by scientific insights" (van Dijck 2001, p. 114). Van Dijck notes the resemblance between The Chess Player and Rodin's The Thinker, and between The Runner (Fig. 8), with its flying skin and muscle flaps, with "futurist art in which movement and speed were represented in new ways" (van Dijck 2001, p. 114). Among the most fascinating of von Hagens' reversals is his flayed plastinate bearing his own skin, an imitation of a similar figure in Juan Valverde's Historia de la composición del cuerpo humano, first published in 1556 and later reproduced in Anotomia del corpo humano... (1559). These two figures will be discussed in more detail in Part II.

Much of the controversy surrounding BODY WORLDS, at least in Europe, has focused on the dual purpose of the exhibits proposed by von Hagens – education and entertainment (in his word, "edutainment") – as well as on his own description of his work as "anatomical art." In part, the contentious nature of such a dual purpose historically reflects the separation of art and anatomical science that began by the end of the 18th century. The cavorting cadavers striding through exotic settings or coyly self-exhibiting their own dissected viscera so typical of 16th-18th centu-

ry anatomical illustrations gradually gave way to a stark realism that eschewed imaginative embellishment, a development nicely documented in the recent Dream Anatomy exhibit at the National Library of Medicine. Thus, according to one reviewer of this exhibit, Gautier

> **Much of the controversy surrounding BODY WORLDS has focused on the dual purpose of the exhibits proposed by von Hagens as well as on his own description of his work as "anatomical art."**

d'Agoty's 1773 mezzotint of a pregnant woman écorché, her musculature and developing foetus "daintly on display," is credibly "Dream Anatomy's most mesmerising image, one in which art and science seem to merge effortlessly" (Smith 2003, p. 829).

The wedge splitting medical schools and art academies soon made such fusions of art and science untenable – at least until von Hagens entered the anatomical scene in the late 20th century with his artistically posed plastinates, including his own version of a flayed pregnant woman with exposed foetus.

The reconvergence of science and art in von Hagens' work, however, is not in itself the most fundamental source of controversy. On one hand, it is the use of the particular medium, human organic material, that lifts the issues surrounding the aesthetic display of plastinates far beyond the tensions or conflicts between scientific and artistic prerogatives. On the other, as is evident in the context of the public autopsy where the artistic element was absent, something akin to sacerdotal privilege is at stake. When the British Inspector of Anatomy Dr. Jeremy Metters

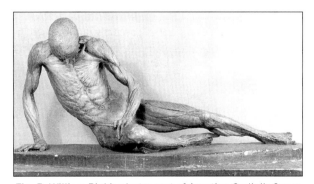

Fig. 5: William Pink's plaster cast of Agostino Carlini's Smugglerius (1775), prepared from the body of a criminal hung for smuggling, flayed by William Hunter and arranged to imitate the position of The Dying Gaul. In the Royal Academy of Arts, London. W. Pink after Agostino Carlini RA, 1834. Copyright: Royal Academy of Arts, London.

Fig. 6: Etching of Fredrik Ruysch's late 17th to early 18th century diorama constructed entirely of foetal and adult human body parts. From National Library of Medicine exhibition, Dream Anatomy, 2002. Image taken from Alle de ontleed- genees- en heelkindige werken...van Fredrik Ruysch.... Vol. 3. (Amsterdam, 1744). Courtesy of the National Library of Medicine.

Fig. 8: Gunther von Hagens' plastinated whole body in the form of a runner with the muscles stripped from their origins and extended from the bone in a spirit of movement illustrating the muscles as mediators of the autonomous will as often portrayed by Renaissance anatomical artists. Copyright: Gunther von Hagens, Institut für Plastination, Heidelberg, Germany (www.bodyworlds.com).

threatened von Hagens with arrest for violating a 1984 Anatomy Act by failing to have a post-mortem license, the latter protested that he was breaking no laws. Metter's attitude, von Hagens added, "reminds me of the times when clergymen reserved the right to read the Bible" (quoted in Record Searchlight 2002, Nov. 21). The body is indeed a sacred text of sorts, with metaphysical attributes of its own that have been read in a variety of ways. Like the Bible, the body is subject to a variety of religious and philosophical interpretations, each with its own healing or therapeutic prescriptions and prophetic visions of the good life – both now and in post-mortem existence. In Part 2 we shall explore the priestly, prophetic and Promethean roles of the anatomist in interpreting the humanistic and spiritual meaning of the human body.

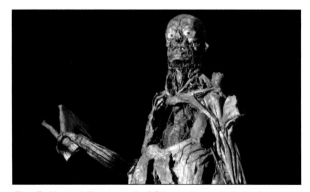

Fig. 7: Honoré Fragonard's 18th century whole body preservation representing Samson holding the jawbone of an ass as described in Judges 15:14-16, in the musée Fragonard de l'École nationale vétérinaire d'Alfort. Copyright: C. Degueurce, musée Fragonard, France.

Charleen M. Moore and C. Mackenzie Brown

Gunther von Hagens and BODY WORLDS
Part 2: The Anatomist as Priest and Prophet

Part 1 of this two-part series highlighted tensions between the anatomical quest for scientific knowledge about the human interior and artistic representations of the anatomised body, contrasting the roles of Goethe's scientific Prosektor and humanistic Proplastiker – roles disturbingly fused in Gunther von Hagens. Part 2 first examines religious interpretations of the human body that fuel the tensions manifest in anatomy art. The body in Western cultures is a sacred text amenable to interpretation as handiwork of God, habitation for the soul and vehicle for resurrection. As handiwork of God the body beckons the anatomist's scalpel, helping establish dissection as the hallmark of Western medicine. The body as divinely designed machine encompasses the idea of an indwelling soul expressing its will in actions mediated through the intricate network of muscles – an understanding reflected in the oft occurring muscle men of early anatomical textbooks. Interconnections of body and soul in medieval somatic spirituality are examined with reference to ideas of resurrection and their impact on anatomical illustration. Part 2 concludes with consideration of von Hagens as priest and prophet, culminating in the Promethean impulse that recognises not God but ourselves as proper owners and moulders of our destiny, embodied in the plastinator's visionary quest to create the superhuman. *Anat Rec (Part B: New Anat) 277B:14–20, 2004.* © 2004 Wiley-Liss, Inc.

KEY WORDS: anatomy; art; anatomical exhibitions; medical education; education; plastination; religion

Introduction

In part 1 of this two-part series (Moore and Brown 2004), we examined tensions between the anatomical quest for scientific knowledge about the human interior and artistic representations of the anatomised body, contrasting the roles of Goethe's scientific *Prosektor* and humanistic *Proplastiker*. We saw how the contemporary German anatomist Gunther von Hagens attempts to fuse these roles as creator of the anatomy art that is displayed around the world in his *BODY WORLDS* exhibitions. In Part 2 we turn to the religious interpretations of the human body that have fuelled the tensions manifest in von Hagens' anatomy art and examine his additional – and more disturbing – roles as secular priest and prophet.

Religious Views of the Human Body: The Anatomist as Priest

Human organic material, however modified, is not simply matter; the human body is not simply an object. Culture in general, and the religious imagination in particular, endow our physical embodiment with metaphysical attributes that both reflect and create an understanding of personal, social, and spiritual identity – including one's final destiny. Within the religious perspectives of the Western monotheistic traditions, three such metaphysical attributes of the body are especially relevant to the anatomical enterprise: the body as God's handiwork, as habitation for the indwelling spirit or soul, and as the vehicle for bodily resurrection.

> **Human organic material, however modified, is not simply matter; the human body is not simply an object.**

The notion of the body as divinely designed, according to Shigehisa Kuriyama, was fundamental to the anatomical quest in the West in the monotheistic traditions, a quest largely absent in India and China. "The evidence linking early anatomical inquiry with the belief in a preconceived plan is abundant and explicit.... The presumption of divine design was absolutely critical to the enterprise of anatomy in just this way. It promised that a cadaver held more than frightening, repugnant gore – that its contents displayed visible meaning" (Kuriyama 1999, p. 124–125). Vesalius was merely standing in a long line of Western anatomical Galenic tradition when in the preface to his *De Fabrica* he explained the inclusion of illustrations as providing – for those unable or too delicate in nature to attend dissections of the human body – the opportunity to attain some degree of anatomical knowledge of humankind that "attests the wisdom (if anything does) of the infinite Creator of things" (Vesalius 2003).

Islamic scholars made similar claims for anatomy; thus the acclaimed Aristotelian philosopher Ibn Rushd (Averroës) proclaimed: "He who does dissection increases his faith in Allah" (quoted in Bittar 1955, p. 357). Somewhat more mystically, the Sufi theologian al-Ghazzali effused: "The science of the structure of the body is called anatomy: it is a great science, but most men are heedless of it. If any studies it, it is only for the purpose of acquiring skill in medicine, and not for the sake of becoming acquainted with the perfection of the power of God. The knowledge of the anatomy is the means by which we become acquainted with the animal life; by means of knowledge of animal life, we may acquire a knowledge of the heart and the knowledge of the heart is a key to the knowledge of God" (quoted in Bakar 1999, p. 195).

Within the Christian tradition, the implications of anatomy for religious thought are made explicit by the 19th century natural theologian Thomas Dick: "Adorable Creator! With what wonderful art hast thou formed us! Though the heavens did not exist to proclaim thy glory – though there were no created being upon earth but myself, my own body might suffice to convince me that thou art a God of unlimited power and infinite goodness" (Dick 1860, p. 111). Dick goes on to emphasise the machine-like quality of the body: "In short, when we consider, that health depends upon such a numerous assemblage of moving organs, and that a single spring out of action might derange the whole machine, and put a stop to all its complicated movements, can we refrain from joining with the Psalmist in his pious exclamation and grateful resolution, 'How precious are thy wonderful contrivances concerning me, O God! How great is the sum of them! I will praise thee; for I am fearfully and wonderfully made. Marvellous are thy works, and that my soul knoweth right well'" (Dick 1860, p. 112).

Dick, in a manner reminiscent of al-Ghazzali, also pleas eloquently for Christians to engage in anatomical study: "Yea, how many are there who consider themselves as standing high in the ranks of the Christian profession, who affect to look down with a certain degree of contempt on the study of the material works of God, as if it were too gross a subject for their spiritual attainments! They profess to trace the wisdom of God in the Scriptures, and to feel gratitude for his pardoning mercy; but they seldom feel that gratitude which they ought to do for those admirable arrangements in their own bodies.... They leave it to the genius of infidel philosophers to trace the articulation of the bones, the branching of the veins and arteries.... But surely such astonishing displays of the wisdom and benignity of the Most High, as creation exhibits, were never intended to be treated by his intelligent offspring with apathy or indifference..." (Dick 1860, p. 45).

Von Hagens is hardly a natural theologian in the mould of a Thomas Dick. Yet he clearly understands the fascination and awe before "the admirable arrangements" within our body. And von Hagens shares with Vesalius the desire to provide those without opportunity or desire to attend a dissection the opportunity to see the wondrous working of the human body, although he sees the design aspect as the product of natural processes that plastination can illuminate: "Plastination... represents a shift in value from a useless corpse to a plastinated specimen, which is useful, aesthetically instructive and produced by nature" (von Hagens 2000, p. 37). He says of visitors to BODY WORLDS: "They will marvel at the diversity and beauty of human nature" (von Hagens, n.d., "Theme of the Exhibition").

The second metaphysical attribute of the body as habitation for the indwelling spirit or soul, defined as an autonomous agent, may well have played a critical role in the development of scientific anatomy in the West. In Kuriyama's analysis, from Galen on the view of the soul as "a self possessing muscular will" (Kuriyama 1999, p. 146) was essential in focusing attention on the body's musculature: "The life of a person cannot be told, therefore, merely in terms of natural processes like digestion and the pulsing of arteries. Beyond processes that happen of themselves, there are also the actions willed by the soul and carried out by these instruments called muscles" (Kuriyama 1999, p. 145).

The muscles "display the soul's decisions" (Kuriyama 1999, p. 151). Such a viewpoint, for Kuriyama, is reflected in the many flayed muscle men or écorchés that are a major motif in Renaissance anatomy books—and perhaps not coincidentally, the covers of von Hagens' BODY WORLDS catalogues.

It is not just the muscles, however, that may reflect the state of the soul, especially when the body-soul relationship is viewed outside the perspective of radical Cartesian dualism. Just as contemporary liberal theology rejects a mind-body dualism, so in late mediaeval thinking, the body was seen as an integral aspect of the human being, both before and after death. Katherine Park convincingly documents the "intensely somatic nature of Christian spirituality in the late Middle Ages" (Park 1994, p. 22). Such spirituality was manifested in the importance accorded to body relics, the penitential use of the body, mutilation and dismemberment as a means of spiritual attainment, as well as in the quest to discern the marks of a sanctified life in the physical body of the truly pious.

Thus, the desire to confirm the physical but interior marks of sanctity—such as the scars of divine love on the heart and other organs—inspired the opening and dismembering of bodies. A particularly instructive example noted by Park concerns one Sister Francesca of Foligno and her fellow nuns, who eviscerated their beloved abbess Chiara of Montefalco after her death in 1308. Cutting through the deceased's back to extract the heart, the nuns discovered in the dissected organ an image of Christ crucified, along with "even more miraculous marks of Chiara's sanctity, all formed of flesh: the crown of thorns, the whip and column, the rod and sponge, and tiny nails" (Park 1994, p. 2).

Von Hagens presents an interesting parallel in which mental and emotional states play the role of the soul: "The external face, the human countenance, has always been considered the mirror to the soul. The soul, on the other hand, also has an effect on the body. Happiness and worry have visible effects on the face within – just look at anorexia or stomach ulcers. Does that mean that an entire plastinated body is also an embodiment, a reflection of the soul?" (von Hagens 2000, p. 38). Von Hagens values the uniqueness of each individual specimen – part of his objection to mere models that only express a generalisation of the body – arguing that each plastinate reveals the particular vicissitudes and anomalies of real individuals. "All models look alike and are, essentially, simplified versions of the real thing. The authenticity of the specimen, however, is fascinating and enables the observer to experience the marvel of the real human being. The exhibition is thus dedicated to the individual face within" (von Hagens, n.d., "Aim of the Exhibition").

Such expressed respect for the uniqueness of individuals does not convince some of the visitors to BODY WORLDS, however. As one medical student wrote after viewing the plastinates in Brussels: "How can von Hagens expose bodies of real people, for everyone to see or touch, without any respect? We learn, during our studies, to respect the human body; a respect anyone would find natural, even necessary, when lying in bed in a hospital, or standing next to a loved one who had just died. A grave mistake has been made, a limit has been crossed. The body should be considered as a whole: a beautiful machine but also the home for the soul. I think we need this limit to orient our lives" (Vertes 2002, p. 168).

> Von Hagens values the uniqueness of each individual specimen, arguing that each plastinate reveals the particular vicissitudes and anomalies of real individuals. Such expressed respect for the uniqueness of individuals does not convince some of the visitors to BODY WORLDS, however.

Part of the student's objection was not just that the human body was presented as a "machine without a soul," but also that the specimens were, in her mind, exhibited in the most disrespectful of ways. After commenting on the skillful dissections, the student added: "But the rest was horror disguised: they had no skin, no face, and looked too beautiful to be frightening. The artistic poses were shocking.... If von Hagens had meant the exhibition to be educational, as he claimed, then why did be put the bodies in these shocking, artificial poses?"

Such remonstrances are not uncommon. The pastor Ernst Pulsfort, in an interview on National Public Radio's All Things Considered, lashed out through the translator: "I think these ideas are perverse. This man is playing with corpses like they are dolls. It makes no anatomical sense to present a dead person playing chess, riding a horse, swimming or fencing. This has nothing to do with anatomy. It is Play-Doh, and he makes it out of dead human meat" (National Public Radio, All Things Considered 2001, p. 12).

Why indeed, we may ask, does von Hagens pose his

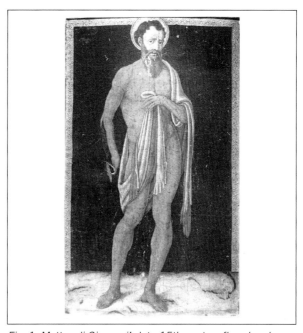

Fig. 1: Matteo di Giovanni's late-15th-century flayed and muscular St. Bartholomew draped in his own skin. © Museum of Fine Arts, Budapest.

whole-body specimens as though they are still engaged in the normal activities of living? As noted in Part 1, von Hagens exalts in imitating representations, in reproducing classic works of art in organic material, yet there is more than just an aesthetic, if morbid, nostalgia at work here. This relates directly to the final metaphysical attribute of the body, as the vehicle or means for the psychophysical continuation of the individual via resurrection.

One of the most powerful doctrines affecting the course and practice of anatomy in the late Middle Ages was the idea of bodily resurrection on the Day of Judgement. This doctrine cut in two directions. On one hand, it emphasised the idea that physical or material continuity is essential to personhood and identity, and thus dismemberment could be viewed as a significant threat to eternal salvation. On the other, God in his omnipotence could reconstitute even the most corrupted of bodies, so that at the Last Judgment the scattered remains of a thoroughly pulverised and decomposed body, gathered, for instance, from the stomachs of carnivores if need be, would be divinely reassembled. Bone would be stuck back to bone, skeletons reclothed with muscles and flesh, and the whole body revivified.

Without such hope in eschatological reassemblage and restitution, the fate of martyrs like the flayed (and according to some versions, beheaded) St. Bartholomew would have been grim indeed. Reflecting the mediaeval fascination with mutilation and dismemberment as a means of spiritual exaltation, St. Bartholomew was frequently portrayed carrying his own flayed skin, sometimes fully clothed but also as a nude wiry athlete, his raw muscles exposed, as in Matteo di Giovanni's 1480 painting (Fig. 1). In Michelangelo's *Last Judgment* in the Sistine Chapel (Fig. 2), the martyr's postmortem vindication is graphically validated. Among the many resurrected souls St. Bartholomew appears fully reenfleshed while holding his own excoriated skin—itself in the form of a drooping self-portrait of the artist, suggesting Michelangelo's own hoped-for restitution through the martyr's intercession and Christ's mercy (Partridge 1997, p. 139). Given the connections between art, religion and science, it is hardly surprising that, as A. Hyatt Mayor notes, "The limp features that sag from his [St. Bartholomew's] hand reappear in the frontispieces of several baroque anatomy books" (Mayor 1984, p. 69). A similar theme is found in Andreas Vesalius's *De Humani Corporis Fabrica*, with its famous engravings of flayed but walking muscle men, which appeared in 1543, two years after the unveiling of Michelangelo's *Last Judgment*.

Anatomical art brought dry bones to life on the printed page, resonating with God's promise in Ezekiel's prophesy in the valley of dry bones: "Thus saith the Lord God unto these bones; Behold, I will cause breath to enter into you, and ye shall live: And I will lay sinews upon you, and will bring up flesh upon you, and cover you with skin, and put breath in you, and ye shall live" (Ezekiel 37:5–6). Giorgio Ghisi's *The Vision of Ezekiel* (1554) reveals its own resurrecting *écorchés* (Figure 3), less than a dozen years after Vesalius' *De Fabrica*. It is in this context that we can better appreciate the religious overtones in Valverde's engraved figure of the flayed man holding his own skin (1556) (Fig. 4). The St. Bartholomewlike *écorché*, knife in one hand, sagging skin in the other, is reminiscent of Michelangelo's restituted saint. Valverde's artist was likely Gaspar Becerra, former assistant to Michelangelo at the Sistine Chapel and an anatomist himself (Roberts and Tomlinson 1992, p. 214).

Von Hagens' plastinated rendering (Figure 5) of Valverde's *écorché*, with its echoes of much earlier representations of the skin-bearing saint, obviously evokes a number of traditional religious ideals. As Ulrich Fischer noted regarding the Mannheim exhibit, "religious associations were unmistakable in this exhibition, such as when plastination was referred to as an 'act of resurrection' or that plastinated specimens had been 'preserved for all eternity'" (Fischer 2000, p. 235). And von Hagens himself notes: "Whole-body plastination joins the ranks of skeletons and mummies as a new means of determining our postmortem existence for ourselves" (von Hagens 2000, p. 36).

The scientifically dissected body in the mid-16th century clearly revealed to those in the anatomical theatres both human and divine handiwork. It also anticipated a yearning for a new kind of immortality and bodily perfection – under human direction – a yearning explicitly voiced by Goethe's *Proplastiker* some two centuries later, and in von Hagens' most recent visions of a superhuman.

The Plastinator as Promethean Prophet or Frankensteinian Monster

The various controversies surrounding *BODY WORLDS* clearly reflect a number of historical tensions between science and art, art and religion, and religion and science that transcend the two cultures of the sciences and humanities. Underlying all these tensions is one major philosophical schism manifested in the question, "To whom does the body belong?" Those, for instance, who desire von Hagens to plastinate their bodies clearly believe it is their own right, whereas Dean Ulrich Fischer offers a very different perspective. As the handiwork of God, Fischer affirms, we and our bodies belong to our Creator. Death does not terminate this status, for the corpse is still the person. He concludes: "Everything that forms a basis of both human confidence as well as human limitations is lost when human beings become works of art in the hands of artists" (Fischer 2000, p. 235). Thus, violation of the body in the anatomical act, includ-

Fig. 2: Detail from Michelangelo's 16th-century Last Judgement portraying the martyred St. Bartholomew fully restored in his resurrected body while holding his own flayed skin. Photo credit: Scala/Art Resource, NY.

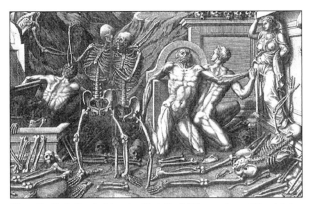

Fig. 3: Detail of Giorgio Ghisi's 16th-century The Vision of Ezekiel representing the reanimation of dry bones through a refleshing of the skeleton as described in Ezekiel 37:1–10. © The Trustees of the British Museum, London. © Copyright The British Museum.

ing von Hagens' hygienic processing of the corpse, inflicts damage on "the human existence of the persons involved" (Fischer 2000, p. 236).

Van Dijck notes the convergence of diverse motivations on the part of those who volunteer to have their bodies plastinated: "To those wishing to donate their own body to science, plastination offers the possibility to unite posthumous altruism and – more egocentrically – eternal 'life.' Since antiquity, people have sought to save their mortal bodies from total decay by having them mummified or embalmed after death" (van Dijck 2001, p. 121–122). And she adds one more motive: "the prospect of having their body transformed into a statue or work of art" (van Dijck 2001, p. 122). The modern quest for plastination seems in one sense not far removed in spirit from the ancient Egyptian funerary prayer to Osiris, that through the embalming process "I shall not decay, I shall not rot, I shall not putrefy, I shall not turn into worms, and I shall not see corruption" (Prayer to Osiris, n.d.).

Individuals intending to be plastinated may be regarded as seeking to fulfill a legitimate quest for an aesthetic postmortem fate, avoiding putrefaction and becoming a beautiful object that perhaps even enhances self-esteem while still living. Alternatively, they may be viewed as deluding themselves by refusing to accept their finitude in a vain attempt to deny divine will. One's view depends in large part on whether we regard ourselves and our bodies as belonging to God, or, ultimately, to ourselves.

Placing these two views in historical perspective, Erwin Panofsky contrasts the mediaeval Christian notion of humankind as being created in the image of God with the later Renaissance ideal of human beings as self-creating. Humankind in the mediaeval perspective was the primary subject of the cosmic drama of salvation, an end in itself, but subservient to God's will. Panofsky notes the great divide between that view of humankind and the one of Pico

della Mirandola of the 15th century, who proclaimed: "Thou, man, masterful molder and sculptor of thyself... may'st shape thyself into whichever form thou wantst"

> The various controversies surrounding BODY WORLDS clearly reflect a number of historical tensions between science and art, art and religion, and religion and science that transcend the two cultures of the sciences and humanities.

(Panofsky 1953, p. 167). No longer Adam but Prometheus is the symbolic representation of what it means to be human.

Those seeking the supposed benefits of plastination and especially von Hagens himself would seem to subscribe to the Promethean point of view. Once again, van Dijck nicely makes the point: "Although in many ways his work is a continuation of age-old traditions in the material production of anatomical objects, he also adds a commentary on the 'nature' of the human body: humans are no longer subject to divine nature, as science and scientists to a large extent control longevity and quality of life" (van Dijck 2001 p. 111). She elaborates: "The most disturbing aspect of Von [sic] Hagens' plastinates, in my view, is neither the transgression of art-science boundaries that purportedly fuelled the controversy, nor the resuscitation of public spectacle or display. Something that remained virtually untouched in the public debate concerning the exhibition was that plastinated cadavers prompted visitors to reconsider the status and nature of the contemporary body, both dead and alive. This body is neither natural nor artificial, but the result of biochemical engineering: prosthetics, genetics, tissue engineering, and the like have given scientists the ability to modify life and sculpt bodies into organic forms that we once thought of as artistic ideals – models or representations. What Von [sic] Hagens does with dead bodies is very similar to what scientists do with living bodies" (van Dijck 2001, p. 124).

Von Hagens' Promethean proclivities are recently manifested in his plans to create a new sort of plastinate, not one reflecting the actual state of a human cadaver, but an idealised "superhuman" of the future. As one commentator notes: "The Plastinator is on to new and ever-more ghoulish horizons. His web site announces, in bold lettering, that he is 'appealing for a terminally ill patient' to film his death, plastination and reconstruction as a 'superhuman'.... Notwithstanding his inability to draw breath, the 'superhuman' is supposed to be free of all the flaws von Hagens faults evolution with bestowing on us. The Plastinator's dead creation will have extra ribs (to protect the vital organs), knees that swing backwards (an attribute that sounds especially unstable), a backup heart (for when the primary organ fails)

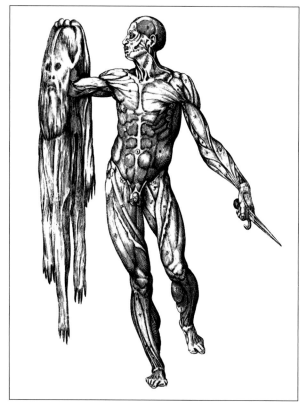

Fig. 4: Sixteenth-century copper engraving of flayed man holding aloft his own skin. From Juan Valverde de Amusco's Anatomia del corpo humano... (Rome, 1559 [first published 1556]). The artist was probably Gaspar Becerra, himself an anatomist, who assisted Michelangelo in painting the Sistine Chapel. Courtesy of the National Library of Medicine.

and a 'retractable penis'" (McGovern 2002). She concludes by quoting the Plastinator's own prophetic vision: "What we do with a real human body today will show what we can achieve in the future using genetic engineering."

Such visions may suggest to many a Frankensteinian nightmare, yet, as one might anticipate from the publicity-seeking plastinator, von Hagens "is quite happy to be compared to Mary Shelley's fictional character, Frankenstein" (Singh 2003, p. 468). As von Hagens himself proclaims, "Hollywood has earned a fortune by blending anatomy with body snatching and playing with ambivalent, gruesome feeling. What can be better than to... put me into this tradition?" (quoted in Singh 2003, p. 468).

For many, von Hagens will ever represent the postmodern Promethean priest, the Frankensteinian promoter of anatomical violence, offending both God and humanity. For others, he is Goethe's idealised anatomist fusing the human urges of the *Prosektor* for scientific knowledge and the aesthetic sensitivities of the ideal *Proplastiker* who delights in celebrating the human power to intervene in nature's processes (and God's designs or evolution's

mistakes, depending on one's point of view) and who transforms the perception of postmortem destiny into something bearable.

The science of anatomy in its long interactive history with art has unavoidably been intertwined with religion and the human aspiration for meaning. The desire to know our bodily interior frequently intersects with spiritual longing for self-knowledge and for immortality. The resulting tensions may be inevitable, given the dual nature of human beings. As Ernest Becker succinctly dramatised this duality, we are creators with minds that soar above nature, yet are "worm[s] and food for worms" who live in conscious awareness of this "terrifying dilemma" (Becker 1973, p. 26). The anatomical enterprise as practiced by von Hagens and many of his predecessors has often served, and continues to serve, to highlight that dilemma, and in the process repeatedly brings science and art into collision, with religion as a catalyst.

Literature Cited

Ashraf Aziz A, Mckenzie JC, Wilson JS, Cowie RJ, Ayeni SA, Dunn BK. 2002. The human cadaver in the age of biomedical informatics. Anat Rec (New Anat) 269: 20–32.

Bakar O. 1999. The history and philosophy of Islamic science. Cambridge: Islamic Texts Society.

Becker E. 1973. The denial of death. New York: Free Press.

Bittar EE. 1955. A study of Ibn Nafis. Bull Hist Med 29:352–368;429–447.

Dick T. 1860. The Christian philosopher; or, the connection of science and philosophy with religion. In: The complete works of Thomas Dick, vol. 2. Cincinnati: Applegate & Co.

Fischer U. 2000. When death goes on display. In: Kelly F, translator. Gunther von Hagens' Anatomy Art: Fascination beneath the Surface. Heidelberg: Institute for Plastination. p 233–237.

Goethe, Johann Wolfgang von. 1947. Wilhelm Meister: Apprenticeship and Travels. Trans. by R. O. Moon. London: G. T. Foulis & Co.

Gould SJ, Wolff RP. 2000. crossing over: where art and science meet. New York: Three Rivers Press.

Kuriyama S. 1999. The expressiveness of the body and

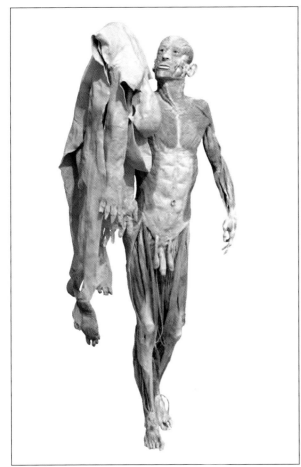

Fig. 5: Gunther von Hagens' late-20th-century plastinated imitation of Valverde's Bartholomew-like écorché. © Gunther von Hagens Institut für Plastination, Heidelberg, Germany (www.bodyworlds.com).

the divergence of Greek and Chinese medicine. New York: Zone Books.

Mayor AH. 1984. Artists and anatomists. New York: Artist's Limited Edition in association with the Metropolitan Museum of Art.

McGovern C. 2002. The plastinator wants you! well, your body. Report: Canada's Independent Newsmagazine (http://report.ca/archive/report/20021021/p46i021021f.html).

Moore CM, Brown CM. 2004. Gunther von Hagens and *BODY WORLDS*, part 1: the anatomist as Prosektor and Proplastker. Anat Rec (New Anat) 276B:8–14.

National Public Radio, All Things Considered. 2001. Body art. Transcript from Livingston, NJ: Burrelle's Information Services. p 12.

National Public Radio, All Things Considered. 2001. No. 8. "Body Art." April 30. Transcript by Burrelle's Information Services. Livingston, New Jersey.

Panofsky E. 1953. Artist, scientist, genius: notes on the "Renaissance-Dämmerung." In: The Renaissance: six essays. New York: Harper and Row. p 123–182.

Park K. 1994. The criminal and the saintly body: autopsy and dissection in Renaissance Italy. Renaiss Quart 47:1–33.

Partridge L. 1997. Michelangelo's Last Judgment: an interpretation. In: Stainton EB, editor. Michelangelo: The Last Judgment—a glorious restoration. New York: Harry N. Abrams. p 8–154.

Porter R. 1997. The Greatest Benefit to Mankind: A Medical History of Humanity. New York and London: W. W. Norton & Co.

Prayer to Osiris. n.d. From the papyrus of Nu, the chapter of not letting the body perish. In: Wallis Budge EA, translator. The Egyptian book of the dead (http://www.lysator.liu.se/(a1)/_drokk/BoD/tchsta.html).

Purcell RW, Gould SJ. 1992. Finders, Keepers: Eight Collectors. New York and London: W. W. Norton & Co.

Record Searchlight 2002. Nov. 21. (http://www.redding.com/news/world/past/20021121topworld023.shtml) Last accessed 9 Aug 2003.

Roberts KB, Tomlinson JDW. 1992. The fabric of the body: European traditions of anatomical illustration. Oxford: Clarendon Press.

Singh D. 2003. Scientist or showman? Br Med J 326:468.

Smith O. 2003. "The Art of the Oldest Science." Science 299 (7 Feb): 829.

van Dijck, J. 2001. "Bodyworlds: The Art of Plastinated Cadavers." Configurations: A Journal of Literature, Science, and Technology 9 (no. 1): pp. 99–126.

Vertes D. 2002. Körperwelten: the fascination of authenticity. Student Br Med J 10:168.

Vesalius A. 2003. In: Garrison D, Hast M, translators. On the fabric of the human body. Evanston, IL: Northwestern University (http://vesalius.northwestern.edu/noflash.html).

von Hagens G. 2000. "Anatomy and Plastination." In: Gunther von Hagens' Anatomy Art: Fascination beneath the Surface. No editor. Trans. by Francis Kelly. Heidelberg: Institute for Plastination. pp 11–38.

von Hagens, Gunther. No date. "Aim of the Exhibition." In BODY WORLDS.(http://www.koerperwelten.de/en/pages/ausstellungsziel.asp) Last visited 25 July 2003.

von Hagens, Gunther. No date. "Theme of the Exhibition." In BODY WORLDS. (http://www.koeperwelten.de/en/pages/ausstellungsinhalte.asp) Last visited 10 August 2003.

"The preceeding articles by Moore and Brown were originally published in Anatomical Records (Part B: New Anatomy) 276B: 8-14, 2004, and 277B: 14-20, 2004, resp. They were slightly edited for formatting style for the reprinting on this catalog."

Dr. Moore is a professor in the Department of Cellular and Structural Biology at the University of Texas Health Science Center at San Antonio. She teaches Gross Anatomy and the History of Anatomy. Her current research interests are in the genetics of aging and the history of medicine and anatomical art.

Dr. Brown is a professor and Chairman of Religion at Trinity University, San Antonio, Texas. He teaches courses in Asian Religions and Religion and Science. His current research interests concern contemporary Hindu responses to modern science and medicine.

*Correspondence to: Charleen M. Moore, Ph.D.,
Department of Cellular and Structural Biology,
University of Texas Health Science Center at San Antonio,
7703 Floyd Curl Drive, San Antonio,
TX 78229-3900. Fax: (210) 567-3803;
E-mail: moorec@uthscsa.edu

DOI 10.1002/ar.b.20003
Published online in Wiley InterScience
(www.interscience.wiley.com).

Franz Josef Wetz

The Dignity of Man

Man is something worth looking at; he presents a picture full of sublimity and dignity. At least, that is what the Renaissance philosophers thought. They one-sidedly emphasised the outstanding importance and sovereignty of this living creature that had the gift of language, and which had already once in its history – in the sculptures of classical Western antiquity – depicted itself, or at least its gods and heroes, as the ideal. With such a self-confident way of looking at themselves, numerous thinkers and artists between the 14th and 16th centuries clearly rejected the dismal mediaeval image, which, in contrast to the glorious Christian afterlife, frequently depicted the misery of existence here on Earth, its wretchedness and worthlessness.

However, what is truly special about the humanistic revaluation of man lies not merely in the emphasis of his worth, but above all in recognition of his beauty. It was as though it was only then that their unique upright posture enabled the inhabitants of Earth to gain an objective view of themselves. Not only at that time was the scope of what the world contained studied, comprehended and painted as an unending landscape as never before – for the Renaissance masters the body of mortal man itself, in ancient times often called the tomb of the soul, had become proof of God's existence. Now it was said that the human body had been designed so superbly in order for it to form a worthy vessel for the immortal soul. The heavenly perfection promised by the church was given an aesthetic earthly counterpart.

It was therefore not by chance that anatomy reached a peak for the first time during the Renaissance and was connected with the art of the time: as shown in countless portraits of the period – realistic even to the extent of dirt under the fingernails – man had become convinced that he could be seen as an individual; and he began systematically to discover the inner as well as the outer features of his form.

Since the Renaissance, artists' representations of the human body have been based on anatomical studies, and from then onwards representations of anatomy, which was only founded as a medical discipline in that period, for a long time followed aesthetic rules and motifs taken from art. The "Dissected Woman with Opened Abdomen and Foetus" by French medical illustrator Jacques-Fabien Gautier (1711–1785), a pioneer in four-colour printing, was painted in 1746.

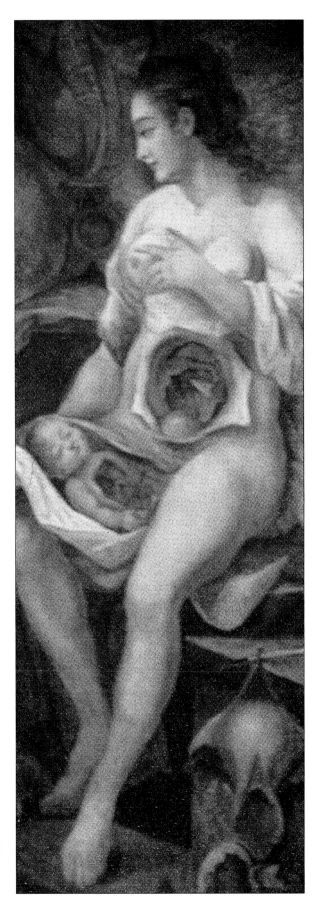

However, to be looked at also means that we offer a target. For however highly developed we may be, we still remain vulnerable creatures, and frail ones at that. It is precisely our vulnerability in many respects and our great and varying sensitivities that cause us to perceive our own visibility as a danger; we therefore conceal ourselves in clothing and housing, and even hide ourselves when we by no means need to shun the light.

Thus on the one hand we consider ourselves worth looking at, do not want to be overlooked, and even seek publicity from time to time, but on the other hand we are also aware of our vulnerability. Ultimately possessing little security, most people are confronted with the need to shape their arduous and worrisome existence themselves throughout their lives. Those who are happy at most experience episodes of a carefree, unworried life.

This recognition of the greatness and misery of man raises the fundamental question of whether the individual also possesses a value that differentiates him from nature. Is he not ultimately only one transient being among others – a naked, narrow-nosed mammal with an overweight head on a spinal column that is rather unsuitable for his upright posture?

Precisely our neediness, imperfection and shortcomings, our insignificance in the boundless universe and our mortality repeatedly raise doubts today about the dignity of man in general, the latter of which, against this sobering background, appears to be a ridiculous presumption. Nevertheless, innate human dignity is a slogan of our time; sadly, however, it is burdened with an unbearable vagueness. Virtually nobody is able to provide clear information on the significance of, and justification for, this great idea. However, everybody uses the expression as if it were obvious. Thus one often reads and hears about the lack of dignity throughout the world, that this or that regime totally disregards human dignity, that something is beneath someone's dignity, even that the dead have a sacrosanct dignity. Unfortunately, what that all really means is generally impossible to find out.

The pathos that is always discernible in the expression all too easily masks its vagueness and openness. Instead of being inviolable, dignity appears to be elusive. One only needs to say the word 'dignity' out loud to be shocked by its hollow ring. Like many big words, this one too has largely worn thin today.

This is cause for concern if one considers the value that should be given to human dignity throughout the world.

All of the United Nations' fundamental documents acknowledge this, and demand that it be recognised by all states and citizens. Accordingly, article 1 of the Universal Declaration of Human Rights from 1948 begins with the sentence:

Marcus Tullius Cicero, the most famous orator in ancient Rome, was the first to proclaim the idea of general human dignity – to be understood both as a distinctive characteristic of each individual as well as a way of individually shaping one's life.

"All people are born free and equal in dignity and rights." But these declarations say nothing about what the expression implies, nor do the numerous state constitutions into which it has been incorporated.

An explanation is therefore urgently needed, especially as many people regard the expression "dignity" more as an empty phrase than a pure introductory word, as a commonplace word to be used in Sunday sermons, that – like edifying words intended as comfort – merely contributes to satisfying the need for general harmony. People like to refer to dignity because this word still sounds good and the fact that it is easy to remember gives the impression that it has a definition.

The fact that in truth it does not have one at all was proven by the examples to be found in the debates about the first major exhibition of plastinated whole-body specimens or plastinates in Germany. Like an all-purpose weapon, it was used against every reasonably justified argument, and was even ideologised. In debates like this, the reference to dignity – or rather to the lack of dignity – was often misused as a rhetorical phrase, either in order to silence unpleasant opponents or in order to help gain general recognition for one's personal interests and ideals associated with the traditional term. Who, by dissenting, would like to give rise to the suspicion that they supported infringements of human dignity? This explains why, in differences of ideological opinion, it can often be played as the joker, and why supporters of the widest range of opinions frequently like to refer to it.

Because dignity was one of the most widely used expressions in the controversy about BODY WORLDS, I shall discuss here in more detail its significance and justification in three general sections and in a fourth section the dignity of the dead.

Sketches from Cultural History

All highly advanced cultures maintain that they respect and protect human dignity. But the expression, if one looks more closely, is mainly of Western origin. In this traditional environment, it is almost always used in two ways.

Firstly, it is used to describe an innate quality. Accordingly, as a result of his humanity, the individual possesses a special dignity as an essential characteristic peculiar only to him, irrespective of his behaviour and the social conditions in which he lives: one comes into the world equipped with it in the same way as with arms and legs.

Secondly, dignity is a question of how to achieve it. Accordingly, it depends on us humans ourselves, on our lifestyle and manners, whether and to what extent we acquire and possess dignity. In this connection, it is sometimes considered more as an individual achievement, and sometimes more as a social skill.

In Western history, both views have almost always been connected with each other. It was said that man should satisfy his innate dignity – the natural characteristic – in his life through his thoughts and actions, i.e., prove himself worthy in accordance with what is required. But only the idea of dignity as a concrete task permeates the whole of Western culture, not its understanding as a natural basic condition and determination of being.

For the ancient Athenians and Romans, the idea that all human beings possessed dignity from birth onwards was foreign. At that time, it was considered to be solely the result of individual achievement and social recognition. Dignity was dependent on the ability and effort made to conquer passions and control feelings. A dignified personality observed the correct moderation and lived according to reason; he bore unhappiness, which did not unduly distress him, in just the same relaxed way as the happiness that he did not allow to result in excessive high spirits. In addition, he displayed dignity in his behaviour, his expressions and gestures, his body care and clothing, and in the calmness that he radiated. Such a person never spoke too loudly, and always walked circumspectly and gracefully. Social esteem, from which dignity could also grow, was bestowed by the general public either on aristocrats or persons with a particular social rank, who – as persons with dignity – generally occupied a high political office.

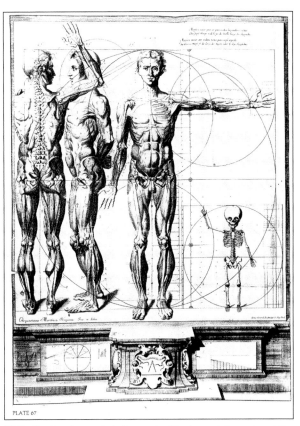

PLATE 67

With the fundamental change in Western philosophy at the beginning of the modern era, a humanistic view of man began to take hold, who now began to investigate both his interiors and exteriors at the same time. Beauty was understood not merely as a superficial quality, but was attributed to internal structures and harmonious proportions. The drawing "Skeleton and muscle figures to illustrate proportions" by the Spaniard Crisostomo Martinez (1638–1694), based on related studies by Renaissance artists such as Leonardo da Vinci and Albrecht Dürer, appeared in print in 1689 in Fontainebleau and in 1692 in Frankfurt and Leipzig.

As far as is known, however, the Roman philosopher and politician Marcus Tullius Cicero (106–43 BC) was the first to express in his writings the idea of general human dignity, describing it both as an unmistakable characteristic as well as a requirement, which he attributed to all men; he based this kind of dignity, on which every individual should base his life, on human rationality. However, Cicero's wider understanding did not gain immediate acceptance; only Christianity brought his ideas to maturity.

If we combine the viewpoints of Christian teaching and of philosophy, the result is the following picture: According to these ideas, the dignity of man is based on the biblical God having created man in His image and allowing him to share His reason and might. As God's special creation, man has an absolute value, as a result of which he differs from all other creatures. In contrast to the natural world, he occupies the center of the universe, which was created for him and for his sake. In addition, according to Christian opinion, the superior worth of man can also be seen in his upright posture, his personality, free will, his immortal soul and from the reason that enables him to recognise the world and God. In particular, however, it appears through God's becoming man – the Almighty becoming flesh – and through the redemption by Christ through His death and resurrection.

In all of these conceptions, human dignity is always seen as an essential characteristic possessed by each one of us, and which is not due solely to an elevated position, aristocratic origins or an impeccable life-style. It must be respected by every individual and all social institutions up to the state itself; all must protect and preserve it.

From the innate worth of man in this respect, however, an obligation is also derived, namely to live in an honest and God-fearing manner and to treat oneself and others kindly. People were convinced that although no-one can destroy the dignity innate in all men, the individual can nevertheless harm himself by allowing himself to revolt against God in sin and disobedience, and by being governed by his inclinations and unbridled egoism – instead of living a thoughtful, virtuous, considerate life.

Unlike the Middle Ages, from the 17th century onwards the dignity of man ceased to be attached to his being the image of God and to his position as the highest being in the world. Knowledge of the immensity of the universe had gradually become widespread, and even today this has the disturbing effect of making man aware of his minuteness and triviality. As a result of rational views, by the beginning of the modern age it had become impossible to deduce further the particular quality of man from his position in the world. Consequently, the fact that the stars do not revolve around man became ever less essential for determining his importance. Man's overriding dignity was seen in the human ability to

According to mediaeval Christian thinking, the dignity of man resulted from his being made in the image of God. In contrast, Immanual Kant, a philosopher of the Enlightenment (shown above in a miniature portrait painted in 1795), based the value of man that he considered unique on man's intellectual gifts.

recognise nature and goodness. Thus, the French philosopher and mathematician Blaise Pascal (1623–1662) confirmed that although man was only one being among others, and as such was of only slight significance, he was a rational being – and as such he was far superior to all other creatures as far as dignity and rank were concerned.

The thinkers of the Enlightenment also speculated that only man possesses self-awareness, freedom, moral standards and reason. Their most important protagonist, Immanuel Kant (1724–1804), based the dignity of man exclusively on his particular intellectual gifts, on his capacity for self-contemplation and moral self-determination. On the one hand, Kant was convinced that man is a transitory part of nature; on the other hand he considered him as a person standing out from nature with a particular, indeed absolute, dignity. By this, Kant meant an absolute, incomparable value, higher than any price; having a price meant having only an external value, and thus capable of being bought, being exchangeable. Conversely, man as a rational being has an intrinsic value – dignity – and is therefore just as irreplaceable as he is unique. As an intellectual and morally rational being, he justly has the right to the respect of his peers, and conversely is obliged to heed others. In addition, the individual also has the same obligations toward himself, and these include never grovelling voluntarily to others. Whoever obsequiously bends the knee in search of favour is insulting himself. Whoever creeps to others should not be surprised if he gets kicked. Only a life in mutual acknowledgement and honest self-respect permits walking tall as the only physical and mental bearing appropriate for man.

According to Kant, the capacity for moral self-determination is expressed above all in the ability of the individual to free himself from his own desires, drives and instincts, and to decide on moral behaviour. One should always ask oneself what would happen if everyone acted like oneself, and then behave in such a manner that everyone in fact could act in the same way as oneself, without its resulting in chaos, injustice or pain.

For Kant, man was master, but not owner of himself. As a rational being with moral standards, the individual does indeed have power over himself, but he should not misuse this power to rid himself of it (that is why the sober thinker was also against intoxicants). Just as the respect-worthy value of the free man forbids his being treated simply as an object or tool, he as a person – that is, as a rational being bound to moral standards – must also never use himself merely as a means to an end or as an object; his dignity therefore forbids him from mistreating, selling or even killing himself. For Kant, human dignity as the embodiment of moral freedom is also a characteristic of man's being and form.

The following is clear: in the modern age, the idea of human dignity has detached itself from old religious bonds, but, as the one innate quality, it has continued to exist and has now found its ultimate foundation in rationality and morality.

Uncertain Ideological Viewpoints

In the meantime, major doubts about the traditional understanding of the term dignity have arisen: doubts about man occupying a special position in nature – whether as a result of his being in the image of God or as a result of his reason. Many reject this superiority over the animal and plant world and the resultant devaluation of all other beings as being doubtful, if not presumptuous or even unworthy. Doubts of a quite different nature weigh even more heavily.

It is still occasionally maintained that the political-legal idea of human dignity is inconceivable without religious assumptions. However, this is countered not only by the fact that in the secular, pluralistic society Christian beliefs have become incomprehensible for many people; the anchoring of human dignity in religion is in contradiction of the constitutionally guaranteed neutrality of liberal communities and of the ideological openness of the United Nations. Accordingly, neither the individual state nor the world community may stipulate an ideology for people – which would, however, be the case if the idea of human dignity were made generally subject to the Christian image of mankind. The liberal constitutional state and the world community should therefore take a neutral stance not only with regard to people's decision to adopt or reject a religion, but should also restrict itself to imparting only ideologically neutral values that are indispensable for the well-being of the individual and the peaceful co-existence of all. The idea of innate dignity based on the ideal of man as being in the image of God does not belong to this.

This is not to say that innate human dignity does not exist. State and law should merely act as though it did not exist, because no one should impose acknowledgement of one particular ideology on another. It should be pointed out, however, that the requirement of neutrality affects only the state and its citizens in their political-legal role; conversely, no one should be denied the right to advocate his religious-ideological opinions in his private and social sphere, or the right to live in accordance with these.

The same objections that oppose a Christian interpretation of human dignity can also be put forward against the rational-philosophical view. The human concept on which it is based is just as invalid universally. The idea of man as a rational being with an absolute value that is distinct from nature is almost as ideologically secure as a religious belief. Hence, the rational-philosophical interpretation of dignity contradicts the constitutionally guaranteed neutrality of our state and the ideological openness of the United Nations; it becomes incompatible with a liberal community and a pluralistic world public as soon as it becomes applicable and binding for all.

However, this does not prevent the individual from having good reasons for being convinced of the truth of a particular ideology. But he should not want to force it onto his neighbor, the State not onto its citizens, and the world community not onto its member states. Only ideologically neutral moral concepts can be asked of anyone and acknowledged by everyone. However, an ideologically completely neutral interpretation of the concept of innate human dignity is not possible; any such attempt must fail as a result of ideological controversies, because the ideas represented cannot be generalized. Consequently, in principle there can be no generally valid interpretation. It would either be definite with regard to ideology or vague with regard to content, for without ideological background assumptions, the assumption of dignity as an innate characteristic remains incomprehensible and empty.

Admittedly one can go one step further. As stated, the need for ideological neutrality merely requires the political institutions to act as if innate human dignity did not exist; modern natural sciences suggest, however, that in fact it does not exist.

The practice of stargazing, one of the oldest sciences known to man, developed from the 15th century into modern astronomy, and broke with traditional mystical ideas. In particular, the knowledge gained only 80 years ago, that even our familiar Milky Way system with its billions of suns, is only one of countless galaxies in the immeasurable universe, made the planet Earth, and thus mankind, into just a fleeting cosmic peripheral phenomenon. The photograph shows a highly active area of star formation in the Rosetta nebula, dark clouds of which will probably also compress and finally collapse to form new stars.

Thus modern cosmology can at least teach modesty to the citizens of Earth: our planet is only one of nine in the solar system, our central star only one average star out of a good two hundred thousand million in the galaxy, and the latter only one of more than a hundred million such galaxies, which in turn form groups and super-groups with immense empty spaces between. Similarly, the knowledge that humanity is a chance result of undirected and often crisis-like biological evolution can place our proud self-awareness in proportion. For example, for about 150 million years of the earth's middle age, reptiles – the dinosaurs – were the predominant creatures living on land; the anatomically modern *Homo sapiens* has only existed for about 100,000 years. Moreover, according to modern genetics and the neurosciences, our behaviour and intellectual life are determined by hereditary factors and unknown cerebral processes to a greater degree than was previously assumed.

Apparently there are no signs in nature that man could point to himself as an indication of his dignity. On the contrary, he is a transitory part of nature, concerned with himself in a world that is not concerned with him. The earliest known traces of hominoids who walked upright were found in a forested area in Tanzania, the Laetoli. These footprints are more than 3.5 million years old. Like the already very human-like primates, who left these behind, we human beings – the last representatives of the species *Homo* – will at some point have disappeared from the surface of the earth.

There is no victory over the briefness of time. The many ruined walls, the weather-beaten columns and the torso sculptures from bygone phases of the very short – measured by geological ages – era of civilization very clearly bear witness to this. What is existentially important is not what the Roman Forum and the Acropolis once were, but what they are today: ruins and piles of rubble, which impressively remind us of the transient nature of everything human. In the nearer or more distant future nothing and no-one with the knowledge that there was once life on earth that claimed a particular value for itself will any longer exist. It requires no excessive pessimism, rather a sober realism, to recognise that man and all his works of intellectual culture have ultimately been condemned to disappear without a trace.

Self-Assertion of Dignity

We shall neither want to accept nor be able to come to terms with complete rejection of the idea of innate dignity, even though it cannot be generalised, and will possibly prove to be merely a fantasy. The excess of suffering, oppression and injustice in the world makes such a rejection appear nothing less than irresponsible; rather, it calls for respect for this idea in everyday practice and for its preservation in philosophical theory. We therefore cannot escape the question of how, despite all reservations, it can be saved.

This question can never be disregarded when humanitarian principles are infringed. This means that our vulnerability and sensitivity in many respects, but also our longing for a successful life, self-determination in freedom and undisturbed self-development, reveal a need for help and protection in which an ideologically neutral right to dignified

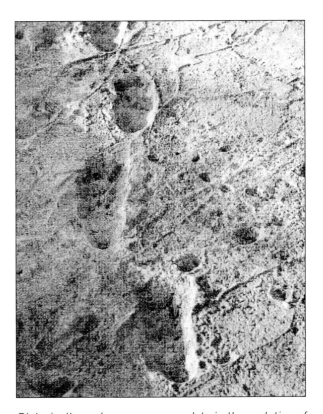

Biologically modern man appears late in the evolution of organisms, and is the last hominoid. Anatomically, we are for the most part the heirs of earlier species of our genus; for example, fossilised footprints discovered in Tanzania confirm that as early as approximately 3.5 million years ago human-like beings were walking upright. Like its ancestors, humanity will not last forever despite all of its achievements in terms of civilization; the end of all life as we know it will come at the latest when the sun inflates into a red giant, and then our planetary system will be destroyed.

treatment is established. Consequently, the expression 'dignity' has a meaning for as long as we can still imagine anything in terms of human degradation and humiliation. The trembling body – ever a symbol of elementary vulnerability and need for protection – stands for such a need for respect, recognition and assistance. One can call this the self-assertion of human dignity as a result of becoming aware of it possibly and actually being disregarded.

This knowledge by no means contradicts the view that man is only one part of transitory nature, only one being among others. For in accordance with the same existentialist premise that each of us is condemned to shaping his needy and worried existence himself, oppression and injustice are perceived as distressingly cruel; nature by no means eliminates the difference between a successful and unsuccessful life.

However, one thing is no longer possible – adhering to the idea of innate human dignity. It is not only difficult to reconcile it with the natural scientific philosophy of our time – it already stands in contradiction to the fundamental principles of our liberal community and of those of the multicultural world community.

Only dignity as an aim can be generalised. Understood in this way, it is less given to us than imposed on us, not a general sign of nobility, but a particular identification of that imperfect being – man. Yet it denotes an ethical ideal and the concrete task of preventing and eliminating intellectual oppression, material need and social injustice. The basis for this is the mutual respect of humans as vulnerable beings concerned for themselves and for others. Considered from the ideologically neutral point of view – that is from the radically secular viewpoint – dignity is not naturally a part of us, but results only from the individual's dealings with himself and his equals, and the dealings of the state with its citizens.

However, if dignity is only a matter of shaping the conditions under which we live, it becomes possible to think that humans have none. Whenever someone is brutally degraded or loses his self-respect, his dignity disappears – albeit not the ethical right to it.

In order to avoid misunderstandings: no-one should be stripped of his dignity; but on the basis of the existence of those who lead, or who are forced to lead, a wretched life without self-respect, one can no longer sensibly say that it has dignity if innate dignity is absent. But even if this existed, it would be of no help to those affected, for such a nobility of being could not give any consolation to them about their undignified conditions anyway. If, therefore, dignity in the religious or rational philosophical sense does not exist, it in no way means that it should no longer be respected as an objective to be striven for. The contrary is the case:

human dignity should be respected precisely when it does not exist as the one so that it exists as the other.

In this ideologically neutral assessment, the rational philosophical principle, which the adherents of religious opinions also share, namely that no one may merely be misused as a means to an end or as an object, continues to be maintained. Such a demand is sensible and ethically justified even if we no longer regard man as a being in God's image or as an intellectual being removed from nature, but merely as a transitory part of nature concerned with himself.

Dignity as an ethical right is one thing, but its guarantee in law is another. In view of the general tendency of man to indifference, egoism and violence, in view of the fact that we cannot be gods creating perfection and general happiness, but are rather animals, the special protection of human dignity in the community – as in Germany as a result of article 1, paragraph 1 of the federal Constitution – appears to be absolutely justified. This arrangement is sensible even without ideological background assumptions.

The Dignity of the Dead

According to general opinion, the right to the protection of dignity also applies to those who have died. In this connection one talks of its continued influence and effect even beyond death. In the debate about BODY WORLDS, the dignity of the dead has become a key concept on which the questions, opinions, assertions and arguments concerning the permissibility and responsibility of a public exhibition of whole-body plastinates are focused.

The Inevitability of Death

Lifelessness is the norm in the cosmos, not a special circumstance; life, in contrast, is a borderline case. What is most natural for us humans – our own existence – is the great exception to which death is the rule.

If the whole of reality were full of life, death would have to remain a puzzle because in that case it would not fit into the world. However, the real puzzle is life, because ever since the big bang the universe has consisted mainly of a field of inanimate particles and forces. Measured against the universe's dimensions of time and space, the entire history of organisms known to us is a fleeting episode restricted to a tiny concentration of matter – the planet Earth.

This applies all the more so for the *Homo sapiens* phase: just as it was by chance that our species appeared in the biotic evolution characterised by erratic mutations and selection (also as a result of catastrophic mass death), the end of humanity is just as certain; and this will not have to wait for the annihilation of our planet when the sun explodes into a Red Giant in about five thousand million years, time.

Like the death of life in general, the death of the individual human being is neither mysterious nor profound. It is the end of a natural course. Admittedly, we can try to postpone this biological actuality with the aid of modern medicine and a healthy life-style, but we cannot avoid it. Our death is as natural as the ageing and decline of the human body, in the course of which nerves and muscle cells die, the skeleton becomes more brittle and the hair less rich in pigment, eyesight and heart and brain functions deteriorate and dark spots develop on sagging skin. For one thing, all these processes are due to the wear and tear to which tissues and cells are exposed in the everyday performance of their tasks; for another, ageing follows a genetic program that determines the life of the individual cells, organs and the entire body. Harbingers of the end of life are age-related illnesses, which often considerably reduce the quality of life. When, finally, the supply of oxygen to the body breaks down, the person who was alive a moment ago is now dead.

Ambiguity of the Dead

But who are the dead after all? Without necessarily having to go into the medical question of definite signs of death, on closer consideration the term itself proves to be ambiguous. On the one hand, we understand the dead to mean the dead body, while on the other hand we mean the deceased.

The deceased is commemorated; the body is disposed of. Nowadays, and in Germany at least, it is either buried in a coffin or cremated and its ashes placed in an urn and interred or scattered at sea. Graves can be anonymous or furnished with names.

However, funeral practices, some of which are very old and carefully handed down, are as diverse as cultures. The ancient Egyptians, who for some of their Pharaohs built the pyramids that subsequently came to be considered wonders of the world, and provided them with costly gifts for the afterlife, were generally buried in a linen cloth. The Parsees placed their dead, naked, on the towers of silence for the vultures. In many tribes, ritual cannibalism took place right up to modern times. The atheist Communist Party of the Soviet Union embalmed their first dictator Vladimir Ilyich Lenin and placed him on show. The Catholic Church allows bones and other physical relicts of its martyrs and saints to be revered as relics. Meanwhile, not only plagues, but above all wars and systematic murder like the fascistic genocide of the European Jews have also filled numerous mass graves.

How a culture treats a body is one expression of the instinctive rejection of the idea that, with death, the definitive end of life has come. The other manifests itself in that, according to general opinion, the wishes of the deceased should remain valid even after death; thus wills that are valid in law must be adhered to by the surviving heirs. The specific instructions of a person concerning the fate of his body after death – such as how it is to be buried and how the grave is to be designed, or whether it is to be donated for anatomical purposes, plastination or transplantation surgery – are also always the provisions of the deceased; they cannot be those of the body. Although we associate the term 'the dead' with both the deceased and with the body, the two expressions do not mean the same thing. How otherwise could one sensibly talk about the "body of the deceased?"

Etymologically, the term 'body' refers to the (dead) physical shell. The expression, which is perceived to be more considerate, is often used instead of 'corpse'; and this latter word in its turn had already supplanted the Old and Middle High German words *hreo* and *re* with their blunt meaning of "cadaver." Yet one also talks about mortal remains, about the part of a human that can decay. The body, which after the death of the individual still retains its form for some time in silent motionlessness, showing features of its personality, is called a corpse until the flesh has disappeared from the bones and any connection with the former unmistakable whole no longer exists as a result of natural decay or other form of decomposition.

The corpse is no longer a person; its ego ceased to exist at the latest after brain death. The corpse as a physical thing or object reveals itself to the unprejudiced view as what it actually is – a possible object for decay or cremation, organ removal, anatomy or plastination. On death, the person comes to an end; he is no longer in this world. He has thus lost his subjective quality and has become an object.

Since time immemorial, man, needing not only direction about reality, but also reassurance about it, has invented symbols and stories in order to cope with death. These make it clear that our need for realism is limited. Glossing over the harshness of reality, even now one talks about peaceful sleep or the resting of the dead, and includes in this picture the body, which, lying on its back with eyes closed and hands folded, is laid out and placed in the coffin. Yet the terms rest, peace and sleep, when related to the body, say less about death itself than about life – its restlessness, restless effort and exhausting difficulty.

Yet the popular image of peace in death is also connected to religious ideas, especially those of the Christians, because they expect re-awakening and resurrection. This concept was often transferred to the body, which is the reason that the Catholic Church forbade cremation for many hundreds of years; the prohibition was only lifted in 1963.

However, if such religious expectations are not, or are no longer, convincing, many people suffer an existential trauma or fear such a trauma. Admittedly, even a religious person cannot seriously believe that a body rests and sleeps. Even though one usually does not wish to know what happens so precisely: A dead person does not rest, he decays; he does not sleep, he decomposes and disintegrates to dust or is burned to ashes. The disintegration of his body into organic and inorganic molecules is inevitable, until, in accordance with the old Latin proverb *terra tegit terram*, earth again only covers earth.

Possibly the dead person remains an object of mourning the whole time. However, this, too, like respecting the last wishes, relates not to the body, but only to the deceased. The body is a lifeless object in appearance, but the deceased is a living subject in memory. Even the visible grave into which the body was lowered, and which those left behind visit, care for and decorate as a place of particularly intensive memories, almost always evokes for them the image of the person who once was, as they knew him, not the image of decaying flesh and disintegrating bones. Not least because this idea is difficult to bear, more and more people are deciding on cremation nowadays, and many are allowing their bodies to be used after death for the living – through transplant surgery, for anatomical purposes or for plastination.

Nameless gardens of rest and communal graves for ashes are a further sign of an absence of illusions in our society. History no longer grows on these grassy areas in many cemeteries. Like the graveyards without individual names that were common in earlier phases of European history, they are in advance of their time, for at some point all graves will reach this state of anonymity and inconspicuousness, and the bodies buried in them will have disappeared without a trace. Even the stone monuments and mausoleums disintegrate if they are not cleared away beforehand.

Memories are of even shorter duration. The mourning for the death of a person cannot hurt forever. The memory of his or her life pales, and finally the once inconsolable ones left behind die themselves; we cannot stop the past from slipping into nothingness. Finally, a veil of forgetfulness covers us all, and even this forgetting is ultimately forgotten.

The Dignity of Plastinates

It should always be made clear in what sense – religious, rational philosophical or ideologically neutral – the word dignity, which can be interpreted in different ways, is being used. If one must apply the word to the dead, in light of all that has been mentioned above, a strict differentiation must be made between the dignity of a body and that of the deceased.

This is not easy. One might think that the word refers only to the body, not to the deceased, since the highest value cannot logically be attributed to something that does not physically exist, that only lives on in memory, which, moreover, gradually pales. However, it is also feasible that dignity apply only to the deceased, but not to the body or even its ashes and the dust, into which it disintegrates, since, with death, the person is extinguished and has lost his subjective quality.

In the debate about plastination and the exhibition of plastinates, there was much talk about infringement of human

Burying corpses or burning them and placing the ashes in an urn are merely cultural conventions – and by no means the only ones, and not the ones that are always adhered to in modern Europe. For example, the Capuchin tomb in Palermo is the largest cellar of mummies in the world. The picture on the left shows a young woman and her godfather, the one on the right the so-called corridor of scholars.

The Christian religious ideas of resurrection are expressed in concrete terms in the traditional picture of the peace of death. Accordingly, the Catholic Church has dressed up relics and whole bodies of saints – here Marie-Bernarde Soubirous (1844–1879), known as Bernadette, in the chapel of the convent of St. Gildard in Nevers. The religious visions that she had at the age of 14 formed the basis for the pilgrimages to Lourdes; she was canonised by Pope Pius XI in 1933.

dignity – that the dignity of the dead, that of their closest relatives, even that of the general public, if not the whole of humanity, had been disregarded. This criticism was expressed by representatives of the two major Christian churches in Germany, namely the Lutheran Curch and the Roman Catholic Church who knew that they had the support of politicians from different camps, and also by doctors; and many journalists made themselves the mouthpieces of these accusations.

It was striking, however, that mostly one only heard or read that human dignity had been infringed, rarely to the extent to which it was supposed to have been. Apparently the critics were confident that those who refer to dignity are correct from the outset, without a precise justification and closer definition of what is meant. Thus the very different questions that arise in this connection, and which I shall discuss below, remained largely disregarded:

- Does the individual infringe his own dignity if he makes his dead body available for plastination?
- For its part, does this type of anatomical dissection and preservation of the donated body infringe human dignity?
- In particular, does the aesthetic form of a plastinated body, and possibly its conversion into a work of art, jeopardise the dignity of the dead?
- Can public exhibitions of plastinates, which are acknowledged to be aesthetically attractive, offend human dignity?

- And to what extent would charging entrance fees for visiting such exhibitions and providing plastinates for scientific and educational purposes in return for money be compatible with the dignity of man?

Limits of Self-Determination

The supporters of the most varied of ideas of dignity are largely agreed that self-determination is one of its essential characteristics. Whether they represent a religious, rational philosophical or radically secular viewpoint – they are all convinced that one of the freedoms of man is being able to make binding arrangements about his estate for the time after death.
Furthermore, it is then often simply maintained that the dignity of a person continues after death and even extends to the dead person.

However, on closer examination, this quite common argument proves to be extremely problematical. For it gives the impression that the dignity of a person can outlive the person himself. However, that is nonsensical, to some extent a misunderstanding of logic: Such use of language presupposes that the deceased, although he no longer exists, must nevertheless continue to be regarded as existent; for only something that exists can have properties such as human dignity. But an existent non-existent is a contradiction in itself.

Respect for the dignity of someone who has died can therefore only mean respect for the dignity that the person had when he was still alive. That therefore means respect not for something that is present, but merely for something that is past. To have this respect is obviously possible, just as the arrangements made by a deceased regarding what he leaves behind can remain binding for the survivors after his death.

The question is, however, where does this obligation come from? It is mainly a social agreement that can be justified both by the wish of the citizens to take decisions that are binding beyond death, and also by their right to self-determination and by the dignity that they can normally demand when they are still alive.

There are nevertheless generally acknowledged limits to the free development of the individual personality. Heading these is the freedom of the person in question. To illustrate the point: the right to swing his arm ends at just the point where somebody else's nose begins. For a similar reason, in some circumstances – despite the right of self-determination – personal disposition over one's body must be withdrawn.

According to religious opinion, man may not dispose of his body in any way that he wishes, because the body, as the image of God, is also God's property; even a corpse has dignity. According to rational philosophical thinking, man may be master of himself, but he is not the owner of himself; accordingly, the individual may not take an entirely free decision about his dead body, because as a former bearer of reason it is given a particular dignity. In contrast, according to radically secular understanding, the mortal remains of a person, considered by themselves, have no dignity whatsoever; only to the extent to which the body is respected and honored is it given a certain dignity.

Does it follow from these three ideas that while the individual is alive he may not decide on the fate of his later dead body? If that were really the case, the dignity of the body would be in direct conflict with the dignity of the person who has died – his former right to self-determination.

Let us disregard the fact that in major natural disasters and epidemics and in wars, when the living count for virtually nothing and the corpses buried in mass graves count for nothing at all, and let us also disregard the numerous anonymous communal graves from former times that also lack special respect for the dignity of the corpses. Whether influenced by this or not – in the meantime man has come to the decision that the dignity of the deceased, i.e., his right to self-determination when he was alive, should be valued over the dignity of his dead body. It is said that the freedom of man includes being allowed to make arrangements about the fate of his mortal remains. Thus what has been said about its not being permissible to decide what is to happen to the corpse has already been partially countered.

Moreover, anyone who can decide between the different methods of disposal after death must decide on one possibility, and as a result of this situation he is inevitably master of his own corpse. Then, however, instead of burial or cremation of his body, he can stipulate that it be given to an anatomical institute for educational and research purposes, or to transplantation surgery for the removal of certain organs, organ parts and tissues in order to save the lives of others; and in view of these long-established possibilities, it would be absurd and inconsistent to forbid individuals from donating their own bodies for the relatively new procedure of plastination.

There is also another aspect. The authorities responsible may only approve a cremation if all suspicion of murder or manslaughter can be ruled out. In order to be sure of this, it is sometimes necessary to perform an autopsy; likewise the legal authorities can order an autopsy and the exhumation of a body that has already been buried – without the consent of the deceased and his relatives – in order

to solve a crime. Not only the supporters of the radically secular understanding of dignity are in agreement with this, but usually also those who hold religious and rational philosophical views. However, by doing this, they also forfeit the idea of the unavailability of the human corpse. For apparently the fact that this is considered to be the property of God or a former bearer of reason, and the fact that relatives, friends and the general public would like to honor the person in the same way as they perceived him at the time of his death, apparently counts for less than the deceased's right to self-determination and the requirements of public safety.

This does not prevent religious or rational philosophical dignity from being conferred on the decaying body, the ashes of a cremated body, the anatomical dissection, the transplantation-surgery organs or a plastinate. It is merely that – as stated above – ideological opinions, which cannot be generalised, may not be imposed on anybody. The liberal State must therefore evaluate the concept "corpse" only from neutral and generally valid points of view, and not from points of view that are bound up with religious allegiance or intellectual history. However, the dignity of the corpse independent of all religious and rational philosophical convictions does not exist. Seen from an ideological point of view, the dignity of a corpse only arises when living persons are handling it; this also includes the respect for the last wishes of the deceased with regard to his mortal remains, as long as public order and health would not be affected by this decision.

Accordingly, with regard to the criticism of plastination and BODY WORLDS, it must be concluded that whoever, while he is alive and in full possession of his mental faculties, voluntarily and after comprehensive information makes his body available for this procedure, and gives his consent to exhibition of the denaturized and transformed dissection resulting from it, is not offending the dignity of his body. In contrast, whoever forbids such a donation of a body is infringing the dignity of the deceased – unless public order and health would be jeopardised.

Objectification of a Dead Body as a Result of Plastination?

The object principle put forward in connection with the Supreme Court's definition and establishment of human dignity has recently also been applied to plastination. There was talk of degrading conversion of the dead into mere objects by making them into organ and whole-body specimens, of demeaning the dignity of their bodies by making them simply objects or things.

This accusation is untenable. It is untenable for the simple reason that while they were alive, the donors contractually agreed to plastination of their bodies after death and because plastination does not indicate contempt for the dead. Above all, the accusation is unjustified because a corpse, as the impermanent remains of a deceased person, is already an object or a thing. It becomes a thing before it comes under the hands of the plastinator. Consequently, the object principle can only relate to living persons, not to dead bodies, as these no longer have a subject quality.

Admittedly, considering the body as an exception to the 'either-or' classes of persons and objects has become established in law. However, this cannot seriously mean that the corpse is still somehow a person, rather that, being the mortal remains of a person who once was, possibly it should not be treated in the same way as other lifeless objects. It can be the object of respect and mourning; and for religious and ideological reasons, out of consideration for the wishes of the deceased and consideration of our own moral feelings, but also, with an eye to public order, we are obliged to treat it with respect. However, none of that would change anything with regard to the status of a corpse as an object. Otherwise in principle, it could not be used for the removal of organs and tissues for transplants or used for anatomical purposes, and it could not even be burned or left to decay in the ground.

According to Gunther von Hagens, the inventor of plastination, during its conversion into a whole-body specimen, a corpse goes through three stages: Firstly it becomes anonymous. Then it is turned into a durable specimen, physically and chemically denatured through and through, which can no longer be identified with the former person. Finally it becomes an object of scientific information. It is simply absurd to consider the rendering of a dead body anonymous (by its not being given the name of the deceased) to be degrading, and to see degradation in the subsequent elimination of its physiognomical individuality (as a result of the anatomical dissection). The person bearing the name did indeed have his own individual life and sickness history; but this is not taken away from the deceased as such, and thus nor is his dignity, whereas the corpse was an object even before plastination.

In this respect, the only thing that is new, and thus unfamiliar, about the otherwise truly revolutionary procedure is that its results, instead of showing the mere frailness and transitoriness of life as anatomical specimens preserved in the usual way do, show the human body in a state that is no longer alive but not yet decayed for a virtually unlimited period of time. In addition to the amazing functionality of our body, its inner beauty can also be revealed if the plastinator is sensitive to this and proceeds with sufficient skill.

Improper Aestheticisation of Plastinates?

As described at the beginning, anatomy blossomed for the first time in the Renaissance, and entered into an alliance with art. At that time, and for a long time afterwards, reproductions of medical discoveries and aesthetic depictions of the human body in paintings and sculptures were very closely connected.

Plastination, as Gunther von Hagens practices it, is in this tradition. A plastinate, if it is to fulfill the task of general enlightenment that is the aim, must be given an appropriate form, which could by no means be achieved with traditional methods of dissection and preservation. If the senses as well as the intellect are to be appealed to, aesthetically attractive solutions to the problem of form almost inevitably result.

However, von Hagens seems to have gone a step further when he oriented the shape of some of his whole-body plastinates on paintings and sculptures. Indeed, the opinion could arise that great works of art had served as models for him: the "Prototypes of Movement in Space" by the Italian futurist painter Umberto Boccioni (1882–1916) for *The Runner*; the "Anthropomorphic Cabinet" by Spanish surrealist Salvador Dali (1904–1989) for *The Drawer Man*; the figure of Bartholomew in the Sistine Chapel by the Renaissance genius Michaelangelo Buonarroti (1475–1564) for the *Muscle Man* with his skin draped over his arm; and "The Doll" by German-French graphic artist and sculptor Hans Bellmer (1902–1975) for the Fencer. However, these similarities came about purely by chance, as Gunther von Hagens did not yet know of these works of art when he conceived these plastinates. Although this may indeed seem astounding, there is nonetheless no doubt about the aesthetic, virtually artistic presentation of his anatomical themes.

Various groups have protested vigorously against this ambitious structural transformation of anatomical specimens. In particular, they maintain that the plastinator is to some degree blasphemously making himself the Creator; in reality he is not concerned with passing on knowledge, but in self-expression. In the process, he is degrading the bodies of the dead in a demeaning manner into mere objects of art that allow the fact that they consist of parts of real bodies to be forgotten. The dead person serves him only as the means for an aesthetic purpose.

In addition, this criticism describes consequences that are to be expected after the supposed taboo has been broken. This leads to the question of how far one wants to go with the treatment of dead bodies. For if the fashioning of corpses so that they can be displayed in museums of art and galleries were once to be allowed, it would only be a small step to transforming dead men and women into armchairs, skeletons into hall-stands, skulls into soup bowls – most definitely infringements of dignity showing contempt for mankind.

The religiously biased accusation that the plastinator is playing the Creator with his whole-body specimens carries as little weight as the suspicion that the workers in a crematorium are behaving like the assistants of the Old Testament's God of Wrath or mythical idols when they push the dead into large incinerators. If one were to argue in this way, one would have to ask whether every surgical procedure performed on humans – whether for health or aesthetic reasons – would not have to be condemned as pride and an offence against the omnipotence of God. Apart from the members of certain sects, the vast majority of people obviously consider this absurd.

Moreover, the criticism of the aesthetic quality of plastinates misses the point here insofar as it is claimed that they are clearly identifiable as objects of art. In principle, however, no object can stipulate how the human mind must perceive it; whether it is perceived as a work of art depends mainly on the eye and judgement of the beholder (although the difficult question of what art or beauty is can be ignored here).

According to what Gunther von Hagens himself says, he makes no claim to be a genuine artist. However, he by no means denies an intended affinity of his works with sculptures – in the same ways as was attempted for the first time with the anatomical portrayals of the Renaissance, and was realised with three-dimensional anatomical models that later became famous. It was for this reason that he even coined the term BODY WORLDS. He can, of course, give his reasons for this: Firstly he owes it to the body donors to give their cadavers an aesthetic form. Secondly, in addition to the functional aspect of the human body, his aim was to reveal the natural beauty of its inner structures. Finally, since traditional anatomy has become increasingly isolated from the public, his plastinates were intended to provide general enlightenment; therefore, among the non-medical lay public, he is trying to prevent the natural fear of death and the horror and revulsion that the usual anatomical specimens can provoke.

In the opinion of almost all the visitors to the BODY WORLDS exhibitions in Germany and abroad up to now, he has, in fact, succeeded in this. Apparently, with his plastinates, many people can be shown things that would otherwise cause existential trepidation and could stir up the emotions, something that, in a natural realistic form, i.e., a form left unaesthetic either through thoughtlessness or by intention, they would not be willing to look at, even if it were to interest them.

The critical observation that this aestheticisation is simply a means to an end that is superficial for, and alien to, a dead body is doubtlessly correct. However, to interpret aestheticisation as an infringement of dignity is nevertheless wrong.

At an early stage in the modern era, anatomy and art joined forces, and medical knowledge was depicted in aesthetic images of the human body. The sculpture "Scorticato" (The flayed one) by Lodovici Cigali (1559–1613) is in the Italian National Museum in the Bargello Palace in Florence, one of the most important collections of works of Tuscan sculptors of the 14th–16th centuries.

Firstly, this reproach does not hold water, because the intentions pursued – dispelling revulsion and creating beauty – are not in themselves offensive, and are fully in accord with the interests of the body donors, who expect their dead bodies to be preserved as perfectly as possible and to be made presentable for lay persons. They would certainly never have agreed to the degradation of their bodies. Secondly, this attack also misses its target because it implies, without explicitly stating it, that the inherently true purpose of a corpse is to be burned or to decay, and that to be plastinated in an aesthetic manner is missing its real purpose. If that were true, it would have to follow that every anatomical or legally ordered autopsy, and even the removal of organs for transplant purposes, would merely be a means to an end that is superficial for, and alien to the true purpose of the body and would thus infringe its dignity. To take that to its ultimate conclusion: the same argument could be used to object to any type of disposal of a body. The reason is that with hygienic disposal of bodies, one is pursuing the remaining superficial remaining purpose of preventing harm to health that would result from their decaying in the proximity of the living – not to mention the intolerability of the appearance and the smell. None of these ways of treating a body can be regarded as an infringement of dignity, because a corpse is no longer a subject and thus there is no purpose inherent to it that could be disregarded.

Does this imply carte blanche to use the dead for any purpose whatsoever? If it is permitted to transform them into aesthetic objects, why not into useful objects – chairs, hallstands or bowls? After all, in the 17th and 18th centuries in France and Germany, corpses were used for supposedly very effective remedies; soldiers believed that carrying the finger of a fallen comrade would bring them luck, and candles made from human tallow were considered to be helpful when seeking treasure. Furthermore, in the Capuchin church in Rome, one can still admire pillars made from skulls, arch supports made from shinbones and chandeliers made from vertebrae, produced by an old monk.

To what extent does a plastinate differ from these? In principle, they do differ: Firstly, these products made from human remains were truly only in fact a means to an end (even though they did not fulfil any rationally comprehensible end). Above all, however, they depicted something that was not human. In order to be truly clear about this attribute, it is necessary to differentiate between relative unfamiliarity with a body and absolute alienation from it: Plastinated whole-body plastinates such as Gunther von Hagens offers to the public depict the human organism as such in order to educate the individual observer about the inside of his own body. In doing so, he uses anatomical specimens rendered durable through unusual techniques – but only relatively, because they still bear the image of man. Conversely, to transform bodies or parts of bodies into bowls or clothes-racks would mean totally alienating the dead bodies, because they would then no longer appear to be anything human.

Nowadays, using bodies or parts of bodies for the wrong purpose would conflict not only with ideological opinions of dignity. Public opinion is almost unanimous in believing that the importance of a body as the remains of a person who has died and respect for his memory would be incompatible in such cases. Even if the deceased, when he was alive, had agreed in his will to his body's being used for useful purposes, or had even demanded this, in the opinion of most people compliance with this wish would not be possible for reasons of observing the established social order and because it would generally be too excessive to be acceptable.

Conversely, the relative (mental) recycling of a body for purposes of serving life, maintaining order and providing education – such as removing organs and tissues for transplantation surgery, performing autopsies for forensic medical purposes or for pathological clarification of the causes of death and dissections for anatomical research and instruction – is basically compatible with any and all ideas of dignity. Plastination, as just expounded, is a relative recycling in the same sense; why then has criticism been sparked by the public exhibition of plastinates?

Offensive Visibility of Plastinates?

Covering dead bodies is a cultural-historical phenomenon of particular importance. Many people find it difficult to bear, or even refuse to look at them. This is an expression of reluctance to face one's own death and the death of others, but also of the need to keep the physical picture of the deceased, whom one has known and loved, intact in one's memory – and possibly of the fear of being reminded of the future decay of one's own body.

This defensive attitude is particularly striking in highly civilised societies. A cloth is placed as soon as possible over the face of the person who has died. The catafalque is covered with flowers and wreaths. In the Federal Republic of Germany, even being waked in an open coffin requires a permit from the authorities.

However, it was not long ago that death was perceived to be natural to a far greater degree than it is today, and dealing with the dead was far more relaxed. Piles of bones and skulls can still be seen in ossuaries, and mummy cemeteries – as in Rome and Palermo – and can still be visited. Unlike Northern Europe, in many places in the Mediterranean countries, it is still the custom to leave the coffin half open until burial so that the immediate family as well as the relatives and friends who have travelled some distance, and all other members of the deceased's community can have a parting look.

In our artificial world, we are rather more inclined to suppress natural facts – the inevitable end of life and the physical disintegration of the body. Confrontation with anatomically dissected and preserved bodies is all the more confusing for many people. Many others, however, want to have them consigned to invisibility, so to speak; thus, in order to deter other interested parties from visiting the BODY WORLDS exhibition, attempts were made to prevent it from opening in Mannheim, with the objection that it lacked dignity; and when that failed, the public was accused of pure voyeurism, of seeking sensation and of having a tasteless thirst for horror. Just as the Jesuits at one time condemned Galileo Galilei because the knowledge that he had obtained

In the not too distant past, dealings with the dead were far more uninhibited than they are today, as ossuaries in many places show. In these, skulls and bones from opened graves were stacked on top of each other. From time to time, however, the limits of piety were considerably exceeded, as in the Capuchin church in the Via Veneto in Rome, where a monk used human bones to make abstruse room decorations.

by looking at the sky through one of the first telescopes threatened their traditional conception of the world, our contemporaries were now to be denied views of the human body that were not possible before the invention and development of plastination, or which, in a different and far less attractive manner were reserved exclusively for members of the medical profession.

There is no doubt that a particular attraction lies in the authenticity and originality of the plastinates. An exhibition of anatomical models that looked confusingly genuine would certainly not have had such enormous success or lasting impact as BODY WORLDS. Certainly many visitors came simply out of curiosity and with the expectation of ambivalent feelings – stunned oppressiveness as well as excited fascination. Yet a representative survey revealed that, instead of these feelings, almost all the visitors had an objective interest in, and concerned thoughtfulness for, the exhibits. The majority proved only to be interested in the structure of the human body, and at the same time recognised its greatness and misery, the physical quality and frailness of the interiors of their own bodies.

What had already been confirmed in the article entitled "Anatomy" published by Denis Diderot and Jean le Rond d'Alembert in the great French *Encyclopédie* that appeared from 1751–1780 all of a sudden became a happening: "Knowledge of oneself requires knowledge of one's body, and knowledge of the body presumes knowledge of such a wonderful chain of causes and effects that one can say that none leads more directly to the concept of an omniscient and omnipotent God; it is, so to speak, the foundation of natural

theology." And further: "In addition to such an important motive, there is a benefit that cannot be disregarded, namely that of being informed of the means by which one feels well, by which one can prolong one's life, which explain the sites and symptoms of disease when one is ill…Knowledge of anatomy is important for everyone."

However, the question remains as to whether the use of plastinates in a way that provides an opportunity for emotional experiences and factual knowledge is generally compatible with the dignity of man. That would certainly not be the case if the public exhibition of anatomical objects were equivalent to a debasing heteronomy of the dead. No one is being debased; and nor is there any heteronomy, as a corpse does not possess any self-determination of purpose. Despite this, those representing a very wide range of ideas of what dignity is or should be are agreed that a body, as the remains of a person who has died, may never be used merely as a means to an end. However, this merely means that one should approach the specimens with a certain respect, and not that the right to view them must be reserved exclusively for the medical profession and should be refused to non-medical laypeople.

Unseemly Exploitation of Plastinates?

Whoever respects the dignity of man respects his neighbour for his own sake and does not regard him merely as a replaceable object. Supporters of religious and radically secular viewpoints also share this rational philosophical principle of Immanuel Kant. Can it also be applied to plastinates?

Many people maintain that selling them (the only possible purchasers are research and teaching institutions and natural history museums) or charging admission to attend an exhibition of them is an infringement of dignity. But even if one concedes that the corpse as a mere thing should be given a certain degree of respect because it is the dead body of someone who has died, that does not apply to payment for a plastinate – considered with reference to Kant's idea regarding goods.

The practices of the Institute for Plastination do not permit any doubt whatsoever on this matter, because they already fulfill the strictest conditions: firstly, the Institute requires that the donation of the body carry no reward; and secondly, it is committed to the principle of never charging for a plastinate itself, only for the costs of producing it – i.e., the cost of dissection and preservation.

Thus the Heidelberg Institute is clearly a service-provider, just like the undertaker who transfers the body to the mortuary and sells the surviving relatives a coffin or urn, the newspaper that accepts death notices, the florist who supplies wreaths, the restaurant owner who prepares the funeral meal, the municipal authority that maintains the cemetery and the layman who speaks at the graveside – but it is also like the church, which is paid for providing spiritual support at the graveside through the church tax.

Conclusion

All in all, it should have become clear that plastination and all of the activities connected with it do not infringe human dignity. These activities are not only compatible with the radically secular understanding of the concept, which as a result of its ideological neutrality can be generalised; but also those who hold an opinion connected with an ideology – religious or rational philosophical – which mainly belongs to the private sphere of the people, do not necessarily have to regard the plastination process or the exhibition of plastinates as an infringement of dignity.

The words 'human dignity' weigh heavily, even though they trip off the tongue so lightly. Precisely for that reason, they should also in future be used more judiciously and with greater circumspection in all respects with regard to plastination.

Franz Josef Wetz has been a professor of philosophy at the College of Education in Schwäbisch Gmünd since 1994. He studied philosophy, German, and theology, and graduated from the University of Giessen, where he did his doctorate and won a prize for his dissertation in 1989. He was employed there at the Center for Philosophy and Principles of Science from 1981 to 1993, latterly as scientific assistant to Prof. Dr. Odo Marquard. Wetz took up deputy chairs in Erfurt and Giessen, and a guest professorship in Warsaw. Since he obtained his postdoctoral lecturing qualification in 1992, he has also been an independent lecturer at the Thüringen Institute for Teacher Training and Curriculum Development. His main areas of work are hermeneutics, ethics and cultural and natural philosophy. Up to now he has published ten books and edited an additional three, broadcast several times on radio and television and written numerous scientific articles.

Readers with a deeper interest will find a detailed discussion of the intellectual, political and legal history of the concept of dignity and a systematic analysis of the image of dignity in modern culture in Franz Josef Wetz's book *Die Würde der Menschen ist antastbar* (*The Dignity of Man is Violable*) Klett-Cotta, Stuttgart, 1998.

Bazon Brock

The Educating Power of the Sciences

Lending Permanence to Happiness

Jeremy Bentham (1748-1832) was a contemporary of Goethe who willed that his body be dissected in the presence of his friends and that his fellow faculty members enjoy his fortune for as long as he remained among them in body. There was more to the challenge of this radical reformer, philosopher, economist and lawyer than met the eye, and the professors met that challenge brilliantly – in keeping with Bentham's utilitarian teachings that the basis of moral codes lies in utility and that everyone recognizes what is to his own advantage. After their colleague died, they adorned his skeleton with a portrait bust and prepared a glass display case for it. This is how it remains to this day, outfitted with one of his hats, walking sticks and suits of clothes, preserved along with his mummified head at University College London.

Jeremy Bentham, the "auto-icon" University College London

"The greatest happiness of the greatest number" was Bentham's general maxim as a social ethicist, and it would seem that he found his own greatest happiness in the knowledge that at least his virtually incorruptible remains would linger among the living for a long time to come. To the extent that this is true, this eccentric gentleman, were he alive today, would most definitely have welcomed Gunther von Hagens as a modern partner, as von Hagens' plastination process makes it (theoretically) possible for more and more confident individuals to follow Bentham's example.

Even as recently as the end of the 19th century, highly devout Catholic monks took those residents of Palermo whom they had comforted during their departure from this world and placed them in the catacombs of this Sicilian city, whose importance dates back to antiquity. The unique climatic conditions prevailing there naturally transform the dead into mummies. As a result, these pious entities sit, stand and lie about in eternity's vestibule, where thousands of calm tourists come each year to spend some time in quiet and, one would at least hope, inspiring communion with them.

Bentham, the residents of the Palermo catacombs and those who have donated their bodies to the Heidelberg Institute for Plastination attest to the fact that members of early advanced cultures that seem alien to us today, such as those of ancient Egypt or pre-Columbian America, have not been the only persons prepared to use their own bodies to represent a central aim of every culture. Radical materialists, devout Christians, and many other modern Europeans have been and are likewise willing to represent that aim, i.e., to lend permanence to existence.

The primary aim of all of the cultural technologies known to us is to fulfill this goal of presenting the world of past, present and future generations as the only world. Mental efforts, at times manifested physically, bridge the vast gulf that we naively perceive between life and death, this world and the next, past and future. These efforts work because they are capable of enduring.

Cultures are a web of relationships between human beings. The less these relationships are dependent upon the discretion of the individual, the more binding they are. This discretion is the result of one's personal temporal horizons, which are, of course, temporary and restrictive. Opening and expanding these temporal horizons means capturing time, bringing it to a standstill; it means escaping time and its ravages, i.e., passing away without a trace.

Cultures make that possible for their members by guaranteeing replicability, in other words by offering the chance of being able to begin and end what essentially has neither a beginning nor an end. This cultural guarantee of replicability defines what we call permanence: the constant presence of the dead and their pasts in the present of the living. Cemeteries, monuments and memorials, museums, libraries and archives, trade routes, old city foundations and architectural styles, field names and city names all embody and represent this type of permanence as an opportunity to repeat, to fathom, to visualise – and to a certain extent, to resurrect.

Historians, archaeologists, theologians and philologists who have learned how to communicate properly with the dead are not the only ones who have the means to achieve permanence by repeating, i.e., by retrieving – today nearly everyone has access to video and audio recording technology. Video allows you to resurrect Marylin Monroe or Adolf Hitler; Enrico Caruso or Elvis Presley can be summoned up by CDs; scenes from your life are permanently available in photos; and at family gatherings you can weave resúmés into biographies, in which time and space can be fitted together or taken apart at will – just as only the cultural elite were

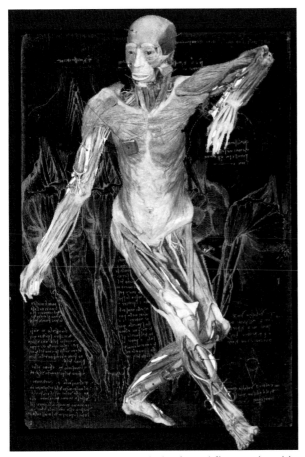

One of Gunther von Hagens' plastinated figures placed in front of an anatomical drawing by Leonardo da Vinci

able to do up until recently. People today have learned this by following the example of the arts and the mass media. The world of TV no longer complains when movies are re-shown over and over and over. Instead, viewers share in the satisfaction of seeing serial happiness return in infinite Warholesque repetition. And sports channel viewers have Friedrich Nietzsche's blessing, as slow motion allows them to watch moments deemed important three, four or an endless number of times, thus helping them achieve Master of Time status, i.e., a cultural giant.

What is described is technical theology: anyone can fulfill the Christian promise of resurrection with no Apocalypse, no Judgement Day. The mass media proves to us every day that we already have the end behind us. That is their Good News.

Gunther von Hagens' plastination is recognisable at first glance as a genuine cultural technology, lending permanence to a biological substrate using a means other than nature, i.e., other than by passing on the organism's intact genetic information.

Techniques aimed at selectively optimising this natural process have thus far been highly successful. Protecting the frail, breeding specific animals, and collecting, selecting and reusing specific plant seeds are methods that have proven themselves to be so efficient that they have come to be the actual pattern for all cultural work – from obtaining a food supply and various forms of preservation, up to and including breeding efforts that reshape nature, thereby expanding useful resources. The requirements for this success are that there be some cultural benefit and that knowledge of the natural processes by which life regenerates itself be preserved. Possession of this knowledge, i.e., being able to apply it and pass it on to others, equates to power. Those desiring a share in this power must submit themselves to rules as they have applied and still apply to priests and doctors, scientists and artists. Yet historical experience shows that breaking rules is also a recognised cultural achievement, as breaking the rules does, in fact, mean having to codify new rules.

In this way, von Hagens is currently breaking the rules governing the knowledge and application techniques that lend cultural permanence to anatomy, medicine, theology and social ethics. At the same time, he is also demonstrating the new, modified rules that will result from this infringement. In so doing, he is acting in accordance with a tendency that has been clear in our culture (i.e., what we refer to as 'Western' culture) for a good 250 years: the tendency toward professionalising to the greatest possible extent the audience and/or clientele of priests, doctors, engineers, artists, craftsmen and those possessing power in democratic societies.

Ever since a large group of associates of French cultural pragmatists Denis Diderot (1713-1784) and Jean le Rond d'Alembert (1717-1783) published all of the practical and theoretical knowledge of their day in what they called an encyclopedia, the principle addressees of such information have not been specialists, but rather all citizens in general. It went without saying that receiving this cultural knowledge would not make these citizens doctors or engineers; they would not be able to paint like an artist or sculpt or produce goods like a craftsman. They were instead to be put into a position to judge the work of artists, doctors or craftsmen, because they would be able to differentiate between what was reasonable (justifiable) and what was less reasonable, between what had been made well and what had been sloppily thrown together, between what was useful and what clearly was not, between effective but bitter medicine and the sweet consolations of a charlatan.

After all, what is the use in producing quality goods if potential buyers are unable to recognise quality? What is the point of performing medicine, painting, or governing according to the rules of the art if neither the ill, nor those who view the art, nor the voters know the existing rules or how to appreciate new ones? Ambitious business people need knowledgeable customers; serious doctors need informed patients; ingenious artists need a discerning audience possessing aesthetic sensibilities and open to new ideas – if not, business people, doctors, and artists might as well abandon their efforts to produce achievements which really would have been worth their price.

The outstanding potential of plastination has been demonstrated by von Hagens' work, which has not only educated the general public (i.e., has made it more discerning and perceptive) in matters that had previously been visually accessible through the use of only moderately useful models. It has also prompted specialists, i.e., anatomists and surgeons, to link their perceptions with familiar ideas and concepts in completely new ways.

If we accept this offer, our trust in the happiness of permanence that culture promises ought to be greatly strengthened. Many of those who viewed the plastinated specimens (human bodies that have been transformed using various means of dissection and preservation) at the BODY WORLDS exhibition in Mannheim indicated in the visitor's book that only upon viewing those immortalised there did they regain a sense of awe for the highest of all cultural aims.

That may well be a melodramatic means of allaying feelings of irritation, even of horror, fear, and mortality. Yet awe does, in fact, result from having overcome highly personal emotional responses in the face of overpowering impressions, and it is those cultural records that embody and represent a claim to permanence that make the most powerful impressions on us. It is in accordance with this premise that we assess not only the tombs of ancient Egyptian pharaohs, Gothic cathedrals, and impressionist paintings in museums, but also disappearing rain forests, faded family photos and the loss of our homes. The plastination substrates have taken the core significance that assigning permanence has for all cultures and impressed it into the minds of exhibition visitors more conspicuously than any other medium presently does.

Real Virtuality

Bridges embody the idea of being able to travel at will from one shore to the other and back again, and represent that idea metaphorically whenever a mental step or leap is being described (bridging a gap between two people or societies, for instance). This unity of embodiment/animation and representation/symbolism is the hallmark of all truly effective cultural achievements, and allows us to recognise them as such.

Heinrich Lübke did, in fact, represent the function of head of state, but he did not embody that function. Gustav Heinemann embodied it, but appeared to have difficulties when it came to representing it. Roman Herzog, on the other hand, has that aura that tells us that he embodies what he represents and represents what he embodies – his body is a sign of his significance. The transformation cue in his case is given by the sirens of his police escort.

In other cases of cultural achievement, the transformation from embodiment to symbolic representation and vice versa ("this is my body, this is my blood") is marked by the ringing of a bell or through acclamation ("this is a work of art and not just material that represents an imaginary work of art"). And do the many voices cheering for a Nobel Prize not drown out the nagging doubts as to whether documentation on a subatomic decay chain reaction indicates the embodiment of a newly discovered particle or whether it merely represents a theoretical assumption formulated in terms of a physical experiment?

When it comes to thoughts, virtuality is conceded as a mere possibility; we evaluate embodiments/materialisations, on the other hand, as something real. Great cultural achievements aim at turning thoughts into reality, but not in such a way that the achievement erases the thought. Instead, it is the unity of embodiment and representation that allows us to distinguish between both levels, i.e., between that which is virtual and that which is real. The product of culture is therefore a real virtuality.

There is, however, a large body of criteria we can use to assess how much reality is contained within an embodiment.

Plastinated voluntary muscles (The Runner) by Gunther von Hagens; Unique Forms of Continuity in Space. 1913, by Umberto Boccioni (1882-1916)

Authenticity is obviously the most highly valued criterion. When touring a castle, a tourist will tap a column to see whether it is really made of marble or simply painted to give the deceptive impression of marble. Is the singing on stage authentic or is it a case of lip-synching to a recording either of the singer's own voice or even of someone else's?

Despite all of the postmodern satisfaction that we get from simulations, fakes, substitutes, reproductions and stylized recitations, we have not yet given up our demands for authenticity. On the contrary: you can only enjoy an imitation when you know how to distinguish it from the real thing.

In general we assign value to the things of this world based on the understandable claim that they really are what they claim to be, i.e., authentic. Was this van Gogh really painted by Vincent or is it the work of an imitator (copier or forger) who was able to make us believe that this van Gogh was real because he himself was extremely familiar with and appreciated the authentic works of van Gogh? Is this Buddha's tooth really an authentic part of the honourable man's earthly embodiment? And is it legitimate to preserve and honour Buddha's tooth? Does this actor really embody the playwright's character that he is currently playing? Or is he just delivering a text, even though he is not supposed to be reciting literature but authentically acting?

This self-evident demand for authenticity is voiced in all cultures, and any objections raised against it fall on deaf ears – such objections, in fact, strengthen the demand. If a relic should prove to be a forgery, the real relics are considered all the more valuable. If artists or architects or craftsmen consciously abandon any claim of embodying their ideas in an authentic manner, they are dismissed as cheap imitators, plagiarists or producers of kitsch or junk who are unable to keep the promises they seem to make.

Plastinated bodies are real virtualities; the extent to which they represent reality is verified to the greatest conceivable extent by their authenticity. One could say that they fulfill the function of relics both of scientific anatomy and of the artistic conceptualisation involved in, for instance, sculpting. If we recall the statue of a runner by Italian futurist Umberto Boccioni (1882–1916), or the surreal, abstract works of French artist Germaine Richier (1904–1959) or the works of Spanish iron sculpture pioneer Julio Gonzáles (1875–1942), we see the conceptual precision with which Gunther von Hagens models his specimens. Their double justification of authenticity – a biological substrate on the one hand and genuine artistic figuration concepts on the other – is especially convincing to those who view the whole-body plastinates. Time and time again, when discussing their reactions to these exhibits, visitors to the BODY WORLDS exhibition emphasise that they were particularly impressed by their authenticity.

Von Hagens does in fact work as a sculptor, creating models of his objects in order to determine how a body must be posed to show precisely what it is intended to show: the fascinating relationship between the external impression that the body makes and its internal structure. The relationship between surface and the functional logic of the human body has guided the conceptual work of sculptors and painters ever since the 4th century BC (as evidenced in Greek and Roman cultures). This work always revolved around two levels, which were used to demonstrate the relationship between internal and external processes. On the one hand artists wanted to illustrate how spiritual/intellectual efforts (such as the will to make a particular movement) manifested themselves through the body; in other words they wanted to show how mental activity or one's frame of mind (sadness or stoicism, enthusiasm or fear) can be embodied. On the other hand they wanted to make comprehensible and perceptible how individual components of the body (skin, muscles, tendons and ligaments, extremities and internal organs) work together to maintain its unity in all of the various states induced by the influence of external forces, particularly gravity.

Making the invisible interior realms of a living body perceptible attracted the attention of early anatomists and doctors who had developed the art of interpreting signs (symptomatology) as a means of drawing conclusions regarding the body's inner workings based on its exterior. This was more or less successful and fulfilled certain limited purposes such as assisting at a birth or healing the broken bones and open wounds that soldiers often suffered. Going a very large step further, however, i.e., creating openings in the body through which surgeons would have access to the inside of the abdominal cavity or chest, was dependent upon the mere possibility of visualising what one had never seen before – insight gained by dissecting and cutting open corpses can only be applied to the living to a very limited extent. The ability to view dead bodies as if they were living was not achieved until plastination and, most importantly, the visualisation concept that Gunther von Hagens developed out of necessity: he needed to give an appropriate form to his incorruptible anatomical specimens.

To perceive dead bodies authentically as living ones is an ancient goal of artists. Not only can that claim be substantiated by stories such as that of the mythical King Pygmalion of Cyprus, who fell in love with a statue of a woman that he himself had made; it is also attested to by countless actual historical accounts of efforts in the art of mimesis (the representation of natural reality) to go beyond purely formal mimicry of contours and surfaces. Michelangelo Buonarotti (1474–1564) would not have been one of the outstanding Renaissance sculptors had he, as a creator of human figures in marble, not attempted to breathe life into his creations – to animate them. "Moving pictures" were, after all, an exciting way to describe early silent films, and 'talkies' described the first movies that had sound.

Animation, i.e., bringing life to a subject, is generally considered one of the loftiest goals of work with inanimate material. Not counting artists' and scientists' demands to create artificial life (a current priority of many cultural creators), plastination methods and concepts have been the most ambitious and successful attempts in the history of art and science at – authentically – perceiving dead bodies in the same way as living bodies.

Machines, for example, could also be understood as dead bodies that engineers can under certain circumstances equip with some of the features of the living. Non-trivial machines, such as self-programming computers and robots capable of learning, are what most often demonstrate astonishing signs of animation. Yet they only represent life simulated via programs – they do not embody it. The substrate required for these machines (generally the chemical element silicon) may well be transformable into highly efficient electronic circuitry; nevertheless it remains far below the level of complexity characterising even a single-celled organism. A machine's body, even for non-trivial machines, is not a sign to anyone, even when designers make an effort to give it a gestalt.

Gestalt, a term commonly used only in German, refers to the unity of embodiment and representation. Gunther von Hagens is an artist/scientist who has managed to lend inanimate matter the gestalt of the living – the gestalt of an authentic real virtuality.

Imaging Science

The ability to lend the real gestalt of the living to a thought process, to an idea, used to be the privilege of the arts, which, as doctor and poet Gottfried Benn (1885–1956) put it, moved in the realm of possibility in which gestalten are created (i.e., in virtuality).

Ever since the time of Goethe (1749–1832), this has been known as the educational power of the arts. A person becomes educated by appropriating the virtual constructs of others, whether in terms of insights, ideas or world views. Once one has embodied, has made completely one's own that which has been appropriated, i.e., once it becomes second nature and an expression of that individual's self, then one not only has an education, one is educated. In that sense, the individual has become a gestalt of the educational power of the arts.

Without doubt, there have been countless educated scientists and representatives of other trades. So why then was there an emphasis placed on the privilege of the gestalt-creating, educating power of the fine arts? If an artist were also to have a scientific education, he or she would have been known as a *poeta doctus*, a scholarly artist, as represented and embodied by author Thomas Mann (1875–1955, Nobel laureate in 1929). Examples of scientists with a sense for artistic creativity are, on the other hand, rare. A sophisticated career requiring an education, it seems, has most often been successfully combined with literary creativity; Arthur Schnitzler, Alfred Döblin and Hans Carossa all worked at least part-time in the field of medicine, just as Benn did; Theodor Storm and Franz Kafka worked in the field of law; Robert Walser was an engineer, and Max Frisch was an architect.

Scientists who place value on being professionals in the fine arts and whose artistic activity extends beyond simply doing it in their spare time or as a sideline have only begun to penetrate the public consciousness in recent times. Neuroscientist and biologist Carsten Höller and Detlef Linke took part in Documenta X ("House of Pigs and People"). A large number of scientists working in the field of artificial life present their findings within institutional and objective contexts in the arts. Several excellent computer researchers see their screen representations as a form of 'imaging,' as a result of giving gestalt to scientific concepts (the term 'imaging science' reflects this).

In a narrower sense, imaging science refers to methods and technologies such as positron emission tomography (PET) that produce images of the interior of a living body; these, however, can only be read, i.e., understood and interpreted, by specialists. In a more general sense, the term refers to processes that open up human perception to aspects of the world that would otherwise elude our natural sensory organs. (It is telling to note that "making the invisible visible" was a credo of painters such as Paul Klee, Wassily Kandinsky, Willi Baumeister and many others who also had their own ideas concerning the theory of art.) Scientists in the field of imaging use their computers to create new languages, and languages have since time immemorial been considered particularly efficient educational forces. Languages are characterised by the relationship that they construct between the internal world of the mind and the social external world of man. The creators of these types of languages are educating scientists in the truest sense. Gunther von Hagens, with his preservation technology and his plastination imaging concepts, is one of these scientists, one of the most interesting in fact. Anyone who puts forth the frequently raised objection that, precisely because of imaging science, von Hagens' process is no longer needed, that the presentation of anatomy that it aims to achieve is already outdated, those who raise this objection fail to see his fundamental achievement. Even the best results from imaging science are only useful in a meaningful way if they are applied in conjunction with displaying the anatomy of dead bodies as if they were living.

The educating power of the science of anatomical presentation can only be even somewhat appreciated if – as I have indicated here – it is understood as a cultural technology that makes it possible to fulfill the ancient cultural aim of presenting the unity of embodiment and representation as a real virtuality and does so in as permanent and authentic a way as possible. Plastination conveys the relationship between interiors and exteriors, between living organisms and inanimate matter, perceiving and making perceptible, viewing and comprehending, and does so at a previously unattained level of authenticity. It follows that plastination may be understood as a linguistic operation that uses artistic concepts to create a gestalt for scientific ideas – a gestalt for mankind living in a cultural context and demanding permanence.

Bazon Brock, born 1936, Prof. em. University of Wuppertal; Dean of faculty for more than 12 years; Head of research family "Culture and Strategy." Since 1995 Professor of Non-normative Aesthetics at the universities of Hamburg, Germany; Vienna, Austria; and Wuppertal, Germany, after his studies in the fields of German studies, philosophy, art history, and political sciences at the universities of Hamburg, Frankfurt, Germany, and Vienna. Since 1957 Brock has organised 1600 happenings, action teachings, and exhibitions; since 1968 he has created and managed schools for visitors at the outstanding international documenta exhibitions in Cassel, Germany; he wrote and performed and produced numerous movies, radio plays, and TV shows. For the past 9 years he has hosted Germany's only long-running TV show on fine arts of today. He has published five volumes of collected works (DuMont Verlag, Cologne, Germany) as well as books on subjects such as aging as a problem for artists and future societies, imaging arts and sciences, the history of looking at floors and grounds. His relationship with Gunther von Hagens is characterised by mutual friendly respect.

Franz Josef Wetz

Modern Anatomical Theatre –
The First Public Autopsy in 200 Years

"At the end of every problem, you'll find a German," wrote Voltaire during the French Enlightenment in the 18th century. Even today, not much has changed, which has to do with the fact that Germany has always been an extremely nervous and very fundamental nation, which as such can be easily disconcerted in order to be able to discuss the issues thus awakened down to the last detail.

This was proven once again by the strong reactions and heated discussions about an "anatomical drama" played out in London. There on November 20, 2002, between 7:00 and 10:00 p.m., the first public autopsy in about 200 years took place. The 'scene of the crime' for this controversial event was the boilerhouse of the Old Truman Brewery in Brick Lane. Together with two anatomists and two pathologists, plastinator Gunther von Hagens uncovered the secrets of the corpse of a 72-year-old German. This unusual spectacle was observed by about 500 spectators on the scene and thousands more on TV screens. As was to be expected, this public autopsy triggered heated debates among Great Britain's citizenry and even more in Germany although it was performed with all due respect for the proprieties of the medical profession.

No matter how understandable such impulses appear to be at first glance, they still seem odd. What is actually so horrible about it when medically interested laypersons for once look over the shoulders of anatomists and pathologists at work in order to inform themselves first hand about the insides of their bodies? It is in fact human nature to have an interest in our own bodies, and it just so happens that the cultural answer to this question is indeed anatomy. In any case, it would be difficult to make medical laypersons understand why they should be barred from taking part in an autopsy while museums of medical history and the BODY WORLDS exhibition are readily open for them to visit.

It is correct to say that today the possibility of taking part in a public autopsy normally does not exist. However, how quickly do we ascribe universal applicability to truths bound up in time and space, which they ultimately never ever possessed as such? Some things that came about historically – and in the meantime have long since become history – were once considered to be perpetually valid. This includes the widespread though mistaken idea of bans on public autopsies. From the close of the 16th century until the end of the 18th and early 19th centuries, there was a long tradition of public anatomy that enjoyed considerable popularity among laypersons.

Anatomical Theatres

In addition to scientific and medical researchers, many artists also showed great interest in anatomy. Hence, Leonardo da Vinci and Michelangelo (1475–1564) not only attended dissections of physician friends of theirs, but also performed anatomical studies themselves – in order to be able to depict persons even more faithfully in their art. Leonardo is supposed to have dissected more than 30 corpses in Florence in order to be better able to incorporate his figures on his canvases more perfectly through a better knowledge of the arrangement of bones, muscles, and tendons as well as of all the other organs. The body, which had been disparaged as the "grave of the soul" for centuries, was ennobled by the Renaissance as the "temple of the soul."

Since this upgrading of the body as an attractive form of expression for the human soul, the general public took greater interest in anatomy, which has been most decidedly demonstrated by the numerous anatomical theatres that were established throughout Europe. However, public dissections first took place outdoors or in temporary structures built out of wood especially for this purpose, which could easily be dismantled when not needed. Such so-called *"temporaria theatra"* could be assembled and disassembled as needed just as quickly as additions to existing buildings. Public dissections were even performed in vacant churches and in the chapels of former monasteries, such as San Francesco in Bologna, Italy, the Church of St. Elizabeth in Basle, Switzerland, or St. Jacob's Chapel in Tübingen, Germany. Nevertheless, permanent *"theatra anatomica"* soon followed in Montpellier, France, in 1530, in Padua, Italy, in 1594, in Bologna, Italy, in 1595, in Leiden, The Netherlands, in 1597, in Uppsala, Sweden, in 1622, in Copenhagen, Denmark, in 1643, in Paris, France, in 1694, in Berlin, Germany, in 1720, and in Halle, Germany, in 1727, to mention just a few places. By the 18th century, nearly every medical school had its own anatomical theatre.

Nearly every dissection was performed in public and was thus accessible to a wider audience. They were not meant solely for a medical forum. This was proven by the title page of Andreas Vesalius' illustrated textbook *De Humani Corporis Fabrica* (1543). It shows Vesalius at the dissection table, closely surrounded by persons of the most widely varied social classes. The same can be seen in Rembrandt's famous painting, The Anatomy of Dr. Tulp (1632), in which Amsterdam mayor and anatomist Nicolaas Tulp is shown dis-

Gunther von Hagens´ Public Autopsy, London 2002

secting a corpse in an apparently private lesson in anatomy before a group of prominent citizens of that city.

In those days, such events gradually developed into social happenings – a new form of sociability and fashion, which soon came to be a part of gracious living. In addition to professors and students, there were also members of the upper class, the nobility as well as numerous clergymen and monks who took part in such events. Moreover, barbers, midwives, battlefield physicians, surgeons and apothecaries were in attendance, even though these were not yet academic professions, but only skilled trades. In addition, many artists, writers, and scholars, such as Johann Wolfgang von Goethe as well as the brothers Wilhelm and Alexander von Humboldt also numbered among the medically interested professional and lay publics. They were bound by a close friendship with the renowned anatomist Justus Christian Loder of Jena, under whose direction Goethe was able to deepen his knowledge of the inner structures of the human body.

Anyone who so desired and could afford it was allowed to attend public anatomical dissections. Even then, admission was charged to take part in such events. Admission to these demonstrations was only free of charge for faculty members, but not for students and medical laypersons.

In general, anatomy lessons resembled more exciting theatre performances than edifying instructional presentations.

It was not only that they – like theatre performances – were announced by engraved invitations and were sometimes even accompanied by music, even the name "theatre" indicates a festive and entertaining framework for anatomical demonstrations that developed more and more into social highlights. They usually lasted several days, starting, for example, with an examination of the abdominal organs on the first day, the contents of the chest cavity on the second day, continuing with the skull on the third day and ending on the fourth day with the limbs, including the muscles, nerves and blood vessels. The attraction of such performances was enormous, but not just because it was so unusual to open and dissect an otherwise closed corpse, but also because of certain non-medical aspects that went beyond the relatively narrow scope of anatomy.

In summary, it can be said that the view the otherwise concealed interior of the body had the following benefits for visitors of anatomical theaters in those days:
- Instructional information (scientific)
- Satisfied curiosity (philosophical)
- Pleasantly spine-tingling experiences (aesthetic)
- Raptly reverent veneration of divine Creation (theological)
- Humble self-realisation on the part of the individual as a vulnerable, mortal, and insignificant part of Nature (existential).

After anatomy as a discipline was sequestered behind the

William Hogarth, The Reward of Cruelty, plaste of The Four Stages of Cruelty, 1750-1751

walls of universities at the beginning of the 19th century, where it has been functioning solely as a scientific discourse ever since and still to the exclusion of medical laypersons. This was then accompanied by a development that left only the scientific interest of experts paramount to all the various perspectives on the deeper structures of the human body. Other forms of perception were either rejected as unscientific or were dismissed as immoral. However, even a non-scientific perspective possessed a certain justification, and what was once considered morally questionable could have been justified as ethically permissible even then.

Renaissance of the Renaissance

This is enlightenment: a kind of thinking with the sun at its zenith, which means the same as maximum light with minimum shadows. Thinking of this kind vigorously defies taboos and shadowy zones, where things seemingly mysterious remain out of the reach of the light of dissection. In this context, anatomical dissections of a corpse can be equated with illuminating the darkness of life with the light of death.

Through Gunther von Hagens, public dissections are being performed for the first time in just under two centuries. In resurrecting this old tradition, the Institute for Plastination

aims to educate the public (and medically interested laypersons in particular) about anatomy, but at the same time he is returning to its proper place the thoroughly acceptable, human need to be curious about our anatomy and to feel a pleasant sensation of horror, a sense of awe, and a humble awareness of ourselves as vulnerable, mortal, insignificant creatures. To venture a glance into an unknown body is virtually the same as to discover our own body therein, as only that which can be uncovered and dissected can be comprehended. There is certainly nothing ethically reprehensible in this.

The criticism that such public spectacles have come to form a part of our thrill-oriented entertainment culture is pointless, as it could also be applied ultimately to almost every cultural event. High culture has been integrated into our general leisure-time activities for years, which have also had a certain justification despite our reservations. Apart from that, high expectations have always depended on the attitude of the beholder. The obnoxiousness of public dissections is primarily also a question of the standpoint, as an anatomical theatre is quite capable of becoming a site for contemplation as well as a place for the imagination. It can thus serve as a venue for thoughtful observation, which invites inquisitive, fascinated, and existentially involved viewers to become engrossed and offers them an unusual kind of encounter with themselves.

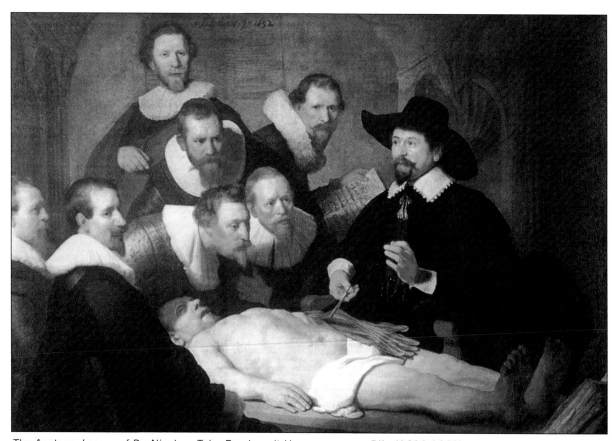

The Anatomy Lesson of Dr. Nicolaas Tulp, Rembrandt Harmenzoon van Rijn (1606-1669)

Whoever becomes earnestly involved in this will emerge from this experience a changed person. For this purpose, the moralisers of our time should stop trying to make anyone interested in public dissections into politico-cultural invalids through their doting condescension.

It is in fact human nature to have an interest in our own bodies, and it just so happens that the cultural answer to this question is indeed anatomy. If, however, medical laypersons are permitted to look at anatomical specimens, then it is not understandable why they should not be allowed to view the dissection of corpses. However strong the fearful desire and pleasant dread may be, which autopsies evoke in their observers, most people will certainly witness such affairs with a straight face. The reason for this is not because the very sight of a dissected body would be shocking for them, but rather because it would be nearly impossible for any of us to treat looking at the fragile bases of our own existence in a light and frivolous way.

Contemplating Oneself without a Mirror – An Eye-Witness Report

Today there is a wide variety of possibilities for producing lifelike pictures of bodily interiors: anatomical atlases in colour, imaging and data technologies such as x-ray, ultra-sound, CT, and NMR. In light of this background, the question arises whether direct viewing of dissected bodily organs while studying macroscopic human anatomy is becoming superfluous?

(Old anatomical plates, Florentine wax models and the figures made out of Plexiglas, aluminum and plastic in the Hygiene Museum in Dresden are as fascinating today as they ever were. To this, the 20th century has added numerous colored anatomical atlases as well as new imaging technologies such as x-ray, ultrasound, CT and NMR, which can be used to generate lifelike images of the body's interiors. And let us not forget the computer-generated 3D representations of the human body, i.e., virtual anatomy, which are at the heart of the Visible Human Project launched in the US in 1988. Does this wide variety of anatomical imaging and data technologies make it unnecessary for students of macroscopic human anatomy to view the dissected organs of a corpse directly?) Are there not already enough books, illustrated reference works and CD-ROMs out there where laypersons can learn all that they need to know about the internal structure of their bodies? Now it is even possible for people to view highly realistic body models on their computer screens and dissect them for themselves. Medical laypersons can use a virtual scalpel to remove the outer layers of tissue to expose the underlying structures. So why would we still need anatomical theaters?

Gunther von Hagens´ Public Autopsy, London 2002

I personally witnessed the public dissection in London. I admit to having been highly sceptical when I went there. I was horrified by the media frenzy surrounding this 'event,' but my own morbid curiosity won out in the end. On the way to the actual venue, I felt a tingle of excitement and a pleasant sense of anticipation – a mixture of trepidation and heightened expectation – no matter how much I tried to visualise just being able to see the inside of a human corpse, i.e., not as something holy or demonic, but simply something natural. Since it was nothing more than this, all of my sensation-seeking voyeurism and comforting horror visions melted away as soon as the demonstration began. Like everyone else in attendance, I earnestly followed the work of the three anatomists and two pathologists. What struck me was how soberly they went about their work, their dispassionate explanations, and the quiet calm in the hall, which at the same time stood in such stark contrast to the heated, often emotional and grim debate conducted in the media and in the public about this demonstration both before and after it took place.

What I was witnessing was what had already been seen at the BODY WORLDS exhibition: a self-disciplined audience that did not first need to be brought to order or to its senses. I think this phenomenon is well worth noting since it is anything but a given in today's world; nevertheless it is not surprising if one realises that both the exhibition and the autopsy reveal a completely new, close-up look at human existence – and we as humans have always been curious about ourselves. In both instances, viewers are looking into someone else's body in order to discover their own, which is the reason that we can even speak of "discovery anatomy." Like a finished plastinate, a dissected corpse also gives us a visual bridge to our own vulnerable, mortal existence. As a result, it is almost inevitable that such a glimpse would function as a way of "viewing oneself without a mirror," which sufficiently explains the earnestness of those in attendance at both the exhibition and the autopsy. This earnestness does not arise because the people are seeing something gruesome that has left them speechless, as might easily be assumed, but rather because these events have simply allowed all of us to see clearly, in a bold or even shocking way, just how fragile the basis for our own lives ultimately is. BODY WORLDS is no more a baroque gallery of curiosities than a public dissection is a Renaissance fair; both provide room for contemplation and imagination, are places to reflect on oneself, and showplaces for contemplative observation that invites curious, fascinated viewers to lose themselves in existential questions.

Nevertheless, a question remains: How is it that knowing the plastinated specimens and dissected corpses to be real can bring viewers closer to themselves? There is, of course, no doubt that the authenticity of the exhibits at events such as these heighten the experience, making it more intense and credible, but it is difficult to say precisely why that should be. What first comes to mind is to reflect on the difference between an original work of art and a copy. The first is usually considered more valuable than the latter, just as encountering a celebrity on the street will arouse greater attention from passers-by than will a life-size photograph of the same person in a store window. This belief in the superiority of seeing an original work of art or seeing a celebrity face-to-face is based on an outmoded superstition, however, and as such I will not pursue this line of thinking any further.

More revealing would be to contrast hiking in a natural setting with paging through a volume of nature photography, or going to the theatre or opera with reading a play or listening to an opera on CD. In these cases, one could also point out that, because we have books and CDs, we would no longer need nature, opera houses or theaters. This is not the conclusion that people would generally draw, however, convinced as we are of the superiority of the latter categories. A similar difference is that between attending BODY WORLDS or a public dissection and merely studying anatomical plates in a book or viewing virtual anatomical specimens on a computer screen. The contrast in this case is as stark as that between walking in nature and simply looking at it in a picture book. The depth of experience is different, and one must understand both to appreciate the difference fully.

I admit, of course, that the need for such an exhibition and for a public dissection has not yet been demonstrated. Where culture is concerned, however, such a necessity simply does not exist. The question we should be asking is not "Is that really necessary?" but rather "Is that really permissible?" When it comes to the permissibility of an event in a liberal state with an open society, the burden of proof does not lie with the organiser, but with whomever would attempt to deny permission in order to forbid it. This is the party that must provide a convincing argument against public dissections. Precisely such arguments, however, simply do not exist. As a result, it is difficult to convince interested parties that anatomical dissections, which medical students regularly attend throughout the course of their studies, must remain solely the privilege of medical experts. Excluding medical laypersons from anatomy can no longer be justified in a liberal democracy with an open society. The opportunity to attend publicly accessible dissections should therefore again become a right granted to all responsible citizens whenever facilities and staffing permit.

The Autopsy Body (2003)

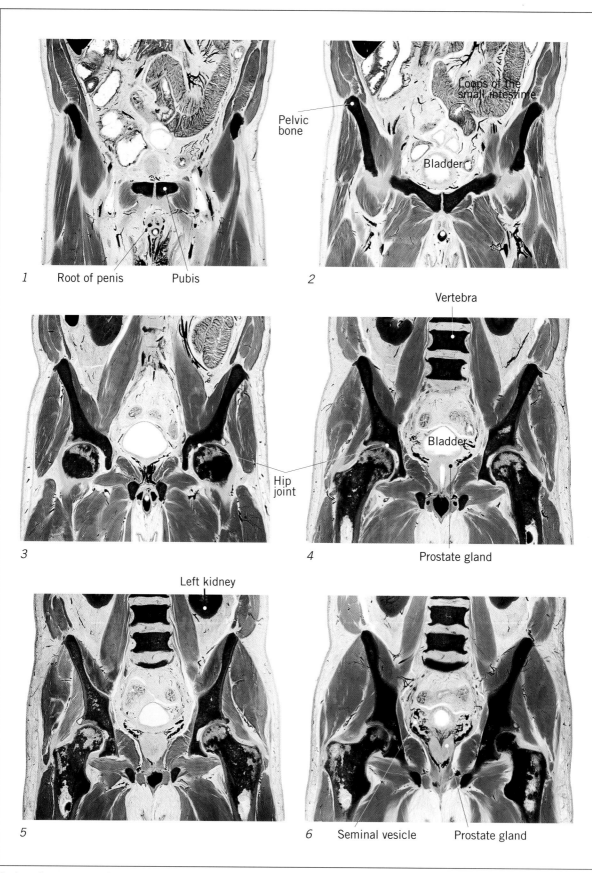

1 Root of penis Pubis

Pelvic bone

2 Loops of the small intestine Bladder

3 Hip joint

Vertebra

4 Bladder Prostate gland

Left kidney

5

6 Seminal vesicle Prostate gland

Series of transparent body slices through a male pelvis, frontal cut

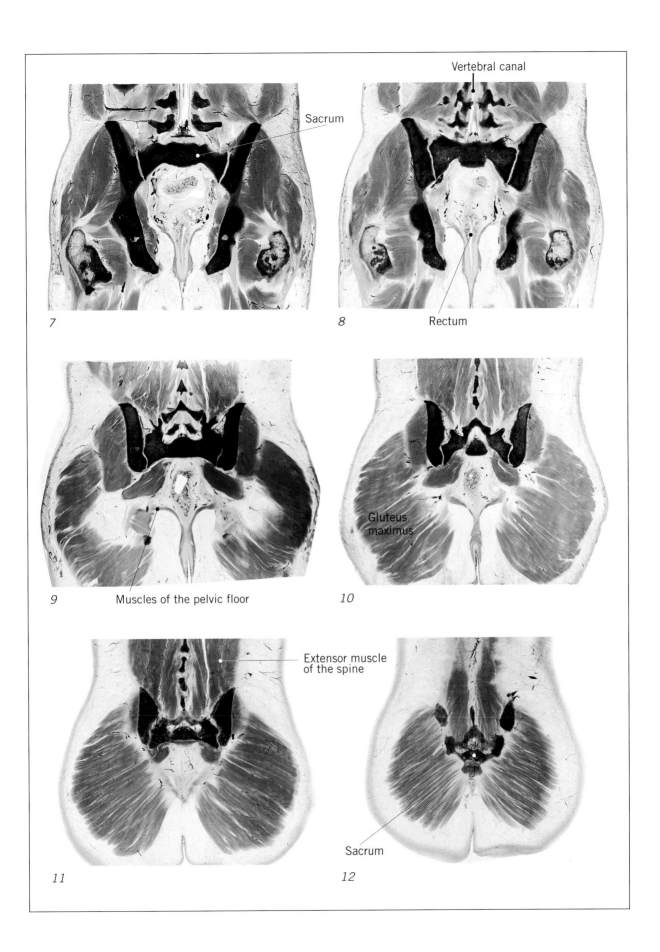

7

8   Sacrum

Vertebral canal

Rectum

9   Muscles of the pelvic floor

10   Gluteus maximus

11   Extensor muscle of the spine

12   Sacrum

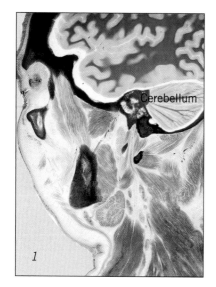

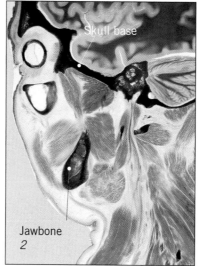

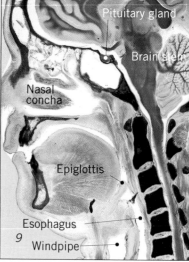

1 Cerebellum

2 Skull base
Jawbone

3 Eye socket
Carotid artery

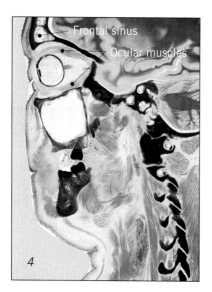

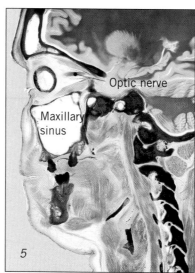

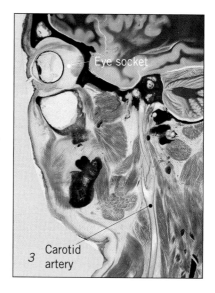

4 Frontal sinus
Ocular muscles

5 Optic nerve
Maxillary sinus

6

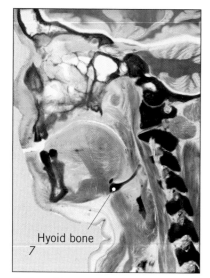

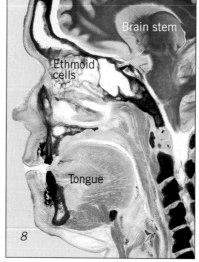

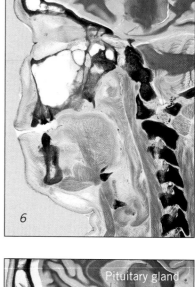

7 Hyoid bone

8 Brain stem
Ethmoid cells
Tongue

9 Pituitary gland
Brain stem
Nasal concha
Epiglottis
Esophagus
Windpipe

Series of transparent body slices, sagittal cut

Publishing Information

Catalogue:
BODY WORLDS – The Original Exhibition of Real Human Bodies
Gunther von Hagens
Angelina Whalley

Editing:
Angelina Whalley

Scientific Consultants:
Eduard Borzyak
Marius Oancea
(Institute for Plastination)

Photographs:
Gunther von Hagens

Design/Layout:
www.die-werbeaktivisten.de, mArc schumacher, Weinheim, Germany

14th printing

© Copyright 2009

Arts & Sciences

Verlagsgesellschaft mbH, Heidelberg, Germany

© Copyright for all photos and sketches
if not mentioned otherwise by
Institute for Plastination,
Rathausstrasse 11, 69126 Heidelberg, Germany

ISBN 978-3-937256-09-2

www.bodyworlds.com